THE ORACLES IN THE
NEW TESTAMENT

THE ORACLES IN THE NEW TESTAMENT

BY
EDWARD CARUS SELWYN, D.D.
HONORARY CANON OF PETERBOROUGH CATHEDRAL, FORMERLY
FELLOW OF KING'S COLLEGE, CAMBRIDGE

Wipf & Stock
PUBLISHERS
Eugene, Oregon

Wipf and Stock Publishers
199 W 8th Ave, Suite 3
Eugene, OR 97401

The Oracles in the New Testament
By Selwyn, Edward Carus
ISBN: 1-59752-635-5
Publication date 4/13/2006
Previously published by Hodder and Stoughton, 1912

And as it is owned the whole scheme of Scripture is not yet understood; so if it ever comes to be understood, before the restitution of all things, *and without miraculous interpositions; it must be in the same way as natural knowledge is come at: by the continuance and progress of learning and liberty; and by particular persons attending to, comparing and pursuing, intimations scattered up and down it, which are overlooked and disregarded by the generality of the world. For this is the way in which all improvements are made; by thoughtful men's tracing on obscure hints, as it were, dropped us by nature accidentally, or which seem to come into our minds by chance. Nor is it at all incredible, that a book, which has been so long in the possession of mankind, should contain many truths as yet undiscovered.*

BUTLER, *Analogy* II, iii.

PREFACE

THE present work is an attempt to discover the use of the Old Testament by the writers of the New. The oracles are precious words, and the words in the New Testament which were precious to the writers are words of the Old Testament. They were precious because they proved the great fact that Jesus was the Christ. The proof is known generally as the Argument from Prophecy.

This volume, instead of being limited to the usual form of that Argument, endeavours to deal with the more extended use of the Old Testament in the New; for while the citation of the oracles is sometimes definite, it is sometimes indefinite, as in John 7^{38} "as the scripture saith," and sometimes, again, where there is no mark of citation at all, they are assumed by the New Testament writers to be known, and whether known or not they are overwritten. They had been under my attention for many years before the conclusion was forced upon me that I was dealing with *Logia*, oracles, of the selfsame sort as those which Papias (about 120 A.D.) says were collected by Matthew in Hebrew. I then saw that by "dominical oracles" Papias meant oracles about the Lord Christ found in the Old Testament, and not, as nearly all writers have hitherto supposed, sayings by the Lord Jesus. This conclusion is so strongly supported by concrete instances that it challenges discussion more securely than many others in the book. It is mentioned here because it has only been obtained by one writer known to me, whose anonymous and valuable work has been much neglected. Chapter XIII below is wholly independent of it, and remains as it was written before I had seen or heard of the anonymous work.

The method here pursued is the same as in two previous works, *The Christian Prophets* and *St. Luke the Prophet*—to discover the train of Old Testament language which actuates the New Testament writer. When Hort marked with uncials in his edition phrases which had not hitherto been recognized as citations, he said that there were many more to be marked. The present volume, working always on the Greek Bible, the Septuagint (LXX), exhibits many more.

The direction of science in detail is always to simplification. When a certain line of study has resulted in finding simple explanations of one passage after another that had not been explained—such as *the portion Macedonia*, where *we were thinking*, and *the spirit of Jesus*, in Acts 16 (see *St. Luke the Prophet*), or again, When *he bringeth in the Firstborn* into the world (Heb. 1^6), her *son The Firstborn*, Jesus *himself when he began*, as *the scripture hath said* (John. 7^{38}), the locality of the Transfiguration, and many more—it is too late to pretend that the line of study is unfruitful or that future expositors can ignore it. My own belief is that the coincidences involved are not fortuitous, even if they seem to come into *our* minds by chance, in Bishop Butler's memorable phrase; but providential, a part of *the purpose of God* of which St. Paul writes. This has been the conviction which has guided the present writer to results which not only demonstrate that the Lord was in no formal or ecclesiastical sense the Prophet of Nazareth (for the alternative to this conclusion is fatal to the credit of the evangelists : Chap. XII), but, further, take us into the mind of the Lord and His apostles and exhibit the trend of their thought. The results have filled me sometimes with astonishment, sometimes with grave concern : they seem to be worthy of consideration.

The Argument from Prophecy can hardly be mentioned to-day without some apology—so much scorn, direct and indirect, has been poured upon it by high authorities, Anglican and other. One of these has recently written : " The question whether Jesus really was the expected Messiah is a question which had a meaning then : it can hardly be said to have a meaning now." This remarkable declaration is perhaps not to be taken too seriously, for it would leave either the facts of the life of Jesus or those of the expectation of the Christ, the hope of Israel, to be ignored—whether by religion or by theology is not clear. Certainly theology can never ignore either. Theology must, as Butler said, *comparing and pursuing, attend to intimations scattered up and down in scripture, which are overlooked and disregarded by the generality of the world.* It must continue *to trace on obscure hints.* And therefore the present volume, in so far as it is a genuine attempt to arrive at the facts of the case, may still hope to arrest the notice of the critic. For it may be that as the Benjamite in search of his father's asses found a kingdom, so we in search of Q or some such document may find the kingdom of David in Ps. 89 (LXX).

I had hoped that some more expert theologian would have taken up the idea and carried it further, but none has done so.

Where the evidence for the use of the Greek Bible by the Lord and the apostles is so hard to obtain, it is probable that this essay will be met with the objection that Jesus spoke Aramaic. Here then may be quoted an observation of Dr. Dalman. In *The Words of Jesus* p. 18 this very high authority says : " In the oral presentation of the " Gospel " at gatherings of the Christian community, as well as in any literary treatment applied to it, the Greek Old Testament furnished the readiest model. This version being the most important book read by the Christians in public and in private, the desire to give to the Gospel a corresponding dress must naturally have existed." If the Greek Bible was the most important book to the earliest Christians, it is lawful to infer that it was the same to the Lord Himself. For it is inconceivable that after His departure the disciples would commence their discipleship with a revolution in the devotional book which they used in His name. Therefore they knew that *the Greek Bible was to Him* " the most important book in public and in private." However, it is claimed for the following pages that they increase the evidence that He used the LXX habitually. As to Dr. Dalman's observation in the last line above, it can only be said here that, the facts being what they are, the continual difficulty is to draw the line between the Lord's sayings (and doings) and those which the evangelists attribute to Him. In " giving the gospel a corresponding dress " how much of the gospel has been sacrificed to the dress? How much of it now is "dress"? And again, did not the Lord Himself give much of the "dress"? In determining the answers a lifetime would be well spent. It is here claimed that the correspondence in question is a correspondence with the Greek Bible immeasurably more than with the Hebrew.

Only readers of the LXX are aware of the enormous divergencies of it from the Hebrew, divergencies which represent undoubtedly in some cases an older condition of the original than that which our Massoretic Hebrew represents. For instance, there is a line of nine words in the Greek of 2 Sam. 17 without a corresponding passage in the Hebrew, where there is no reason to suppose interpolation by the Greek translator, and where on the other hand the omission of the corresponding Hebrew may very well date from the Jewish Synod of Jamnia (A.D. 90), the members of which were within a lifetime of the act of betrayal (see Chap. XII below, also p. 213). However, it is beyond the scope and space of this essay to discuss the original meaning and bearing of the Hebrew Old Testament: the LXX is here treated as the book which the apostolic writers and the Master Himself used. It need not be said that only a portion of the Argument from Prophecy which is so conspicuous in Luke 24 and Acts 1–4 as a foundation of the new faith is covered in these pages. But so far as they go, they compel the conclusion that the "deposit" of the Christian faith has grown out of the Greek Bible, as it could hardly fail to grow, while out of the Massoretic Hebrew it could hardly have grown. In the controversy between Jew and Christian upon the given conditions of the

Argument from Prophecy, the Jew had no chance of winning.

An argument involving words that were in the mouth of the Lord and His apostles again and again is one that, however obsolete or obsolescent to-day, must be capable of scientific treatment, and such treatment of it will assuredly yield valuable conclusions. The importance of the LXX for the understanding of every page of the New Testament is immense. The study of textual criticism cannot go much further with present materials, but the study of the oracles can be greatly extended. May the present work serve, in however humble a degree, to promote that extension!

Just as the embryonic stages of the individual existence are obscure, and the discovery of them is attended with startling results, so are the beginnings of the Body, which is the Church. As the former are discovered experimentally, so are the latter; and part of the experiment, or the experience, lies within the literary sphere : *it must be in the same way as natural knowledge is come at.* There was a time when the Church of Christ was " the sect of the Nazarenes." To that time we moderns must needs look back, and make out of it what we can. This need not and ought not to blind us to the Life, which is beyond analysis, and greater than literature and science.

That this Life as the Lord lived it should be mixed up with the question of what is called " the Messianic consciousness " is somewhat unfortunate. What sort of consciousness descended, like a heavenly rain, upon Him, or crept like a haze upon His coloured view, or hung round Him with haunting spell, or enveloped Him as a phase of thought, or passed to Him as an endowment? Is this the sort of consciousness that a Messianic purpose assumes or in which it is invested? Is consciousness a proper term at all? Is it not rather purpose, volition, resolution, determination, in which we are to base His Messiahship? The history proves, on any shewing, that while others had uttered predictions and talked of fulfilments, He set Himself deliberately " to fulfil all righteousness." The moral effort " to do Thy will, O God " was not a work of any less continuous determination, nor an easier exertion of the will. It must needs continue until " it is finished." This is a use of human language, but it is no further removed from philosophic accuracy than to speak of Messianic consciousness. Instead of this unscriptural term—and He was scriptural so far as we know anything of Him and His thought, and His study and His language and also His action—the terms purpose, resolution, determination seem more appropriate.

The materials before us consist of a number of facts, practically speaking texts of scripture, which have not been put in relation to one another for many centuries. If an expression in the New Testament resembles or repeats another in the Old there is a possibility, which may or may not finally be raised to a certainty, that the resemblance or repetition is deliberate. This book endeavours to discover the extent, the cause, and the mode of that deliberation. Undoubtedly some imagination is necessary to discover this, but it must be imagination working on the lines of history. And it should be a form of sympathy with dead authors.

To a number of persons the pages of Holy Scripture contain, and were always meant to contain, a cryptic armoury of texts which support the idea of a Catholic Church under a supreme infallible ruler. These persons bridge over their gaps with an imagination in sympathy with their object but not with their authors, to whom they attribute a prescience of which they never dreamed of being capable. Another set of persons finds on every page a proof of the Calvinistic or other doctrine of the Atonement; they too use their imagination through highly coloured spectacles. May it, however, be possible to see the scriptural facts and texts through the spectacles of the first Christian century? to use the imagination which they used and as they used it? These pages contain the result of an effort to do this for some portions of the gospel narrative. It is an effort of imagination and sympathy working on historic lines—imperfect and incomplete, as the author is aware.

That any one should ever be the Christ is a matter of recognition, a subjective matter for those who like the term, which involves no sort of disparagement. If Christ is *the anointed son of David*—and this is the narrowest and closest sense which the word can carry—he is such only by the recognition of men, even when men are represented only by the Baptist. The act of God is invisible. The coronation of the King would be meaningless without the concurrence of men, who must endorse the right divine or human. If Christ is the universal Saviour—and this is the largest sense of the term—still more is he such by the recognition of men. Who is to proclaim him but men? That Jesus should be Christ

PREFACE

without any meaning in the identity is not conceivable. Consequently, the act of God being assumed, the act of men is required to follow, and its following is a matter of history and can be investigated. Investigation can go no further now into the question of Joseph's descent from David. That has either to be assumed on the evidence or else we must say that the divine Adoption of Ps. 89, "I will adopt him my firstborn," suffices on the side of Jesus' connection with David : but the identity with the Christ which forthwith commences after the resolution of Jesus to be the Christ is a public matter, of history, as well as of inner life. And as history it depends upon evidence of various kinds, including testimony, which includes recognition as its correlative. Hence the prominence given in John 1^6 to the Baptist's witness, a prominence which is secured by a sharp interruption of the sublime train of thought which has begun to be set forth in that opening chapter.

On the other hand it may be worth while to say here that *Jesus* and *Christ* are not interchangeable terms, and never can be, though they are currently often interchanged. Jesus is the Man, Christ is His title. He entered upon it in a way which has no parallel. But it has so been ordained that we owe it entirely to the argument from prophecy that we speak of Jesus " Christ " at all. And in regard to the Virgin-birth—a doctrine to which these pages refer frequently, and they will be found at issue with both sides of the controversy on St. Luke's declaration of it in Luke. 1^{35}, the one verse which has seemed to commit to that doctrine not only Luke 1, 2, but all Luke and therefore all Acts—there should be no hesitation in saying that He was born of "the Virgin" Mary of prophecy just as He was Jesus "the Christ" of prophecy. Without prophecy and the study of it we could not have known of Jesus "Christ," nor of "the Virgin" Mary. And how few know and reflect that He was made flesh " of (ἐκ) the Holy Ghost " in the words of the Nicene creed! There is no authority for ὑπό instead of ἐκ, and never has been.

This is not the place to enlarge upon Messianism, whether national or not, whether as "a consistent dream" or the reverse, nor upon the Messiah supposed to be waiting behind the clouds. But if Dan. 7 was in any sense a source of inspiration to the Lord Jesus, there is room for the opinion that Ps. 89, though strangely overlooked by the authorities, is another and far more present source. It contains not only the clouds, but His Pre-existence, the guidance for His travels, His claim as David's son, His Prayer, His rejection, His disappointments and encouragements, the defeat of His adversary (Herod as identified by Justin Martyr), His ultimate Resurrection, His names, Firstborn, Elect, Christ, and a strong confirmation of His name, Son of Man. Unless He applied Ps. 89 to Himself the Gospels are not intelligible. To the title, *The Son of the Man*, not only has Dan. 7 contributed in Aramaic *bar-nāšā*, but Ps. 89[47 f] *ben-ādām* (implied in the plural there used) and *geber* (*strong-one*, ἄνθρωπος).

I have been unable to find that any writer has treated the subject of this book, with the exception of the volume on Papias mentioned above. Obligations have been acknowledged when I was conscious of them, including obligations to standard works such as the *Encyclopædia*

PREFACE xvii

Biblica and Schürer's *History of the Jewish People* (Eng. Tr.). Only after going to press have I seen Dr. Abbott's latest and most valuable work on *The Son of Man*. Had I read it before writing, I might perhaps not have written at all, for, as Horace says, (Urit enim, etc.)

> They who outshine their age with brilliant torch
> Depress the lesser qualities they scorch.

In England Dr. Abbott outshines his age. For the thoughtful his studies form an essential guide-book. He seems to appreciate in an increasing measure the importance of the LXX as a main factor in the production of the New Testament. I venture to quote two sentences of his which go to confirm results obtained in the following pages : " But it will also be found that there are probably few or no traces of Enochian influence in any words assigned, on the best authority, to Christ." " Confusions apparently caused by the doubt in the minds of evangelists . . . parallel to the doubt about the saying in Ezekiel." For " parallel to " I would suggest, with less apparent caution, " caused by." But few of the trains of thought here followed have been anticipated by that accomplished theologian, by whom we still hope to be instructed, and, what is more, uplifted as few indeed can without seeming to do so. I am also conscious of indebtedness to the comprehensive and appreciative criticism of the Fourth Gospel by Prof. B. W. Bacon. The addition of Chapter XIV on Dr. Schweitzer's *Quest of the Historic Jesus* was an afterthought.

Italics have been used to denote the verbal coincidences, rarely otherwise. The oracles are quoted as from the Greek Bible.

b

If the tone of this essay strikes the reader as too confident in places, the writer can only state his conviction that he could never have written it without the aid of which St. Paul speaks : Such confidence have we through Christ to God-ward. This is a safeguard, but not against error. As the late General Butler says : "When you cut down the forest or clear the brushwood in a new colony, the first crop that springs from the soil has many weeds in it. It is inevitable that it should be so : perhaps it is even necessary. The man who doesn't know how much he doesn't know may have his uses in a new land, where there is plenty of space." At the same time the present writer's purpose has been more limited—only to cut down wood for the Building of the House of the Great King that is builded in glory for evermore.

HINDHEAD,
November 1911.

CONTENTS

CHAPTER I

THE MAGI

Preliminary p.1. The "fanciful element" in time-honoured prophecies p. 3. The peril of the Assyrian king p. 8. The approach of the Kings from the East p. 11. The escape to Egypt p. 13. Kings, or magicians? p. 14. The Babe of Bethlehem p. 18. The star p. 22. The gifts of the Magi p. 24. Other features of the Magi-story p. 28.

CHAPTER II

HEROD THE ASSYRIAN

The possible origin of the appellative p. 30. The name "Assyrian" confirmed by scripture texts p. 32. Interpretation of prophecy as affected by catastrophic events p. 36. Oracles of the fall of Jerusalem p. 40. Oracles of Baptism p. 44. The dreams of Joseph p. 46. The flight into Egypt and the return p. 47. Difficulties of the Rachel oracle p. 49. The Immanuel oracle p. 52. Hellenism in Palestine p. 53.

CHAPTER III

THE SHEPHERDS

The secret of the Messiah p. 61. The locality of the Shepherds p. 62. The valley of Achor for a resting-place p. 65. The direction to Bethlehem p. 68. The angel calls His name p. 70. The paradox of peace, and the thing of price p. 72.

The arrangement of words in the *Gloria in Excelsis* p. 74. The Book of Wisdom in Luke p. 77. Was Herod's will and testament discovered in Isaiah ? p. 79. St. Luke's preface to his Gospel p. 80. St. Luke was not a Gentile p. 84. Note p. 88.

CHAPTER IV

HEROD AGRIPPA I

A reference in Isaiah p. 89. Had the author of Acts seen Josephus ? p. 90. Herod's fatal symptoms p. 93. Modern physicians on the data of Herod's death p. 95. Josephus compared with Isaiah p. 97. The prophetic view of Agrippa's death p. 99. Agrippa both Babylonian and Assyrian p. 103. The fatal symptoms of Antiochus Epiphanes p. 108. " Worm-eaten " and " fowl-eaten " p. 110.

CHAPTER V

THE FIRSTBORN

The oracles in the *Book of James* p. 115. The cave of Bethlehem p. 116. The Virgin-birth not in St. Paul p. 121. The paramount importance of Ps. 89 p. 123. The Epistle to the Hebrews on our Lord's tribe p. 125. " The Holy Ghost shall come upon thee " p. 128. The Firstborn in St. Luke, St. Paul, and *Hebrews* p. 132. The Firstborn of the Dead p. 135. Other scriptural bases in *James* p. 138.

CHAPTER VI

JOSEPH

False ingenuity refuting Luke on the Census p. 141. Herod the Ethnarch or the King p. 144. " Jesus himself when he began " p. 146. The Building of the House p. 153. Cyrus, Cyrius, Cyrinus p. 155. Cyrinus' antecedents p. 159.

CONTENTS

Questions for Luke as a historian p. 162. Some questions answered by Luke the Prophet p. 165. The Rod from the root of Jesse p. 167. Nazareth and Nazarene p. 171. Joseph's name and circumstances p. 173. The Remnant or Residue p. 175.

CHAPTER VII

JOHN THE BAPTIST

The Benedictus a Levitic cradle-song p. 179. John's ministry based on Malachi p. 184. Josephus on the Baptist and the Son of Sirach on Elijah p. 186. John's charter and mission to the Levites p. 188. The Sadducees and the Pharisees p. 190. John's message out of Malachi p. 193. The locality of John's witness p. 195. "Behold, the Lamb of God" p. 198. Two trances of John p. 199. The Covenant of Noah p. 202. The Purgation of the Temple p. 204. Is Justin's tradition earlier than one in the Fourth Gospel? p. 206. The Chananæans p. 208.

CHAPTER VIII

JUDAS

A trace of a list of the oracles p. 214. The Potter's Field in Matthew p. 215. The Falling-asunder in Acts p. 218. Postscriptural accounts of Judas. The bag, the bursting, the curse, the crushing p. 223.

CHAPTER IX

PETER AND PAUL

Christ the Rock p. 230. The Smitten Rock p. 231. Peter's confession p. 234. Peter and Eliakim p. 236. The Porter and the Keys p. 238. The power of the Keys put in commission p. 240. The Martyr's crown p. 243. The precious test and the precious word p. 244. St. Paul and St. Peter at Babylon p. 247. The doctrine of Kenôsis, emptying p. 249. The Chaldeans the enemy p. 252. The Chaldean Elymas or Hetoimas p. 255. Other Chaldeans p. 262.

CHAPTER X

THE TRANSFIGURATION

The bases of the narrative p. 265. Sion is Hermon p. 270. The trance of Peter on Hermon p. 272. General conditions of a vision p. 274. Particular conditions of this vision p. 275. The voice from the cloud p. 280. Peter's study of Holy Scripture p. 282. The expulsion of the dumb spirit p. 286. The raising of the Widow's Son p. 286. " Elijah restoreth all things " p. 289. The result of the Transfiguration p. 291. " Transfiguration " in St. Paul's view p. 292. Did St. Paul know the Transfiguration narrative ? p. 295. Is another explanation of the origin of the Gospel narrative possible ? p. 297. Deliberate fulfilment of Zechariah by Jesus is the true solution of the coincidences p. 300. The Lord's movements governed by prophecy p. 302. " The compensation," " the sons of men," and " The Man " p. 306. Further guidance of Ps. 89 p. 310. The Charter of the Lord p. 313. The Messiah-secret p. 315.

CHAPTER XI

THE OLIVET DISCOURSE

False attribution of discourses to a genius p. 320. The form of the Olivet discourse p. 322. The matter of the Olivet discourse p. 323. " The blessings of David " p. 329. The fig tree p. 332. " Not a hair of your head " p. 333. Was the discourse constructed by the Evangelists with a predictory

CONTENTS

purpose? p. 335. Certain features of the discourse and an attempted reconstruction p. 337. The Lord without Eschatology p. 344.

CHAPTER XII

THE BETRAYAL

One day of David's life p. 346. The Greek narrative of David's flight p. 347. Points of identity in the gospel narrative p. 349. The Agony in the Garden p. 357. The Bloody Sweat p. 360. Rejection of the Agony in the Fourth Gospel p. 362. The Ode of Moses, and Ps. 92 concerning Malchus' ear p. 363. The "Agony" connected with Hosea p. 365. "The Lord reigned from the Tree" p. 367. Justin on the Argument from Prophecy p. 369. Is the Betrayal narrative manufactured or does it describe deliberate fulfilment? p. 370. The Triumphal Entry p. 371. The eating of the Passover p. 373. The two swords p. 375. How far is the Malchus story manufactured? p. 379. Are the swords for fighting? p. 381. The sword of Justice p. 384. The irony of anguish p. 385. The name Gethsemane. The Cup p. 387. The opportunity of Judas p. 390. Judas deliberately fulfils Scripture p. 393.

CHAPTER XIII

WHAT, THEN, DID PAPIAS WRITE?

Title of the work of Papias p. 396. "The oracles" in the New Testament p. 398. "The oracles" in the Apostolic Fathers and in Philo p. 402. The Apostolic Fathers in their regard for the Old Testament p. 407. The extant contents of Papias p. 408. Translation of some of Papias's expressions p. 413. "Peter's instructions" p. 416. The oracles of Papias still founded on the Old Testament p. 418. "The vine with ten thousand shoots," etc. p. 421. Ignatius and St. John on "filtration" of the Church from Judaism p. 425.

CHAPTER XIV

DR. SCHWEITZER'S QUESTIONS

The Messianic secret p. 429. The MAN in the Book of Wisdom p. 430. The resolution of the Christ p. 433. Partial discoveries of the Christ p. 434. The Lord and the Forerunner p. 435. Jesus, the Twelve, and the multitude p. 439. " The cities of Israel " p. 443. " I will go before you " p. 446.

LIST OF ORACLES p. 450.

CHAPTER I

THE MAGI

To pronounce the words Jesus Christ is to assert a coincidence, a coincidence which is by no means accidental but providential, in accordance with the purpose of God, and inseparable from the belief in that purpose. The expectation of the Christ was held by a considerable body of opinion in the first century B.C., and may be described as a faith or trust or belief: when Jesus came He was pronounced to fulfil many terms of that expectation. A coincidence was discovered between the facts of His life and the ideas of the previous faith. Jesus was identified with the Christ, the Man was found to correspond with the Opinion, the Life to fulfil the Faith. It is therefore vain to say that in these modern days we, whether Christians or not, have no interest in the question whether Jesus was the Christ. Neither the person Jesus nor the title Christ can be ignored. Nor can it be argued that coincidences can be put aside as a secondary matter. Historically the great coincidence, the great providence, lies at the very basis of the Faith, and the Faith can never cease to be a matter of history.

Nor can the coincidences which supported the Faith cease to be the subject of study. For it is not yet known how the popular belief that Jesus was the Christ was formed between the years A.D. 30 and 70, and between 70 and 120. But it is quite clear that the apostolic writers held that it was largely formed upon coincidences between what happened and what had been written

2 ORACLES IN THE NEW TESTAMENT

centuries before. The four Gospels contain a hundred passages of Old Testament which are treated as fulfilled in the events which they relate. Fifty of these are introduced by expressions which show that the evangelists considered them to be fulfilments. They write, " then was fulfilled what was written," " as it is written," or something similar. Fulfilment cannot fail to imply the recognition of a coincidence, whatever else and whatever more it means. About eighteen more fulfilments are claimed in the Acts, where it is evident that St. Peter, St. Paul, and other apostolic men are building the Church by means of fulfilments of passages from the Old Testament. The Epistles contain a hundred passages which are introduced by a similar formula, which would appeal to Jews and any others who knew the Bible, with a necessary, crowning and conclusive force. There was—and this is always to be remembered —the force of a life and a love behind the words quoted and greater than all, but this cannot now be estimated and is to be put on one side for that very reason. What we are now concerned with is merely the rational machinery employed towards the formation of the faith. This with all the coincidences involved is a proper matter for scientific treatment.

The modern mind has a natural dislike for what it considers to be fantastical and farfetched. But it has also an affectation of dislike for the same. This affected dislike is apt to be imported whenever any train of reasoning is submitted which conflicts or seems to conflict with its established or habitual modes of thought, and especially with its prejudices. But it should not be allowed, and perhaps the best way to avoid it will be to notice, first of all, some fantastical and farfetched coincidences which have become time-honoured as fulfilments of prophecy. If the half-dozen prophecies here to be adduced are not considered to be fantastical and farfetched, then their acquittal will serve for hundreds more of the same sort which can be adduced hereafter. For it may here be stated that if the fulfilments of prophecy declared to be such by the writers of the New Testament are only as one-half of those which have been recognized in modern times as actuating them, they do not stand in the proportion even of one-quarter or one-eighth to the number of those which a more careful study discloses. To use a simile from physiography, as there are mountain-ranges on the land, so there are mountain-ranges under the sea which have to be counted and charted as much as the former, and sometimes the results will be no less startling and momentous than when the land-ranges were brought into the map. Why have these submarine quotations, if we may use such a term concerning quotations which have only imperfectly been brought to the pen, not been noted before? In the first place, because we are all inclined not to see what is before our eyes, as the history of mechanical discovery abundantly proves. In the second place, because the Greek Bible has for practical purposes been little better than a sealed book to the ordinary Greek scholar till the last twenty years, when Dr. Swete's Cambridge edition appeared. And the Greek Bible is the real cradle of all Christian thought and doctrine.

The " Fanciful Element " in Time-honoured Prophecies.

To begin, then, with the half-dozen prophecies which a candid reader now would consider fantastical and farfetched if he came upon them for the first time. Let us start with the early pages of St. Matthew's Gospel. " Now all this has happened that it might be fulfilled that was written by the Lord through the prophet, saying . . . And they shall call his name Emmanuel, which is, being interpreted,

4 ORACLES IN THE NEW TESTAMENT

With us is God." Granted that the birth of the future son was fraught with Messianic import, it can hardly be maintained that the prophet's words were without some meaning for his contemporaries, that in fact they bore no meaning that could be seen for upwards of seven hundred years. It must therefore be admitted that his own son, or another, was to be born, and was subsequently born and was named Emmanuel. Of this son we know nothing more. Of the Son, whom he prefigured, as is granted, we know also nothing further from the pages of Scripture under that name, *Emmanuel*. Nowhere else is he introduced, no reference is made to him as so called. It is never shown that Emmanuel is another name for Christ or for Jesus. Nothing but an indulgent habit on the part of Christians has caused us to forbear with this farfetched and fantastical application of a specific prophecy, a prediction referring to a definite person by name having been taken as if it referred to another person whose name bears no relation to the other. It is no more related to the other than if it had been "Solomon"* as meaning our Peace or one of many others. And, further, the verse is not quoted from either the Hebrew (*she shall call*) or the Greek Bible (*thou shalt call*), and both are very different from *they shall call*.

The second is, "That it might be fulfilled which was spoken by the Lord through the prophet, saying, Out of Egypt have I called my son." The original of this is in the Hebrew, where it is said of the Israelites at the Exodus, "When Israel was a child, then I loved him, and called my son out of Egypt." "My son" here is Israel personified. Now it is a little farfetched and fantastical to take a passage of the clearest and simplest meaning, applied by

* The *Psalm of Solomon* (17^{37}), which describes Messiah as king, deliberately contrasts the old Solomon and his future antitype. See Ryle and James *in loc*.

THE MAGI

Hosea to the whole people, and to make it apply to the infant Jesus on the occasion of the flight to or from Egypt, though Matt. $2^{13, 14, 20}$ (*arise, by night*) indicates the hour of the Exodus. To regard Him here as the first of the Israel of God, the Jacob or the Abraham of the Israel of God, is a fancy, fanciful, fantastical. Before the fulfilment can be understood we have to pass through three stages of identification: first, that the Lord is The Firstborn (on which see below); next, that "My Firstborn Son is Israel" (Exod. 4^{22}); and thirdly, that "I called my Son Israel out of Egypt."

The third is, " Then was fulfilled that which was spoken through Jeremiah the prophet, saying, A voice was heard in Ramah, weeping and great mourning, Rachel weeping for her children; and she would not be comforted, because they are not." The original passage is a poetical reference to the stalwart men of the tribe of Benjamin, Rachel's son, departing, as the prophet saw them, into hopeless exile, as it then seemed, along the way to Babylon. This Ramah was north of Jerusalem in the territory of Benjamin, ten miles from where the tomb of Rachel was supposed to be, near Bethlehem, south of Jerusalem. To suppose that Ramah in Benjamin would be included in " the borders of Bethlehem " is straining a point. To suppose that there was another Ramah—certainly a common name—near Rachel's tomb, and therefore near Bethlehem, is not enough, for we still have to strain a point in considering that the murdered Innocents, to whom the prediction is made to apply, could be called Rachel's children, her " offspring," just because they had lived near Rachel's tomb. It is somewhat fantastical to discover this coincidence, and the basis of it is fetched from afar.

The fourth is a passage which, as it stands now, forms part of a discourse of Christ, but many commentators,

6 ORACLES IN THE NEW TESTAMENT

from Neander and before him, would fain have it to be no more than a gloss. " For as Jonah was three days and three nights in the belly of the sea-monster, so also," etc. Those who do not feel that this is fantastical, and far-fetched, and untrue to all the records we possess in the Gospels will probably not take the trouble to read this further. With this we pass from the first Gospel, and go to the Acts.

The fifth and sixth passages bear, like the fourth, upon the Resurrection. St. Paul's speech at Antioch in Pisidia is reported by St. Luke thus (Acts 13^{33}): "This promise God hath fulfilled to our children in that he raised up Jesus, as also it is written in the second psalm, Thou art my Son, this day have I begotten thee. Now that he raised him up from the dead, now no more to return to corruption—he hath spoken on this wise, I will give you the holy and sure blessings of David." But this latter promise, as the speaker and the reporter well knew, was unintelligible by itself, and must not be dissociated from the following verse, " Because he saith also in another psalm, Thou wilt not give thy Holy One to see corruption." The first of these three quotations seems at first to have no bearing upon the Resurrection, but to declare a recognition of sonship, heirship, kingdom, and withal some figurative new birth on a particular day. This, however, is the chief passage (and probably the only passage which does not involve a certain amount of special reasoning for its application, since Ps. 89^{27}, where *Firstborn* ($\pi\rho\omega\tau\acute{o}\tau o\kappa o\varsigma$) occurs, might not have carried its special force into Christian doctrine without this, and it has actually failed to carry it to the translators of the Revised Version) which has caused St. Paul's expression, *The firstborn from the dead* (Col. 1^{18}). And yet the original in Ps. 2 has no bearing on the Resurrection except upon one assumption, which we know was made by St. Paul

THE MAGI

(Rom. 1⁴), that Jesus was "defined" or "declared" to be God's Son by the resurrection of the dead. If we moderns shrink from that idea of his definition (ὁρισθέντος)—and certainly we cannot but take the definition, the ὅρος, as a sharp dividing line, shutting out as well as shutting in, not merely as a line to be pulled about at choice—then we have to admit that the use of the psalmist's words is both fantastical and irrelevant, which is worse than farfetched. If we follow St. Paul in this idea, we are precluded at any moment preceding the Resurrection from some measure of the conviction which, for instance, was uttered by the centurion in front of the cross, "Truly this man was God's son." We note that St. Luke is different here from the two synoptics, for he gives the words as "Certainly this was a righteous man," and we naturally suppose that St. Luke herein shows his acquaintance with his friend St. Paul's definition.

The second text, from Isa. 55³, "I will give you the holy and sure blessings of David," in its application in St. Paul's discourse, if not wholly irrelevant, is farfetched and fantastical until taken in close connection with Ps. 16¹⁰. But it is not contended that Isaiah wrote this psalm. The commentary treatment of the Bible, as if one writer filled with meaning the passage of another and so made it applicable and possible of fulfilment, receives in this case a good illustration. It is an instance of the oracular treatment of the Bible, as the collection of "the oracles of God." For these oracles were consulted by the apostolic writers not historically, not critically, nor yet as heathen oracles were consulted, but with a belief in the unity of scripture which at that time was inevitable. The wonder is that they were ever supposed or expected to be treated in any other way.

8 ORACLES IN THE NEW TESTAMENT

The Peril of the Assyrian King.

Now with this amount of cautionary preface let us take the story of the Magi in St. Matthew and trace it back to its origins in the Greek Bible. It may be premised that the oracles which follow have no relation known at present to a collection of "Matthæan oracles." This perhaps may be discovered. Nor again is it pretended that there is no foundation in fact for the Magi-story. The year A.D. 70 was destined to mark a division between Jewish and Christian interpretations of the Bible as the oracular source of guidance to both parties: it was to be their watershed from which the two currents of thought, one Jewish and the other Christian, were to pour in opposite directions from the same hill-country of Holy Scripture, no part of which was to be found more full of springs, more like a "many-fountained Ida," than the book of the prophet Isaiah. As soon as the Christian Jew resorted to the oracle, he struck his finger on the place where it was written (Isa. 8^5) in the passage that he already knew as one of the most Messianic, that is to say the most Christian, of the whole Bible,

> Isa. $8^{5\text{-}8}$ And the Lord added to speak unto me further, Because this people doth not choose *the water of Siloam* that journeyeth quietly, but chooseth to have Rezin and Remaliah's son to be king over you, therefore behold the Lord bringeth up against you the water of the river, strong and great, *the king of the Assyrians* and his glory: and he shall go up against every one of your valleys, and shall walk round against every one of your walls, and shall take away from Judea *a man who shall be able to lift up a head* or capable of some performance, and his encampment shall be so as to fill the breadth of thy country. With us is God.

THE MAGI

This is nothing but a prediction, in the given circumstances, that the water of Siloam that journeyed so quietly in the golden tankard, into the silver basin beside the altar, from which it flowed by a pipe to the Kidron eastwards, as the crown * of the ceremonial at the Feast of Tabernacles, the greatest and most crowded and jubilant feast of the Jews, should by the Jews' own choice journey no more. In A.D. 70 the Feast of Tabernacles, after an existence of some five centuries with few interruptions, could no more be celebrated at the Holy City which was demolished. As a prediction, indeed, the text, though so ancient, could hardly have been expected to have any pointed fulfilment apart from the grander issues which included it; but after their fulfilment it must have appeared to carry its own point, its own sting, when the glory of the great feast of the nation was gone for ever. "My people loved to have it so, and what would they do in the end thereof?" They chose to rebel against Rome, and their choice was their extermination.

This will seem a small point at the first reading, however stinging to the Jewish opponent, if not supported by further fulfilment in the first century A.D. But the context also had its fulfilment in the eyes of those who lived then. For that "a man should be taken away from Judea who *should be able to lift up a head* or capable of some performance" was clearly another prediction fulfilled, in Christ who was made to be "*the head* of the corner" (Acts 4^{11}), "*the head* over all things to the Church," "the fulness of him that filleth all in all" (Eph. 1^{22}). But what is more strange is that the intervening passage had also its recognized fulfilment. *The Assyrian king* is Herod. This is proved beyond all doubt.

---

* On the connection between the imagery of this usage and that of Baptism, see the *Journal of Theological Studies*, Jan. 1912.

10 ORACLES IN THE NEW TESTAMENT

In Justin Martyr's argument with the Jew Trypho * (about A.D. 140) we find that Justin has to prove that Isa. 7^{14} refers to Christ, in answer to the Jews' contention that it refers to Hezekiah himself, and he shows that the words (Isa. 8^4) "before the child shall know how to call father or mother" make it quite inapplicable to Hezekiah and applicable only to "our Christ."

"For at the time of his birth" (says Justin) "Magi from Arabia came and worshipped him, having before come to Herod who was then reigning in your land, whom the word calls king of the Assyrians because of *his godless and lawless mind*. For you know that the Holy Spirit often says such things in parables and similitudes: as he has done even to the whole people in Jerusalem, in saying to them often, 'Thy father was an Amorite, and thy mother an Hittite'" (Ezek. 16^3).

That this identification of Herod with the king of the Assyrians in prophecy was no random or temporary fancy of Justin is proved by the fact that he recurs to it several pages later, and applies the same prophetic title to Herod the Great's second successor. "But when Herod (Antipas) had succeeded to the power assigned to him, to whom Pilate by way of a favour sent Jesus bound, God having foreseen that this also would happen had said thus"—

Hos. 10^6 Having bound him they brought him away to the house of the Assyrian † as a friendly gift to the king.

The same passage of Isa. $8^{9 \text{ f}}$ enables us to see the way

* *Dial.* 77 (303).
† *Dial.* 103 (331) εἰς Ἀσσυρίου (LXX Ἀσσυρίους) ἀπήνεγκαν ξένια τῷ βασιλεῖ (LXX adds Ἰαρείμ, but of this addition Justin says not a word). For the variation of Justin from LXX and Hebrew, see later (pp. 25^{ff}). Tertullian, too, recognizes Hos. 10^6 as "de Christo" (*Adv. Marc.* 4^{42}).

THE MAGI

further to the device of Herod, of which we shall see more later.

> Isa. 8⁹ If ye again wax strong, again shall ye be defeated. And whatsoever device ye devise the Lord will scatter it away, and the word that ye speak shall surely not abide in you, for with us is God. . . . Fear ye not his fear nor be troubled.

The Approach of the Kings from the East.

And here we are struck by finding an alternative Magi-story within the limits of the New Testament, and also by way of a fulfilment of the same Isa. 8⁷, and still following upon the sure ground that Herod is the king of Assyria. This text clearly identifies him with "*the water of the river that is strong and great*, which the Lord bringeth up against you." What river is this? For as surely as it was, by hypothesis, an instrument of punishment on the people of God, it must have a local habitation and a name. At present it is a plague and peril which in some sort must be removed. It is a *device* which must be scattered. We ask, therefore, Is it the Tigris, most proper to Assyria? Is it the Euphrates, rather more proper to Babylon? Or is it another? There is little doubt that one solution of this question is to be found in Rev. 16¹², where we read that the sixth angel "poured out his phial upon the river, the great river Euphrates; and his water was dried up that there might be prepared *the way of the kings from the rising of the sun.*" For Isaiah had long ago said that—

> Isa. 60³ *Kings shall journey at thy light* and Gentiles at thy brightness—

and just before this verse he said in connection with the river—

Isa. 59¹⁰ And they from the west shall fear the name of the Lord, and *these from the rising of the sun* the glorious Name: for there shall come *as a violent river* the wrath from the Lord, it shall come with anger; and there shall come on behalf of Sion *the rescuer*, and he shall turn away impieties from Jacob.

The seer of Ephesus, in fact, saw in his vision the Euphrates, which had been a symbol of the wrath of the Lord, dried up for the beneficent purpose of enabling kings to come from the East to worship at the light that was to appear in the city of David.

And yet was it certain that the river was the Euphrates and no other? Was it possible that any reader of Isaiah could fail to answer that the Nile was predicted in the great vision of Egypt in Isa. 19⁵⁻¹⁰ to be dried up? The Old Testament seemed to point this way and yet the Christian prophets have not seen the Nile in the dried-up river; the Nile is not mentioned nor meant. But there was another passage in Isaiah that must have been brought under consideration—

Isa. 10²⁴ Fear not, my people, ye that dwell in Sion, from *the Assyrians*, that he shall smite thee with a rod (Herod's rod had been mentioned in 10¹⁵): for I will bring a plague against thee, *to see the way of Egypt*. For yet a little and my wrath shall cease, and my anger shall come upon *his device*, and God shall raise against them a plague like that of Midian in the place of affliction, and his anger shall be at *the way by the sea unto the road towards Egypt*. And it shall be in that day that his yoke shall be taken off thy shoulder, and his fear from off thee, . . . for he shall come to the city of Aiath . . . Megiddo . . . Michmash . . . fear shall take hold of *Ramah* the

THE MAGI 13

city of Saul . . . Gallim . . . (Laish) . . . Anathoth
. . . Madmena . . . Gibbeir.

We seem to be drawing very near to the visit of the Magi, the flight into Egypt, the wrath of Herod, and the massacre of the Innocents in Bethlehem *and all its borders,* as narrated in Matt. 2. We note that there is mention here of a plague on the way to Egypt, but not of a river.

The Escape to Egypt.

There is yet another train of visionary thought to be mentioned in this connection. The seer of Ephesus has written, in Rev. 12^{13}, a reference to a river which is not the Euphrates or the Nile, and yet might, if it received a geographical location, be placed on the way to Egypt. " And when the (dragon or) serpent saw that he was cast to the earth he pursued the *woman who had borne the man-child.* And there were given to the woman the two wings of the great eagle that she should *flee* unto the wilderness unto her place, where she is nurtured three times and a half from the presence of the serpent. And the serpent cast out of his mouth behind the woman *water as a river*, that he might make her to be carried away by the river. And the earth assisted the woman, and the earth opened her mouth and devoured the river which the serpent had cast out of its mouth. And the serpent *was wrath* against the woman, and departed to make war with the rest of her seed, *them that keep* the commandments of God and *have the witness* of Jesus: and he stood on the sand of the sea." This passage, like the rest of the Apocalypse, has been interpreted in countless ways, and it is capable of more than one meaning because more than one element has entered into its composition—the eagle, the wilderness, the times, the assistance of the earth. We shall see later (Chapter V) that there is some reason to think that it may be connected with the infancy of the Baptist. But it seems probable that it bears upon the persecution by Herod of the child Jesus and his mother, in accordance with the prophecy of Isa. 8[7]. The description of the wilderness and the river precisely suits the so-called " river of Egypt," now the Wady-el-Areesh, which is occasionally in winter a turbulent rushing torrent, but for the rest of the year a wide, dry river-bed, serving as the natural boundary of Egypt. It forms the subject of a specific promise in—

> Isa. 27[12] And it shall be in that day that God will stop up from the channel of *the river* as far *as Rhinocorura* (Wady-el-Areesh), and shall draw together the sons of Israel.

If we suppose that the seer of Ephesus had been pondering Isaiah, we can see how naturally Isa. 8[8] in the Hebrew, which he so often preferred to the Greek, would have suggested the rescuing *wings*. The birth of *the man-child* had been mentioned just before. Even the " *witnesses*, faithful men " (Isa. 8[2]), are perhaps in his mind.

There is a certain difficulty in regard to the serpent casting forth a river which is the king of Assyria, but this is a kind of difficulty inherent in the interpretation of visions. (We have, however, in the pages of Justin, an illustration of the nearness of the ideas of a persecuting Herod and a devouring serpent. After identifying the roaring lion of Ps. 22 with Herod he proceeds : " *Or else he meant the devil, whom Moses calls the serpent.*") In other words, Herod shall persecute like a violent river as far as the boundary of Judea on the way to Egypt, but his limit is Rhinocorura. Once across that, the violence is harmless to the true Israel of God.

Kings, or Magicians?

But this is an anticipation. Let us ask next, how did *the kings from the East* become *Magi*—an evil name in

THE MAGI

the first century, as that of Simon *Magus* and Elymas the *Magus* demonstrates, though translated here favourably " wise men " ? Why should men whose entire class was associated with evil, be represented as coming to visit the infant Christ at Bethlehem ? Kings they were in Isa. 60^3. They continued to be kings as late as A.D. 68 or later, when Rev. 16^{12} was written. But in Matt. 2 they are magicians—idolaters of that most insidious form, the false prophets who contended with the work of the Divine prophets. The answer must be that when Matt. 2 was written it was felt to be more important to recognize their character as idolaters, or till recently such, than their position as kings, since their homage to the infant king—

Isa. 32^1 Behold, a king, *a righteous king*, shall reign—

betokened from the first his coming triumph over idolatry, the opening of the eyes of the blind, the bringing the bound out of bonds (Isa. 42^7), the bursting of every yoke of iniquity (Isa. 58^6). Many kings of the East were past masters in the magic art. Cicero had written that nobody could be king of Persia without a previous knowledge of the training and science of the Magi. Idolatry was the enemy of the Christian faith, but kingship was not. An incident that betokened the death-blow to idolatry under the form of false prophecy might well be placed in the forefront of the life of the Son of God, who was on earth the Prophet of Nazareth. Moreover, before Matthew was written, the time had come in which the old charge of casting out devils by Beelzebub was magnified into a more general argument that the alleged miracles of Christ were wrought by the aid of magic in order to produce the belief that He was God's son. This argument would find at least a preliminary answer in the homage of representative Magi. Lastly, none but the astronomical caste could be expected to understand the heavenly phenomena.

16 ORACLES IN THE NEW TESTAMENT

The astronomy of Babylon was four thousand years old.

By Justin's time there is no recognition that they were kings : they are *magicians from Arabia*, as he calls them repeatedly. Why from Arabia ? At first we should be disposed to answer in the words of

> Isa. 60⁶ *All from Saba* shall come bringing *gold and frankincense, and precious stone* shall they bring—

along with—

> Ps. 72¹⁰ *Kings of Arabia and Saba* shall *bring gifts.*

But it is strange that Justin hardly quotes from Isa. 60 at all, and appears not to have seen its bearing on the story of the Magi. His view is different. He says of the Magi, "that they had been carried away as spoils* unto all doings of the devil, but when they came and worshipped Christ evidently had revolted from the power that had spoiled them, which the word mysteriously indicates for us as *dwelling in Damascus, then part of Arabia* though now annexed to Syrophœnicia, as you Jews must all admit," while the evil power is called Samaria because it is sinful and unrighteous. Samaria is famous to this day as the site of Herod's palace and his colossal statue of the Emperor Augustus. At the same time, Justin insists that the Ramah in question is in Arabia : he says "Because, then, of the voice which was about to be heard from Ramah, that is to say from Arabia (for there is to this day a place in Arabia called Ramah), lamentation was about to fill the place where Rachel, wife of Jacob, surnamed Israel, the holy patriarch, is buried, that is to say Bethlehem, of the women lamenting their own children that had been killed, and having no comfort in their misfortune." Justin can only mean that a voice

---
* *Dial.* 304 D. (78).

THE MAGI

from Arabia was to cause lamentation in Bethlehem for the massacre of the Innocents there, and that this voice had been heard by the Magi in Arabia (Damascus), and served or tended to convert them. What guidance then had been found concerning the conversion of idolaters in Damascus? In *the burden of Damascus* we find clear indications of it.

> Isa. 17$^{7\text{ff}}$ In that day the man shall be confident in him that made him, and his eyes shall look unto the Holy One of Israel, and they shall no more be confident in the altars nor in the works of their hands which their fingers have made, and they shall not see the trees nor their abominations.

The voice from Arabia would of necessity be a voice of "woe!" Now we actually find a denunciation of woe in

> Isa. 17$^{12, 14}$ *Woe*, O multitude of many nations! Towards evening (the west) there shall be grief: before morning it shall have ceased. This is the portion of *them that ravage you.*

These passages, though not cited by Justin, were present to the minds of those who formed the tradition which he has followed. Moreover, the name of *Arabia* appears in close union with *Damascus and Samaria* in Isa. 10^9, and Arabia may be regarded as the firstfruits of idolatry destined to be taken from under the face of Herod as spoil by the new-born Child.

> Isa. 8^4 Before the child knoweth how to call father or mother, he shall take the power of Damascus and the spoils of Samaria from (under) the face of the king of Assyria.

And yet, after all, why should we wonder at the voice being heard from Arabia? For was it not the voice of the Lord?

Isa. 30³¹ For, because of the voice of the Lord, the
Assyrians shall be defeated, with the plague where-
withsoever he smiteth them. And it shall be round
about him, whence had been his hope of assistance,
on which he had trusted.

The "Assyrian" tyrant had counted on his subjects
in the city of Jerusalem, and now they were put to
confusion together.

The Babe of Bethlehem.

However, the burden of Damascus, with its two kindred
points, the conversion of Arabia and the voice in Arabia,
receives confirmation from Isa. 33, which itself leads on to
another constructive idea.

Isa. 33³ ᶠᶠ By reason of *the voice of fear* peoples were
startled from the fear of thee and *the Gentiles were
dispersed*. And now shall your spoils be gathered
together of small and of great, just as if one has
gathered locusts, so shall they *mock you*. Holy is
God who dwelleth on high . . . *our salvation is
among treasures*, there has come *wisdom* and *knowledge* and *holiness* unto the Lord, these are the
treasures of righteousness.

We begin to picture here the infant Saviour lying among
the threefold symbolic gifts of the Magi. But then we
pass on a few verses and we read what will strike us, in
the light of the Magi, as one of the most touching and
remarkable passages ever composed.

Isa. 33¹³ ᶠᶠ They *who come from afar* shall hear what
things I do: they that draw nigh shall know my
strength. *The lawless men in Sion* stand aloof:
fear shall take hold of *the godless men*. [And he
shall say] Who will announce to you that *the fire*

THE MAGI

burneth? Who will announce to you *the place everlasting?*

The Magi have then come to Herod, *the lawless and godless* man in Sion, as Justin said of him, and Herod has asked them how they knew that *the fire* in heaven was "his star," and how they would find the place of Christ's birth. Next follows a graphic picture of the Babe, born on a journey, a pilgrim upon earth, waving His tiny arms and stuffing them into His half-open eyes.

> *Journeying in righteousness*, speaking the straight way, hating lawlessness and unrighteousness, and *waving his hands away from gifts*, burdening his ears that he may not hear a *judgment of blood*, stopping his eyes that he may not see unrighteousness, he *shall dwell* in a lofty *cave* of a strong rock : *bread* shall be given to him, and *his water* is faithful. *A king* shall ye shall see with glory : your eyes see land from afar.

The picture of the Babe, born on a *journey* because His father was *righteous*, destined soon to a longer journey to Egypt, endowed from the first with perfect expression and sinless thought, shunning the gifts of the Magi as if He could have been conscious of them, is inimitable and captivating. But, in fact, every line of this passage of Isaiah receives its commentary in Matt. 2, which is built upon it in a spirit of childlike confidence that what was predicted of *our Salvation* was actually fulfilled. Thus the *judgment of blood* anticipates Herod's decision to kill the Innocents, which outrage is further indicated in *unrighteousness*. The *cave* is the one and only origin of Justin's* idea which, through Origen and Epiphanius, has survived to this day. *Bread*—for he was in Bethlehem, "the house of bread"—should be plentiful. *His water* is that of Baptism, as we know it was interpreted

* *Dial.* 296 D (70), 304 (78).

in the Epistle of "Barnabas" (11⁵). But the passage is here broken by a dramatic change of address, where the prophet Isaiah is supposed to turn first to the Magi, with the words: "You shall see the king in the place you have visited from afar," and then to the *troubled* Herod (Matt. 2³) and his forces to say—

Isa. 33¹⁸ *Your* soul shall meditate fear of the Lord.

This is the reading of the Alexandrine MS., representing the text which the apostolic writers followed (so far as I have been able to judge). To which Herod replies by a sudden summons for his counsellors—

Where are *the scribes?* Where are the counsellors? Where is he that counteth them *that gather together, the people* small and great?

This is the right reading. But what is most remarkable is that, apart from the MSS. evidence, it is proved by the word in Matt. 2⁴ *having gathered together* (συναγαγών, the active participle, corresponding to the passive συστρεφομένους in Isa. 33¹⁸). What Herod seems to say is, "Fetch them all here and count them." The counsellors of Isaiah are the high-priests of Matthew. *The scribes* (γραμματικοί, γραμματεῖς) are in both : *the people* are in both.

Isa. 33¹⁹ But he took no counsel with it, nor uttered (knew) his deep bass voice, that they should not hear —a people whom he had scorned and [said] there is no sense in him that heareth.

Herod insists on a full meeting of the Sanhedrim, each member to be counted in his place, but after all, though he inquires of them where the Christ is to be born, he does not take counsel of them, and so Matthew represents them as answering the question and quoting Micah, but he says

THE MAGI

no more about them, and passes to Herod's inquiry of the Magi what time the star appeared.

The inquiry by Herod of the Magi and his instruction to report to him was, however, but a dark device of the tyrant pretending his own homage to the new-born king—

> Is. 31[6] Turn ye about! (or, convert ye!) say ye that devise a dark *device* and a *lawless*.

(The words "sons of Israel" which follow after "lawless" are a false reading). This was, moreover, a foolish device because—

> Hos. 11[5] Ephraim (the babe born at *Bethlehem-Ephratah*) *dwelt in Egypt* and Asshur (Herod) [was] his own king, because he did not choose to convert, and he did weakly with the sword among his cities (in massacring the Innocents)—

and—

> Isa. 32[6] The foolish man will speak foolishness and his heart will think vanity, to perform *lawless* deeds and to speak misleading against the Lord, to disperse hungry souls, and he will make the thirsty souls empty.

The latter words refer to the newly-arrived Magi. But their return is also to be found prefigured. They know that—

> Isa. 31[8] Asshur (Herod) shall fall: no sword of a man nor sword of mankind shall devour him.

But meanwhile they must baffle the device of the Assyrian by a better device of their own.

> Isa. 32[7] For *the device* of the evil men will devise lawlessness, to destroy *humble* men by unrighteous words and to scatter the words of the *humble* by

judgment. But the *godly* men devise prudently and *this* device shall abide.

It is not difficult to recognize the Magi in the *humble* and the *godly* men.

The Star.

The appearance of the star was predicted by the Mesopotamian Balaam, the typical Magus, and false prophet—

> Num. 24^{17} There shall *rise a star* (ἀνατελεῖ ἄστρον) out of Jacob, and there shall *be raised* A MAN out of Israel . . . and Edom (Herod the Idumæan) shall be his inheritance.

But to see how closely Balaam's "parable" belongs to Isaiah for the purposes of early Christian interpretation we have only to read four verses further—

> *Strong* is thy *dwelling*, and if thou settest *thy nest in a rock*, and if there be for Beor a nest of wickedness, *the Assyrians* shall make thee a captive of the spear.

What would this seem to be but a warning against "Herod and his men of war" employed to butcher the Innocents near the rocky refuge of Bethlehem? Herod's own expression in Isa. 10^{14} was—

> I will take the whole world in my hand like a nest, and remove them as forsaken eggs.

Therefore Bethlehem, too, would become his captured birds-nest with its precious spoil. But the star of Balaam had become merged in the light, the glory, of a far more magnificent prediction, that of—

> Isa. 60$^{1\,\text{ff}}$ Lighten thou, lighten thou, Jerusalem, for *thy light* has come and *the glory of the Lord* has risen (ἀνατέταλκεν) upon thee. Behold, darkness shall cover the earth and blackness come upon the Gentiles,

THE MAGI

but upon thee shall *dawn the Lord* (ἐπὶ δὲ σὲ φανήσεται—the first occurrence of the *Epiphany*), and *his glory* shall be seen upon thee; and *kings shall journey at thy light* and Gentiles at thy brightness.

The idea of the star is becoming identified with that of the Lord to be. The child Christ is the Dayspring. So we find in—

Zech. 6¹² Thus saith the Lord Almighty, *Behold a man, Dayspring* (ἀνατολή) is his name, and he shall rise from under him, and he *shall* * *build the house of the Lord* . . . And *they that are afar off* from them shall come, and shall *build in the house of the Lord* (the Magi shall worship at Bethlehem), and ye shall know that the Lord Almighty hath sent me unto you : and it shall be so if *hearing ye shall hear the voice* of the Lord your God.

This would point out once more to *the voice* being audible in Arabia whence they came.

There are still some more particulars in prophecy concerning the heavenly phenomenon, including the evidence for Bethlehem itself as the birthplace.

Mic. 5² And thou, Bethlehem, house of Ephratha, art fewest to be among the thousands of Judah : out of whom there shall come forth to me (one) to be a ruler of Israel, and his outgoings are from the beginning, from the days of an age everlasting. Wherefore he shall give *them* until *the time of her that beareth* and *she shall bear* (a child) and the rest of their brethren shall convert to the son of Israel. And *it shall stand* and shall see, and the Lord will shepherd his flock in strength, and they shall be *in the glory of the name of the Lord* their God : for now he shall be magnified

---

* See further below, Chapter VI.

unto the ends of the earth. And there shall be *peace here.* . . . and he shall rescue from the Assyrian when he cometh against your land and when he goeth against *your borders.*

(The explanation of the text of Matthew differing from both the Greek as above and the Hebrew will be given later.)

Micah has thought fit to connect Bethlehem with Ephraim, for some archæological reason unknown. The fact justified the Christian interpreter in taking Hos. 11^3 to mean the child of Bethlehem-*Ephratah.*

Hos. 11^5 Ephraim dwelt in Egypt when the Assyrian himself was his king because he would not convert.

This is evidence for the flight into Egypt, as Hos. 11^1 "Out of Egypt have I called my son" (Heb.; but LXX has *his* children) is evidence for the summons out of it. The other italicized words indicate the Magi, the Mother and Child, the star standing over the holy place of birth in all its glory. Further oracles are—

Isa. 60^2 His *glory* shall be seen *upon thee.*
Isa. 60^{17} I will make thy rulers to *be in peace* and *thy visitors* in righteousness.

The mention of *the borders* (ὅρια) of Bethlehem very clearly indicates the range of the massacre of the Innocents by the tyrant. The list of places passed by the Assyrian in Isa. 10$^{28\text{-}31}$ very fairly answers to the expression in Matt. 2^{16}, "Bethlehem and all the borders thereof" (p. 13 above).

The Gifts of the Magi.

The gifts of the Magi, to which we now return, constitute a problem of quite unusual interest, and furnish a crucial test of the theory propounded in these pages.

THE MAGI 25

We have already seen that " our *salvation* is among treasures: there has come *wisdom* and *knowledge* and godliness unto the Lord " (Isa. 33^6). But we are to learn how these are symbolized by material gifts by comparison with another oracle—

> Isa. 60^6 All from Saba shall come bearing *gold*, and *frankincense* shall they bring, and *precious stone*: and they shall preach the gospel of the *salvation* of the Lord (see p. 16 above).

This is the right reading supported by the Alexandrine and the Sinaitic MSS. The comparison of *wisdom* and *knowledge* with *gold* and *precious stone* is in Job 28^{16}, while frankincense stood for ceremonial piety. But Matthew has myrrh for the third gift where Isaiah has precious stone. How the *precious stone* of Isa. 60 became the *myrrh* of Matt. 2 has now to be explained. First of all we may observe the divergence of Matthew from Hebrew and LXX here. This is paralleled by the like divergence in the neighbouring verse (Matt. 2^6) where, though Matthew quotes the prophet Micah, he does not agree either with Hebrew or with LXX. In this case we can only suppose that Matthew quotes from the list or collection of oracles which are said to have been collected by Matthew in a Hebrew language by Papias as quoted by Eusebius (see Ch. XIII below). In translating from the original into Aramaic—the " Hebrew language " in question—and back from Aramaic into Greek, there was more room for divergence than if he had merely resorted to the Hebrew or the Greek. This theory, however, was hardly present to me when I discovered what the true reading of Isa. 60^6 is: it was nothing but an idea; but it was clear that here, if anywhere, was an opportunity to test the theory that the Magi story was built upon the LXX from beginning to end.

26 ORACLES IN THE NEW TESTAMENT

The question, then, being whether *precious stone* of Isa. 60 had been converted into *myrrh* of Matt. 2, if we first consult Dr. Gwynn's *Apocalypse in Syriac* we find that *môrâ* was the Syriac for myrrh and *miq'râ* was precious stone. This leaves little doubt that the theory is going to stand the test, for the change of *miq'râ* into *môrâ* is of the slightest and easiest kind, whether orally or in writing—a change that an editor would not hesitate to propose in nine cases out of ten in any classical work where sense was concerned. The proof, however, is not complete. Some word from the Hebrew root YQR, *to be precious*, must be found, not in Syriac, but in Aramaic. And here we find that *môq'râ* is *a precious thing*, which is even nearer to *môrâ*, the R of which is strongly and roughly guttural, though the oral affinity is hardly greater than the written.* The intervals of meaning, sound and writing are thus reduced to the smallest minimum.

If any doubt still remains as to the etymology it is removed by pursuing this word *môq'râ* into the Greek and Latin languages. Pausanias † speaks of μορρία along with crystals as vessels made of stone. Pliny expressly says that the conquest of Mithradates first sent the Romans mad after *myrrhina,* as the word came to be spelt after being *murrhina* and *murrhea*. The variation in the spelling suffices to prove how little the Romans and Greeks knew its meaning. King shows that they were agate vases, saucer-shaped, valued not for the workmanship but for the material. He supposes that they were imported ready-made from India. Pliny also tells us that " the East sends us the *murrhina,* found in several places all within the Parthian dominions (Propertius 4^5),

---

* Buxtorf, *Lex. Chald.* 980.

† Paus. 8^{18}; see King, *Natural History of Gems,* 179, on *Murrhina,* who also quotes Pliny, *N.H.,* 36^{66}. My thanks are due to my friend Mr. Robin Fausset for drawing my attention to *murrhea.*

THE MAGI 27

but the finest sort in Carmania." In the "Periplus of the Red Sea" they are an export of the modern Malwa. Neither King, however, nor the dictionaries venture on an etymology of *murrhea*. I therefore suggest that the above Aramaic is correct. The word *môq'râ*, being to purchasers as rare as the agate to which it belonged, was as easily mistaken for *môrâ*, losing its Q before the strongly guttural R, in Aramaic as it was in Greek or Latin, where naturally it was conjectured to have to do with *myrrha*, myrrh, which it sometimes resembled in colour.

It is clear that this oracle at least has found its way from the Greek of Isa. 60 into Aramaic, and from Aramaic back into Greek in Matt. 2. Can it be doubted that as it is an oracle, and as Matthew made a collection of the oracles in a Hebrew language, this very collection was the medium of its passage from the one to the other, from the Greek Isaiah to the Greek Matthew, which always has been Greek, though it must be uncertain whether it is the work of the same "Matthew" who made the collection? Probably the Gospel is called after Matthew just because it was known to contain several of the oracles that were known to be in the collection made or believed to be made by Matthew. The question how the words *and precious stone* came into LXX is one that must not be asked any more than why they were dropped out of the Hebrew text. I hold they are original and the Hebrew has omitted them. But we cannot now embark upon the causes of the divergence of LXX from Hebrew in places which are innumerable. The fact of *precious stone* in Isa. 60^6 being in the singular number favours the idea of an agate vase. When once myrrh was substituted, fancy was naturally busy with the symbolic fitness of myrrh for the occasion. Indeed, this fancy may well have contributed to the substitution;

it may have turned the scale first of all in favour of a more intelligible name. But an agate vase is really more natural than myrrh as the offering brought by a king or magian from the further East to Bethlehem.

Other Features of the Magi Story.

Lastly, the rejoicing of the Magi *with exceeding great joy* when they saw the star for the second time was clearly intimated in—

Isa. 9$^{2\,f}$ O people that walk in darkness, behold great light : ye that dwell in *a land a shadow of death*, light shall shine upon you. The most part of the people which thou broughtest home is enjoying thy pleasure, and they shall rejoice before thee as men that rejoice in harvest, and like them *that divide spoils*.

The reference to *darkness* is taken of the previous heathen state of the Magi. They were now to be triumphantly rewarded with the sight of the king who should actually *spoil the Assyrian*.

Isa. 33^4 And now shall be brought together your spoils both from *small* and *great*.

The *persecuting* Herod (Isa. 33^1) should live to see his spoils, both the *great* of Arabia (Damascus and Samaria, Isa. 8^4) in the person of the Magi, and the *small* of Bethlehem in the person of the Infant, taken from before his eyes (ἔναντι) by the new-born King.

One more reference to Arabia on the return of the Magi which Justin has not noticed, perhaps because the title is obscured in many copies of the Greek Bible—" The title *of Arabia.*" Its very beauty adds to its obscurity.

Isa. 21^{13} To meet the thirsty man bring ye water, O inhabitants of Teman, *with loaves* (from Bethlehem)

THE MAGI

meet ye *them that flee"* (the Magi are escaping Herod: "For *the device* of the evil will devise *lawlessness, to destroy humble men* by unrighteous words. . . . But the godly devise prudently and *this device* shall abide," Isa. 32⁶ ᶠ). " For the multitude of them *that have been massacred* . . . and for the multitude of them *that have fallen in the matter of the Child* (ἐν τῷ παιδίῳ). Therefore, thus saith the Lord unto me, " *Yet a year* as a year of a hireling, and *the glory of the sons of Kedar* shall fail " (the star of the Magi shall be eclipsed, ἐκλείψει).

The Innocents were slaughtered *in the matter of the newborn Babe.* And the heavenly phenomenon faded within the year.

CHAPTER II

HEROD THE ASSYRIAN

The Possible Origin of the Appellative.

Now can we possibly discover how, why, and when first Herod was identified with the king of the Assyrians in prophecy? If we can discover this, we may have some clue to the time at which the legend began to take shape. We have already seen that three Herods, and we shall see that four, were identified with the "king of Assyria." Can we determine which of these was the first to bear that prophetic title? I am inclined to think we can. The story is a strange one, though the appellative "Herod the Assyrian" is not dependent upon the story alone, as we shall see later. The Assyrian king says in all his arrogance—

> Isa. 10^{14} *My hand hath reached as a nest* the riches of the people, and as one gathereth forsaken eggs I have gathered all the earth, and there was none that fluttered a wing, nor opened a beak, nor chirped.

The figure was one of the commonest with the Assyrian kings, who were proud of being the "birds-nesters" of the world. And long ages before Sargon king of Assyria, his namesake Sargon I. king of Babylonia had written on his cylinders, "the nests of the birds he swept away." *
The Egyptian monarchs wrote likewise. Isaiah therefore is very literally true to fact, and his figure of speech would be familiar.

Now it was a cruel transgression of the law of birds

---

* *Records of the Past*, ii. p. 61. Scores of passages could be quoted involving the same metaphor.

HEROD THE ASSYRIAN

nesting* as given in Deut. 22⁶ to take the hen bird with the young. But obviously the Assyrian monarch's boast was that he took the parent birds first and then even took the forsaken eggs, for the usual catalogue is "their warriors I slew, their cities I burned, their sons, their daughters, their families I cut off."

But now comes the curious fact in connection with Herod. We are told by the Rabbis † that Herod the king brought wild pigeons from the desert and domesticated them. They were called by some *Herodians* (and by some *The Dorsians*—this, however, is a mere blind—by a change of order in two consonants of the name) and they were said to be trained to say Kirî, kirî, by way of acclaiming Herod as "Lord, lord" (κύριε). One day a pigeon was silent, and when advised by its mates to coo as they did, it began kirî (with a kāhph) kirî (with a kooph), meaning "slave lord," which reference to Herod's low origin caused its neck to be wrung. The *Mishna* takes the matter of pigeons seriously and says, "Now the law of letting go the nest holds only of birds, and then only of birds not prepared (*i. e.* which have not a nest prepared in houses and dwellings by themselves or by men for them). What, then, are birds not prepared? For instance, geese and hens that nest in the garden. But if they nest in houses as do domestic pigeons, a man is not obliged to let the mother go." It follows from this that Herod, the law-breaker (ἄνομος), added one more to his long list of lawless actions in bringing entire broods of pigeons from the desert, though after they were domesticated in the dove-cotes of his palace he was free to treat them as he liked.

* "If a bird's nest chance to be before thee in the way in any tree or on the ground, young ones or eggs and the dam sitting upon the young or upon the eggs, thou shalt not take the dam with the young," etc.
† Buxtorf, p. 630. See also Schürer, *Jewish People*, etc., I. i. 440. Josephus refers to the wild pigeons being tamed.

82 ORACLES IN THE NEW TESTAMENT

Now everyone knows from his school-experience how a nickname is most often bestowed from a trifling occasion, and it sticks long after the occasion is forgotten. It is highly probable that such was the occasion of Herod earning the name of a bird-nesting " king of Assyria." It may be thought that no incident so slight as this would be necessary to qualify Herod for the title, and certainly his savage truculence was always behind it, so that if he were to be identified with the king of any great empire in mockery, it would not be Babylon which stood for superstition, nor Egypt which stood for ease. It would be Assyria. But a slight incident is, I believe, just what would originate the comparison, and the Rabbis of the time were just the class that would delight to point it by such an appellative, which would pass from them into currency with the Jewish community at large.* If this conjecture were correct it would follow that the evil antagonist of the Christ in prophecy was recognized as Antichrist before Jesus was recognized as the Christ by His disciples. This may prove to be a consideration of no small importance.

The name " Assyrian " confirmed by Scripture Texts.

However, the appellative once bestowed would be made good by many minds busy with the study of the prophets.

---

* The *Mishna* is strangely silent about him. Schürer has not noticed the name of Assyrian. But it is worth while considering whether it does not lie hid in the corrupt passage of *Seder Olam* (Schürer, *H. J. P.* § 16, E. T., p. 5, note). *The War of* אסוירום is more likely to mean the *war of Assurios* by a slight misplacement of only two letters than to mean the *war of Varus* by the rejection, which Schürer has to suppose, of the two first and the fourth letter. Besides, he has to admit that his eighty years do not even then work out between the war of Varus and that of Vespasian. If, however, we read *Assyrios* (Herod) we have his war with the Arabians about 10 B.C., which makes just eighty years. It was a small affair, but he had an " army," permission from Rome to chastise, and a " battle."

HEROD THE ASSYRIAN

The same passage in Micah that spoke of a ruler of Israel to come from Bethlehem, a ruler whose goings forth have been from everlasting, in contrast with the Assyrian (p. 23), proceeded within two pages of jerky and disjointed prophecies to say—

> Mic. 6⁹. The voice of the Lord crieth unto the city . . . hear ye the rod, and who hath appointed it. Are there yet the treasures of wickedness in the house of the wicked? . . . therefore I also have smitten thee with a grievous wound : I have made thee desolate because of thy sins.

In these words Micah seemed to denounce the sinful hellenizing Herod. Josephus informs us that when the plague broke out in Judea soon after Herod had put his wife Mariamne to death (29 B.C.), it was believed to be a divine judgment, causing as it did great mortality both of the populace and of Herod's honoured friends.[*] But the blood of judicial murder still flowed, and then came the erection of costly public works, the theatre and amphitheatre in Jerusalem, the rebuilding of Samaria named Sebaste in honour of Augustus (27 B.C.), the royal palace, the fortress and port of Cæsarea (22–10 B.C.). All these undertakings meant grinding taxation rendered more grievous by years of famine and pestilence. The Temple itself was begun in 20 B.C. But this pious enterprise did not conceal the fact that the temple-building Herod was "godless and lawless" throughout his career, as Justin calls him in order to justify the Assyrian title. Meanwhile Micah proceeds in the same context to predict, as it might well seem, his domestic discords.

> Mic. 7⁶ For the *son dishonoureth* the father, the daughter riseth up against her mother, *the daughter-*

---
[*] Josephus, *Antt.*, XV. vii. 7.

in-law against her mother-in-law; a man's enemies are they of his own house.

And meanwhile Herod's sons Alexander and Aristobulus were returning his suspicion inflamed by Salome with undisguised aversion, till he journeyed to the emperor Augustus at Aquileia to accuse them to him (12 B.C.). Herod's mother Cypros and his sister Salome had succeeded in instigating him to get rid of Mariamne. These were the most palpable and historic discords of his discordant house, in which he had nine wives alive at one time, and children by seven of them, while the women in the court constantly excited new disturbances.

But, again, we know from Justin* that the Jews of his day asserted that Herod was a native of Ascalon, while Josephus further says he was an Idumæan of honourable family. Now there was a prophecy of Amos which was at all times ominous for Herod.

Amos 1⁶ ff Thus saith the Lord, for three transgressions of Gaza, yea for four, I will not turn away the punishment thereof, because they carried away captive the whole people, to deliver them up *to Idumea* . . . and I will cut off *him that holdeth the sceptre from Askalon*.

And here we come upon what is probably the reason why Herod was determined to keep pigeons about his palace. Ascalon was symbolized by its doves, which commemorated the worship of Astarte, for which it was once known. Traces of the doves are found in its monuments to-day.† And the Arabic name of the adjacent village is Ḥamāmeh, "Dove." Herod wished to have about him the living heraldry of his origin. As the caged wolves are to the city of Rome, as the captive

---

* *Dial.*, 272 (52). Schürer, *Jewish People*, I. i. 314.
† *Survey of Western Palestine*, III. p. 243.

HEROD THE ASSYRIAN

bears are to Berne, so were the Hôrôdôsiyôth pigeons, domesticated from the desert, to Herod, king of Judea. After his death a palace at Ascalon was presented to his ever-loyal sister Salome, by Cæsar, and there she ended her days.

The connection with Ascalon does not, however, bring us much nearer than before to the identity with the Assyrian. For though, geographically speaking, Ascalon is within ten miles of the site of the Assyrian Sennacherib's camp when he besieged Libnah and took Lachish and Ascalon in the most memorable campaign of the whole history of Judah, yet since Ascalon is not named in the Bible in that connection it is doubtful whether it can be admitted to the present consideration. The course of ancient prophetic interpretation was ruled exclusively by the literary content. At the same time, when Herod died universally hated the words of Isaiah would be quoted with more force of conviction than ever before.

> Isa. 31^5 As birds flying (as his own pigeons), so will the Lord protect Jerusalem, he will protect and deliver it, he will pass over and preserve it. Convert ye unto him from whom ye have deeply revolted, O children of Israel. For in that day they shall cast away every man his idols . . . *Then shall the Assyrian fall with the sword* not of a man, and the sword, not of men, shall devour him.

Here, then, is a considerable body of fulfilled prophecy, and yet its momentum, like that of a solid body moving through space, though considerable, would not be appreciated until there occurred some impact or collision with another body equally solid. Obviously, one such body would be that of the believers in the destined antagonist of Herod. Let us assume that, when Herod died, his identity with the Assyrian, instead of depending on the Greek text, was inferred from matters of fact as elucidating and elucidated by the Hebrew text, for there was no reason why the Jewish clergy, the Soferim, the scribes, the Rabbis, of the school of Hillel, who lived to a great age and actually survived Herod three years, and of Shammai, should condescend to honour the Greek version by their notice. Against the hopes of the people for the appearance of that mysterious king who was to deliver them from Herod and from Cæsar, hopes which found daily expression in the life of the people, Hillel's views of the prophecies merely resulted in words of very sceptical caution. "No such king," he said, "will ever appear."* Such an authority would carry much influence, but it would not extinguish the hopes, and if meanwhile we do not know what the verdict of the rival and frequently opposing school of Shammai said upon the subject, we know that the scribes had to deal sincerely with a prophecy in Hosea, which did but increase the bitterness of the outlook for the downtrodden people.

Hos. 11[11] The Assyrian shall be his king, because they refused to return (to Egypt) . . . the Lord shall roar, and the children shall come trembling from the west, they shall come trembling as a bird out of Egypt, and *as a dove out of the land of Assyria.*

And there were the doves of Assyria fluttering before his very eyes!

Interpretation of Prophecy as affected by Catastrophic Events.

In Chapter I. we saw that in the first half of Matt. 2 there is not one statement, and hardly a single word save *Jesus* and *Mary* that does not rest upon the prophetic oracles. For those who assumed and asserted the birth of

* *Sanhedrin,* quoted by Etheridge, *Hebrew Literature,* p. 37.

Messiah at all, it was not only probable, it was necessary, that they should construct the mode and circumstances of it in this particular way, believing as they did in the truth of prophecy, believing that they possessed the very words of the prophets, and that the prophets had supplied the details to the last particular. We know to-day that their belief was wrong on the second of these three heads, though we may share their belief on the first head, as St. Paul knew that Herod Agrippa II. believed the prophets, and to some extent on the third. But in the absence of any other evidence for the historical truth of the Magi story, we can but allow it to occupy the place of a legend, the origin of which is completely verified within certain limits, though not as to the nucleus of it.

The latter part of Matt. 2—and very different it is—remains for some further consideration, though the main feature of it, the flight into Egypt, has been before us already. The first business of the narrator is to dispose of the Magi, and this he does by means of a dream.* But he uses the same device to remove Joseph later, on a similar occasion, to his native land, and he introduces the dream in the same language, " And being warned in a dream he (they) departed (or better, as the Revised Version the second time, *withdrew*)." At first the idea is likely to occur that a dream is the undramatic resource of a romancer, and it is important to notice that there is no place for dreams in the New Testament but here, and on the lips of Pilate's wife (Matt. 27^{19}). Visions are for young men and for men, but dreams only for the old and sapless, as Joel implies (Acts 2^{17}).

Before going further with the dreams let us consider the interpretation of prophecy in the phase which the above passages have illustrated in the time when Justin

* Justin seems to commit an inaccuracy here in saying their withdrawal was " in accordance with *a revelation*."

wrote, about A.D. 150, the Dialogue with Trypho the Jew, purporting to report a conversation of 136–140. There is no reason to suppose that the controversy had differed greatly in character during the years that had passed since A.D. 70.

The effect of the fall of Jerusalem was of necessity first to promote and afterwards to check the further progress of discovery of passages in the Old Testament which proved that Jesus was the Christ. References, however oblique or circuitous, obscure or far-fetched, as moderns would consider them, would be pressed into the service, but eventually the reserves would be exhausted, and the list fairly complete. The great historical event had effaced the Holy City and the Holy Place, and had left the idea of a House not made with hands, a City that had foundations whose builder and maker was God. It was a lesson on a gigantic scale to show that the local and temporary in religion was for the Jews abolished without any hope of its renewal. Until it should be renewed by the reconstruction of the Temple, the Jew must find his solace still in repeating the Psalms and Scriptures that in by-gone centuries had pointed forward to the new Temple of Zerubbabel and the possible, but dimmer, glories of centuries to follow. He was put back to the times of the Babylonian captivity. He had existed for intervals in former ages without a temple. In the year 71 he would cherish a hope that history would again repeat itself and out of his fresh captivity a new restoration would arise. And as surely as the sacred cycle of seventy years (three times and a half time), dating from A.D. 70, neared its completion, that hope culminated in the insurrection of Barcocheba in A.D. 132. The Jews crowned him king and hailed him as Messiah and attempted to rebuild the Temple. Hadrian summoned from Britain his best general, Julius Severus. Two years were spent in warfare before Jerusalem was taken and the new Messiah killed, and not till 135 was the war ended by the capture of Bether and a wholesale slaughter (the Rabbinical historians say 580,000 !) of the Jews. Justin's conversation with Trypho is placed a year or two after this catastrophe.

On the other hand, what would have been the effect of the former catastrophe in A.D. 70, which the later would but aggravate, upon the Christian side of the controversy? The argument from prophecy drew its main supports on either side from Isaiah, but it is easy to see that the preponderance was enormously on the Christian side for all who found in ancient prophecy a guidance among current events and an interpretation of them. The force of this statement will appear as we proceed. The Christian faith had the positive and constructive ideas which could only be overthrown by a Jew who denied the value of prophecy altogether. Meanwhile the people of Israel was almost the only source from which the ranks of the Christian Church could be recruited. " Jews and proselytes " were the only persons who could appreciate the argument from prophecy at all, for they alone were acquainted with the Old Testament. This is a self-evident fact, and wherever we can test the statement, it is proved to be true. In A.D. 70 the number of non-Jewish Christians was exceedingly small—a few handfuls were to be found in Antioch, Rome and the larger cities—and only Jewish and proselyte converts need be considered for at least a generation.* Wherever the Gentiles are mentioned in the Acts and Pauline Epistles, they are

* The evidence is next to nothing apart from the character of the literature, on which an attempt will be made to treat the question later. See Schürer, *Jewish People,* § 31, and Harnack, *Expansion of Ch.,* Eng. tr., p. 60, who quotes Havet's doubt if in St. Paul's lifetime a single pagan became Christian without previous knowledge of Judaism and the Bible, and adds " substantially this is accurate."

to be understood as proselytes of the synagogue. And this is not surprising, for the strength of the argument from prophecy in the teaching of those books is enormously greater than it is in the Gospels. I assume that the substance of Acts was not unknown in Palestine long before 70, and it is possible that a first draft of Acts was circulated there before St. Luke left for Rome, without, of course, the latter portions and without the dedication. It can well be understood that in the forty years before 70 the effect of books would be but small in comparison with that of the " living and abiding voice " of St. Paul and St. Peter, not to mention SS. Luke and Jude and Barnabas. But an accurate estimate of those personal spiritual forces is beyond our powers.

Oracles of the Fall of Jerusalem.

At the same time there were many prophecies of the Old Testament which were so palpably fulfilled on a large scale that none could fail to see their fulfilment. The destruction of Jerusalem by fire had been predicted in the clearest terms by the ancient prophets. First we notice—

> Isa. $4^{2\,\mathrm{ff}}$ And in that day God shall shine out *in counsel* ($\dot{\epsilon}\nu\ \beta o\upsilon\lambda\tilde{\eta}$) with glory upon the earth, to exalt and glorify the remnant of Israel : and it shall be that that which is left in Sion and the remnant in Jerusalem shall be called holy—all they that are written for life in Jerusalem. For the Lord will wash away the filth of the sons and daughters of Sion, and will purge away the blood from the midst of them with the spirit of judgment and the spirit of burning.

The Authorised Version is as follows—

> In that day shall the branch of the Lord be beautiful and glorious, and the fruit of the earth shall be comely for them that are escaped of Israel. . . .

HEROD THE ASSYRIAN

This passage is remarkable. The LXX, as above, used a good Greek word (ἐπιλάμψει), *shall shine out*, which it uses nowhere else, to translate the Hebrew *shall be beautiful*. But then it ought to have used ἀνατολή, *Anatolê*, "Dayspring," for the Hebrew *the Branch*, as it has elsewhere (Zech. 3⁸, 6¹², Jer. 23⁵, 33¹⁵), although ἀνατολή cannot mean *Branch*. Instead of ανατολη we find ευβουλη. Now there is every reason to think this is merely a primitive error of a very early copyist. Since it would only have been consistent to translate by *Anatolê* here, how tempting to a Christian controversialist to find or to make *Anatolê* by a very slight change of four letters instead of the mistranslation which we have! But no trace of such a substitution have I discovered anywhere. It was enough for the apostles that the Greek did not recognize here a reference to the Dayspring or by implication to the Branch in Hebrew—a conclusive evidence of the overpowering influence of the Greek Bible. It need hardly be said how much the passage would have gained for Christian controversy had it been shown that the appearance of the Dayspring, Christ, caused the destruction of the city.

Next we notice—

Jer. 20⁴ Therefore thus saith the Lord, Behold, thee and all Judah will I give into the hands of the king of Babylon (Rome), and they shall remove them away and cut them in pieces with swords. And I will give the whole strength of this city and all its labours and all the treasures of the king of Judah into the hands of its enemies, and they shall carry them to Babylon.

And—

Jer. 21¹⁰ The king of Babylon shall burn it up with fire.

This prediction was so abundantly repeated and was

so clear both in Greek and in Hebrew that the fulfilment of it must have been followed by the conversion of thousands to Christ in the time A.D. 70–100. In those years of anguish and despair to patriotic Jews the effect of what follows in Jer. 23^{4f} must have been great—

> Behold, the days come, that I will raise up to David a Dayspring in righteousness. And I will gather the remnant of my flock out of all countries whither I have driven them, and will bring them again to their folds . . . and I will set up shepherds over them which shall shepherd them : and they shall fear no more nor be dismayed. . . .

This prepares the mind for the thought of the Good Shepherd.

The fact that these predictions had received their fulfilment six centuries before was no sort of reason against their second fulfilment, but this was rather a confirmation of that. There was again the famine and the sword, there were the false prophets and diviners, their omens and their spells (Jer. 27^9), as the prophet foretold, and how many more besides those which we can now read in his pages! Even individuals had been predicted by Jeremiah and answered to their names in the fall of Jerusalem,—Ananiah the false prophet (28^1), Eleasah and others. The trench had been cast against the city, as Jeremiah said. But if the predicted woes were thus fulfilled, should not the predicted new heart, new way, new covenant everlasting (Jer. 32^{39}) find their fulfilment equally ? Then how apposite was—

> Jer. 50^{17} Israel was an erring sheep, lions thrust him out : the first that ate him was the king of Assyria (Herod), and now more lately his bones are eaten by the king of Babylon (Vespasian) !

HEROD THE ASSYRIAN

But further this passage has a remarkable correspondence—

> Isa. 4⁵ And he shall come, and it shall be that every place of Mount Sion and all her neighbourhood shall be shadowed by a cloud by day, and as of smoke and the light of burning fire by night, and in all the glory he shall be sheltered.

To the Jew this would bear a Messianic meaning,* with a reference to the Tabernacle and the Feast of Tabernacles : but no Christian after A.D. 70 would hesitate to apply it to the burning of Jerusalem, the concluding words pointing to the Saviour.

However, this event greatly modified the activity of prophecy in the sense of revelation by ecstasy, first because it showed a clear fulfilment of much ancient prophecy; next because it cleared the air of much recent prophecy which in regard to the second Advent had failed of fulfilment : thirdly, because it enabled a plain reader of the Old Testament to discover minor fulfilments for himself. The Seer of Ephesus who saw his visions in 68–69 could never be so full of prediction again, because he had foretold the fall of Rome as Babylon and the whole of that prediction had failed through the fall of Jerusalem instead. Affection did not allow these discredited prophecies to perish, and it may be true that they " saw the light in the end of the reign of Domitian " in the sense of a further publication, but certainly not as a fresh composition. It was certain that an end was in sight for the prophetic gift, concerning which St. Paul had written, " Desire earnestly to prophesy." Within a limited range apocalypses continued, indeed, as long as " the days of the elders who had prolonged the time with Jesus and who

---

* Schoettgen, *Horae H.*, ii. 485; Edersheim, *Life and Times of Jesus*, App. ix.

had known all the works of the Lord which he wrought to Israel" (Josh. 24[31]) continued.* The latter words would more than cover the time to A.D. 100. And later than that, Ignatius wrote that if he should have such apocalypses to impart to the Ephesians he would impart them. Montanism still continued the gift, but it was destined to decline before the rising sun of organized Churchmanship in the second century. This sun shone upon the fourth Gospel, which was winning its way first into Asia Minor, and then into other parts of the Catholic Church.

Prophecy, therefore, would be engaged chiefly in a gathering of the fragments that remained that nothing should be lost. Obviously one class of the fragments would include those texts which received light from the fall of Jerusalem and could hardly have received it before. One example is the passage which was found to refer to the rejection of Siloam's healing water. No prophetic vision would be needed to discover the fitness of that application. The allegorical mode of interpretation of the Old Testament once started could proceed rapidly upon its own lines unassisted by ecstasy, and this fact alone would cause ecstasy to pass out of use. In 80-100 it was a disappearing gift.

Oracles of Baptism.

Meanwhile a wholly new circle of ideas was growing up with an imagery of its own, drawn perforce from the Old Testament language and principally from the most sublime and noble poetry of Isaiah. The centre of this circle was Christian baptism, of which the Water-bearing seemed to be an acted prophecy. This solemn rite had from a very early date associated with it the two texts from Isaiah—

* See *The Christian Prophets*, p. 236; *St. Luke the Prophet*, p. 62.

HEROD THE ASSYRIAN

Isa. 12^3 With joy ye shall draw water from the wells of salvation—

and—

Isa. 8^6 Because this people doth not choose the waters of Shiloah that flow softly, etc.

The fact was suggestive that other passages of the same prophet might also be applied to Baptism. Elsewhere the present writer* has shown a great number of references in the newly-discovered Odes of Solomon to precisely three chapters of Isaiah (60–62) ; in fact, the imagery of those very poetical works is chiefly drawn from that source : and they are instinct with the baptismal ideas. But here we may just mention a few more Isaian passages on baptism.

Isa. 55^1 Ho ! ye that thirst, journey to the water.

Isa. 54^8 f Said the Lord who rescued thee, From the water of Noah's time have I this, even as I sware to him then that I would not be wrath with the earth any more for thee.

Isa. 44^3 I will give water in the time of thirst to them that journey in the waterless place, I will set my spirit upon thy seed, and my blessings upon thy children, and they shall rise as grass in the midst of water, and as oziers on flowing water.

Isa. 43^{20} I give water in the desert and rivers in the waterless place, to make my elect race to drink, my people whom I purchased to declare my righteous deeds.

Isa. 35^7 In the desert doth water break forth.

It so happens that we find the first and the last of these (at least) as part of the lessons for the Epiphany Rite of the Blessing of the Waters.†

* *Journal of Theological Studies*, Jan. 1912.
† Conybeare, *Rituale Arm.*, 430.

46 ORACLES IN THE NEW TESTAMENT

The Dreams of Joseph.

With these observations we return to the second part of the Magi story, which we left on the subject of dreams. The New Testament writers were powerfully influenced by the Greek Wisdom of Sirach (Ecclesiasticus). Perhaps there was no one line that impressed them more strongly than Ecclus. 42^{24}: "All things are double one against other, and he hath made nothing imperfect" ($ἐλλιπόν$), for in it they saw a scriptural confirmation of all their fulfilments of prophecy. But the same book, which again and again sings the praises of prophecy, contains, on the other hand, a vehement disparagement of dreams. (Ecclus. 34^{1-7}) "Dreams lift up fools. Whoso regardeth dreams is like him that catcheth at a shadow, and followeth after the wind. Dreams have deceived many, and they that put their trust in them have failed." However, it is possible that the evangelist found some guidance for his narrative here in the words of—

Isa. 29^9 Be undone ($ἐκλύθητε$) and *amazed* ($ἔκστητε$), be drunk not with liquor nor with wine: for the Lord hath given you to drink of the spirit of torpor; and shall tightly close the eyes of them and of their prophets and of their rulers; *ye who see secrets* ($τὰ κρυπτά$).

Matthew may have thought the address in the concluding words was to the Magi, whom Isaiah made to see some admonition in their torpor, while the eyes of Herod and his scribes and his Sanhedrin were to be sealed. For Isaiah continues—

Isa. 29^{14} Therefore, behold, I will furthermore change the place of this people, and I will change their place ($μεταθήσω$ is correlative to $ἀνεχώρησαν$, *they withdrew*, Matt. 2^{12-22}), and I will destroy the wisdom

HEROD THE ASSYRIAN

of the wise and hide the prudence of the prudent. Woe unto you that form a device deeply.

Here, again, is the deep device of Herod. Though there is an objection to this application of 29^9 in so far as it prescribes *be amazed* (ἔκστητε), which should rather mean *ecstasy* than *dreams*, whereas the plot of the Magi is not helped out by ecstasy but by dream, it is easily overcome by a reference to Gen. 2^{21} " And God cast a deep *sleep* (ἔκστασιν) upon Adam *and he slept.*" We conclude that Matt. 2 was written at a time when visions in trance were becoming rare. The Magi are supposed to sleep heavily in order to dream.

But there is a third dream, a fourth, a fifth, for our "undoing," in which "behold the angel of the Lord appears" (1^{20}, $2^{13, 19}$ with $2^{12, 22}$). It is evident that the story has not been made out by revelation in trance to a prophet but by careful study of the Old Testament.* Probably the evangelist was not a prophet, for he is the only New Testament writer who mentions dreams. And he certainly does not make us think that Joseph was a prophet: Joseph, like the Magi, is qualified to receive only the secondary and lower form of divine communication by means of a dream, as if he resembled his namesake in Genesis. This accords with the law of Num. 12^6—

> If there be among you a prophet of the Lord, I will be known unto him in a vision, and will speak unto him in a dream.

And it may be that Matthew intimates that Joseph was "an old man" because he read in Joel 2^{28} "Your old men shall dream dreams."

The Flight into Egypt and the Return.

Besides "the plague" of having "to see the road to Egypt" (p. 13) and the other predictions already men-

---

* *In sobriety*, ἐν καταστάσει, as Justin would say: *with undistorted mind*, ἀπερισπάστῳ διανοίᾳ, as Ignatius would say.

tioned (p. 21), the flight into Egypt was clearly foretold in—

> Isa. 19¹ Behold, the Lord sitteth upon a soft cloud and shall come into Egypt : and the handiworks of Egypt shall be shaken at his presence.

The meaning must have been understood *as lightly as* if he sailed through air.* It seems that this was partly the basis of the vision in Rev. 12¹⁴ "There were given to the woman the two *wings of the great eagle* that she should flee unto the wilderness unto her place." But in that vision the train of thought which is implied is rather more complex than in Matthew. The coming of the Lord into Egypt is to be attended with grievous plagues to the Egyptians, as a sequel to the ten plagues.

> Exod. 19⁴ Ye have seen what great things I have done to the Egyptians when I took you up as *upon eagles' wings* and brought you unto myself.

And again—

> Deut. 32¹¹ *As an eagle* he spread out his wings and received them, and took them up upon his pinions.

The *great things* included conversion, as is shewn by—

> Isa. 19²¹ ᶠ The Lord shall be known to the Egyptians . . . they shall convert unto the Lord and he shall heal them.

There is a fact that goes some way to proving that the flight to Egypt is based on Isa. 19¹ ᶠᶠ—that in Pseudo-Matt. (23)†, where a story is told that the idols in the temple at

---

* " Sometime we see a cloud that's dragonish,
   A vapour sometime like a bear or lion,
   A tower'd citadel, a pendant rock,
   A forkèd mountain, or blue promontory . . .
   They are black vesper's pageants."—*Antony*.
† Cowper, *Apocryphal Gospels*, 63.

HEROD THE ASSYRIAN 49

Sotinen, where the Holy Family tarried first in Egypt, were all prostrate on the earth, broken in pieces, we read, " Then was fulfilled," Isa. 19¹, quoted above.

The return from Egypt was supported, besides other passages, by—

> Isa. 43⁵ Fear not: for I am with thee: from the east I will bring my seed, and from the west I will gather thee.
>
> Hos. 12⁹ I the Lord thy God bring thee out of the land of Egypt: I will yet settle thee at home in booths even as the days of the feast.
>
> Hos. 11⁵ Ephraim dwelt in Egypt, and Asshur (Herod) was his king, because he did not choose to convert.

This meant that the Child born at Bethlehem-Ephratah continued in Egypt so long as Herod reigned (see above, p. 24).

Difficulties of the Rachel Oracle.

The design of Herod to destroy the newborn King of Israel has been shown above (p. 21). We bear in mind that Herod's wrath is the violent river let loose, and in the light of this identity we must consider the oracle—

> Isa. 32² And THE MAN shall be hiding his words (in parabolic teaching), and he (the righteous king) shall be hidden as from rushing water (or water being borne, $\varphi\varepsilon\varrho o\mu\acute{\varepsilon}\nu o\upsilon$), and he shall appear in Sion as a rushing river glorious in a thirsty land.

This admits of more than one interpretation in a Christian sense. It may mean that the infant King is to be hidden from Herod's wrath, by the flight into Egypt; or it may mean His obscurity before John's imprisonment by Antipas as the Assyrian (Mark 1¹⁴); or it may mean His retirement in Galilee for most of His life, during

50 ORACLES IN THE NEW TESTAMENT

the continuance of the Feast of Tabernacles and the Waterbearing of Siloam, crowned by His appearance (see Chapter X) in public shortly before His death. This oracle is the reason for the concealment of His Messiahship, as we shall see. It is the origin of the Messiah-secret, about which so much has been written. Later, especially after A.D. 70, it would be taken to mean the previous obscurity of the Church down to the cessation of the Waterbearing, to be followed by the large influx of converts after that date.

Then we have had some references to Herod's feeling that he had been mocked by the Magi (pp. 17, 22), and to the massacre of the Innocents (24, 28). We have already observed that Jer. 31^{15} has to do, not with a massacre, but with the exile of his people: he watches the sons of Benjamin son of Rachel going into exile, and he figures Rachel weeping for their exile and uncomforted. Nevertheless, he proceeds to say that they shall return to their native land some day when they have been chastened. Naturally, as Jeremiah is speaking of the sons of Benjamin, he must imply that Ramah is the Benjamite Ramah, the most famous of all the Ramahs, though the Ramah of Ephraim, otherwise called Ramathaim-Zophim, was also famous. It is clear, then, that Jeremiah has nothing to do with a massacre and nothing to do with Bethlehem. This does not seem to help with Matthew. How, then, and why does Jer. 31^{15} come to be applied by Matthew here? We have seen already Justin's explanation that Ramah was in Arabia, that a voice heard from Ramah caused the journey of the Magi, which caused the massacre, which caused the lamentation. And though there may well have been many Ramahs in Arabia, there is no apparent reason why Rachel should be connected with an Arabian Ramah. Justin's interpretation fails to supply such connection, and, in fact,

HEROD THE ASSYRIAN 51

emphasizes the disconnection to the point of absurdity. Rachel is, however, connected by Matthew with Rachel's tomb, which as the memorial of the touching story of her death was claimed to be in the territory of more than one tribe, even as Homer's birthplace. In 1 Sam. 10^2 it was claimed for Benjamin's territory, but in Matthew's time it was popularly placed, as in Gen. 35^{19}, a mile north of Bethlehem in Judah, and that is its traditional site to-day.

The evangelist also remembered that Isa. 10^{29} had mentioned "Ramah the city of Saul," *i.e.* the Ramah of Benjamin, as one of the places suffering from the invasion of the Assyrian. But then Isa. 8^8 showed that the Assyrian's object was " to take away *from Judea* one who shall be able to lift up a head." Now Ramah, though not in Judah, was *in Judea;* what, then, did the tribe matter? There was no Judea indeed when Jeremiah wrote, but Judea is in the Greek Bible frequently, and this name was known to the readers of Matt. 2. That was enough. Again, he found that Bethlehem was called by Micah Bethlehem-Ephratah, *i.e.* of Ephraim, for some archæological* reason or other, but every one knew that Bethlehem was in Judah, and that alone was the important point. At last all was in order for the two quotations (Matt. $2^{6,18}$) to support the King's nativity in Judah and the massacre there: Bethlehem and Rachel's tomb and Ramah were all in Judea. At the same time it must be observed that for any critic or reader who shuts his eyes to the contents of the Greek text, and especially to the words *from Judea*, which are likely to escape notice and belong to a wholly different context, a large crop of difficulties covers all this piece of ground, and the evangelist will be seen heavily burdened in trying to remove them.

* See Dr. King's Note on Ps. 132.

52 ORACLES IN THE NEW TESTAMENT

The Immanuel Oracle.

We now come to that which for various reasons, ecclesiastical, artistic and traditional, has become to many persons one of the corner-stones of their faith. The Nativity of Jesus is the virgin-birth of the Christ *who was to come* (ἐρχομένου), and this doctrine originates in the Greek Bible. The Isaian passage was taken over by a logical necessity into the Christian Church during the period A.D. 70–100. The doctrine of the virgin-birth has been pronounced by Dr. Sanday, whose authority carries much weight, to be non-essential to the orthodox faith, one of the strongest grounds being that it was not essential to St. Paul, who in a crucial passage seems rather to have chosen to pass it over. He says (Gal. 4^4) "But when the fulness of the time came, God sent forth his son, born of *a woman.*" The meaning of *'almah* (παρθένος LXX, νεᾶνις Aq. Sym. The., *a virgin* R.V., *the maiden* R.V. margin) may be seen in commentaries and especially in Robertson Smith, *The Prophets of Israel*, p. 424. He translates *'almah* by *young woman.*

The Hebrew is thus translated in R.V. margin.

> Isa. $7^{14\,ff}$ Therefore the Lord himself shall give you a sign; behold, the maiden is with child and beareth a son, and *shall call* his name Immanuel. Curds and honey shall he eat, *that he may know* to refuse the evil, and choose the good. For before the child shall know to refuse the evil, and choose the good, the land whose two kings thou abhorrest shall be forsaken. The Lord shall bring upon thee, and upon thy people, and upon thy father's house, days that have not come, from the day that Ephraim departed from Judah; (even) the King of Assyria.

The Greek diverges in the following particulars: Behold, the *virgin shall be* with child and *shall bear*

HEROD THE ASSYRIAN 53

a son (ἕξει is probably the right reading (א A Q) and not λήμψεται, and the two expressions are distinguished in meaning by Philo) and *thou shalt call . . . before he knoweth or preferreth evil things, he shall select the good thing.* For before the child knoweth good or evil, *he disobeyeth evil to select the good thing, and* the land which thou *fearest* shall be forsaken *from before them* [*their two kings*]. God shall . . . that *he took away* Ephraim from Judah; the king of the Assyrians. The sense is cloudy both in Hebrew and in Greek. But after the disputed first line the sense will probably be admitted, that before the child to be born develops into intelligence, the lands of Pekah and Rezin shall be laid waste, and Judah shall be reduced to wild pasture ground whose inhabitants feed on sour milk and honey. And plainly there emerges an antithesis between a saving Emmanuel and the destroying king of Assyria. This sharp conflict is foretold from the first. The sign is the Nativity, and almost simultaneous with it is the onset of the Assyrian.

Hellenism in Palestine.

But it mattered little for the Jewish interpretation of prophecy what the Hebrew original said in its clear-obscure. In the Greek version it had not only a translation, but a commentary, which, though it often enough explained the obscure by the more obscure, was still a commentary, a standard of comparison, a stimulus to thought. We know that in certain conditions the popular mind prefers the more obscure, and loves the mysterious even when it is least necessary. The popularity of the Greek version was advancing apace. How could it do otherwise? Herod had set his face against everything Hebrew and in favour of everything Greek.* His am-

* Schürer, *Jewish People*, § 22, somewhat minimizes the total effect, but the mass of evidence he has collected under the heads

bition was a Roman ambition throughout, and a Roman, in the East especially, must be above all things Greek. Herod would foster the liberal arts and culture, but what form of culture was known in the East save that of Greece? He employed the scholarly historian Nicholas of Damascus, a Gentile Greek, to teach him philosophy, rhetoric and history. In the non-Jewish towns of his kingdom he actually erected heathen temples. Thus, indeed, he fulfilled the prophecies of the violent river (Isa. 8[7]) that swept away the softly-flowing rivulet of Siloam. The tide of Hellenism swept away the profound learning and gentle wisdom of Hillel from its moorings in Jerusalem, and in the next generation the liberal and refined Pharisee, Gamaliel, pressed by the distresses of the times, transferred the synedrial schools from Jerusalem to Jamnia, near Joppa, where about A.D. 90 a synod was held concerning the Canon of the Old Testament, and where the next generation witnessed the creation of a standard text of the Hebrew not materially different from what is translated in the English Version.

Consequently the public ministry of Jesus commenced in a community far more hellenized in opinion than that which had rejoiced at the death of Herod, more accessible to the ideas which the Greek Bible conveyed, in spite or because of all its blunders, puzzles and uncertainties. And it had manifest advantages over the Hebrew Bible. The future lay with the Greek language, not with the Hebrew, as the people at large must have seen. The Greek language was that of common life everywhere outside of Jerusalem for a Jew. It was far more pliant, expressive, practical, than the Hebrew. It was civilization and trade and commerce embodied

---

of government, games, buildings, art, industry, coinage, etc., abundantly proves the flowing tide of Greek language amongst Jews of Palestine, and, further, that Herod swelled it.

HEROD THE ASSYRIAN 55

orally. During the three centuries which had passed since the translation of the Bible commenced, the Jews had thriven throughout the world as it seemed they had not thriven before. Alexandria and Egypt were a sort of nearer West to them, but the farsighted genius of Alexander the Great had opened to them the further West of Spain and Gaul when he made the Israelites to be the cement of all Eastern commerce overland and of Mediterranean oversea. The vast proportion of Jews in the year A.D. 30 throughout the world spoke Greek, and there was no other language that they had in common. Then again, foreign culture was a fact, and the Jews, who were incessant travellers, could not be blind to it. They must be aware that there was a kind of narrowness in the Jerusalem Rabbis.* The saying of the Pharisees in John 7^{49}, "This people that knoweth not the law are cursed," has its exact counterpart in that which is ascribed to the great Hillel, "The unlettered cannot fear God, nor yet the ignorant be pious." When the near kinsman of a great Rabbi inquired of him whether having mastered all Jewish lore he might not turn to that of the Gentile world, the teacher, referring to Ps. 1^2, bade him inquire what hour was not of the day nor of the night, that he might devote it to study that was not of the law. Such narrowness could not satisfy a worldwide people. Moreover, long before Philo, some venturesome Jews of Alexandria had, like Aristobulus (150 B.C.), imported Greek philosophies into their own commentaries on the Pentateuch, or like the pseudo-Aristeas, identified Zeus with the God of the Jews. This was the rapidly growing spirit of Hellenism which, far from meaning anti-Judaism, nevertheless meant a wider view than that of the Jerusalem Rabbis. At the same time it brought a narrowness of its own. For when Hellenism began

* *Dict. Christ. Biography*, "Philo," p. 358,

to capture Jerusalem, it began to intensify party spirit, and to promote all the factions and fierce animosities and discords that for so many centuries had been the feature of every city of Hellas. That way led shortly to the city's ruin. The individual " to whom, with his brother," says Josephus,* " our ruin may almost entirely be attributed," was one skilled in Greek literature and confident in his acquaintance with it. And no Palestinian Jew was more completely and continuously hellenized throughout his lifetime than Josephus himself.

Now remembering the transformation wrought by this violent tide of opinion, this transvaluation of values, let us revert to the prophecy of Isa. 7^{14} which we have read as it was in the Hebrew, and consider what would be the effect on a Jewish reader of the Greek version of the same passage, which is this—

> Isa. 7^{14} Therefore the Lord himself shall give you a sign : Behold the virgin shall conceive and shall bear a son, and thou shalt call his name Emmanuel : butter and honey shall he eat before he knoweth or preferreth evil [things] and he shall choose the good thing : because before the child knoweth good or evil, he scorneth wickedness to choose the good thing, and the land which thou fearest shall be forsaken from before them [the two kings]. But God shall bring upon thee and upon thy people and upon thy father's house days that have not come since the day when he took away Ephraim from Judah, the king of the Assyrians.

At once he would be struck with the astounding character of the promised sign, and would be constrained to say that the announcement heralded by the *Behold* was far more worthy of wonder according to the Greek

* *Life,* 9^6.

HEROD THE ASSYRIAN 57

than according to the Hebrew. Next, the difference in tenses, *shall conceive and bear*, would not be very important in prophecy, and yet the future tense of the Greek might easily tell more with those who were less well informed of the history of the time of Ahaz : it would lend itself more to a continuous future. Next, *thou shalt call* seems to come straight to the reader, to whom the name is made of more interest than to the mother. Then comes an obscure passage, more obscure than in the Hebrew, in which frugality of life* seems to be the outward token of a good inner disposition : while the Greek, on the other hand, lays stress upon a definite selection of all goodness as the line of the child's career from boyhood. The next sentence is clear in the Hebrew, that before he arrives at years of discretion the hostile land of the two allied kings shall be laid waste; but in the Greek we have a slovenly translation, because the translator has inserted after *good or evil* a paraphrase of his own as if in brackets [*that is to say he scorneth wickedness to select that which is good*], by way of merely repeating his previous mistranslation, after which he has to struggle out of his own difficulty by inserting *and* before *the land*. Again, *he took away Ephraim* (Flight into Egypt, see p. 24) is more forcible though less correct than *Ephraim departed*. Finally, in these two verses in the Greek we have more emphasis on the person of the Child to be born, for more is said about Him; and less emphasis on the hostile land, which falls quite into a background in consequence of the intrusive *and*. What that land was or could be is by no means clear in the Greek, but it would be certainly interpreted to be Rome by every Jew who looked for this prophecy to be or to have been fulfilled and who lived in

* If we take it as Cheyne, *Prophecies of Isaiah* (1880), p. 48, "*when* he shall know," it means compulsory privation even till he has reached years of discretion.

the years 50–100 A.D. For, even if we do not follow A (see p. 20) in reading *them* in verse 14, the LXX has lost all idea of *the two kings* being kings of Rome or one of them a king of Rome; it would even permit the idea of Rome being destroyed by two Parthian kings or a Parthian and another, and the fear of Parthia* was very much present to the Romans themselves throughout that century. Consequently the whole essential import of the Hebrew, in regard to the boyhood synchronizing with the deliverance, had been quietly lost by the Greek. What was preserved, however, was the prediction of Herod, the king of Assyria, not as the destroyer of the hostile land as the Hebrew made him, but as the savage antagonist of the Child, like a plague of wild bees ($7^{18\,ff}$), like a rasping razor, like a violent river.

Here, then, was a total alteration of the Hebrew by its Greek version. Wherever Hellenism pushed its way among the multitudes whose centre was the Temple, there this version of *the sign which the Lord Himself would give them* became predominant. So long as the Hebrew text enjoyed undisputed sway in the minds of expectant Jews, they would expect a person called by the name of Immanuel from his birth, a lad of the highest character, who should witness, if he did not in person promote, the fall of Rome, and the peril of Herod. But how could this opinion, however zealously entertained, succeed in uniting a faction or rallying a fraction of the Jewish people? Nothing whatever was gained by the interpretation of the King of Assyria as Herod. Nothing was gained by the understanding that before Immanuel was ten or fifteen years of age, in other words "in that time from now," the fall of Rome would take place. The interpretation was too insipid for

* Philo, *Leg. Cai.*, 1023 c, ἐφόβουν δὲ αὐτὸν (Petronius) καὶ αἱ πέραν Εὐφράτου δυνάμεις.

HEROD THE ASSYRIAN

the taste of a single individual. For Immanuel was unknown.

But once let this dull, quiet, opaque body conflict and collide with another body of opinion which was founded on the Greek text, and fire flashes from their impact. The *virgin* shall conceive . . . *thou shalt call* . . . his name . . . *he scorneth* wickedness. . . his deadly foe is *Herod*—this is the body of Greek opinion, not less Jewish than the other, not with any conscious intention of becoming less Jewish. We read a few verses further and find (Isa. 8⁷) that Herod " the river strong and great, the king of the Assyrians and his glory, will go upon every one of your valleys and walk upon every one of your walls, and will take away from Judea one who shall be able to lift up a head or powerful to accomplish a deed: and his encampment shall be so as to fill the breadth of thy land. With us is God." To the Greek translator here the image of the Assyrian is rather that of the plague of bees than of the mighty river. The *valleys* (8⁷) are *yours* instead of the *channels* being *his;* the wells are *yours* instead of the *banks his.* But he has totally altered the sense once more by the creation of *a man* (ἄνθρωπον, person, *i.e.* the babe) *who shall be able to lift up a head or powerful to accomplish a deed* (δύνατον συντελέσασθαί τι). This is indeed a creation of the Greek translator, for the Hebrew of verse 8 is as follows: " and he [the king of Assyria] shall sweep onward into Judah; he shall overthrow and pass through; he shall reach even to the neck; and the stretching out of his wings shall fill the breadth of thy land, O Immanuel (or, With us is God)." *The man* in question would be identified with Emmanuel by any reader of the Greek who knew that " With us is God " is the translation of that name. The synagogue-readers would be competent to make the identification. Emmanuel, then, is of Judea, as Herod is. And he shall be able to lift up the head of his fellows and accomplish a great work. Here again the Greek translation is slovenly, for *powerful* (δύνατον after ὅς δυνήσεται by mere repetition) is not wanted. But there is one declaration here in the Greek which must have given it in comparison with the Hebrew the stamp of transcendent importance—that the object of the Assyrian's jealousy is a human being, not an angel (as the opponents of Heb. 2[16] maintained), not a monster (as the Book of Enoch, Ch. 90[37] : 161 B.C. Charles), not a tendency (as the Assumption of Moses, written by a Zealot, A.D. 1 or later). We may not yet say that Emmanuel is identical with Messiah (Christ), but at least the subsequent life and career of Emmanuel become henceforward invested with unique interest and expectation, as those of a human being. And we shall see later how the *Man who shall be able to lift up [his] head or is powerful to accomplish a [great] deed* is Isaiah's forecast of *the Man who shall live and shall not see death,* for God *will deliver his soul from the hand of hell,* of whom the Psalmist speaks in Ps. 89[48].

CHAPTER III

THE SHEPHERDS

The Secret of the Messiah.

WHEN we pass from the story of the Nativity in Matthew to the corresponding account in Luke we notice two points of contrast. First, though Matthew is usually considered the Gospel for the Jews and Luke for the Gentiles, we observe that in the present case Matthew has described the visit of Gentiles, Magi, to the cradle of the infant king, and Luke the visit of Jews in the person of the Shepherds. This is a very strong point against those who assert that Luke was a Gentile. Secondly, unlike the Magi, whose science, inherited from immemorial times, has endowed them with a precision of calculation that issues in confidence (Matt. 2^2), the Shepherds are smitten with surprise and great fear (Luke 2^9), and, even after reassurance by the angel and the heavenly host, appear to resolve after some doubt ($διέλθωμεν\ δή$) upon their journey to Bethlehem. To them the Saviour, the Lord Messiah, is one whom they have to find where he is hidden,* asking no question of any man but themselves, whereas the Magi inquire as if with the certainty that they would soon know. We are reminded of—

Isa. 32^{1f} For, behold, a king, a righteous (one) shall reign . . . and *he shall be hidden as* ($κρυβήσεται\ ὡς$) *from rushing water.*

* John 7^{27} But when the Christ cometh no man knoweth whence he is. See also John 7^{10} He went up not openly but *as* ($ὡς$) *in secret.* But this, we observe, is the occasion of the Feast of Tabernacles and of the water-bearing from Siloam. See John 7^{38} for *the rivers of living water,* $ῥεύσουσιν\ ὕδατος\ ζῶντος$.

On a later occasion the words *hidden as* are clearly reproduced in John 7^{10} (see Chapter X.); the *rushing water* is the violent river which is Herod Antipas. The heavenly light which to the Magi was itself a sign (*his star*) is not so to the Shepherds, but is the occasion, or rather the circumstance, of the angel appearing to them and giving them the sign (Luke 2^{12}), Ye shall find a babe wrapped in swaddling clothes and lying in a manger. The manger is thus the hidden object of the Shepherds' quest.

The Locality of the Shepherds.

The original motive of the story in Luke, as in Matthew, was certainly some Jewish tradition. Edersheim* says: "That the Messiah was to be born in Bethlehem was a settled conviction. Equally so was the belief that He was to be revealed from Migdal-Eder, ' the tower of the flock.' " He refers to the Targum of Jonathan, so-called, in Gen. 35^{21}, which is this: " And Rahel died, and was buried in the way to Ephrath, which is Bethlehem. . . . And Jakob proceeded, and spread his tent beyond the tower of Eder, the place from whence, it is to be, the King Meshiha would be revealed at the end of the days." We are further to distinguish the Temple-flocks destined for Temple-sacrifices and their shepherds from ordinary flocks and their shepherds, who from their manner of life were unable to observe the requirements of the Law, because they kept their flocks in the wilderness all the year round. The Temple-flocks are mentioned more than once in that most Messianic prophet Zechariah, where they are called *the flock of slaughter* ($11^4,\ ^7$) " that is kept for Me " (11^{11}). And they are noticed in Mal. $1^{8,\ 13}$ (and Malachi is only the latter portion of Zechariah) where the prophet complains, " when ye

* *Life and Times of Jesus*, 186.

THE SHEPHERDS 63

offer the blind for sacrifice, the lame and the sick and the injured, it is no evil!" On the other hand, the advent of the Good Shepherd was prepared in Jer. 23^4, as we have seen.

Now it is Luke who puts the two apparently diverse thoughts of a *flock of sheep* and a *King* into connection in the words, "Fear not, little *flock*, it is your Father's good pleasure to give you the *kingdom*" (Luke 12^{32}). But perhaps neither this relation of ideas nor even that of the "sheep for sacrifice" with the birth of "the Lamb without blemish and without spot" is so likely to account for Luke containing the visit of the Shepherds as the simple consideration that they represented (1) the ministry of the Jewish Law, (2) the tradition of David as Shepherd, when in their humble fashion they came to do homage at the first. But is it possible to discover the place where Luke supposes these flocks to be kept, or Migdal-Eder to be?

When we come to examine the details of the story, we can see that the Tower of the Flock was not very near to Bethlehem, because the Shepherds say, "Let us *go through as far as* Bethlehem." This expression is not consistent with a short walk of only a mile. The shortest distance of which it is used, and it is used by Luke (Acts 9^{38}), is the ten or twelve miles between Joppa and Lydda. Thus it exactly suits a journey such as will presently be made. Such a distance, too, is by no means inconsistent with the other expression, "Now there were shepherds in *the same country*," for it would take them only four hours to cover it. It must be said that for the present purpose, which is to discover what St. Luke thought, we must be content to put aside all traditions of the Crusaders' times and of Jerome regarding "the Field of the Shepherds" and "the House of the Magi" (Beit-Sâhûr, *House of sorcerers*), which sacred sites are exhibited to pilgrims near Bethlehem. Nor, again, is any help to be derived from tracing the steps of Jacob's journey in Gen. 35 as to " Ephrath *which is Bethlehem.*" There is every likelihood that the last three words are a gloss, for no solid ground can be discovered why Bethlehem, six miles south of Jerusalem, should be connected with the tribe of Ephraim or should ever have been called Bethlehem-Ephratah. Consequently the way is open to Dr. Cheyne to suggest that Ephrath is a "correction" in early times of the original *Beeroth* (el Bîreh), some nine miles north of Jerusalem, though it is not clear what etymological reason there is for this supposition. The alteration, however, would be easy. Let us then suppose it and see what results follow. Every traveller on the one road which joins the south of Palestine with the north, the only road through the central highland that has ever existed—and this is indisputable—knows that Jacob would have passed Beeroth whichever his journey was, if he passed between Jacob's Well at Shechem on the north and Bethlehem on the south. He also knows that the water there is good, as the name Beeroth, "Wells," implies; and that the panorama there, commanding the site of Jerusalem and all the southern mountains of Judea, is remarkable. A point on the road there is about 2820 ft. above sea, and if, as we are told in Gen. 35^{20}, Jacob set up a pillar upon Rachel's grave, it is probable that the author or redactor knew of a pillar or tower or conspicuous rock near the roadside which he chose to identify with the historically touching incident of Rachel's death. Another pillar is mentioned as existing at Beth-el just before this (35^{14}), and the tower of Edar is mentioned just after it (35^{21}). We thus have two pillars and a tower, and considering that we have both J and E at work here, we may safely reduce the three structures, or quite probably natural rocky

THE SHEPHERDS

eminences, to two, if not even to one, at Beth-el (2890 ft.) and at Beeroth. But we have another datum: for (Gen. 35) "from Beth-el there was *but a little way* to come to Ephrath," where Rachel died. Now this suits the position of Beeroth, less than three miles off,* much better than Bethlehem, which is fifteen miles further. The one safe postulate is a panorama from the roadside; for such a place is always one where a tower or pillar is likely in all ages to be built. The circumstances attributed in Gen. 35^{9-15} to the erection of the pillar at Beth-el —" to thy seed after thee will I give the land "—demand a panorama, or, we might say, the panorama and the patriarch suggest the conversation.

The Valley of Achor for a Resting-place.

The reason of this digression will appear presently. We find that the originating passages of the story of the Shepherds are principally three.

The first of these in Hebrew gives an indication so feeble that hardly any one who consulted the oracle could discern an answer from it.

> Isa. 65^9 And I will bring forth a seed out of Jacob and out of Judah an inheritor of my mountains; and my chosen shall inherit it, and my servants shall dwell there. And Sharon shall be a pasture of flocks, and the Valley of Achor a place for herds to lie down in, for my people that have sought me.

But we pause for a moment to notice that there is no more suitable occasion for Luke to find a fulfilment of the blessing upon Jacob delivered in Gen. 35^{9-15} than the Nativity, and if he did identify the Tower of the Flock (Eder) with the neighbourhood of Beeroth and Beth-el there is a remarkable fitness in his association

* Saadiah and Kimchi translate "about a mile" (Kalisch).

of the Valley of Achor with that fulfilment, for this valley was near it. It is obvious that Isaiah here mentions the western and the eastern sides of the hill-country—"my mountains"—of Judea. But the Greek turns it:

> Isa. 65⁹ And I will bring forth *the seed* out of Jacob and out of Judah, and he shall inherit my *holy mountain*, and my elect and my servants shall inherit, and they shall inhabit there. And there shall be *in the wood* habitations (ἐπαύλεις) of sheep, and the Valley of Achor for a *resting-place* (ἀνάπαυσιν) of the herds *for my people*—(*to them*) *who sought me*.

At once we note in these words their particular and quickening force; they elate expectation, and kindle curiosity. We wish to know more about *the seed, my holy mountain*—which is beyond a doubt the hill-country of Judea, but the singular form is more particular. Then *Sharon* has disappeared, but *in the wood* is a phrase offering wide range of possibility, and *they who sought me* (aorist) in that connection suggests forthwith a reference to another oracle—

> Ps. 132³ I will not go up to the tabernacle of my house or give a *resting-place* (ἀνάπαυσιν) to the temples of my head until I find a place for the Lord, a habitation for the God of Jacob. Lo, we heard (of) it (the *resting-place*) at Ephrathah, we found it in the thickets *of the wood*. We will go into his tabernacles, we will worship unto the place where his feet stand. Arise, Lord, into thy *resting-place*, thou and the ark of thy holiness. Thy priests put on righteousness and thy holy ones (ὅσιοι) shall rejoice. For thy servant David's sake, turn not away the face of thine Anointed (*Christ*).

This is a very astonishing correspondence. The two passages Isa. 65 and Ps. 132 have three things in common,

THE SHEPHERDS 67

the *resting-place*, the *wood* and the *seekers*, who seem to say the actual words, " we will go and worship at the place where his feet stand "—*the place Eternal* of Isa. 33^{14}. Furthermore, it appears from Ps. 132 that *the wood* is near Ephrathah and there is a *hearing* and a *finding* there; these are parellel or identical actions, according to the rules of Hebrew poetry. Again, since wherever there are sheep there are shepherds, it appears plainly that the shepherds are to be identified with them *that sought me*. And once more: the Greek permits us to see that *the herds for my people* (singular) may easily be detached from the second dative case (plural) which immediately follows, *to them that sought me*; in any case *the herds for my people* naturally means the temple-herds of oxen for sacrifice. Lastly, when we place the two passages together, we can see that the guardians of these temple-herds and temple-flocks are naturally called holy (ὅσιοι, *lawful*, but not ἱεροί) as being occupied in however a menial capacity about the provision of beasts for sacrifice.

And where was the Valley of Achor? The geographical authorities agree that it was one of the many gorges which descend from the central ridge to Jordan, dropping 3,000 feet in a very few miles, pictures of rocky desolation without verdure. Nor does Isaiah say that there shall be verdure in the Valley of Achor. We are hardly concerned to ask if Luke considered the question whether Achor was fit to be called a resting-place of herds of oxen. It is unlikely that either the Greek translator or Luke had visited the place: to them it was only a matter of literature. All that we know of it is that " it is a great heap of stones unto this day," that it was east of Beth-el, and formed the north boundary of Judah. A writer * who has no thought of its being identified with

* *Enc. Bibl.*, "Achor." See also Bädeker's *Palestine* (Socin).

"a land the shadow of death" (Isa. 9^2) describes it as "a dark and dismal place," and probably that is the very reason why Isa. 65 says that it shall be made to smile with flocks and herds. Its "gloomy associations" would be entirely changed. Or Isaiah may have meant (what is less likely) the lower parts of the valley, which open near Jericho in richly fertile country. Whether it is the Wâdy Hârith, or Wâdy Fârah, or Wâdy Ḳelt,* or another, the head of it was close to Beth-el and Beeroth, which we assumed to be Ephrath. So far the localities correspond closely.

The Direction to Bethlehem.

We now come to the second oracle, hoping for some light upon the relation of the hearing to the finding and the seeking, and upon the resting-place at Ephrathah and "thy resting-place."

Micah 5^2 And thou, Bethlehem, house of Ephrathah, art fewest to be in the thousands of Judah: from whom shall (one) come forth unto me to be for a ruler of Israel, and his goings forth are from the beginning from days everlasting. Therefore he shall grant them until the time of her that beareth; (and) she shall bear: and the rest of their brethren shall convert unto the children of Israel. And he (or, it) shall stand, and shall see; the Lord shall shepherd his flock in strength; and in the *glory* of the name of the Lord their God shall they be: for now shall he be magnified unto the ends of the earth; and this shall be our *peace:* when Asshur shall come against your land and when he shall go against your

---

* Conder, *Tent-work in Palestine*, ii. 21, is rather too confident for the Ḳelt, for Josh. 7^{2,24} "brought them up unto the Valley of Achor," postulates an upland valley, and Ḳelt is only the lower portion of one. Ai was a highland town.

THE SHEPHERDS 69

country, then shall be raised up against him seven shepherds, even (or, and) eight bits of men (δήγματα ἀνθρώπων). And they shall shepherd Asshur with the sword, and the land of Nimrod in her trench, when he cometh against your land, and advanceth against your borders.

The shepherds, therefore, being seven or eight in number, having found something in the thickets of the woods, where they kept their flocks in or near the Valley of Achor eight or nine miles north of Jersualem, are directed not to Ephrathah, if that is Beeroth, but to Bethlehem-Ephrathah, six miles south of Jerusalem, as the birthplace of one who shall become a ruler of Israel, one of ancient and lofty, if not also mysterious lineage. Then follows a most obscure passage, of which one interpretation would be this: God would let His people, them that sought him, be absent from their appointed task in the sheepfolds and byres of Achor until the time of the Nativity, their mission being ultimately to convert their brethren to the true Israel. Meanwhile God would stand over them as a glory, beholding them from on high, and bathing them in light; and He would shepherd their flocks in their resting-place as part of His own mighty flock. To them the name and majesty of the Lord their God should be a glory, not only in the figurative but in the literal sense; for now He shall be magnified throughout the earth. This infant King to be born is the token to them not of war, however, but ultimately of peace: when the persecuting Herod attacks Judea, these seven or eight " bits of men," leading men, shall form the nucleus of a resisting force.* However provisional such an interpretation might be, it would,

* Micah goes on to mention "sheep at grass" (ἐπὶ ἀγρωστιν, a word which occurs only five times in the Bible). Luke 2[8] comes near it with ἀγραυλοῦντες (very rare, nowhere else in the Bible).

so far as it went, mean the identity of that which they found in the woods near Achor with the glory that stood over them, or perchance a bright angel or heavenly phenomenon that shone round about them, and they must make their way to Bethlehem.

The Angel calls His Name.

The third oracle is one that clears up some difficulties of the other two.

> Isa. $9^{1\,ff}$ Do this first, do it quickly . . . Galilee of the Gentiles *and the parts of Judea* : O people that sit in darkness, see ye a great light : ye that dwell in a land, even the shadow of death, light shall shine upon you. The most part of the people which thou leddest home (is) in thy rejoicing, and they shall rejoice before thee as they that rejoice in harvest, and as they that divide for themselves spoils. Because the yoke that was laid on them shall be removed, even the rod that was on their neck : for the Lord shattereth the rod of them that oppress them as in the day against Midian. For every armament that had been gathered against them by craft, and every suit (of armour) shall they pay without profit, and (the foes) shall wish that they had been burnt with fire. For a child is born to us, a son is given to us, and *an angel shall call his name,* of Great Counsel, Wonderful, Counsellor, Mighty Authority, *Ruler of Peace,* Father of the world to come. For I will bring peace upon the rulers and health unto him.

In this passage the Alexandrine MS. has been followed, as usually in these pages. The noteworthy variations of reading are at the beginning where *and the parts of Judea* are included along with the northern and eastern parts, and at the end where *an angel shall call* his name.

THE SHEPHERDS

The great light in heaven illuminates those who *sit* in darkness, as the shepherds did, dwelling in a land that was "just the shadow of death" for its dismal desolate gloom of appearance and association. The obscure statement in Micah about the conversion of their brethren is here cleared up, for there is a general conversion from misery to rejoicing in the person of their deliverer. The spoils were to be taken, as Isa. 8^4 said, by the growing lad—the power of Damascus and the spoils of Samaria—from before the eyes of the Assyrian Herod. The angel announces the full style of the infant King. Once more the promise of peace is the feature of his reign. The strange expression in Micah, "seven or eight *bits of men*," is not explained. (The origin of the blunder is easily seen by a Hebrew scholar in the indistinct pronunciation of a reader: there is a corresponding error in the previous words, "he shall see and he shall shepherd"). The translator's meaning was perhaps that these should be biting men, for a *bit* is merely a *bite;* men who could deal biting strokes as with a dagger, or as the adder that biteth in the mountain path, like the men of Dan "that bite the horse's hoof" (Gen. 49^{17}). There is, however, in Micah 5^5 only one meaning possible, that of physical resistance to the Assyrian: and yet, as by a paradox, this militant resistance to Herod is to be overcome by *peace*.

There is another reference in the same context of Isaiah to the end of the Assyrian, which was to be by fire.

> Isa. 9^{13} And the lawlessness (of Herod) shall be burned as fire, and as dry grass it shall be eaten by fire, and shall be burned in the thickets of the wood: and it shall devour therewith all the hills round about: for the exceeding wrath of the Lord the whole land hath been burnt together, and the people shall be as it had been burnt up with fire.

The Paradox of Peace, and the Thing of Price.

If St. Luke attributed to the Shepherds a knowledge of Isaiah and Micah, as he must have done, he would further, perhaps, attribute this much. Indeed, Isaiah says—

> Isa. 10^{17} The light of Israel shall be as a fire, and he shall sanctify it with burning fire, and it shall eat the undergrowth like grass.

If so, we can understand why Luke 2^9 says "the shepherds feared a great fear," for if they knew of a devouring fire to consume the adversaries, this might deal havoc among friends as well as foes. The oracle continues—

> Isa. 10$^{18\,f}$ In that day the mountains and the hills and the woods shall be extinguished, and it shall devour from the soul to the flesh: and he that fleeth shall be as he that fleeth from burning fire: and they that are left behind of them shall be a cipher, and the (or, a) little child shall write them.

But the child is further described as the rod of God's wrath upon Herod.

> Isa. 10^5 Woe unto the Assyrians—the rod of my wrath and of my anger is in their hands.

The words might mean by themselves that the ordained rod is in their power, as the Child was for a time in Herod's grasp, or that his kingdom contained within it the agent of his overthrow. The context was to make this clear—

> Isa. 11^1 And there shall come forth a (or, the) rod out of the root of Jesse and a flower shall go up out of the root. (See Mic. 5^2 above.)

And after the great passage which follows he passes on to the general tokens of peace which are to be displayed even in the animal kingdom. But in Isa. 11^8 the

THE SHEPHERDS

Greek breaks off sharply from describing these tokens and bears naturally and directly a specific meaning which in the Authorized Version would never have occurred to us.

> Isa. 11^8 And the infant child [shall be found] upon a hole of adders, and upon a den of adders' offspring shall he set his hand. And they shall not do harm and they can by no means destroy any one upon my holy mountain, for *the whole* [*land* ?, or *dwelling*—a feminine] is filled so as to know the Lord as much water for to cover up the seas. And there shall be in that day the root of Jesse, even he that is being raised up to rule the Gentiles : upon him the Gentiles shall hope. And his *resting-place* shall be a thing of price (τιμή).

It is not difficult, indeed it is inevitable, for any inquirer of the oracle to read in this passage an answer to the question, What *did we hear* of *the resting-place at Ephrathah* (p. 66), when, after *finding* the heavenly light in the thickets of *the wood* of Achor, *we sought* instruction further and received it from *an angel?* The resting-place of the flocks at Achor has led the Shepherds on to another resting-place at Bethlehem-Ephrathah. And a fine paradox is here. The Child's *resting-place* shall be a thing of price, a precious thing—a den of adders ! This is the picturesque description of *the manger* at Bethlehem, the cockatrice's den. The cockatrice is a kind of basilisk that haunts caverns and pits, and such a pit would be a country manger in Judea, to which the holy mother was reduced because there was no room for them in the inn, the proper *resting-place*. The Greek Bible has succeeded, not for the first time, in being literal in a sense other than that in which it attempted to be literal, for it has given the form of words which the inquirers of the oracle were able to fill with meaning just by reason of the question which they brought to it. Who has not seen in the paintings of Correggio and earlier masters the room at Bethlehem filled, *the whole of it*, with light from the divine Child? There is nothing in the New Testament to prompt this painter's fancy. And yet without the faintest thought * of it they have had meanwhile a scriptural authority for what they painted, " for *the whole resting-place* is filled with light so as to know the Lord in the person of the new-born Child." For any reader who had passed over the doubtful feminine in the Greek, as if " land " or " dwelling " had to be supplied would, when he came to *his resting-place*, go back and supply that feminine substantive and no other.

The adders and the cattle and the asses shall do no manner of harm in this manger which is in *my holy mountain* (p. 66), where *my holy one* lies (Ps. 89^{35}). And why? Because—

Isa. 1^3 *The ox* knoweth his purchaser, and *the ass* the manger of his Lord.

And here we have once more the scriptural authority for the picture of these animal friends of man sharing in the peace of the Nativity. They, too, are in " the place eternal," where they see the King with glory (Isa. 33^{14}, ^{17}).

The Arrangement of Words in the Gloria in Excelsis.

Two or three more points remain to be noticed. It has long been a vexed question whether in the *Gloria in Excelsis* we are to read " good-will toward men " or " unto men of good-will." The rhythm of the sentence appears to favour the former, so that we should have three qualities, glory, peace, good-will ascribed in the

---

* The LXX was unknown to them. The Vulgate here has *terra*. They followed the Apocryphal Gospels.

THE SHEPHERDS 75

three respective spheres of God, the world, mankind; and this is rather the idea that impresses the modern reader, who regards the need of the world as it is, without troubling about the conditions in which St. Luke wrote. And in Westcott and Hort's Appendix we read the reason why this opinion is allowed in the margin of their text, in deference to Westcott's opinion. But the latter form, "unto men of good-will," is both better attested and intrinsically more probable. And now we ask if any light is thrown upon it by the above supposed discovery of its origin. The answer is strongly in favour of the latter form.

We must put aside all possible applications to the modern world, all broad-minded desires for the general advancement of mankind, which are not inseparable from either of the two forms, and we turn again to the originating passages as given above. We noted that Isaiah 65^9 has fixed the dwelling-place of "my elect and my servants" as "my holy mountain." The believer in "the seed out of Jacob and out of Judah shall inherit" Bethlehem by virtue of His inheriting it in the obvious though figurative sense with which Luke 2^4 ($\pi\alpha\tau\varrho\iota\tilde{\alpha}\varsigma$) has invested the words. But Isa. 65^{10} goes on to hint to the inquirers of the oracle who the first of these believers shall be—the shepherds of Achor—"those who seek me." And Luke expressly gives the angel's words, which are followed by the song of the angels by way of reassuring the fear-stricken shepherds. Consequently we require a particular reassurance for them and not a general promise to mankind at large. They must be able to take the message as meant for them, and identify themselves with "men of good-will," as the reader of Isa. 65_9 would identify them when he finds them the first among "my elect and my servants." The good-will is not of necessity God's good-will towards them, though that would be involved clearly enough in their being His elect, but it can easily be understood of their good-will in obeying the angel, their docile faith, and a much less virtue than this is implied in the use of the term elsewhere in the Greek Bible. There is some further support for the idea of "men of good-will" in Mic. 5⁴: "They shall be in the glory of the name of the Lord their God," where there is no thought of the good-will directly towards mankind at large.

The Angel-song follows as a necessity from the oracle of—

> Isa. 33⁷ For angels shall be sent forth (apostolically ἀποσταλήσονται) requiring peace (ἀξιοῦντες A).*

The first clause of it is based, if any basis is required for the spontaneous burst of praise to the Holiest in the height, upon the Hallel of—

> Ps. 148¹ Praise ye the Lord from the heavens, praise him *in the highest*. Praise him all his angels, praise him all his powers. Praise him sun and moon, praise him all the stars and the light.

This had been already applied by the Son of Sirach in his description of the moon—

> Ecclus. 43⁹ The beauty of heaven, the *glory* of the stars, an ornament giving light *in the highest* of the Lord.

In the second clause, "and upon earth peace," we have already seen the references in—

> Mic. 5⁵ And there shall be *peace* here—

---

* The Alexandrine MS. which Luke used, especially in Luke 1, 2, continues: "bitterly weeping, exhorting peace." This symptom of emotion Luke passes over. Sterne's sentence: "The recording angel, as he wrote it down, dropped a tear upon the word and blotted it out for ever," was anticipated in this beautiful expression.

THE SHEPHERDS

the preceding words being " unto the ends *of the earth.*" This thought recurs in—

> Isa. 9⁷ Great is his rule and of his *peace* there is no bound.

It appears that these passages do not support Hort's opinion, marked by him in brackets, that we might divide the song thus: Glory to God in the highest and upon earth: peace among men of good-will. In Isa. 11¹⁻¹⁰, the most graphic of all, the tokens of peace after the smiting of the ungodly, though *peace* is not named, are found distinctly *upon the earth*, and not *among men*, but in the sphere of the non-human animal creation.

The mention of the " multitude of the heavenly host " (Luke 2¹³) takes us back to the early vision of the prophet Micaiah before Ahab.

> 1 Kings 22¹⁹ I saw the God of Israel sitting upon his throne, and *all the host of heaven* stood around about him on his right hand and on his left.

The Book of Wisdom in Luke.

When the angel says " *This shall be the sign* to you: ye shall find the babe wrapped in *swaddling-clothes* and lying in a manger," he enforces one prediction by another as—

> Isa. 37³⁰. *This shall be the sign to you:* eat this year what thou hast sown.

The swaddling clothes are from a very remarkable source—

> Wisd. 7⁴. *In swaddling-clothes* was I nurtured and *in careful thoughts.*

For the *careful thoughts* are, beyond a doubt, reproduced by Luke 2¹⁹ " And Mary kept all these things, pondering them in her heart." That Luke had concluded that what was predicated of Wisdom in the book of that name, as well as of Solomon the son of David, was predicated of Christ as the Wisdom of God and the Son of David, is clear from his other statements. Thus, Luke 2^{40} "And the child grew and waxed strong, being filled with *wisdom*;" with which compare—

Wisd. 7^7 And there came upon me the spirit of *wisdom*.

So again Luke 2^{52} supplies *wisdom and stature* to the terms expressing Samuel's "advance in favour with God and man" (1 Sam. 2^{26}). So again Luke 7^{35}, "*wisdom* is justified of all her children," *i.e.* of those whom she repeatedly addresses as "my son," "children" (Prov. 8^{32}, etc.). The identity of wisdom with the Word and Son of God was so entirely established in the fourth century that one of the most cardinal texts in the Arian controversy was that of Prov. 8^{22} concerning wisdom: "The Lord possessed me as the beginning of his ways unto his works." And here may be mentioned the fact that Wisdom also contains an anticipation of one of the three Temptations of Christ—

Wisd. 7^8 I preferred her above sceptres and thrones, and esteemed riches nothing in comparison of her.

Again, the incident of Christ among the doctors is dimly foreshadowed in—

Wisd. 8^{10}. For Wisdom's sake I shall have estimation among *the multitude*, and honour with *the elders* though I be young. I shall be found of a quick conceit in judgment and shall be admired in the sight of able men: when I hold my tongue they shall abide my leisure, and when I speak they shall give good ear unto me: if I talk much they shall lay their hand upon their mouth.

THE SHEPHERDS

The multitude here is the company which came up (συνοδία Luke 2⁴⁴) to the feast, *the elders* are the doctors in the Temple. The latter portion is expressed by "both hearing them and asking them questions." They were "amazed at his understanding and his answers." There is no verbal citation. Yet what proves the underlying presence of Wisd. 8 in Luke 2 is that immediately after this we read—

> Wisd. 8¹⁶ After I am come into my house, I will repose myself with her.

And what is this but the basis of "Wist ye not that I must be in my father's *house* (or *business*)" (ἐν τοῖς τοῦ πατρός μου)? The ambiguity is naturally intentional: He was engaged in His father Solomon's pursuit of wisdom.

Was Herod's Will and Testament discovered in Isaiah?

Lastly, since Luke records the visit of the Shepherds immediately after his mention of the enrolment, to which we shall refer in a later chapter, it may be well to observe here that in Isaiah the connection of the Nativity with some important writing, but not, I think, the enrolment, is almost as close as in Luke.

> Isa. 10¹ Woe unto them that write (γράφουσιν) wickedness; for *writing they write* wickedness, making judgment to swerve from beggars, robbing a verdict of the poor of my people, so that they have a widow for robbery, and an orphan for plunder.

And again—

> Isa. 8¹ And the Lord said unto me, take thee a volume of fresh large (paper), and write in it with a man's pen to make a *plunder of spoils* sharply: for it is at hand.

What could be the meaning of these passages to those who consulted them but that *the writing* was fraught with defeat and disaster for some one—it might be the Assyrian Herod, or it might mean oppression for the Jewish poor! No wonder if the people began by resisting it. Josephus * follows up his mention of Herod's second will, in which he enriched Cæsar with a thousand talents and Cæsar's family with five hundred more—some £360,000 sterling wrung from oppression— by narrating the conspiracy of Judas and Matthias, who were most learned (λογιώτατοι) expositors of the laws and popular teachers. He considers the writing of the will caused the outbreak. It is highly probable that these learned scribes were actuated by the study of Isa. 10^1. And again it is probable that St. Luke, reviewing in his mind the history of Herod's death 4 B.C., and the partition of his kingdom and possessions and property followed by disturbances, discerned the fulfilment therein of the prediction concerning *plunder of spoils*. But at any rate all notion of resistance to oppression is absent from Luke, who never mentions Herod the king after his first line (Luke 1^5). And here in 2^1 we have something quite different—the vague phrase which Luke is to employ so often (about fifteen times) in his work, "And it came to pass in those days."

St. Luke's Preface to his Gospel.

This leads to the remark that a rigid chronological order ought not to be expected of this writer, who reserves to himself in the clearest terms his right to group events together in accordance with his purpose, which is that of a prophet first of all, and only after that a historian. It is unfair to Luke to accuse him first of professing to be a historian and then of falling short in his dates. What he promised in his preface was to write consecutively, uninter-

* *Antt.*, xvii. 6^1.

THE SHEPHERDS

ruptedly (καθεξῆς γράψαι), after a close parallel study of all his prophetic authorities from the first (παρηκολουθηκότι ἄνωθεν πᾶσιν ἀκριβῶς). And what were these authorities? Obviously oral in regard to the explanations of the oracles and not written. We do not know the date when "Matthew collected the oracles in Hebrew" (see Ch. XIII), but even after this collection was made, the interpretations or translations of them were left to the individual's unassisted powers, as Papias has told us. Nobody can read the observations of that brilliant and original and suggestive scholar Friedrich Blass,* too early taken from us, on the proem of St. Luke, without feeling that he has put the matter in a new light, if only by proving that ἀνατάξασθαι is *bringing together*, repeating *from memory*. This statement of Luke can never now be controverted. The predecessors whom he mentions were oral narrators of the explanations of oracles, and their subject matter was "the things that have been fulfilled amongst us" in Palestine, in the usual prophetic sense of fulfilment. But then, in speaking of authorities at all, we must remember that the word *all* is just as likely to be neuter † as masculine in gender, and that his authorities

---

* Blass, *Philology of the Gospels*, p. 18, comparing Acts 11[4].

† The Greek of Luke 1 [1-4] is given for convenience: Ἐπειδήπερ πολλοὶ ἐπεχείρησαν ἀνατάξασθαι διήγησιν περὶ τῶν πεπληροφορημένων ἐν ἡμῖν πραγμάτων, καθὼς παρέδοσαν ἡμῖν οἱ ἀπ' ἀρχῆς αὐτόπται καὶ ὑπηρέται γενόμενοι τοῦ λόγου, ἔδοξε κἀμοὶ παρηκολουθηκότι ἄνωθεν πᾶσιν ἀκριβῶς καθεξῆς σοι γράψαι, κράτιστε Θεόφιλε, ἵνα ἐπιγνῷς περὶ ὧν κατηχήθης λόγων τὴν ἀσφάλειαν. With this may be compared another preface, that of the Greek *Wisdom of Sirach* (Ecclus.) which Luke knew and has rather mitated (πολλῶν, line 1; ἠκολουθηκότων, line 2; καὶ αὐτὸς, line 8; συγγράψαι, ib.; ὅπως, line 9) where we notice ἠκολ., meaning the other books which have since followed in the line of the prophets. Luke's παρηκ. is quite different of course in meaning, and implies careful thought. Thus I cannot think that Prof. Burkitt does quite justice to St. Luke's endeavours when he says (*The Gospel History*, etc., p. 207), "He wrote history as we write it, by putting together such materials as came to his hand." Prof. Burkitt is hard put to it in holding that Luke was the evangelist and companion of St. Paul and also a reader of Josephus. I hope he may see his way to drop the latter burdensome condition.

G

82 ORACLES IN THE NEW TESTAMENT

whom he followed from the first had before them things which were far more ancient than the "eyewitnesses." Jerome is here right in taking *all* as neuter, and Eusebius wrong in taking it as masculine and meaning the eyewitnesses. The things in question are the same that the Bereans found by examining the scriptures (ἀνακρίνοντες τὰς γραφὰς εἰ ἔχοι ταῦτα οὕτως, Acts 17[11]), *whether these things were so.* St. Luke says that he followed in *parallel* observation all things related, to see whether and how far the related stories agreed with the prophecies and so fulfilled them. This is the force of the παρηκολουθηκότι, which is plainly something more than ἠκολουθηκότι would have been. Nowhere else does Luke use this compound, but its other usages in the New Testament are of distinct prophetic application ([Mark 16[17]] 1 Tim. 4[6], 2 Tim. 3[10]).*
Then *from the first* (ἄνωθεν) naturally means from Gen. 1[1] onwards through the Old Testament. The whole expression conveys precisely what Luke did, it implies a careful study of the parallels of the Lord's life with the Old Testament scriptures. He does not mention any written histories, though there is room for Mark and, if necessary, Q among the authorities (πᾶσιν). He was probably aware that he was but the second narrator, or the third, of the Christian Church, and so far from professing to write history he is at pains to show that his object is to make Theophilus know the certainty of his information, hitherto oral, henceforward written. The oral information that

---

* In spite of the uncertainty attending portions of the Pastoral Epistles, I contend that St. Paul has mentioned here the same leading which is exhibited in *St. Luke the Prophet*. He says to Timothy παρηκολούθησάς μου τῇ ἀγωγῇ—" Thou didst follow with prophetic parallels my leading," as well as with thy footsteps. For ἀγ. *conduct, manner of living,* is quite too insipid a translation. No wonder that he writes to the Thessalonians, as to no other church, that the Gospel came among them at first in the holy *spirit* (the prophetic interpretation of Joshua) *and much fulfilment.*

THE SHEPHERDS 83

Theophilus had received did not amount to tradition, which is assumed to be unalterably delivered as received, but was rather a somewhat tentative exposition of the fulfilments of the oracles of the Lord. It was tradition in a fluid state, wanting *certainty*. Hence the need of a fresh study of the prophetic parallels by Luke before writing.

His predecessors had undertaken to give from memory oral descriptions * (διήγησιν) or reports or narratives principally based upon oracles, rather than histories; and he does not dissociate his work from theirs, nor does he dream of disparaging them. If the modern reader speaks and thinks of Luke as " the sacred historian," a character that he never professed, he will only find that he has exacted too much and must suffer a painful reaction of thought. The exacting tendency is fostered by the idea that Luke was a Gentile. Does the proem favour this idea? It says " the matters which have been fulfilled *among us*." Hardly any will assert that *us* means *Gentiles*; but how improbable on every ground it would be that when by *us* he means *our generation* or *our countrymen* in Palestine or *our order of prophets*, there should be found not one Jew to succeed to the pen of the writer, but only a Gentile! The notion that there were many Gentiles in the whole Church when St. Luke began to collect materials is altogether untenable and contrary to all evidence. As to whether *us* refers to time or to space or to rank more especially, the question is not easy to decide, but whichever is meant, there is simply no room in the expression for a Gentile. In the next line of the proem *us* is used again, and surely in the same sense as before, and therefore, since tradition takes time, a later time must be assumed. I venture to claim that by *us* is meant *the order of prophets* whose function it

* *St. Luke the Prophet*, p. 35.

was to deal with the facts delivered and reported to them and to determine how far they were fulfilments. Perhaps on the whole the meaning *our generation* for *us* is the least tenable. Blass holds it to be *our Church in Judea*, and perhaps if he had spared more of his busy thought from the classics to theology he would have come to see that Luke could hardly have understood the prophets so well and mixed with the Christian prophets so closely and incessantly without having been one of the order himself.*

St. Luke was not a Gentile.

Dr. Harnack rather slightingly says that the mention in Acts 28² of the *barbarous* people at Melita is quite enough to show that Luke was a Greek, that is a Gentile. Is Dr. Harnack, then, prepared to assert that the prophet Ezekiel was a Gentile, for he says (Ez. 21³¹), " I will give thee over into the hands of *barbarian* men who fashion destructions " ? Will he maintain that the author of Ps. 114¹ was a Gentile ? " When Israel came out of Egypt and the house of Jacob from a *barbarian people.*" Egypt, with perhaps the oldest civilization in the world, was called *barbarian* by a Jew who was in Egypt when he translated the Psalm ! After this it may be superfluous to ask whether the intensely patriotic Jew who wrote 2 Maccabees was a Gentile, because he uses *barbarian* for Gentile three times or more, as *applied to Greeks* of all people in the world ! Dr. Harnack has failed, like the rest of us, to see what was before his eyes in the LXX.

But perhaps the assertion that Luke was a Gentile rests mainly on a misconception of a verse (Col. 4¹⁴) where it is maintained that Luke the physician and Demas are mentioned as if they belonged to a different

* In *St. Luke the Prophet* the present writer tried to show this at length, also to prove that Luke is Silas.

THE SHEPHERDS 85

class from " those who start from (ἐκ) the circumcision." Now, even if they do, we have only to ask to which of those two classes St. Paul would consider himself to belong. The inevitable answer is, to those who do not start from the circumcision. St. Paul, " the Hebrew of the Hebrews, circumcised the eighth day," holding as he did that circumcision was nothing nor uncircumcision, was not one who started from circumcision, τῶν ἐκ περιτομῆς: neither, though circumcised, was his friend Luke. Moreover, Luke, in his diary, not only wrote of " the fast being already past " as a mode of marking the time of year which no Gentile would dream of using, especially in a ship full of Gentiles, but he shows in every line of his writing an intimate knowledge of the law, the prophets, and the psalms, such as no Gentile could ever have possessed.

So general is the conspiracy to believe that Luke was a Gentile that when we come to Luke 1, 2 we have to listen to all sorts of apologies for Luke having become remarkably Jewish in these chapters, and so again in Acts 1–12; and then search is made for his Hebrew sources. Great waste of time! Both Luke and Acts have to deal with Jewish characters, atmosphere, usages, modes of thought, with very few exceptions. The writer is a prophet. He admits no dreams as in the story of the Magi. Throughout his narrative there is the underlying warp of the Old Testament, just as there is in Acts concerning Pentecost, Philip, Peter at Joppa, Saul at Damascus, Paul and Silas at Philippi, etc. And no explanation can be given of the familiar difficulties, such as why Paul circumcised Timothy, why Philippi was the first city of the portion Macedonia, why at Philippi " we were thinking that there was a place of prayer " on the Gangas, why St. Paul had to be escorted by a considerable army out of Jerusalem, until these conditions of the case as moulded by prophetic considerations are understood as St. Luke understood them.*

But the chronology of the times of which he treated must have been far the greatest of all his difficulties. Some notion of it may be gathered from the fact mentioned and set forth by Schürer (*Jewish People*, § 3) that almost every one of the more important cities in Palestine had during the Græco-Roman period its own era, indeed its own calendar. On this subject the most hardhearted critic may grant indulgence to St. Luke!

After reading Usener on the Nativity† the question of the authorship of Luke 1, 2 seems to demand here a few remarks. He argues that these two chapters are inconsistent with the rest of the Gospel: that Luke appeals ($1^{1\cdot 4}$) to those who were eyewitnesses and ministers of the word; and that in saying "from the beginning" and "from the first" ($ἀπ'\ ἀρχῆς,\ ἄνωθεν$) he implies that the baptism of John was *the beginning*, if we compare Acts 1^{22}, 10^{37}. Therefore, says Usener, on critical grounds and by Luke's confession, Luke began his Gospel with John's baptism and preaching in Luke 3, and Luke 1, 2 have been prefixed to it later by a reviser. He submits that these additions, including the corresponding passage of Matt. 1^{18}–2^{23}, must come from quite other hands— the substance of them, not necessarily the form. He then goes on to say that the story of the Nativity arose and took shape at a time when the consecration of Jesus to the Messiahship had already become firmly associated with the baptism in Jordan, otherwise "the miracle at the baptism could not have arisen at all; the one excludes the other." And he adds that "the two verses in Luke $1^{34\ f}$, the only verses in Luke in which the supernatural

---

* For the discussion of these questions see *St. Luke the Prophet*.

† *Enc. Bib.*, 3347 ff.

THE SHEPHERDS 87

birth of Jesus is stated, are incompatible with the rest of Luke 1, 2, and thus must have been interpolated by a redactor. These two verses once removed, what remains is a purely Jewish-Christian account of the birth of the Messiah, still resting upon the foundation of the old and genuine tradition that Jesus was the offspring—the firstborn offspring—of the marriage of Joseph and Mary."

Now in the pages of this book, which have been written without special reference to Usener's theory, it will be seen that there was no miracle at the baptism, for a vision in trance is no miracle: that there is no miracle implied in Luke $1^{34\ f}$ in the sense of a Virgin-birth: that the firstborn son has no reference to uterine brethren, though it does not forbid the idea of them, but it has the same meaning as *the Firstborn of all creation* (Col. 1^{15}, etc.). Consequently there is no necessity to separate Luke 1, 2 from the rest of Luke, or to suppose the hand of a reviser in this very homogeneous Gospel, as Harnack has otherwise shown it to be. I assume with Blass, whose Latin authorities are confirmed by the Lewis palimpsest of Sinai, that in Luke 2^5 the reading is " with Mary his wife," for the reading and the translation also of the Revised Version " who was betrothed to him " are, to my reason and faith, incorrect and more than incorrect.

With regard to the date at which the ideas of Luke 1, 2 took shape, it seems from the results hitherto obtained that when St. Paul wrote to the Romans, about A.D. 55, he had clearly seen that the Firstborn was an attribute of the Lord. There is nothing, therefore, to surprise us in the fact that Luke, his intimate friend, writes that Mary brought forth *her son The Firstborn* (*the son, the Firstborn*, as Blass reads, makes it all the more clear that Luke means *The Firstborn* in the Pauline sense) in (say) A.D. 75, for he would have written the same in 55. What is there in this title inconsistent with the baptism by

John? That this was the beginning of His ministry in such a way that *eyewitnesses and ministers of the word* could not be found, with the exception, perhaps, of Mary and her kinsfolk, to give a tradition of still earlier years is obvious, and it is natural that in most cases *from the beginning* should mean *from the baptism*, but we must retain the right on certain occasions to discover an earlier beginning and study it when found. We have seen above that *from the beginning* means something totally different from *from the first*, which refers to the first page of Genesis. But the sources of the information contained in Luke 1, 2 may, it seems, be properly included in the title "eyewitnesses and ministers of the word," for *the word* is a term comprehensive enough to include this information.

NOTE

Another illustration of the meaning of *the spirit of Jesus* (the expression is quite unique) in Acts 16⁷ as *the prophetic interpretation of Joshua* is here added to those in *St. Luke the Prophet*: it is one that escaped me before under my very eyes. On the occasion of St. Paul's first visit to Europe—the Promised Land which he and Silas were sent by Jesus to reconnoitre and occupy—the first visible land adjoining the portion Macedonia ($\tau\tilde{\eta}\varsigma$ $\mu\varepsilon\varrho\iota\delta\varsigma$ *Μακ.* Acts 16¹²), which as *the portion of Benjamin* (Josh. 18⁹,¹¹) he claimed as his own, was the territory of Abdêra in the land of the Bistones, the Abdêrîtis Bistonôn. Now when he found in his handbook, the book of Jesus (Joshua), that he was bidden to take his bearings by *the Mabdarîtis Baithôn* (Josh. 8¹²) he concluded that he had the leading of Providence. And who shall say that he was wrong? This is *the leading* ($\dot{\eta}$ $\dot{\alpha}\gamma\omega\gamma\dot{\eta}$) of the Greek Bible, which readers who were intent upon the Hebrew have failed to see.

CHAPTER IV

HEROD AGRIPPA I

A Reference in Isaiah.

WE have no right to expect to find in an Old Testament prophet any detail so particular as the prediction of the disease which carried off Herod Agrippa I. in the year A.D. 44. Nevertheless we find it, or, to speak more accurately, we find that Luke saw the suggestion of it. It is not enough that we should know—

> Isa. 31^8 Asshur shall fall: no sword of man shall devour him—

but—a sufficiently astounding disclosure—we are to know the particulars of his death.

> Isa. 10^{18} On that day shall be extinguished the mountains and the hills and the woods, and *it shall devour him* (the ruler of the Assyrians, 10^{12}) *from the soul to the flesh*, and he that fleeth shall be as he that fleeth from burning fire.

"By means of the voice of the Lord," says Isaiah, as if in solemn contrast to the shout of the populace of Cæsarea, "It is the *voice of a god*, not of a man" (Acts 12^{22})—

> Isa. 30^{31} By means of the *voice of the Lord* the Assyrians shall be defeated with *the plague* wherewithsoever he shall *smite* them.

The same word *smite* is used by Luke on this occasion. His *angel of the Lord* is the same that Isaiah mentions—

Isa. 37³⁶ And *the angel of the Lord* went forth and *smote* in the camp of the Assyrians.

Acts 12²³ And immediately *the angel of the Lord smote* him *because* he gave not God *the glory* : and he was eaten of worms and gave up the ghost.

Luke is careful to give the reason for the punishment, which is closely similar to the words of Isaiah upon the Assyrian in the context—

Isa. 10¹⁶ But the Lord of hosts will send ($ἀποστελεῖ$) upon thine honour dishonour, and upon thy *glory* burning fire shall burn (for he said, I will act in my strength, 10¹³).

It is clear that Luke considered that Agrippa I. was the Assyrian of the time.

Had the Author of Acts seen Josephus?

But here a very important question arises affecting the credibility of Acts which cannot be passed over. Some persons maintain that the author of Acts wrote later than Josephus, and had read and borrowed and blundered over his writings * It is further contended that the account of Agrippa's death is a case in point. It may be argued thus : Josephus, who is well informed and particular in detail, has described the symptoms of Herod the Great's mortal illness (4 B.C.), which will here be called *morbus* for short, declaring that it was thought at the time, and in fact was, a divine punishment for the tyrant's transgressions of the law ($ὧν\ παρανομήσειεν$) and great impiety ($τοῦ\ πολλοῦ\ δυσσεβοῦς$), more particularly for his latest execution of some forty persons for pulling down his golden eagle from the Temple gate, the ring-

* *Enc. Brit.*, "Acts," etc., by Schmiedel. Burkitt also, *The Gospel History and the Transmission*, p. 110, " a somewhat careless perusal of the *Antiquities*."

leaders being burnt alive. Josephus has also described the death-symptoms of the pious and conscientious king Agrippa I., who died beloved of his people at Cæsarea (A.D. 44) after a reign of three years. The author of Acts, it is argued, has taken Josephus's account of the *morbus* of Herod, and with a bungling recollection of it has attributed it to Agrippa.

There seems at first sight to be something in favour of this opinion if we set aside the extraordinary and overwhelming evidence furnished by the texture of nearly every page of Acts that it is essentially a primitive work mostly contemporaneous with the events—and this is a very large " if " indeed. Let us look, then, at the dates of the two writers. Josephus's earliest work was *The Jewish War*, and it may have appeared about 75 A.D., when he was thirty-eight. This is what he writes—

" I was general of our so-called Galileans as long as resistance was possible, and then, being made a prisoner of war, I was with the Romans. Vespasian and Titus kept me in custody, compelling me to be at their elbow, at first in chains. I was set free again and was sent from Alexandria with Titus to the siege of Jerusalem. Of the events as they occurred at that time not one escaped my knowledge. I used to write up carefully the doings of the Roman leaguer as I saw them, and I alone understood the news that was being brought by deserters. Later, when I got leisure at Rome and had the whole work in preparation, I employed some assistants for the Greek (the notes being in Aramaic), and so composed the history. And so abundant was my confidence in its accuracy that I ventured to take, first of all, as my witnesses the commanders-in-chief, Vespasian and Titus. They have been the first recipients of my books, and after them I used to sell them to many Romans who had served with me in the war, and to many of our own people, men versed in Greek culture, including his excellent majesty king Agrippa."*

The latter wrote to Josephus no less than sixty-two letters of cordial testimony, and he, in return for such friendly patronage, would describe his royal father's death in the most friendly terms. Now if Acts was written in A.D. 75–80 the author might have seen or heard the contents of the *War*, published in 75 or thereabouts. The later we place Acts, the more opportunity for some years there was for this advantage. But if we put Acts twenty years later there is less excuse for the bungling of two Herods by the author, for by that time, 93–4, Josephus' great work, *The Jewish Antiquity*, was completed, and it contains a fuller description of Herod's death than the *War*, and also a full description of Agrippa's death.

The author of Acts is so careful in most of his work that the idea of a colossal blunder, such as this would be, is not lightly to be entertained. He is so peculiarly well informed on some matters of the Herodian family (Acts 13^1, etc.) and of Cæsarea and its neighbourhood, as many writers have demonstrated, that the event of A.D. 44 is not likely to prove an exception. If he wrote as late as A.D. 100 he would presumably have known what Josephus wrote in the *Antiquity*. No writer of common intelligence could possibly confuse the two pictures drawn by Josephus of the two dying Herods, as if in the sharpest possible contrast, one in the seventeenth book and one in the nineteenth, the former a brutal and detested tyrant, tortured by heaven for his crimes, at seventy years of age, the other cut off in his fifty-fifth year, too soon for his people's hopes, but not too soon for their affection, by a painful attack which he bore with the courageous yet tearful

* Jos. *c. Ap.* i. 9. See *Life*, 65.

philosophy of a fatalist who recognized the rebuking will of God for his acceptance of the unholy flattery. Confusion here is not conceivable. The only possibility is that the author of Acts had not seen the later but only the earlier work of Josephus.

In the *War* he describes Herod's death at Jericho, but only mentions that of Agrippa at Cæsarea in the briefest terms. A very ignorant and stupid writer—such as ours was not—could conceivably blunder anywhere, but he is more likely to mix two events of which one is described and the other only mentioned. But as soon as we come back to the relatively early date, we come back also to the Lucan authorship, and Luke was born many years before 37, the birth of Josephus. His experience, not in childhood but in manhood, included Agrippa's reign. And so far from deriving information from Josephus about Agrippa's death, he could have gathered it from his friends at Cæsarea long before Josephus wrote the *War*. The theory of Luke's borrowing in this case puts too much strain upon our own intelligence in requiring us to understand his stupidity. In other cases of his supposed borrowing, those of Lysanias and Judas and Theudas, for instance, other considerations* come in. It cannot be shown that Acts and the *War*, though they appeared about the same time, have any reference to one another.

Herod's Fatal Symptoms.

Before we proceed to a further examination of the language of Acts it will be well to have what is said by

---

* Schürer has, I think, completely proved that the Lysanias who was M. Antony's victim was not the only tetrarch of Abilene, and he says Luke is "thoroughly correct." I have endeavoured to show that the Theudas of Acts 5[36] was Athronges, who would naturally, like many more rebels, be also called (Theodatos) Theudas, in *St. Luke the Prophet*, pp. 331–337.

JOSEPHUS ON HEROD'S DEATH (4 B.C.)

In the *War*, A.D. 75 (i. 33, 5)—	In the *Antiquity*, A.D. 93 (xvii. 6, 5)—
Then the disease pervading his whole body distracted it by various torments. For the fever became more intense, the itching of the whole surface was insupportable, and the pains of the lower abdomen were incessant. On his feet were swellings as of one labouring with dropsy.	But his disease became daily aggravated. . . . A fire glowed in him slowly, not so much apparent to the outward touch as it augmented the wasting (κάκωσιν) within. For it brought a vehement insatiable appetite for food. His intestines also were ulcerated, and the chief violence of the pain lay in his colon. An aqueous and transparent humour also had settled about his feet.
And there was also an inflammation of the abdomen, and a septic state (σηπεδὼν) lower down generating worms (σκώληκας).	And there was a similar disorder about the abdomen, in fact a rottenness (σῆψις, septic state) beneath, producing worms.
Besides this there was an orthopnœa (upright breathing) and difficulty in breathing	There was, too, an upright tension of breath, and this (tension) was very unpleasant both from the offensiveness of the effluvia and the quickness of the asthma.
and a convulsion of all the limbs.	There was, too, a convulsion about every limb, imparting an intolerable strength.
(He caused them to carry him across the Jordan to the warm springs of Callirhoë, where the physicians prescribed a warm oil-bath: after which, though brought back apparently dead, he revived and took energetic and cruel measures of massacre, including the murder of his son Antipater, and five days after this murder he died. Age 70.)	

HEROD AGRIPPA I (died A.D. 44)

(grandson of Herod on paternal side and grandson of Herod's sister on maternal side) is said by St. Luke (Acts xii) to have died " eaten of worms " (σκωληκόβρωτος).

HEROD AGRIPPA I

JOSEPHUS SAYS (*Ant.* xix. 8, 2)
he had a pain across the heart. And there supervened a sharp pang of the stomach (κοιλία), violent from the first. . . .
The symptoms continued for five days, when he was overcome by the abdominal (γαστρὸς) pain and expired. (Age 54.)

Modern Physicians on the Data of Herod's Death.

With regard to Herod, my friend Dr. Fleming Sandwith, M.D., late physician to H.H. the Khedive, has favoured me with the following observations, which are the more valuable from his great experience of oriental diseases—

"The details of Herod's illness are too vague to form a diagnosis with certainty, but I guess that he suffered from *myiasis*, which means that he may have had a collection of maggots or larvæ of any kind of dipterous fly. *Myiasis* may be confined to the skin, or the subcutaneous tissue, or the intestines, which become infected through swallowing larvæ of flies. This would account for the description "eaten of worms," but it would not account for his *orthopnœa* (upright breathing), which may have been caused by heart disease or kidney disease. I therefore suggest that Herod, who richly deserved it, suffered from *myiasis* plus heart or kidney disease.

"It is true that there is a disease caused by worms in the intestines which gives rise to certain abdominal symptoms, including difficulty of breathing and dropsical swellings. This is what we call *ankylostomiasis*, and I enclose a paper on the subject.

"The worm itself was not discovered till A.D. 1843, and it was not till after that that the Egyptian anæmia was recognized as being associated with this worm, which has only been brought to light by means of post-mortems and by the microscopical examination of fæces. As there were no microscopes and probably no post-mortems in Herod's time, I fail to see how any one could have known that he had internal worms (*entozoa*). Hence my suggestion that he had *ectozoa*, and maggots would be called worms, even by Luke, if he was a physician."

The above observations are confirmed by the experience of Surgeon-Major Bernard Kendall, I.M.S. (retd.),[*] who says of *myiasis*—

"My friend C. J. Jackson, at Cawnpore, showed me a case . . . suffering from (fly-blow) maggots in his nostrils. With great care and trouble these were removed, and the man, when well, was discharged to duty. Not long after the same man was readmitted suffering in the same way, but to a greater degree, as the maggots had penetrated to the throat, and, eating into an artery, the man died. This man was a very heavy sleeper, and slept with his mouth wide open, which will account for the access of flies to his nose. I also had under my own care a soldier who had maggots under his long finger-nails, but these were easily removed."

It has been commonly said that Herod's disease was *phtheiriasis*, an old name for *pediculosis*. Dr. Sandwith says of this : "It is still rampant, but it is rather difficult to die of it."

The late Sir R. A. Bennett[†] wrote : "The two accounts (Acts and *Antiquity*), considered together, leave scarcely any room for doubt that the cause of death was perforation of the bowels by intestinal worms, inducing ulceration and acute peritonitis. Medical records contain such cases, and the condition of the stomach and bowels after

---

[*] *The Lancet*, Feb. 11, 1911.
[†] *The Diseases of the Bible*, by Sir Risden Bennett, M.D., LL.D., F.R.S. 1896[3].

indulgence at a feast would favour the occurrence of the fatal termination at such a time. Any abnormal distension of the bowels, especially if associated with bodily exertion, would be sufficient to account for rupture of the intestines at spots previously eroded and thinned by ulcerative disease. And there is scarcely any suffering more severe than that which attends peritoneal inflammation thus induced." Add to this the fact that Agrippa was the grandson of Herod on his father's side, and of Herod's sister Salome on his mother's side, and it is certain that whatever the family tendency to abdominal disorder may have been, he inherited it. It is therefore credible that the cause of his death was akin to that of Herod's death. Dr. Fleming Sandwith says : " It is quite true that a round worm, like a garden worm in appearance, can push its head through an ulcer of the intestine, and so produce peritonitis. I have seen this at post-mortems. No such diagnosis of Agrippa's fatal illness is justifiable without a post-mortem, and I don't suppose for a minute any post-mortem was done."

Josephus compared with Isaiah.

When we pass from the pathological to the literary side of the question and see what Josephus says and does not say concerning Herod, it seems that we can get perhaps a little behind him. There is no necessity to turn the tables upon him, but we notice that he, or rather his writing, like St. Luke, was not free from prepossessions in the case. Luke, as a member of the prophetic order, had set his mind on the fulfilment of prophecy. But Josephus on this occasion was not dissimilar, for his account of Herod's death is partly based on the reports of those who equally sought the fulfilment of prophecy. He says in the *War*—

"It was said, therefore, by those who are conversant with divine things * (οἱ ἐπιθειάζοντες) and to whose wisdom it appertained to declare such things, that God had inflicted this punishment upon the king for his great impiety."

And in the *Antiquity* he says—

"So that they who referred to a divine agency (οἱ θειάζοντες) said that this disease was a punishment."

Josephus's authority for this account is undoubtedly the large history of Nicolas of Damascus, a Greek, the trusted friend and counsellor and instructor of Herod. Both the accounts are circumstantial, the later (*Antiquity*) adding nothing of value here to the earlier (*War*), but though we can recognize the group of divines or diviners as separate from that of physicians, it seems hardly possible to discriminate the respective contributions of either party to the story. For a closer analysis of it exhibits four or five points in which the medical symptoms, as he describes them, are based upon the very words of Isaiah!

1. Isaiah had said (10^{16}) of the Assyrian, "Upon thy glory burning *fire* shall burn." Josephus says of Herod, "It was a slow *fire*," but he would naturally have spoken only of a fever (πυρετός), not a fire (πῦρ), and in the *War* he has said *fever*.

2. Isaiah wrote, (10^{18}) "It shall devour (him) from the soul to the flesh." Josephus says of Herod's fire "not exhibiting to the *touch* a heat corresponding to the gradual wasting *within*." The form of this expression is peculiar and artificial, as if forced into shape by the above quotation.

3. Isaiah had used the rare word *corruption* (σῆψις), which he says shall be strewn underneath the body (14^{11}).

* Josephus elsewhere uses the term of Moses and of Solomon but in a different sense.

HEROD AGRIPPA I

This is said of the King of Babylon, on which see below. Josephus says *corruption* (σῆψις) produced worms.

4. Isaiah had said "*worms* shall cover thee" (14¹¹). Josephus uses the same word (σκώληκας).

5. Isaiah had said, "As he that fleeth from burning fire." Josephus speaks of the repulsive stench.

Now upon the assumption, which seems to be more than probable, that Herod was popularly known as "the Assyrian" before his death, it may be granted on the one hand that those who recognized it as an act of divine punishment would do so on the strength of Isaiah and the Old Testament scriptures, and they would be inclined to report his symptoms in accordance with the scriptural predictions, by a process of assimilation. On the other hand, Nicolas of Damascus * was on the spot, a competent person of sixty years of age, a Gentile, a follower of Aristotle, a cultured and eloquent man, qualified singularly well to report the statements of the physicians. Therefore, before we adopt Josephus's account of Herod's illness, a certain balancing of judgment appears to be necessary. And at the same time it is quite possible that Luke may have been acquainted with the history of Nicolas—a contingency which does not seem to have been considered enough hitherto. In any case, we are obliged to suppose that this historical work was the basis for all time of the received account of Herod's end.

The Prophetic View of Agrippa's Death.

After these conjectural and provisional results concerning Herod's *morbus* and the inconclusive results on the question of borrowing, we turn again to Acts 12²³ concerning Agrippa : " and he became worm-eaten and

---

* Schürer, *Jewish People*, § 3, 11. Rhetorically he identifies himself with the Jews in pleading before M. Agrippa, but he was not a Jew.

expired" (καὶ γενόμενος σκωληκόβρωτος ἐξέψυξεν). Is this very terse expression capable of a poetic interpretation, we are inclined to ask first, in the sense of a poetic contrast of death and glory—the pomp and the shining hopes of Agrippa cut short? We think of—

> *Hotspur.* No, Percy, thou art dust,
>   And food for——
> *Percy.* For worms, brave Percy: fare thee well, great heart!
>   Ill-weav'd ambition, how much art thou shrunk!

But the presence of *he became* (γενόμενος) forbids this in the narrative, which, after all, is not a drama, though dramatic. Luke asserts that Agrippa became what he had not been before, and *after* this change of condition expired.*

Failing the poetic interpretation, there is a good deal to be said for the extreme prophetic, "He proved to be the prey of worms, as said the prophets concerning the king of Assyria, and so expired." This assumes that it was well known at the time of writing (say A.D. 70–80), if not also at the time of the event (A.D. 44), that every king of Assyria, every ruling Herod, was to be worm-eaten in or before his death, and that this ruler, Agrippa, proved it manifestly. Does not this assume too much and explain too little? The term *worm-eaten* was not universally familiar, very far from it, as we shall see later. Theophilus, for whom Luke wrote, would know its meaning, but even he must have been startled at the word, which he had never seen before unless he had read Theophrastus on botany—a most remote contingency. But then Luke intended to startle the reader. And then at first one thinks that γενόμενος could not support the stress which this interpretation would throw upon it. But here we have to consider what had happened to the

* The use, *e. g.*, of κελεύσας, Acts 23[35], appended to the main sentence, cannot be taken to support the contrary: the order of γενόμενος at the beginning of the sentence forbids it.

HEROD AGRIPPA I

three previous Assyrians. Herod had answered to the prophetic prediction of his mode of death, but what had become of his son and successor, the ethnarch Herod Archelaus, with his half-brother the tetrarch Herod Antipas? The gentler Philip, whose dominions were remote, we need not consider, but both these rulers emulated their father in luxury and rapacity though not in ability. Both ended their lives in exile after deposition, for Babylon-Rome here again overthrew the Assyrian Herod. Jerome* says that a *tumulus* of Archelaus was shown near Bethlehem, but it is not conceivable that he should have lived or been buried in the dominions from which he was deposed, and the *tumulus* must have been either not a tomb at all, or the tomb of some other Archelaus whom Jerome wrongly identified. Archelaus was banished to Vienne A.D. 6, Antipas to Lyons A.D. 39. These events fulfilled Isaiah's prediction in a remarkable way—

Isa. 31^8 And Asshur shall fall: no sword of a man nor sword of a human being shall devour him : *and he shall flee, not from before a pursuer.*

After they had gone 2,000 miles away, it is too much to expect that the manner of their death was verifiable, and we do not now know what it was. Dio Cassius implies that Caligula put Antipas to death, but he wrote as late as some 180 years after this event. Thus all the three Assyrians who passed away before A.D. 44 fulfilled the predictions of Isaiah, and the fourth, Agrippa, now fulfilled in his sudden death the *plague* of *the angel of the Lord.* Perhaps this might be considered enough to justify Luke's categorical mention of Agrippa's end. He could not be included in the list of two Assyrians *fled—deposed;* he must belong to the other category, *worm-eaten.*

* About 400 A.D. See Schürer, § 17, *E. T.*, p. 42.

102 ORACLES IN THE NEW TESTAMENT

But the fact remains that we do not find in the ancient prophets anything quite so precise as the term *worm-eaten*. The question, then, occurs whether it can have been inserted by Luke with what we might call a rubrical purpose. This is a supposition which would involve the assumption that Acts was a book to be read in church, or at least contained references for the church-reader. We recollect that when an obscure expression, *the abomination of desolation*, is mentioned in two Gospels (Matt. 24^{15}, Mark 13^{14}), it is followed by the direction " Let the reader mark ! "—the church-reader of Daniel (9^{27}, etc.) being intended. Now Luke, who omits the expression, omits also the direction : and yet he was well aware of the practice in the synagogues generally, and the Lord's practice (Luke 4^{21}), and St. Paul's, which he had heard himself.* The above supposition, therefore, seems to lack support in the case of Luke, and therefore of Acts, though the suggestion was always there even without the rubric. Then there is another frequent expression which must have puzzled every modern reader, " He that hath ears to hear, let him hear," and which had probably a similar use as a sort of rubrical direction. This occurs in Luke as well as in Matthew and Mark. From the fact of Rev. 2^7, etc., giving the additional expression " what *the spirit* saith unto the churches," one must conclude that it had a prophetic bearing; that is to say, *spiritual* being *prophetic*, as in Rev. 11^8, *the spirit* here means the *prophetic inspiration* of meaning—whether typical in the usual sense, as when the rubric is appended to a passage about Elijah, or

---

* Acts 18^4. " Paul conversed in the synagogue inserting the name of *the Lord Jesus*." Such is the Bezan (D) reading supported by the Fleury and Stockholm MSS. and the Philoxenian Syriac, and read in the Latin Vulgate to-day. This was just the crucial difficulty—how to familiarize Jews with the name for JHVH of the Old Testament as applied to Jesus. See *St. Luke the Prophet*, p. 369.

parabolic, as when it is placed after a parable, or allegorical, as in Rev. 2^7, etc. In each of the Epistles to the Seven Churches it occurs in connection with words or thoughts of the Old Testament. In all these cases we may suppose that there is an implicit reference to—

Isa. 32^3 And they shall no more have confidence in men, but they shall give their ears to hear—

and that the *men* in question mean the Jews, in accordance with the oracle of Isa. 6^{9f}, Hearing ye shall hear . . . which is quoted so often in New Testament; and further, that the warning was remembered as from the Lord's own lips. Since, however, in Acts 12^{23} there is no rubrical or other direction mentioned, we cannot insist that *worm-eaten* was specially intended to point back to the Isaian account of the Assyrian's destruction. But we have yet to see whether Luke himself was not very well aware of the fulfilment of Isaiah in Agrippa's case by other tokens. And it must be remembered that the preaching in the synagogue, following the reading, still offered a large opportunity for the Argument from Prophecy, as it had to St. Paul at Antioch in Pisidia, where " the rulers of the synagogue sent unto them saying, Brethren, if ye have any word of exhortation for the people, say on."

Agrippa both Babylonian and Assyrian.

Now we have mentioned a passage which comes very near to this word, only that it is uttered in regard to the King of Babylon, not of Assyria—a point to which we now recur—

Isa. 14^{11} Thy glory cometh down unto hell, thy much gaiety: underneath thee they shall strew *corruption* (σῆψιν), and thy coverlet is the *worm* (τὸ κατακάλυμμά σου σκώληξ).

104 ORACLES IN THE NEW TESTAMENT

Here * Isaiah intended, and we may suppose that his Greek translator in Egypt recognized, a contrast between the Babylonian king and the Egyptian king whose mummified body was never allowed to become a prey to worms. This consideration, however, is by the way. The point to be noticed is that Isaiah does use the term *worm* in connection with the death of an Eastern potentate, and in such a way that the reader of the lesson might suitably comment upon it by reference to Agrippa in Acts. The converse is also true. But then the obvious objection is that a prophecy about the King of Babylon's death in Isaiah is not the same as if it related to the King of Assyria. Now it may be admitted that if we were dealing with the years A.D. 60–70, this would be true. By that time the study of prophecy, at least within the Christian Church, had been carried very much further than in 4 B.C., and Babylon had been identified with Rome by a distinct phase of mental imagery which was only to be shattered by the fall of Jerusalem, and not wholly even then. This fact is proved by the evidence of Rev. 16–18, which is insuperable. But in 4 B.C. there was no clear distinction between Babylon and Assyria: Herod was the Assyrian, but Rome was not yet Babylon. And there was hardly such a person yet as a king of Rome; for in the twenty-seven years since the battle of Actium Augustus had veiled his supreme power under the forms of the republic, and who could then possibly foretell the future succession of the twelve Cæsars or *the seven heads?*

There is no evidence in the Messianic literature before 4 B.C. of anything like an identification of Babylon with

---

* I am unable to see that Enoch 46^6, which certainly is based upon this text, has any relation to Herod's death except as showing that there was a tendency in the first century B.C. to discover generally a judgment upon a sinful ruler in his death—a fact almost as old as human nature.

HEROD AGRIPPA I 105

Rome. The natural and historical way of regarding the king of Babylon was, and is to this day, to identify him with the king of Assyria, who was the actual overlord of Babylon during most of the historical centuries, until the brief period when Nebuchadnezzar, King of Babylon, became overlord of Assyria, after which for two centuries the king of Persia was overlord of both. Moreover, the very context in the dirge of the king of Babylon appears to sanction this identification—

> Isa. 14$^{23-25}$ And I will make Babylon desert ... as I have spoken, so it shall abide, to destroy *the Assyrians* upon the *land that is mine and upon my mountains*.

It would seem then that the fall of Babylon was predicted as being less an end in itself than a means to the fall of the Assyrians, and any description of the king of Babylon's destruction was meant to apply to him as king of Assyria. Such would be the interpretation of " those conversant with divine things " as Josephus calls them, at the time of Herod's death in 4 B.C.

But Josephus neither made a medical nor a theological diagnosis of Herod's disease. Nor does he connect or compare Herod's case with the classical cases of Sulla and Alkman the poet, and the four other cases of *morbus* mentioned by Plutarch. He makes no reference to Isaiah or the prophets. It is left for us to discern, if we can, the traces of the warp which underlies his writing. But " Acts " was not a part of this warp. That he had heard of a small treatise written by another Jew at Rome, a Nazarene, and taken notice of it, is an idea not worth considering. He could only have done so, if at all, by mixing with the same higher literary and social circles of Rome with which St. Luke, like St. Paul, had possibly been in some sort of contact : but the society of the

Flavian emperors in A.D. 73 was very different from that of the Neronian court in A.D. 63. On the whole, it is more likely that Luke had time and opportunity to read Josephus than Josephus to read Luke. Josephus was ignorant of Luke's statement about Agrippa's death, whatever he knew of the pathology of Herod's case, or of Isaiah as the basis of the divines' verdict upon the Assyrian. In the hundreds of pages that he wrote upon Herod, he never implies that he knew of the Assyrian appellative or identity. But considering that Herod's great-grandson, Agrippa II., was his friend and patron, he would hardly have said so if he had known.

With Luke it is, as we have seen, far otherwise. Of Herod the Great's death he has said nothing : of Agrippa's he has written one word *worm-eaten*. In regard to the attendant circumstances, the appointed day at Cæsarea, the array in royal apparel, the shout of the populace that he was a god, the acceptance of the impious flattery, the violent pain as the stroke of doom, there is actual agreement between Luke and Josephus, yet without any appearance, I think, of borrowing. Josephus says nothing, moreover, which opposes the idea of *morbus*. " He became quite exhausted by the pain in his stomach for five days." So much is clear on the negative side. But on the positive side we must recognize the fact that Luke must have known, nearly throughout his life, that Herod the Great was " the Assyrian," and that according to the contemporary opinion which Josephus reported in history Herod had died by the stroke of God.

Still again it may be urged that Luke, who did distinguish between Babylon and Assyria, would not have attributed to the Assyrian king what Isaiah had predicted of the Babylonian. But just here we have to consider the facts carefully. Luke, writing (say) in A.D. 75, had before him the tradition which time had crystallized for

HEROD AGRIPPA I

nearly fifty years before Agrippa's death, and for eighty years before he wrote "Acts"—the tradition that Herod the Assyrian fell by the avenging stroke of the angel of God. During those fifty years the league between the Assyrian family of Herod and the Babylonian line of Cæsars had been very much strengthened and closed. One result of this fact is that if ever an Assyrian was also a Babylonian, it was Agrippa. Bearing a Roman name, brought up at Rome with Tiberius's son, the friend of the emperor Caius the would-be polluter of the Temple, the friend of Claudius who succeeded the assassinated Caius, Agrippa was *a* king of Babylon, if not *the* king. To expect, therefore, that Luke would analyze the established tradition about the head of the Herodian line and deduct from it precisely that element of it connected with the agency of worms in death, which originally referred only to the king of Babylon, would be indeed to run the line of prophecy rather fine. Even if we look, on the other hand, away from the fulfilments in Roman history back to the prototypes in Chaldean history we find that the Jews did not discriminate as we moderns do between Assyrian and Babylonian. We consider that we are right in calling Nebuchadnezzar a Babylonian king, but the book of Judith says " he reigned over the Assyrians" in Nineveh (Jud. 1^1), and frequently calls him the king of the Assyrians. To those who admit that Luke recognized every Herod as potentially the king of Assyria there is no difficulty except the pathology in ascertaining the actual cause of Agrippa's death. Theologically speaking, Agrippa, the astute and popular, had persecuted " those of the way, and had killed James the brother of John with the sword." He thus seemed to deserve the family name of the Assyrian bestowed by those who feared and hated him. He was cut off prematurely and swiftly after what he himself admitted was a sin of overweening pride. Was not this death a divine punishment closely in accordance with scripture prophecy?

The Fatal Symptoms of Antiochus Epiphanes.

Even this, however, does not bring us to the precise point of the terse, sharp expression of "worm-eaten." We have seen that neither Isaiah as translated and understood and reported, nor the report of Herod's death by Josephus, amounts to a statement of *morbus*. For this more definite idea we have to read in another and very different writer, the author of 2 Maccabees, who had to describe the death of the savage persecutor Antiochus Epiphanes. The treatise of this wordy and rhetorical epitomizer—his notion of an "epitome," of the work of Jason of Cyrene, is certainly not ours: he is a sort of anthologist—is considered to belong to the latter part of the first century B.C., and may even have been written as late as the death of Herod. In that case the writer may actually have been influenced by the ideas current about 4 B.C. concerning that event. But of such influence it is not easy to discover any traces, except in the expression that arrests our notice (2 Macc. 9^9), "till from the body of the impious wretch worms began to seethe up" (ὥστε καὶ ἐκ τοῦ σώματος τοῦ δυσσεβοῦς σκώληκας ἀναζεῖν). There, too, was the plague of God that smote him for his contumacy.

The passage in 2 Mac. $9^{5f.}$ concerning the death of Antiochus Epiphanes is worth giving at length—

> "For he had spoken overweeningly in this sort, I will make Jerusalem a burying-place of the Jews (¹) when I come there. But the all-surveying Lord the God of Israel *smote* (ἐπάταξεν) him with an incurable and invisible *plague* (πληγῇ): and as soon as he had ended these words, a pain of the bowels that was remediless came upon him, and

sore torments of the inner parts : and that most
justly : for he had tormented other men's bowels
with many and strange calamities. Howbeit he
nothing at all ceased from his bragging, but still was
filled with overweening pride, breathing fire in his
rage against the Jews, and commanding to haste the
journey : but it came to pass that he fell from his ([4])
chariot carried violently, so that having a sore fall,
all the members of his body were dislocated. And
thus he that a little afore thought he might command
the ([2]) waves of the sea (so overweening was he
beyond the condition of man) and weigh ([3]) the
heights of the mountains in a balance, was now cast
on the ground ([5]) and carried in a horse-litter, manifestly exhibiting unto all men the power of God.
So that even from the body ([6]) of the impious wretch
worms did seethe up, and whiles he lived in sorrows
and pains his flesh fell away, and the filthiness of
his smell was noisome ([7]) to all his army. And him
that a little afore thought to reach the stars of heaven
no man could endure to carry for his intolerable
smell. Hereupon, therefore, he began to leave off
most of his overweening pride, being utterly crushed,
and to come to the knowledge [of himself] by the
scourge of God, his pains increasing every moment.
And when he himself could not abide his own smell,
he said these words, It is meet to be subject unto
God, instead of a mortal man overweening."

The tiresome fivefold emphasis on overweening pride
($\dot{v}περηφανία$) is remarkable in this passage : the notion
exactly applies to Agrippa. [The bracketed numerals
show the parallels with the overweening intentions of
Sennacherib, p. 112 below.] To these may be added the
expression in 2 Macc. 9^1 of Antiochus's retreat in
disorder ($ἀναλελυκὼς ἀκόσμως, ἀσχήμονα τὴν ἀναζυγήν$)

compared with Isa. 37[28]: "I know thy sitting down and thy going out and thy coming in." Antiochus was turned back, like Sennacherib, by the way by which he came. And, like him, he had swelled with anger (ἐπαρθεὶς τῷ θυμῷ) like that of Sennacherib (Isa. 37[29]: ὁ θυμός σου ὃν ἐθυμώθης). That 2 Macc. 9 is indebted to Isaiah there can be little doubt.

But it is not so clear how far Luke is indebted to 2 Macc. 9. We know that Heb. 11 is very much indebted to 2 Macc. 6. The reference in Hebrews to the drum of torture is certain, and is universally admitted (Heb. 11[35] = 2 Macc. 6[19]). Again, the reference to "the living Lord being angry with us a little while for our chastening and correction" (Heb. 12[5 f] = 2 Macc. 7[33]) is highly probable considering that this is more than anything else the theme of the writer of 2 Macc., as he clearly avows. Again, the reference to the creation (Heb. 11[3] = 2 Macc. 7[28]), "of things that were not," is still more probable. Then 2 Macc. is one of the very few scriptural books which admits the title "the Hebrews" (2 Macc. 7[31]). If, then, Hebrews found a valuable source of suggestion in 2 Macc., about the year 70, it is very probable that Luke found the same within the same decade. Indeed, as it is certain that 2 Macc. was composed well before A.D. 44, and as there is every reason to suppose that Luke had it before him in that earlier time, he may even then have formed the conclusion that Agrippa resembled Epiphanes in being worm-eaten. He was like Epiphanes in being a persecutor of the faithful; he was like him impious; like him he had time before he died to avow, and did avow, his impiety; like him he recognized the judgment of God.

"*Worm-eaten*" and "*Fowl-eaten.*"

But there is one touch of style in Luke which I believe points conclusively to the origin of the term. 2 Macc.

HEROD AGRIPPA I   111

(9^{15}) has used the rare word " fowl-eaten " of the unburied victims of Epiphanes; Luke uses the equally rare word " worm-eaten " of the impious monarch, *smitten* with the *plague* of God.

It is somewhat difficult to convey to an English reader the force of this remark. Here is a five-syllable word, not exactly one " that on the stretched forefinger of old time sparkles for ever," but a fine, tragic-sounding word that one would least expect to find in a medical writer, and, in fact, it does not occur in the great classic master Hippocrates, son of Herakleides of Côs. We have to go a century later in history to find it in Theophrastus, who uses it of vegetable life. The equivalent, worm-eaten, is by no means a true equivalent, but no other word is possible—" worm-eaten " is an ordinary word as applied to wood, paper, etc. But 2 Macc. has the word which seems to have suggested the former to St. Luke: " fowl-eaten," which is a fair equivalent of the Greek, but again fails to do justice to the fact that the Greek οἰωνόβρωτος is also a five-syllable. This also has a tragic sound, yet does not occur in classical literature till three centuries later than the other, and is then found in the geographer Strabo (66 B.C.–A.D. 24), so that the author of 2 Macc. may be credited with the composition of οἰωνόβρωτος until he is made to resign the credit to his original, Jason of Cyrene. It is a striking word, and most readers of the classics would be inclined to say it was almost indispensable, and one which they had seen before. Consciously or unconsciously, it would be likely in the same way to impress St. Luke, and it would suggest to him to recoin or to coin the word σκωληκόβρωτος, for it is hardly probable that he had read Theophrastus' botanical works, though there are some who will fancy that he read them in the course of his medical diploma. Certain it is that in the use of this term by St. Luke there is no light whatever thrown upon the question whether he was a physician of the body, though there is much light upon his literary character as a prophet. Neither of the two component parts, σκώληκες, *worms*, and βιβρώσκω, *I eat*, illuminates the question : a layman would as naturally use them as a physician.

Two considerations seem probable. One is that Herod's contemporaries had the account of Epiphanes in 2 Macc. 9 before them and were influenced by its contents, the details in Josephus being the more particular and rather more gruesome of the two : and this improvement of the occasion is what we should expect if the account of 2 Macc. were the earlier model. The other is much more tangible—that 2 Macc. was written, whatever its date, after a perusal of the prophecy of Isa. 37[24 ff] against Sennacherib, for it has several ideas in common with it. These are connected with (1) the intended desolation of the country; (2) the conquest of the *waters* of the sea; (3) the *height of mountains;* (4) the use of *chariots;* (5) the *overthrow of insolent pride*. And at the same time it shares two more ideas with Isa. 10[18], the (6) flesh-disease and (7) the flight of men, whom it was fair to interpret in Isaiah as meaning the attendants on the dying king, and at any rate 2 Macc. so represents them. However that may be, we are safe in holding that Luke had 2 Macc. before him as early as A.D. 44 when Agrippa died, and that *morbus* is suggested by the expression already cited, and, further, that whereas Epiphanes was called in this scripture an impious wretch, Agrippa was one who avowed his own impiety, and recognized, as did Epiphanes in 2 Macc., the judgment of God as justly visited upon him. Would not the effect upon St. Luke's mind be to confirm his belief that persecutors of His chosen were punished as he says?

Finally, it may be urged that, after all, if Agrippa died of *morbus* there is no need to discuss the question why

HEROD AGRIPPA I

Luke conveyed the fact in the language used, which only explains briefly and in untechnical phrase the main feature of the disease. This objection ignores some plain facts—first, that the disease was so rare and obscure that not many physicians in many myriads had met with a case of it; next, that it is, or was then, a subject of literary tradition, a choice if unsavoury subject, usually but not always reserved, since the time of Sulla, for the great monsters among mankind and quite beyond the ordinary diagnosis even of theologians; thirdly, that the point and climax of the narrative is that this disease was the punishing stroke of the angel of God. It is indeed the climax and the close of the first half of Acts, the most indispensable, perhaps, and the most literary of all the primitive Christian treatises. The author, so far from giving to this incident what we might suppose to be the position of a footnote, has intended its very sharpness and suddenness and its position in the narrative to mark its importance, and it is not for modern readers to minimize or ignore it. We have not to be content to accept what is written unless we can discover the relation between the act of man and its consequence, the act of God, which is so plainly declared to be such. If it should prove that neither the physician nor the theologian could throw light upon that relation, then only should we be justified in adding one more incident to the agnostic category of so-called faith which has already reached a considerable length during the last hundred years, and has encroached to a precisely corresponding extent upon the understanding. But the bounden duty of every man in every sphere of life is to recover what ground he can for the understanding, gaining it from that ocean of wasted and suspended judgment which is too often content to say it does not know when it really does not care, and is reluctant to care.

I

CHAPTER V

THE FIRSTBORN

IT is not easy to determine what the importance of the *Protevangelium Jacobi*, or First Gospel of James, is. " An apocryphal work by a fanciful fatalist, unhampered by knowledge of Jewish affairs," we may certainly agree that it is, and also that it " furnished subjects for former Christian art " (Usener), and also for the art of the Renaissance. And it is clear that Origen mentions it, probably in A.D. 245, by name, and one of its contents. But we can trace it no earlier than about that time. When, then, Hort says that the reading " cave " for " manger " (Luke 2^7, see Matt. 2^{11}) is " doubtless by confusion with the Book of James," we require to know how it got into James, and the theory propounded in these pages is that it came from LXX not only into James, but, like so many other statements, into the earliest traditions. How popular the book became, whether it ever became in some measure a rival of our Gospels so that such " confusion " was ever possible, is unknown, but until it can be shown that it was so widely current, and popular, we are not at liberty to suppose that it has affected the canonical Gospels. The simpler explanation which is here offered is that all Gospels were based on LXX. But, considering how much stress has been laid upon the Book of James, and its importance for the Nativity story,* it is worth while to examine into its indebtedness to the Greek Bible.

* Usener, *E. B.* 3344 says : " All further treatments of the story rest entirely on the three sources Matthew, Luke and *Protevangelium* —as Conrady has shown (*Quelle der Kindheitsgesch.* 172 ff.). Later

THE FIRST-BORN 115

The Oracles in the Book of James.

The *Protevangelium of James* does not follow the text of LXX very closely, but it shows, nevertheless, its frequent obligations to it. The author is one who had considerable powers of imagination within closely prescribed limits. If he had to describe a birth, he could imagine that a midwife's presence was desirable; if the birth was premature or took place in abnormal conditions, he could imagine the concern of the midwife, or, again, the delay of her arrival on the scene; he could imagine the anxiety of the husband to secure her assistance, and the other emotions awakened in the characters concerned. In this story there is no such thing as a journey from Nazareth to Bethlehem. Joseph appears to belong to Bethlehem of Judea, when the command from Augustus the king is received, that all who were there should be enrolled. Joseph is embarrassed with " this damsel (παῖδα), whom he cannot enrol either as his wife or as his daughter." He concludes, however, that "*the day of the Lord* will bring it about as the Lord willeth it. And he saddled the ass, and set her upon it, and his son led it, and Joseph followed. And they *drew near* (ἤγγισαν) within three miles (of what, we are not told). And they came in the midst of the road (or, came up in Bethlehem). And Mary said to him, Take me down from the ass, for my burden urgeth me to be delivered. And he did so, and said to her, Whither shall I take thee and hide thy shame? for the place is *desert*."

About this point it becomes clear that some scriptural ideas are at work in the writer's mind. " The pangs of a woman in childbirth " are connected with *the day of*

---

additions, such as that of the ox and the ass, to the manger, are due to popular imagination, partly influenced by the liturgy." As to the ox and the ass see Ch. III., p. 74 above.

the Lord in Isa. 13⁸, ⁹, and this again with the idea of a "*desert.*"

> Isa. 13⁸ *Pangs* shall take hold of them as of a woman in childbirth, and they shall . . . *be amazed*, and they shall change their countenance as a flame. For, behold, *the day of the Lord* cometh, past healing of wrath and anger, to make the world *desert*, and to destroy the sinners out of it.

More remarkably still, the same oracle continues—

> For the stars *of the heaven* and Orion and all the order *of the heaven* shall not give their light.

Now the Book of James is about to say what he saw in the heaven. "And I, Joseph, walked, and walked not: and I looked up into the air, and I saw the air *amazed*, and I looked up into the vault *of heaven*, and I saw it standing still." The indebtedness is clear.

But there is another oracle in Micah which has also influenced the narrative.

> Mic. 4⁹ And now why knowest thou evil things? *Was not a king thine?* Or doth thy purpose perish because pangs take hold of thee as of childbearing? Endure thy pangs and be manful and *draw near*, O *daughter of Sion*, as one in childbirth: because now thou *shalt come out of the city* and shalt sojourn (κατασκηνώσεις) in the plain. . . .

The Cave of Bethlehem.

Perhaps we may suppose that this somewhat enigmatical original has been the cause of the somewhat enigmatical journey which Joseph is made to take in the Book of James. For Mary and Joseph seem to have been together either in Jerusalem or in Bethlehem, before the journey is started. The "three miles" taken with "the middle

THE FIRST-BORN 117

of the road " seems to show that it was either a journey of three miles out from Jerusalem, where they had been pronounced blameless by the priest just before, or three miles out from Bethlehem, and in any case there is some distance to cover before the cave is reached. The actual distance is nearly six miles from Jerusalem to the cave at Bethlehem.

"And he found a cave there, and took her in, and set his sons by her, and he went out and sought a midwife in in the country of Bethlehem."

There is no MS. authority for " a cave " instead of " a manger " in our Gospels : perhaps Epiphanius (A.D. 400) might have had such; but it is quite certain that Justin Martyr was persuaded that the Nativity took place in a cave. And to-day the visitor to Bethlehem is shown the cave, and, five yards from it, the manger. The tradition is therefore a strong one that the Babe was born in a cave.

Justin, however, does not agree with the Book of James, for he says : " Since Joseph had no place in that village to sojourn (καταλῦσαι), he sojourned in a certain cave *near* (σύνεγγυς) the village; " after which the Babe was laid in a manger. We cannot help noticing in passing, that the idea of *drawing near* is still prominent in this account also. But is it not also in—

Isa. 33[13] They that (come) from far (*i. e.* the Magi) shall hear what I do, they that *draw near* shall know my strength ?

The cave certainly originates in the LXX, which gives, in Isa. 33[13-19], one of the most graphic descriptions of the new-born Babe that we can possibly conceive. (See p. 19.) No wonder if Papias of Hierapolis (about A.D. 100) took and incorporated it in his important work in five books entitled *Exposition of the Oracles concerning the*

Lord, by which he meant the precious words of the Old Testament which foretold the Messiah. From that work we may suppose Justin took his account of the cave.

The book of James continues: " And (I saw) *the fowls of the heaven* still (or, *trembling*); and *I looked at the earth* and saw a table set (or, a vessel lying—but this makes nonsense) and labourers set beside it, and their hands on the table, and they who were chewing did not chew, and they who were lifting took not up, and they who were bringing to their mouth brought not, but the faces of them all were looking up: and behold, sheep were being driven, and they went not forward but stood still, and the shepherd was lifting up his hand to smite them with the crook, and his hand stood uplifted: and I looked upon the river-torrent and I saw the mouths of the kids set thereto and not drinking, and all things that were in movement were driven from their course." Here the author has given play to his imagination, and has produced a picture quite idyllic: the birds of the air, the labourers at their noonday meal, with their hands on the table, the sheep in the field, the shepherd with his crook, the kids of the goats by the river-side, are a very fair piece of literature. The sympathy of nature in expectancy is rendered with a poetic feeling that Milton would love.* But it is easy to see that what prompted his imagination is the oracle of—

Jer. 4^{23-31} *I looked upon the earth*, and behold nothing, and *unto the heaven*, and his lights were not. I saw the mountains, and they were trembling, and all the hills in confusion. I looked up, and behold there was no man, and all *the fowls of the heaven*

---

* We may note, by the way, that Tischendorf has made an unhappy choice of his reading in putting a *vessel* on dry land in the hill-country, as if the author did not know what he was talking about. *Evangelia Apocrypha*,[2] 1876.

THE FIRST-BORN

were *fluttered*. . . . Thus saith the Lord, *Desert* shall be all the earth, and yet I will not make completion. They went down into the caves (εἰσέδυσαν εἰς τὰ σπήλαια). . . . *For* I hear the voice of thy groaning as of *a woman with child*, as of her that beareth *her firstborn :* the voice of *the daughter of Sion* shall be let loose.

The first part of this passage might leave some doubt as to the origin of the suggestion, but when *the fowls of heaven* are brought in, the doubt disappears, and when the whole picture is taken as a series of effects antecedent to the cause, a woman in childbirth, and she the daughter of Sion, the connection is quite certain. That they went, or had gone, into the caves is a superabundance of prophetic wealth, and so is the *desert* (see p. 116) of the earth.

The interview which follows between Joseph and the midwife is most insipid, but the "bright cloud overshadowing the cave" which they see is doubtless based upon—

Isa. 4^5 And (He) shall come, and it shall be that every place of Mount Sion (including Bethlehem, to wit) and all the neighbourhood thereof, shall be *shadowed* by *a cloud* by day, and as if a smoke and *light of fire* were burning *by night*, and with all *the glory* [of it] he shall be *sheltered* (or, of the Lord it shall be filled).

So says, in like manner, the Book of James: "And suddenly the *cloud* withdrew from the cave, and there appeared a great *light* in the cave, so that their eyes could not bear it. And gradually that light withdrew until the babe was seen." There is much closer following by the author of his original in this passage than we might suppose from the analogy of other haloes and bright lights in later history, whose stories indeed are, in many cases, founded upon this.

Then follows further converse between the midwife and Salome, who is the unbelieving Thomas at this outset of the Life of Christ. We now come to the Magi. " And behold, Joseph made ready to go into Judea " : we are to understand away from Bethlehem. " And there was a great tumult in Bethlehem of Judea; for Magi came, saying, where is he that is born king of the Jews ? " etc. The idea of the tumult ($\theta \acute{o} \varrho v \beta o\varsigma$, excitement, as we should say) is probably only a natural accessory of narrative, but it may perhaps be based upon an oracle which has produced so much of the picture already.

Isa. 33[7] Behold, now, these shall be afraid in the midst of your fear.

The course of the story follows that of St. Matthew except in a few particulars. Herod sent his servants to the Magi. He examined them, saying, What sign did ye see *of the king* that is born. " And the Magi said, We saw a very great star shining among these stars and *dimming* them, so that the stars were not seen. And thus we knew that a king was born unto Israel, and came to worship him. The star stood at the entrance of *the cave*. They took out of *their scrip* gold and frankincense and myrrh." There is nothing here but the ordinary adornment of a simple story which, after all, is not quite so close to the ideas of Isa. 33[14f] as is Matthew, except in regard to the cave. There is a divergence where James says that the Massacre of the Innocents caused Mary to be afraid, and she took the Child and swathed it and put it in a manger for oxen, for Matthew contains no reference to the manger at all. James also differs from Luke as to the occasion, for Luke says, " She brought forth her son, the Firstborn ($\tau \grave{o} \nu$ $v \acute{i} o \nu$ $a \grave{v} \tau \tilde{\eta} \varsigma$ $\tau \grave{o} \nu$ $\Pi \varrho \omega \tau \acute{o} \tau o \kappa o \nu$, see below, Ch. VI.), and

THE FIRST-BORN

she wrapped him in swaddling-clothes and laid him in a manger, because there was no room for them in the inn." The importance of the correct translation, " her son, the Firstborn," is obvious when we remember—

Ps. 89[27] And I will make ($\theta\dot{\eta}\sigma o\mu\alpha\iota$, *adopt*) him (David) my *Firstborn*, high above the kings of the earth—

and when we observe that David has been mentioned twice in Luke 2[4], and his name is to occur again in 2[11]. The idea of the two Gospels is that Joseph, *son of* David (Matt. 1[20]), of *the house and* lineage of David (Luke 2[4]), conveyed his Davidic lineage to the Firstborn, who was thus *adopted* in the words of the psalmist into the line of David, so that he is called long before this by St. Paul (Rom. 1[3]), " born of the seed of David according to the flesh." St. Luke, then, in his use of the term *Firstborn*, silently points to Ps. 89, as if he had added : " Let the reader understand "—the Firstborn of David being the primary meaning, then the firstborn among many brethren, then the firstborn from the dead, and the firstborn of all creation.

The Virgin-birth not in St. Paul.

At this point we may observe that the great difference between the Book of James and the New Testament writers is that the former is the protagonist and champion of the Virgin-birth as it is commonly held in England now, the New Testament writers are only coming to it. First of all, St. Paul, when he wrote Rom. 1[3], has no idea of such a doctrine, so far as his words prove anything. There is an entire lack of evidence to show that Mary was of the seed of David or was believed to be so. The whole family history, so far as it goes in Luke 1, goes to imply that Mary was, like her kinswoman Elizabeth, of the tribe of Levi. And the Messiah had been expected to come from that very tribe for the greater part of the second century before Christ.* Then, in the same Epistle (Rom. 8³), St. Paul goes on to say, " God, by sending his own son in the likeness of sinful flesh, and for sin, condemned sin in the flesh " : and these words are not consistent with any other statement than that which he made in 1³, where "according to the flesh " is the equivalent of " in the likeness of the flesh of sin." If the latter expression did not imply actual human flesh, St. Paul would indeed be guilty of the Docetic heresy which asserted that the crucified was not a human body, but either " a bodiless demonium " or some other kind of spirit. No possible escape can be found from actual human flesh in the use of the term "likeness," which includes all humanity as like humanity. Therefore the Lord's human flesh was of the seed of David. And it was never heard that a man's seed was reckoned by his mother's side unless this was specified for sufficient reason.

Next, in Gal. 4⁴, " God sent forth his son, made of a woman, made under the law, in order that he might redeem them that are under the law, in order that we might receive the adoption of sons." Here it is worth while to consider whether St. Paul had not already considered the bearing of Ps. 89²⁷ on the question of the sonship of the faithful in Christ. This passage closely resembles Rom. 8¹⁵ : " the spirit of adoption whereby we cry aloud, Abba, father : " it is essentially the same whether Galatians was written as a later abstract or as a preliminary sketch of Romans. Certainly there is nothing very tangible about this expression " the spirit of adoption." In the Jewish law there was no such thing as adoption. It is not conceivable that St. Paul should resort to the practices of Egypt or of Persia for his illustration. He goes to Greece or Rome,

* See Dr. E. G. King, *Yalkut on Zechariah*; Appendix.

THE FIRST-BORN 123

for his readers were well acquainted with Greek and Roman law. Consequently his phraseology is to be taken with considerable freedom. "The law of the spirit of life in Christ Jesus" is the fullest expression of his meaning in the passage; "the spirit of Christ," "the spirit of God," "the spirit of adoption," "the spirit," are shorter expressions of the same truth, that we as faithful in Christ Jesus are enabled by the argument from prophecy to see that we are made sons, whereas before we were only in the position of slaves. Children we always were of God, but sons, representatives, of God, we become by adoption and by the sense of it.

The Paramount Importance of Ps. 89.

Now is it not clear that the entire passage in Rom. 8 and Gal. 4 is based upon Ps. $89^{20 ff}$? Ten or eleven consecutive sayings corresponding in the two writers seem to prove this. Ps. 89^{19} had said: "Then didst thou *speak in a vision* to *thy sons*." But St. Paul says (Rom. 8^{14}) "As many are led by *God's spirit* are *his sons*." The prophets are addressed *in a vision*, and the prophets are chief among those who are led *by the spirit*, for they are often "in spirit:" the prophets are therefore chiefly, if perhaps not solely, intended.

Again, Ps. 89^{20}, said: "I have exalted *an elect* one out of my *people*." But St. Paul says (Rom. 8^{33}) "Who shall bring charges against the *elect people* of God."

Again, Ps. 89^{20} said: "I have found David *my servant*." But St. Paul says (Gal. 4^1) "The heir differeth nowise from *a servant* though he be lord of all." David was the heir.

Again, in Ps. 89^{21}: "For my hand shall *assist* him" is just what St. Paul says (Rom. 8^{26}): "The spirit *assisteth* our infirmity ($\sigma\nu\nu\alpha\nu\tau\iota\lambda\alpha\mu\beta\acute{\alpha}\nu o\mu\alpha\iota$ * in both places).

* This word occurs only once more in the New Testament, and twice more in the Old Testament.

Again, in Ps. 89^{22} " The *son of lawlessless* shall not hurt him" means, as elsewhere so often (Acts 2^{23}, etc.), the heathen. So Rom. 8$^{31\,\text{ff}}$: " Who can *be against us ?* Not persecution . . . nor sword . . . nor powers."

And Ps. 89^{23} said : " And I will bruise his enemies." So Rom. 8^{37}: " We are more than *conquerors* through him that loved us."

And Ps. 89^{26} said : " He shall call upon me,* Thou art *my father* " (âbi), which certainly finds its fulfilment in Rom. 8^{15}, Gal. 4^{6}: " God sent forth the spirit of his son into our hearts crying aloud, *Abba, father.*"

Again, Ps. 89^{26} : " My God and *the helper* (ἀντιλήμπτωρ) of my salvation," is precisely the idea of the spirit's *intercession* for us (Rom. 8^{27}), " he *helpeth* (συναντιλαμβάνεται) our infirmity."

Then Ps. 89^{27}: " And I will make (θήσομαι, *adopt*) him *my firstborn*, high *above the kings* of the earth," reappears in " The heir . . . being *lord of all*, is under governors " (Gal. 4^{1}).

Again, Ps. 89^{28} said : " My testament shall stand fast for him." This is the source of all that idea of expectation which pervades Gal. 4$^{2-5}$, " *until* the term appointed of the father," and " we receive in full the adoption," and Rom. 8$^{18-25}$: " *earnestly waiting* for the redemption of our body."

Lastly, Ps. 89^{29} said : " And I will (θήσομαι) *adopt* his seed for ever and ever." " Who shall separate us, the elect," says the apostle (Rom. 8$^{33,\,35}$), " from the love of Christ ? " and his answer is eloquent upon this theme.

This comparison makes it fairly clear that St. Paul had the idea of adoption *as based upon Ps.* 89 in his mind at the time when he wrote Galatians and Romans. But now does this imply that the heir of David born at

* No notice of Ps. 89^{27} here in Lightfoot ! Nor in Dalman, *The Words of Jesus*, p. 192, which see for the Aramaic idiom. It is not impossible that it represented *Our Father*.

THE FIRST-BORN 125

Bethlehem—though St. Paul ignores His birthplace altogether—was *adopted* in the sense that He was not of the seed of David until He was pronounced to be so by God? Does it leave us free to infer that Mary was a Levite, that Joseph was only His putative father? There can only be one answer to this question. If St. Paul had insisted only that Christ Jesus was *the son* *i.e.* " the representative," of David, it might have been otherwise; or if he had called Him only " the Firstborn *of the house* of David." But as he has laid stress upon His being of *the seed* of David, in accordance with Ps. 89^{29}, (τό σπέρμα αὐτοῦ), the answer must be in the negative. He held Him to be the Son of David by direct lineage through His father, whom the two evangelists call a son of David. And his " definition of Him as God's Son " —to use the words of Rom. 1^4—was made, as he there describes it, " with power in accordance with the spirit of holiness by (ἐξ) the resurrection of the dead." Had there been any reserve whatever in St. Paul's mind in regard to the abnormal character of the Nativity he would not have said, in Gal. 4^4, " born of a woman, born under the law," but " born of a virgin, born under the law." In fact, however, this latter expression would have involved an inconsistency, because his object is to show that Christ was entirely Man and entirely a Jew. He could not redeem the Jews without entirely becoming a Jew (Gal. 4^{5a}), nor mankind without becoming entirely Man (Gal. 4^{5b}). And the inconsistency would, it is almost needless to say, have defeated his argument and made it absurd.

The Epistle to the Hebrews on our Lord's Tribe.

There is another explicit declaration of our Lord's tribe in Heb. 7^{14}: " For it is openly evident (πρόδηλον) that our Lord hath arisen as the Dayspring (ἀνατέταλκεν) out of

Judah, upon which tribe Moses spake nothing concerning priests." This remark has a directness which ought to satisfy every doubt concerning the relative importance of Mary's tribe. No scriptural writer has ever stated that Mary's tribe was Judah. The two evangelists declare that Joseph was of Judah. Before Hebrews was written, St. Paul had written, and the Apocalypse was either written or about to be written, and the writer speaks of "the Lion out of the tribe of Judah" (Rev. 5⁵). And Hebrews says, "it is *palpable*" (πρόδηλον), as if nobody disputed the question in the author's day. The observation: "Our Lord hath *arisen* (ἀνατέταλκεν) out of Judah" declares not merely that He is born out of that tribe, but that His birth has been the rising of a new dawn of day to the tribe which had long been in obscurity. It is based upon the oracle of—

Zech. 3⁸ Behold, I bring my servant the *Dayspring* ('Ἀνατολή).

If we translate *arisen* instead of *sprung*, it recalls Isa. 60¹: "The glory of the Lord is *risen* (ἀνατέταλκεν) upon thee." Thus it seems clear that a choice must be made between the renderings *Branch* and *Dayspring*. And this choice is easy when we observe that the passage in Zech. 3⁸ has the conclusive words, "Hear now, *Jesus the great priest*," which show that Hebrews is here based on the Greek of Zech. 3. But on further examination it is evident that the LXX of Zech. 3⁸, 6¹², in translating 'Ἀνατολή has intended it to mean Dayspring, or if not intended has left the reader free to understand it so and to dismiss from his mind the meaning of Branch. The original of Zechariah is obscure for the purpose of the argument in Hebrews, but the fact of Joshua being called *the great priest*, though of the tribe of Levi, by implication enhances the greater priesthood still of One who holds under a

THE FIRST-BORN 127

changed law and is to arise as the Dayspring ('Ανατολή). Zech. 6¹² is not, indeed, actually quoted till we come to Heb. 10²¹, but there it is clear that LXX is used,—"*a great priest* over the house of God." Consequently we infer that Hebrews has used the Greek also in Heb. 7²⁶, "made higher than the heavens," which represents freely Zech. 6¹³, "he shall sit and shall take precedence upon his throne."

Westcott, on Heb. 7¹⁴, has a remark that might mislead : "There is nothing to show in what exact form he held that the Lord's descent from Judah through David was reckoned : whether as the legal representative of Joseph, or as the son of Mary, *who was herself known to be of Davidic descent.* The genealogies (Matt. 1, Luke 3) are in favour of the former view." Who, we must ask, has ever known her to be of Davidic descent ?. No man, so far as we can tell. For those who assert her Davidic descent support their assertion by an inference from three passages : first, the very one (Rom. 1³) which we have considered; then Ps. 132¹¹, which is a curious means to prove or disprove a fact of centuries later ; * and lastly, Luke 1³², "the throne of David his father," where, as before, we may not assume that the Davidic descent of Mary is implied when that is the very question that we are seeking to solve. Why was it not "David *thy* father," if so ? If there is any Jewish law by which a man inherits on his mother's side when his father is known it should

---

* This is in Heb. *of the fruit of thy body*, but in Greek ἐκ καρποῦ τῆς κοιλίας σου. So also is the same promise in 2 Sam. 7¹², 1 Ch. 17¹¹, of David as progenitor. But since the Greek expression is so frequently applied to a mother, it is not surprising that it was claimed that it applied to the mother in this verse also in support of the Virgin-birth. The silence of St. Peter, who comments on the text in Acts 2³⁰, is significant on this point—if we are to read κοιλίας with Blass. But if with Westcott and Hort we read ὀσφύος we have a term which is never used of child-bearing once in the whole Bible. Still more significant !

be produced. Even "the legitimacy of the children did not depend on the form of the marriage,"* but so far as we know they were the father's not the mother's. There was no case for the mother's rights unless they were specially reserved, and there appears to be no recorded case of such a reservation. We must conclude that Westcott's words quoted above, so far from stating that Mary was known to be of the tribe of Judah, mean *as if* she were herself known to be of Davidic descent.

Besides this difficulty in regard to the tribe, the supporters of the Virgin-birth as it is commonly held are faced with another. If Joseph was only the putative father of Jesus, the question of his tribe is unimportant, while that of Mary is all-important. How then does it come to pass that the scripture-writers declare Joseph's tribe to be Judah, but ignore the tribe of Mary?

"*The Holy Ghost shall come upon Thee.*"

Then it is contended, or even rather assumed, that Luke 1^{35} proves that the conception was due to the physical agency of the Holy Spirit: " The Holy Ghost shall come upon thee, and the power of the Highest shall *overshadow* thee" (ἐπισκιάσει σοι). But there is nothing in these words to suggest any such agency. Ezekiel uses the expression "The spirit [of the Lord] came upon me." Isaiah says, "The spirit of the Lord [came] upon me": so that there is nothing even uncommon in the terms of it or in the idea. The word "overshadow" is the same as that mentioned above (p. 119) as applied to the bright cloud overshadowing the cave, and this we have seen probably originates in—

Isa. 4^5 A cloud *shall shadow* . . . and with all the glory [he] shall be sheltered (σκιάσει νεφέλη . . . καὶ πάσῃ τῇ δόξῃ σκεπασθήσεται: or, δόξῃ κυρίου πασθήσεται, A).

* *Enc. Bibl.*, "Family," 1502.

THE FIRST-BORN

The amount of meaning that has been read into Luke 1^{34f}, not only by believers in the Virgin-birth, but by opponents of it, is really astonishing. If it be possible to dismiss undue prejudice for a moment, the reader may be willing to consider a few points which may conceivably moderate his opinion. " The angel said, The Holy Ghost shall come upon thee," and on the same page the sequel is, " And [Mary] said, My soul doth magnify " etc. What, then, is the meaning of the angel's words? Simply two things : first, that the prophetic spirit should come upon Mary, and, secondly, that she should conceive and bear a Prophet who should be great and be called the Son of the Highest. The Magnificat fulfilled the first and the Nativity the second prediction. There is nothing said about a physical conception of Mary *by* ($ὑπό$) the Holy Ghost, while the words of the " Nicene Creed " say quite accurately *by* ($ἐκ$) the Holy Ghost. Unfortunately the doctrine as commonly held in England is the former, and the right doctrine is the latter.

If there is still room for doubt, let the corresponding passage in Luke 1^{67} be noted : " And Zacharias was filled with the Holy Ghost, and prophesied, saying, Blessed be," etc. Every prophet prophesying *was filled with the Holy Ghost*, but let us ask the question, Which is the stronger expression, " He was filled with the Holy Ghost, and said," or " The Holy Ghost came upon her, and she said " ? If anything the former seems to be the stronger. In fact they are exactly equal in strength. But why did not Luke say of Mary what he has said of Zechariah? The answer can only be either that he did or that he did not dream of the possible perversion of his words to mean physical conception by the Holy Ghost. If he did, then he has intentionally avoided the perversion; if he did not, then why the perversion of later days ?

The Holy Spirit of whom the angel speaks is the spirit

K

of prophecy, " which spake by the Prophets," which came upon the Virgin as it *came upon* Ezekiel (Ezek. 2^2, etc.), as it *should come upon* the rich women in Isa. 32^{15}; Zachariah was *filled with the spirit* of prophecy as Elisha was (Ecclus. 48^{12}) and as Micah was (Mic. 3^8). Both expressions could be abundantly confirmed from the Old Testament. The whole substance of the angel's annunciation is in Isaiah, and most of the phraseology—

LUKE I	ISAIAH
31. *Behold, thou shalt conceive and bear a son.* [^{27} *The virgin's name* (τῆς παρθένου).] *And thou shalt call his name* . . .	7^{14}. *Behold, the virgin* (ἡ παρθένος) *shall conceive and bear a son, and thou shalt call his name,*
32. *He shall be great,*	9^6. *Angel of great counsel.*
and shall be called Son of the Highest.	7^{14}. *Emmanuel* (God with us).
The Lord God shall give him the throne of David his father and he shall be king	9^7. *the throne of David and his kingdom*
. . . *for ever*	*from henceforth and for ever*
33. *and of his kingdom there shall be no end.*	*and of his peace there is no bound.*

Thus the article of the creed, Born of the Virgin Mary, bears the meaning which it bore from the first, from the date of Luke I at least—Born of Mary who fulfilled Isa. 7^{14}.* It does not bear the meaning which the Book of James would have it to bear, and perhaps few who uphold it would commit themselves to that book, which is the first, however, after Matthew, to set it forth as a professed history.†

* In Luke 2^5 I hold the true reading to be, with A and other authorities, " his wife who had been espoused to him " (σὺν Μ.τῇ ἐμν. αὐτῷ γυναικί), as was said in Luke 1^{27}, from which passage it is not improbable that ἐμνηστευμένη is imported.

† As this goes to press I notice that Dr. Harnack, who becomes generally more and more conservative, writes (*Date of the Acts*, etc., E. T. p. 145) : " Hence one may, indeed must, cherish very serious doubts as to whether the idea of the Virgin-birth would ever have made its appearance on Jewish soil *if it had not been*

THE FIRST-BORN

The idea of "the power of the Highest *overshadowing* thee" is in any case that of the cloud (Shechinah is an unbiblical term) overshadowing the tabernacle as—

> Ex. 40³⁵ And Moses *was unable* to enter into the tabernacle of the witness, because the cloud *overshadowed* (*upon*) it (ἐπεσκίαζεν ἐπ' αὐτήν), and the tabernacle was filled with the glory of the Lord.

In the application the body of Mary is regarded by St. Luke as the earthly tabernacle over which brooded the cloud of the Most High, while within the holy place, the shrine of the Holy Ghost, there was tabernacled or sheltered the earthly body of the Christ. Hence we have a close agreement with the words of John 1¹⁴, "the Word became flesh and *tabernacled* in (or amongst) us, and we beheld his glory, a glory (however in this case) as of an only-begotten from a father, full of grace and truth." There is a decided contrast implied here between Moses (as in John 1¹⁷) and his greater successor Jesus. The *inability* of Moses to enter the tabernacle is contrasted with the *power* of the Most High to place Jesus in it. *Glory* is used by St. John, *Power* by St. Luke, both terms being justified by the pentateuchal references. At the same time there was nothing to indicate a physical agency of the Holy Spirit in the conception, and everything to indicate a dynamic.*

---

for Isa. 7¹⁴." (The italics are his.) But I venture to think that Dr. Harnack has not yet begun to assign its full importance to the Greek Bible. Nor does he come to close quarters with the actual meaning of ἐκ πνεύματος ἁγίου, which he considers to be coloured by ideas which became popular in A.D. 100. I hold that St. Luke could and would have said γεννηθεὶς ἐκ πν. ἁγ. in accordance with what he has written in Luke 1. He could not have prefixed to it the words which Matt. 1¹⁸ has prefixed.

* So we might say κατὰ δύναμιν τοῦ πνεύματος, and ἐκ τοῦ πνεύματος, but not κατὰ φύσιν τ. π. Far less would it have been possible to assert ὑπὸ τοῦ πνεύματος.

The Firstborn in St. Luke, St. Paul and Hebrews.

We now return to the idea of the Firstborn in Luke 2^7 as showing the emphasis which St. Luke by implication lays upon the prophecy of Ps. 89, as proving the Messiah to be of the house of David, and we have traced the same train of thought in St. Luke's companion St. Paul (Rom. 8^{29}), "That he should be the firstborn among many brethren." The manner in which he introduces this statement is the more remarkable because it comes in parenthetically, breaking a climax of four stages between the first stage and the second. Foreknew—foreordained, foreordained—called, called—justified, justified—glorified. What he means to say is that the use of the term Firstborn implies of necessity other children of the same birth—"many brethren"—by a mere logical process, and these in this case are "foreordained to be conformed to the image of his son," but he has omitted to state that Firstborn is a term drawn from Ps. 89^{27}, and yet upon this prophecy and its whole context being known and recognized and assumed as a *datum* the whole of this part of his argument is based. It is unfortunate that in Westcott and Hort's Greek text the πρωτότοκον is not printed in uncials, both in Luke 2 and in Rom. 8^{29}. The same observation applies to πατήρ in "Abba, father" (Rom. 8^{15}), for this also takes us back to Ps. 89^{27} and to no other passage whatever. Here is the brotherhood of man, and its limit.

This, however, is not the only passage in St. Paul where he draws out the meaning of the Firstborn of Ps. 89^{27}. In Col. $1^{15, 18}$ He is not only the Firstborn as regards His brethren but (1) the Firstborn of all creation, and (2) the Firstborn from the dead. He is the Firstborn of all creation because (ὅτι) in Him were created (ἐκτίσθη) all things . . . and through Him and for Him.

THE FIRST-BORN 133

There is a very long and learned note of Lightfoot on this passage in which the connection with Ps. 89 is fully recognized, but in such a way as to let us lose sight of its previous use by St. Paul and by the authors of Hebrews and Revelation. It happens that these two other writers have employed the ideas (1) and (2) just mentioned, though both wrote later than Colossians. Heb. 1⁶, after speaking of the idea of Son as the "effulgence" and the "impress" of the glory and substance of God; says "And when again *he hath introduced the Firstborn into the world* (οἰκουμένη), he saith, And let all the angels of God worship him." On this text, again, there is a long and learned note of Westcott. There is, however, no real difficulty. The rule of ὅταν with the aorist subjunctive is one to which there is no exception, and it means "when (he) has (done)" or "after (doing)"—whether of future time or not. Therefore we look into the citation and examine the context. As *the world* here is not κόσμος, but οἰκουμένη, we have a clue at once.

There are two passages from which it may be drawn, and we have to decide between them. For the words naturally mean, "After introducing *in the previous context* the Son into the world the scriptural authority proceeds to say, And let," etc. We therefore look into one of these authorities (Ps. 97⁷), and there we find the verse in question following shortly after *the world*, οἰκουμένη (Ps. 97⁴), which again follows shortly after "The Lord reigneth" (Ps. 97¹), which follows closely on Ps. 89.

Ps. 97, ¹, ⁴, ⁷ *The Lord* reigneth, the earth shall rejoice . . . His lightnings shined (in) *the world* (τῇ οἰκουμένῃ) . . . *Worship him*, all his angels.

There is therefore no further doubt about the origin and the meaning of the words of Heb. 1⁶. The Firstborn and the Lord are identical and the terms are interchangeable. For the original usage of "the Lord" as meaning Jehovah has for the writer of Hebrews passed over to Jesus, as his subsequent citations prove.

This discovery, which is of the simplest kind, ought to clear the way to the writer's meaning, and show us its limits. Hebrews shows that the psalmist has represented the Firstborn, whose name he assumes to be intelligible already to his readers, as King of all the world, including the angels. Not only is He King, He is Maker of the heavens in the sense that they were made by His agency ($δι'$ $οὗ$). For we cannot consider Ps. 97, which he has quoted, to be far apart from—

Ps. 96^{13,10} The Lord will judge *the world.* . . . The Lord setteth up *the world.* . . . The Lord made ($ἐποίησεν$) the heavens.

And all this region of the Psalms is full of the praises offered by the creation to Jehovah. When Jesus is once substituted for Jehovah, the only cause for surprise is that Romans and Hebrews have used such moderation of terms that the due measure of sovranty is still found to be reserved for the God who is over all : and our punctuation of Rom. 9^5 must be in accordance with this deliberate reserve, " He who is over all, God, be blessed for ever and ever, Amen." This was the ancient doxology which concluded each of the five books of the Psalter, and it is not conceivable that just at the moment when St. Paul professed his absolute unity with his brethren who were his kinsmen, the Israelites, he should attempt the least innovation in the meaning of that solemn and venerable formula of Israelite praise. He quoted it for the very purpose of proving his unity with them, and he used it in the same sense with them.

THE FIRST-BORN 135

The Firstborn of the Dead.

The other extension of the meaning of the Firstborn to which we have referred (2) is to the resurrection—St. Paul so extends it, and Rev. 1^5 so extends it. "The Firstborn of the dead and the Ruler of the kings of the earth." But here we observe a peculiarity. The writer prefixes to these words, "And from Jesus Christ, the faithful witness." *The faithful witness* is a quotation from the same Ps. 89^{37} which has been before us so often : but there it is intended to refer to the sun, or rather perhaps to the stars, "and as the witness in the sky is faithful" (King). But which is right? At first one is inclined to assert a mistranslation on the part of LXX, which both separates the line from the previous line by a colon, and omits *as*, thus making "the witness" to be distinct from that of the heavenly bodies. Even so, the meaning which it cannot bear even in the LXX—since David was not "in heaven"—is that which the author of Rev. 1 has placed upon it, by making it refer to David himself or as represented in his greater Son. He has made it to be a sentence unrelated to the simile which preceded it, and has transferred the thought to the glorified and exalted Jesus, "And the witness in heaven is faithful." But, on the other hand, it must be remembered that the LXX is here quite strictly literal in not inserting *as*, for the Hebrew should be translated "and the (a) witness in the sky is faithful." Then, since rhythm is not an infallible guide and punctuation is not a guide at all, we have to exonerate the LXX from blame in this verse. Then LXX leaves us with a rather cryptic meaning. The author of Rev. 1, probably in a state of trance, found in it the reference that we know.

Here, then, we have the third New Testament writer who has recourse to this psalm. From it he has also drawn "the Ruler of the kings of the earth" (89^{27}). From what has he drawn "the Firstborn of the dead"? It seems almost certain that the same difference of punctuation which affected him in 89^{37} affected him also in—

> Ps. 89^{48} He shall rescue his soul (life) from the hand of hell" ($ᾅδου$).

The line before is—

> Who is the man that shall live and shall not see death?

The answer to this may very well be supposed to be conveyed in the next words, "He (God) shall rescue this man's life from death." In other words, "Who is he that shall live for ever? He whom God shall rescue from death": that is, the Christ. If the apostles disjoined verse 37c from its context—and it is apparent that they did so—much more easily can we understand their making 48b an affirmative statement, in answer to 48a, which is a question and which need not be followed by a second question. The LXX gives no sign of the presence of a question except in the punctuation, although it is usually held that the Hebrew intended—but is not this intention altogether doubtful?—the interrogative to continue. Thus what the psalmist perhaps put as a contemplation of the frailty of man has become, in the Greek, a prediction of the resurrection. This is noteworthy, considering the fewness of the testimonies to the resurrection which are contained in the Old Testament.

We have now seen that Ps. 89 has been used as the basis of teaching the brotherhood of man in Christ, the headship of Christ in creation, His place in the act of creation, the resurrection of Christ from the dead. We have also seen that St. Paul in Col. 1 combines the last two of these doctrines, that Hebrews declares the second;

THE FIRST-BORN 137

but assumes on the part of his readers an understanding of Firstborn as an attribute of Messiah, and that Revelation declares the third. One might be inclined to infer that the writer who combined most of these thoughts was later in time than those who expressed one or other of them severally, to say, therefore, that Colossians was later than Hebrews and Revelation. But we must bear in mind that St. Paul would in any case be master of a greater power of synthesis than either of the others, and also that it would be probable that Colossians had been seen and read by St. John of Ephesus before A.D. 69, and as the first three chapters of Revelation are very likely the latest of all to be composed, there might have been longer time still for the circulation of Colossians. The assumption by Hebrews that the readers were acquainted with the meaning of Firstborn is not so much an assumption that they knew what we call Rabbinic interpretations of Ps. 89, as that they knew the usual Christian interpretation of that and other scriptures. The writer would not open his Epistle with so many texts of scripture unless he had credited them with a considerable familiarity with it, but that would not suffice by itself. As Jews they must have read it and heard it read, but he presumes their acquaintance with "the argument of the origin of the Christ," in other words, the Argument from Prophecy (τὸν τῆς ἀρχῆς τοῦ χριστοῦ λόγον, Heb. 6^1. See Ch. XIII. below). Few Psalms would be found to support it more strongly than this. The inference seems to be that Ps. 89 began very early to form part of the basis of the Argument from Prophecy. It hardly needs to be said that Ps. 89$^{20, 26, 27, 38}$ prove that the Messiah (ὁ χριστὸς τοῦ θεοῦ) is the Son of God.*

* Lebreton says (*Histoire du Dogme*, i. p. 121), "Neither in the Old Testamant nor the Apocrypha does one find the title 'Son of God' applied by the writer to the Messiah.' This, though literally correct, is not practically. See Ch. IX. below.

138 ORACLES IN THE NEW TESTAMENT

Other Scriptural Bases in James.

The massacre of the Innocents in the Book of James has two remarkable sequels, apart from causing Mary to "swathe the child and put it in a *crib for oxen*," which last expression confirms the idea that the crib or manger is based upon—

Isa. 1^3 The ox knoweth his owner, and the ass the crib of his Lord.

The first sequel is the flight of Elizabeth with the infant John to the hill-country for concealment. "She cried aloud, Mount of God, receive a mother with her child. And suddenly the mountain was divided and received her. And light shone through to them; for the angel of the Lord was with them, preserving them." It seems that we have here simply a commentary on a verse or two in Rev. 12$^{13\,ff}$. Herod is the dragon. "And the earth assisted the woman, and the earth opened her mouth and devoured the river which the dragon shot out of his mouth." But here the parallel is upset, for instead of the woman being swallowed, the river of persecution which the dragon vomited from his mouth should have been swallowed. Perhaps, however, this is only the way in which James understands it. Another parallel between the two books lies in the fact that the dragon had angels (Rev. 12^7), and James says that Herod had sent out assassins ($\varphi o\nu\varepsilon v\tau\grave{\alpha}\varsigma$) to kill the innocents. And immediately afterwards we find a further comment on Rev. 12^{17}, "And the dragon was wrath with the woman, and went forth to make war with the rest of her seed, that keep the commandments of God and have the witness of Jesus."

What inference is to be drawn from these phenomena? Are we to argue that Rev. 12$^{7\,ff}$ contains as a Nativity-story of Jesus what had been formerly a Nativity-story

THE FIRST-BORN 139

of John and was in course of being transferred to Jesus ? and that James preserves traces of the older form of the tradition ? Or are we to hold that James has ignorantly taken Rev. 12⁷ ᶠᶠ as a suggestion of images, and used it merely in order to eke out an idyll of its own for the completion of its own copy ? Either argument seems possible, but space forbids further discussion of Rev. 12, which appears to contain doublets in 12³⁻⁶ and 12⁷⁻⁹, ¹³⁻¹⁷, and which can perhaps be explained by reference to Justin Martyr.*

For the second sequel is Herod's rage against Zacharias. "And Herod sought after John, and sent his servants to Zacharias, saying, Where hast thou hidden thy son ? And he answered and said to them, I am the minister of God, and I am busied with the temple of the Lord, I know not where my son is. . . . And Herod said, His son is going to be king of Israel. And Zacharias said, I am a witness for God, if thou dost shed my blood; for the Lord will receive my spirit, for thou sheddest innocent blood in the porch of the Lord's temple. And about daybreak Zacharias was slain." *The minister* of God, *the witness* for God, are expressions which recall Rev. 12¹⁷, and they are in fact suggested by it. In the same way the murder of "Zacharias [son of Barachias, Matt. 23³⁵] whom ye slew between the temple and the altar" is here attributed to Herod by a somewhat ingenious and as it seems intentional confusion of dates and history. At the same time it is dangerous to pronounce upon this question. James is probably more anxious to add one chapter of lively incident to his Book than to prove the fulfilment of an ancient prophecy. And yet the prophecy in question was one that seemed especially to invite the narrative of its fulfilment by the ominous words of the dying priest in 2 Chron. 24²², "The Lord look upon it

* *Dial.* 330 c. See p. 14 above.

and require it," and by the fact that they are implied in the reference of Matt. 23^{35} and yet no precise fulfilment is given in our Gospels. What James says is that the priests, not knowing Zacharias was slain, " stood waiting for him to greet them with prayer and to glorify the Most High "—a strange mode of action to attribute to the priests, that they should wait " for the blessing of Zacharias that should meet them according to custom," even if he were high priest, as James appears to consider that he was. " And when he tarried, they were all afraid; but one of them ventured and went in and perceived near the altar blood congealed, and a voice saying, Zacharias is murdered, and his blood shall not be wiped out until his avenger cometh. . . . And the wainscotings of the Temple shrieked out, and were cleft from top to bottom. And they found not his body, but found his blood turned into stone. . . . And after three days of mourning, the priests took counsel whom they should appoint in his stead. And the lot fell upon Simeon : for he it was who was admonished by the Holy Spirit that he should not see death, until he saw the Christ in the flesh."

The narrative is a good instance of the false and artificial kind of fulfilment of prophecy. Zacharias is, as we suppose,—for we have no other evidence of this fatal end to his life,—unhistorical in this portion of it; but merely because his name is identical with that of Zacharias son of Jehoiada, what is told of the latter in 2 Chron. is attributed to the Baptist's father. There the two murders are made to agree in detail as happening " between the temple and the altar." And as if it were not enough to have the words of the son of Jehoiada, " The Lord look upon it and require it," " the voice " near the altar is inserted as pointing to the avenger.

CHAPTER VI

JOSEPH

False Ingenuity refuting Luke on the Census.

ST. LUKE has done his utmost to fix the date of the Nativity by that of a certain census or enrolment, and by nothing else. He had fixed the birth of John by saying, " It came to pass in the days of Herod, king of Judea." He is about to fix the preaching of John by a variety of dates. And yet in fixing the Nativity he has not satisfied his readers, modern or ancient, and they have commented on his dates in large volumes of criticism, now friendly, now adverse. Since every writer who touches the subject is bound to make his profession of approval or disapproval, or else add to the least profitable multitude of those who suspend judgment on this point of history *ad infinitum*, the present writer respectfully submits that Luke should be considered apart from Matthew, and be judged by his own words and not by presuppositions, or rather, since Matthew is really later than Luke, by postsuppositions. The conclusion to which this leads is that Luke, disregarding other traditions if he knew them, such as that which Matthew was destined to follow, maintained that the Nativity took place at the time when Quirinius was *legatus* of Syria in A.D. 6, and that there is nothing in Luke which conflicts with this statement, which he has made as clear as any one could make it. He recognizes that there were other enrolments since that date, for he had lived to see several during his lifetime, but this, he says;

was the first. There was none before it, and so it was the first. Now it is very strange what ingenuity and determination have been exerted by those who assert against Luke, and as if they were supporting and making good his declaration, that it was not the first—that though it *took effect* in some wonderful way, though it was "first [really] carried out"* when Quirinius was governor, there was a something before it. All this is special pleading, of a sort that does small credit to Luke "the historian." It is not easy to find an authority, whether friendly to Luke or not, except perhaps, Mommsen and Schürer, who will allow him to mean what he so positively says. Is not the evangelist very unfortunate that he cannot be let alone? Misinterpreted first and then mistranslated on the same page in his second chapter, it is a wonder that he is esteemed at all. He nowhere claims to be a historian. If he was a historian he made a poor commencement of his history by saying that it was the first when his friends have to show that it was not exactly the first, but the second. In the present work it is maintained, not that he was a historian, but that he was a prophet, who thoroughly understood prophecy, and an attempt is made more than once to support his accuracy; but it seems that those friends who claim him as the historian are more clamorous for the harmonization of his date with that of Matthew than for the justice of that title.

Here, for instance, is a remark in one of the latest commentaries on Luke 2^2: "The meaning of it is not really doubtful. *This took place as a first enrolment, when Quirinius was governor of Syria.* The object of the remark is to distinguish the census which took Joseph and Mary to Bethlehem from the one undertaken by Quirinius in A.D. 6, 7, at which time Quirinius was

* Edersheim.

JOSEPH

governor of Syria." But why make the first appear the second census? Why do as the Sophist? Why *deuteroprotize*, if we may coin a word for this time-honoured piece of special pleading? Why suppose that Luke, when he mentions only one, wished to make any distinction whatever between two censuses, the first census and one before it? One cannot and does not suppose that Luke had seen Matthew and knew the difficulty of harmonizing with him. Where has Luke thrown out any hint that there was another census before the first? Could he possibly have said more plainly that this was the first, and there was none before it? *This took place*, etc., though put in a parenthesis by some, is no clearer on that account. Luke did not write the marks of parenthesis, nor is the sentence "intercalated," nor is it a perplexing footnote. He has no thought of suggesting that the decree of Cæsar was a long time or a short time before the census. His one idea is that Quirinius was connected with it. The reason of this idea we shall presently see. Luke *had followed carefully the parallels* of prophecy (παρηκολουθηκότι, Luke 1³) in this case as before, and he indicates the result in the one mention of Quirinius. He has no intention of raising the question whether Quirinius was governor of Syria twice, and though Mommsen thinks he was, and though the Tivoli inscription seems clearly to prove that he was, although nobody else ever held the honour twice—the fact does not help our question, because his former governorship fell still too late for the time of Herod.

Apart from the chronological difficulty, the editors have imported into Luke 2² a difficulty of style. It is a law of Greek, as of all literary language, that a term used twice in two lines bears the same meaning in both places unless the contrary is plainly stated. Where, then, Luke says *enrolled . . . a (the) first enrolment*, it is hard to say what but perversity can maintain that *the enrolment* is not identical with the being *enrolled*. But to insert another enrolment between the two actions, that is before the enrolment here declared to be *the first*, is more than any scholar can justify. Had there been the smallest suspicion in Luke's mind that his writing was not even yet clear, he would doubtless have made it so, but he has shown us in Acts 5^{37} that he knew what he was writing about, for he there refers to *the days of the enrolment*, in which Judas the Galilean revolted. It is not contended that this was at a previous supposed enrolment; therefore *the enrolment* was a sufficient description there; therefore *the enrolment* would have been a sufficient description in Luke 2^2; therefore it is clear that Luke has added πρώτη, *first*, here, out of abundance of caution, so that nobody could mistake which enrolment he meant. Nevertheless, it seems his effort has been in vain. But harmonization, though as old as the second century, and correction of Luke by his own friends, though equally old,* are both in vain. For even if successful here, there are yet scores of passages where they cannot succeed. The gospel traditions are three, sometimes four, and though they cannot be harmonized they become increasingly interesting as three. The price of harmonization is the loss of the characteristic features, and the result of it is dulness and vagueness withal.

Herod the Ethnarch or the King.

It may be said that there is one overwhelming objection to this view of Luke's date—that he dates the birth of John *in the days of Herod the king*, and the Nativity follows shortly. But it would be a sufficient answer to say that though John's birth was announced in the days of Herod the Great, there was an interval of some nine

* Tertullian says Sentius Saturnius instead of Quirinius.

JOSEPH 145

years between the Baptist and the Lord. What objection is there? Only on the part of those who maintain that the Annunciation synchronized with the Conception. But this is not a necessary corollary even to the doctrine of the Virgin-birth. It by no means follows from Luke $1^{30\text{ff}}$. There seems to be nothing whatever in favour of it but tradition, and when it is seen that the tradition rests solely on the desire to harmonize, it must lose its evidential value. On the other hand, there is no serious objection to another explanation of *Herod the king of Judea*, one which would have the effect of reducing the great discrepancy of nine years between the ages—as meaning Herod Archelaus. Though he was not *de jure* king, though he did not coin money " of King Herod " as his father did, though he awaited Cæsar's pleasure, which never came, to enjoy the title dependent on his good conduct, and so was never more than ethnarch, yet his coins prove that he was called Herod, Josephus styles him king,* and he had been saluted king by the soldiers. Matt. 2^{22} also calls him king. Now in the first line of the Gospel we can hardly imagine how Luke, if he meant Archelaus, could begin by an over-refined accuracy *in the days of Herod the ethnarch*. It would have been only hair-splitting. The title ethnarch reminded the Jews of 5 B.C. of the great days of Simon the Maccabee, but by A.D. 5, after Archelaus had borne it for nine years, all the lustre was gone, and no more ethnarchs ever held sway in Judea. The associations, therefore, of *ethnarch* being of no account, what did the rule of style demand? Style is sometimes more than minute accuracy, and it would have been meticulous on Luke's part to call Archelaus anything but *Herod the king*. Thus Luke leaves us a choice for the date of John's birth between Herod

---

* δῆθεν δὲ ἔπρασσεν ὅμοια τῷ Ἡρώδῃ καὶ ὁ ἐπικατασταθεὶς αὐτῷ βασιλεὺς Ἀρχέλαος υἱὸς ὤν.—*Antt.*, 18, 4, 3. See Schürer, *Hist. J. P.*, § 16.

L

the Great and his son Archelaus; nor is it a matter of such great importance as the seniority of the Baptist to the Lord. The date of the Nativity is important, and it must be said, while leaving the question of chronology to those who are learned in the subject, that these pages are not written without a sense of responsibility for making the age of the Lord younger in his ministry than is traditionally supposed, but the only verse which causes the difficulty (Luke 3^{23}) is known to be of dubious reading, meaning and authority.

"*Jesus Himself when He began.*"

The reading of Westcott and Hort here is: *And Jesus himself when he began was about thirty years of age, being the son as was supposed of Joseph* . . . καὶ αὐτὸς ἦν ὁ 'Ι. ἀρχόμενος ὡσεὶ ἐτῶν τριάκοντα, ὢν υἱός, ὡς ἐνομίζετο, 'Ιωσήφ). [After *began* A.V. supplies *to be*, R.V. supplies *to teach*.] This reading has not satisfied the mind of Blass,* whose critical remarks are the more valuable that he entirely deprecates being considered a theologian. He points out that *when He began* is unintelligible, and that instead of it Clement and Irenæus (here in the Latin) about A.D. 190–200 read (ἐρχόμενος ἐπὶ τὸ βάπτισμα *cum veniret ad baptismum*) *coming to the baptism* (the latter, however, retaining ἀρχόμενος and reading *as it were beginning to be of thirty years when coming to the baptism;* this is obviously an attempt to combine Clement's reading with the Received, and is merely valuable as a witness to the former). Tatian (A.D. 170) also seems to have read and written *coming*. Moreover, the authorities which read *beginning* place it in various positions, and several omit it, while one cursive (700) which is often remarkably trustworthy, reads *coming* and omits *to the baptism*. While, therefore, the weight of authority may favour Westcott and

* Blass, *Evangelium S. Lucam*, praef. xxxviii.

Hort as editors following sound laws of evidence for edition, there is very much in favour of a special exception to those laws in this case, simply because the origin of the change of the single vowel is so easily seen. That Clement was correct in supplying *to the baptism* is a pure hypothesis; he simply overlooked the fact that *coming, he that cometh*, is a prophetic term of Messiah, which originates in—

> Mal. 3^1 Behold, *he cometh*, saith the Lord Almighty.
> *Cf.* Mal. 4^1 the day *that cometh*, saith the Lord Almighty.
> Hab. 2^3 For *he that cometh* shall come and shall not tarry (ὅτι ἐρχόμενος ἥξει).

This part of the argument was probably not present to Blass, who therefore has been content simply to place *coming* (ἐρχόμενος) within brackets in his text of Luke. This is a pity; for *He that cometh* is the vital point of Luke's sentence here.

And the remarkable thing is that *He that cometh* (ἐρχόμενος) has no article, just as (χριστός) *Messiah* has none. One is a title as much as the other. This text is only visible in LXX, the Hebrew having "though it (the vision) tarry, wait for it." And yet it is fully quoted in Heb. 10^{37} with the verse that follows it. It is therefore certain that ἐρχόμενος was present to some N.T. writers. Luke was fully aware of it as a technical term (Luke $7^{19\,f}$) and makes it part of the Baptist's disciples' message. But in order to see how much it impressed him, we must observe that it is also part of the Hosanna cry—

> Luke 19^{38} Blessed is *he that cometh*, the king, in the name of the Lord: peace in heaven, and glory in the highest. (R.V. is sadly misleading here.)

This passage shows the close kinship of the idea with that of *the king*. And we forthwith conclude that in Luke 3^{23} it is not far removed from a kingly meaning.

But first let us translate without the meaningless and awkward *beginning* which would require us to supply *to teach*, whereas we have not yet had any authority at all for *the teaching* of Jesus. How can we possibly tell that He is going to teach? Mark said that He taught, but Luke has never referred us to Mark, rather the reverse. "He shall baptize with fire;" yes: "I am not worthy to unloose his sandal;" yes, for He is a King. But it is not usual for a king to teach. Nor is baptism a necessary preliminary to teaching. There is no warrant for the expectation at this point that He would teach, and there can be no warrant to supply the words *to teach* after *beginning*. What, then, is to be supplied? Can we find another translation?

The translation *beginning to be about thirty* has long ago been rejected by scholars. Therefore there is no meaning to be attached to this reading. There is great meaning to be attached to *The Coming One*, but it was slightly obscure to Clement, and he, while preserving for us unconsciously the ancient and true reading, has put a wrong gloss upon it by adding *to the baptism*. We therefore get *Now Jesus himself was The Coming One*. And the meaning is that the Baptist had hitherto been the only person visible to the world as either *the Coming One* or *the Messenger* before His face (Mal. 3^1). Henceforward it was declared that John was the Messenger and Jesus the Coming One. This was by no means clear to the people, least of all to the disciples of John, and Luke does not say that it was, but he mentions the vital fact in closing the baptismal declaration in the words of Ps. 2^7, "Thou art my son, this day have I begotten thee."

The evidence for the reading just quoted, in the actual words of the psalm, is very equally balanced according to Hort, though he does not say so. Blass accepts it, and

JOSEPH

rightly says that the fact of Gnostic heretics asserting that the Sonship dated from the baptism is a strong evidence for it. Whence could they have derived their tenet except from the reading *to-day*, which they did not obtain from Mark, Matthew, John, and must therefore have found it in Luke? Justin's testimony in favour of it—he quotes it twice—is peculiarly strong because he would have been careful not to give a handle to Cerinthian and Valentinian doctrine * by a false reading of this verse. On the other hand, those who came after him might be glad to escape from the reading *to-day have I begotten thee*, by means of a paraphrase. Justin quite boldly says, " The Father asserts that His birth took place for men at the moment of their knowledge (γνῶσις) of Him."

We now pass on to the next words, *as it were of thirty years, being the son* . . . Bearing in mind the fact that *he that cometh, the Coming One* is closely connected with *the king* in Luke 19^{38}, we see, of course, that this is the fulfilment of David. Just in the same way we have seen that Luke 2^7 declared *her son, the Firstborn* (not merely *her firstborn son*) in fulfilment of Ps. 89^{27}, " I will make him my Firstborn." And " Blessed is *he that cometh* in the name of the Lord " is directly quoted from Ps. 118^{26}, which is made Davidic by the insertion of *the king*. So that, whereas it has been usual to connect the age of thirty with the legal age of the Levites' ministry in Num. 4 (in the LXX this is twenty-five, not thirty), it should be rather considered whether there is anything whatever in Luke to connect Jesus with the Levites; whether it is not more true to say with Heb. 7^{14} that it is palpable that our Lord hath sprung out of Judah—a tribe which hath nothing to do with priests in what Moses said; whether instead of the

* Lightfoot, *Col.*, 1879, p. 264.

150 ORACLES IN THE NEW TESTAMENT

Levites' age Luke is not thinking of David's age; and whether, in fact, the statement which he considers fulfilled is not rather—

2 Sam. 5³ᶠ They anoint David before all Israel. David was *a son of thirty years* when he began to reign.

This seems to represent the train of thought in Luke's mind. But instead of *son of thirty years being the son* (υἱὸς ἐτῶν τριάκοντα, ὢν υἱός) which occurs only in the Syriac MSS., where it represents their native idiom, we have *as of years* (ὡσεὶ ἐτῶν). It is worth while to consider what the late F. Blass, a Greek scholar of almost unrivalled knowledge, has written on this verse. Blass thinks that there was, however, in Greek originally the double *son*, and, being misunderstood, this caused the trouble: but as the idiom *a son of* = *aged* occurs nowhere in the New Testament, he does not uphold it. Yet how easily it would drop out if it were once there (ερχομενοςῡςωςειετων)! However, he decides first to bracket *coming* (ἐρχόμενος), which does not appeal to him on the ground of prophecy— a subject which he generally ignores: and then to read *as of thirty years as was supposed son of Joseph* (ὡς ἐτῶν τριάκοντα ὡς ἐνομίζετο υἱὸς Ἰωσήφ), omitting (ὢν) *being*, as a later addition to help the sentence out. He has, however, not observed the force of *as* (ὡσεί, ὡς), which is particularly used when a prophecy is marked as fulfilled * in the New Testament. For instance, "tongues *as of* fire" at Pentecost, means tongues that were not of fire but fulfilled the prophecy with a close enough resemblance to fire; and certainly the meaning cannot be the same as if the *as* had not been mentioned. So here *as of thirty years* means that He was near enough to that age to fulfil the prophecy of David. An approximate age over twenty would fulfil it. Blass further thinks that *as*

* *St. Luke the Prophet*, 301.

JOSEPH

was supposed was meant by Luke to apply both to what precedes—the age—and to what follows—the descent, " for Luke must needs have learnt from Paul that Christ really had existed from all eternity."

But, as we have seen, there is no necessity to apply *as was supposed* to the age, because the ὡσεί, *as it were*, already sufficiently expresses the same meaning, when rightly understood. Therefore we are free to make *as was supposed* to apply to the descent from Joseph only. After this we are free to consider it merely as part of the pedigree. But what we do want is *son of David* (τοῦ Δ.), which is a fact embodied, but also embedded, very deeply in the pedigree. This alone answers the implied question (from Luke 3[15]) *whether John were himself the Christ*. On the other hand, the relationship to Joseph is not in question throughout the whole chapter. The pedigree, therefore, is an afterthought, if not also an interpolation.

Thus I venture to claim that the writing of Luke was καὶ αὐτὸς ἦν Ἰησοῦς ἐρχόμενος, υἱὸς ὡσεὶ ἐτῶν τριάκοντα τοῦ Δαυείδ, and all the pedigree is a later addition. *Τοῦ Δ.* is needed to justify καὶ αὐτός. Translate: "And [so] Jesus himself [not John] was He that cometh, being as it were thirty years of age [like David] [when he began to reign], [the son] of David."

If the above considerations are just—and they involve no violence to the text or to the interpretation—the verse in question allows a great liberty to the age of Jesus at the Baptism. That Luke had so learned it and held it is beyond all doubt, especially for those who translate *her son the Firstborn* correctly. Luke held the Eternal generation of the Son, but not the Virgin-birth in the modern sense of the term. He found support for it in

Ps. 89[4] Unto eternity (ἕως τοῦ αἰῶνος) I will prepare thy seed.

Ps. 89[36] His seed shall endure for ever (εἰς τὸν αἰῶνα).

152 ORACLES IN THE NEW TESTAMENT

The chronology of the life of Jesus is almost always based on the supposition that the Baptist was six months older than Jesus, and this rests upon the idea that the Annunciation synchronizes with the Conception. But this idea is not by any means certain, it is not more than antecedently probable. The probability is ready to vanish in the presence of tangible considerations. And so far as Old Testament precedents are concerned, there is nothing to show that the annunciations to Manoah's wife and to Hannah were simultaneous with conception. Again, everything seems to show that the Baptist died six months before Jesus. This provides a striking coincidence, if John was six months older than Jesus, that they were of precisely the same age at death. But it also suggests the possibility that many persons reasoned backward from the times of their death to those of their birth, and fancied that Luke recorded the Annunciation accordingly.

Again assuming that the one date which Luke precisely marks by several concurrent computations is correct, as we are fully entitled to do—the date of the preaching of John (Luke $3^{1\,f}$), is it reasonable to suppose that no time is to be allowed for the growth of John's influence before he declares Jesus as the Christ? Let the preaching be A.D. 29. The date of John's death is not driven by the proceedings of Antipas to fall in the same year, nor by inference therefrom is the Crucifixion driven to A.D. 30. The most commonly received chronology really does not allow time for John to have gathered such a following as Josephus implies that he had (see Ch. VII.), nor for the strength of his condemnation of Antipas' conduct, nor for John's prolonged imprisonment as the Gospels represent it, nor for the exceedingly wide diffusion, implying great numbers, of the adherents of John's baptism which Luke attests (Acts 19^3). Luke, therefore, cannot mean to imply that the ministry of John ended almost as soon as it

JOSEPH 153

began. Its actual duration, whatever it was, permitted Luke to allow a later relative date for the ministry of Jesus, as well as a younger age at His ministry than is commonly supposed.

Among minor considerations of chronology, the expression "forty and six years was this temple in building" (John 2^{20}), is really of no primary or particular value.* But one fact must here be urged, that when Luke 2^1 opens the account of the Nativity by saying, "Now it came to pass *in those days* that there went forth a decree," he does not mean to refer the reader to 1^5, but rather to the verse which has immediately preceded (1^{80}). "And the child grew and waxed strong in spirit, and was in the deserts *till the day* of his showing unto Israel." This *day* must imply numbers of *days*, and Luke has reserved a large margin of *these days* in which the Nativity might occur. Nothing but the powerful presupposition of harmony of Luke with Matthew has induced so many writers to make the Nativity occur six months precisely after John's birth in Luke's account.

The Building of the House.

Let us now approach the passage (Luke 2^1) concerning the enrolment under P. Sulpicius Quirinius, from the prophetic side of the question, which has not been treated at all, and on this side we shall find that there are facts which claim attention from learned and unlearned alike. The prophet Isaiah must be heard upon the subject, and also Ezra the scribe. We may begin by referring to the great idea of the Christian Church as the building of the house

* The authorities on the chronology of the New Testament can be seen in Moffatt's *Historical N. T.*, the *Bible Dictionary* and Schürer. But Keim, who places the apprehension of John as late as A.D. 34, is an authority nearly always worth considering. In dating the crucifixion A.D. 36 he has a few supporters. The chronology is still very far indeed from settlement,

of God—an idea which the apostles * have made familiar to us, following the announcement in the Book of Enoch, " Then shall the House of the Great King be builded in glory for evermore." Here are only a few of the very many passages which show that the common word " edify " would never have existed without this great and leading thought. Eph. 2^{19}, " Ye are of the household of God, being built upon the foundation of the apostles and prophets, Messiah Jesus himself being the chief corner-stone, in whom the whole building groweth unto a holy sanctuary, in whom ye also are being built up together for an habitation of God in the spirit." 1 Pet. 2^5, " Unto whom coming, a living stone, rejected indeed of men, but with God elect, precious, ye also as living stones, are being built up a spiritual house for a holy priesthood, to offer up spiritual sacrifices, acceptable to God through Jesus Messiah. Because it is contained in scripture—

> Isa. 28^{16} Behold I lay in Sion a chief corner-stone elect, precious, and he that believeth on him shall not be put to shame. . . ."

Jude ^{20} " Ye building up yourselves on your most holy faith." Acts 4^{22} " He is—

> Ps. 118^{22} The stone which was set at nought of (you) the builders, (which) was made the head of the corner."

The *edification* of the House of the Great King and the members of it is one of the most prolific images of the New Testament, including the Sermon on the Mount (Matt. $7^{24\,\text{ff}}$). And yet it was, of course, a great Restoration, a putting-back (and very much more) of a house that had been before.†

------
* *St. Luke the Prophet*, pp. 128, 141^{ff} 187.   " House of the Great King," Index.

† For the Restoration of paradise, the first Adam, etc., see *St. Luke the Prophet*, p. 137 ^{ff}.

JOSEPH

The Restoration was the first duty and work of Elijah: who " shall first come and *restore* all things." The words are not in Luke, but he had read them in Mark, and he determined to preface his Gospel, as Mark had not, with the parallels of prophecy from the first (παρηκολουθηκότι ἄνωθεν) concerning Elijah's coming into the world. This he has done in 1$^{5-80}$. But the restorer's birth must be followed by its sequel, and, without further preface, we are brought to the restoration of the house of David. In the very psalm which declares the Firstborn we read—

> Ps. 89^4 I sware unto David my servant, unto everlasting I will prepare thy seed, and will *build up* (οἰκοδομήσω) thy throne unto all generations.

Consequently we revert to our sources, and we read concerning the House of God which was restored—

> Ezra 5^2 Then arose Zorobabel [son] of Salathiel, and *Jesus*, son of Josedek, and *began to build the house of God* that is in Jerusalem, *and with them the prophets of God helping them.*

It was, and it is, very remarkable how history repeats itself in some ways. For here were the prophets of God helping another *Jesus*, son of Joseph, to build the house of God. A few verses later the letter of Tatnai to Darius says—

> Ezra 5^8 The house is being built *with elect* stones, and wood is being laid in the walls. . . . And a great king of Israel built it. . . . But in the first year of *Cyrus* the king, *Cyrus* the king took counsel that this house of God should be built (or, edified).

Cyrus, Cyrius, Cyrinus.

Previously we have read how—

> Ezra 1$^{1\,\text{ff}}$ In the first year of Cyrus king of Persia, that

it might be fulfilled which was spoken by Jeremiah, the Lord stirred up the spirit of Cyrus, King of Persia, and he made proclamation in all his kingdom *and put it also in writing*, saying, Thus saith Cyrus, King of Persia, All the kingdoms hath the God of heaven given me, and he hath charged me to build him an house in Jerusalem in Judah.

So far Cyrus, King of Persia, speaks as if he were conscious of the divine will and himself a servant of God. And the same idea comes out more strongly still in—

Isa. $45^{1\,\text{ff}}$ Thus saith the Lord God *to my Christ* (or, anointed) *Cyrus*, whose right hand I have holden, that the nations should hearken before him, and I will burst the strength of kings, I will open doors before him, and cities shall not be shut. I will go before thee and will level mountains, I will shatter brazen doors, and break iron bars in pieces, and I will give thee treasures, dark, hidden, unseen [treasures] will I open for thee, that thou mayest know that I am the Lord thy God, who call thy name, the God of Israel.

Perhaps no better instance than this can be found of the gross ignorance of history which marked the first century of Christian writers. Barnabas (12) quotes this as "The Lord said to my Christ Lord (τῷ χριστῷ μου κυρίῳ)," to show how David calls him Lord and does not call him Son, and how Isaiah supports him in doing so, as if there were no question of *Cyrus* and never had been! Barnabas is blindly followed by Tertullian (*Prax.* 11, 28, *Jud.* 7), and by Cyprian (*Test.* 1^{21}), and by Novatian (*Trin.* 21). After this catena of carelessness we are still rather surprised at the audacity of Gregory of Nyssa, who, after giving the reading Κύρῳ (Cyrus), proceeds to say that " some take it of Cyrus, the Persian, but *this is*

JOSEPH

ridiculous, for how do the following words suit Cyrus?"*

And what follows is still more remarkable, both for what it says and what it denies.

> *For the sake of my child* (παιδὸς) Jacob and *Israel who is my elect I will call thee by my name* and will receive thee : but thou knowest me not. For I am the Lord God, and there is none beside me : I girded thee with strength, and thou knewest me not, that they may know from the rising of the sun and from the west that there is none beside me.

So the Anointed One, Cyrus, is, after all, not conscious of God who anointed him—he remains a heathen. But what could be clearer than this, that Cyrus (Κῦρος) is, in some sense, the Christ of God, and that God *will call*, or has called, *him by his name* (Κύριος) *for the sake of His Child*, the Lord Christ (Κύριος χριστός)? So it must inevitably have been understood by the apostles. The whole of this point is lost in the Hebrew, which says : " I have titled thee by *thy* name " : or rather, the point is wholly made by the Greek Bible, owing to the fact that Κῦρος nearly = Κύριος, while Koresh has no relation to (Messiah) Māshiākh. Again, the mention of *my child* takes us back to Isa. 9, 10, 11, etc., while the Hebrew has only *Jacob my servant*, meaning the Jewish people.

But if the name Cyrus is to be considered as bestowed by the divine purpose in imitation of the divine name, the inference is neither untrue nor unimportant that when the first syllable of the name appears in another name, in connection with the same great object, the building of the house of God at Jerusalem, this also is part of the divine purpose. For what else is Cyrinus (Κυρῖνος) but a sort of lesser Cyrus? (The spelling is now given as

---

* See Hilgenfeld, *Barn.*, p. 113.

158 ORACLES IN THE NEW TESTAMENT

Κυρήνιος, Κυρεῖνος, but there is good authority for *Κυρῖνος* being the actual spelling in Luke 1² by St. Luke. The officer's true name is Publius Sulpicius Quirinius.)

Now Cyrinus is the diminutive or, at least, derivative from Cyrius (*Κύριος*), not from Cyrus, as Saturninus from Saturnius, Antoninus from Antonius, Flamininus from Flaminius. But the names in -ius are themselves derivatives from earlier names which are usually obvious enough, Saturnius from Saturnus, Flaminius from Flamen, Antonius from Antius, and that probably from Ancus (servant of Mars), like Pomponius from Pompeius from Pomptius, Pontius, from Pomptus *Πέμπτος* (fifth son). Therefore the direct and natural succession of names, to speak purely etymologically, is Cyrus (*Κῦρος*), Cyrius (*Κύριος*), Cyrinus (*Κυρῖνος, Κυρεῖνος*) which the Luke MSS. give us. Josephus, on the other hand, knowing nothing about the prophetic association of the name, has given it as *Κυρήνιος* (Cyrenius). Yet the Roman spelling, in Tacitus and in the inscription from Beyrout,* is Quirinius, which Josephus ought to have spelt as Strabo spells it, *Κυρίνιος* (Cyrinius). But Josephus probably did not know that Quirinius had been praetor-proconsul at Cyprus and Cyrene, and that while there, in what was usually a sinecure billet, he had been called upon to repulse and conquer, with a mere handful of troops, or with a force hurriedly gathered from Egypt, the two "hinterland" tribes of the Marmaridæ and Garamantes. This is what Mommsen thinks, but he does not suggest that conceivably the cognomen *Cyrenius* (as spelt by Josephus) might have been assumed from this exploit. P. Sulpicius was a smart soldier and active administrator (*impiger militiæ et acribus ministeriis*, Tac. *Ann*. 3⁴⁸). The chief objection is that the name, if drawn from Cyrene, would

* Mommsen, *Res Gestae divi Aug.*, p. 166, has worked out this subject fully, but without reference to the spelling.

JOSEPH 159

then have been probably *Cyrenæus* (Κυρηναῖος) : for he would not have taken *Cyrenaicus* (Κυρηναϊκός), which was already appropriated by the school of philosophy. However, this stout Latin soldier, born at Lanuvium, may very well have chosen a name that, while truly Latin or Samnite, going back to Romulus Quirinus, would yet serve to remind his friends of his successful brush with the African natives, in *Quirinius*. Some ten years after this he conquered the utterly impregnable tribe, as they were considered to be, the Homonadenses,* a hill-tribe in Pisidia, and was awarded the honours of a triumph and two days of thanksgiving. In taking 4000 men of them alive and settling them in cities he imitated the historical clemency of Cyrus. Four years later still he is *rector* to C. Cæsar.

Cyrinus' Antecedents.

Had, then, Cyrinus nothing to do with the building of the house of God ? He was very much the cause of it in St. Luke's mind, for it was he who conducted the census for Augustus Cæsar—in whatever capacity or by whatever influence and at whatever time—and the census was the occasion of the birth of *the Christ Lord* (Χριστὸς Κύριος, Luke 2^{22}) in the city of David. So much is the difference of one Greek letter.

But, on the other hand, there was, strange to say, an historical parallelism between Cyrinus and Cyrus. For P. Sulpicius Quirinius had come from the old Persian kingdom to rule Syria. He had been sent out at an extreme and most difficult crisis, and was appointed *rector* or aide-de-camp to C. Cæsar, the grandson of Augustus, who, at the age of nineteen, was sent to win his spurs by pacifying the troubled land of Armenia. He needed, as we can well understand, the help of one of the most

* Strabo, xii. 569.

eminent military men of Rome, and this he received, first in the experience of M. Lollius and, after his death, in his successor the consular Sulpicius (consul 12 B.C., d. A.D. 21). The young Cæsar was wounded and died on his way home in Lycia (Feb. A.D. 4). But, before he left his responsible post, Cyrinus had set up a Median as king of Armenia, and this Roman *rector* of a Roman prince, who could achieve wonders in Persia, might appear to have had the mantle of Cyrus resting on him. Considering there had been a general state of peace all round the Mediterranean coasts for thirty years, P. Sulpicius Quirinius had managed to see very much military service, gaining conspicuous success, and the prestige of his name was considerable. He had, in the words of Isa. 45^1, made *the nations hearken before him*, he *had burst the strength of kings*, he *had opened out cities*, and by conquering mountain tribes had practically *levelled mountains*. When, then, this keen soldier and active administrator took in hand the enrolment of property and population in Judæa in A.D. 6, the event would recall the similar action of Cyrus, who made proclamation and *put it also in writing* that he was charged *to build the house of God* in Jerusalem, and yet meanwhile *knew not the Lord* God though actually called by His Name. Such a combination of paradoxes was now in a wonderful way repeated, and was repeated, too, by one of nearly the same name.

These considerations supply the chief, if not the sole, reason why Luke mentioned the name of Cyrinus. Had he merely said *at the time of the first enrolment*, his friend Theophilus would probably have been able to supply the name of the governor of that as of the other enrolments that fell within his memory. But the associations of the name were the important matters, and these were more likely to be awakened by the mention of it, and to become a theme of commentary.

JOSEPH

It seems, too, as if an answer can now be provided to some questions that are put by both parties in the controversy. Ramsay asks, after concluding his argument,* which in the later part is very much more convincing than in the earlier : " But why did Luke not name Varus, the ordinary governor, in place of dating by the extraordinary officer? If he had had regard to the susceptibilities of modern scholars, and the extreme dearth of knowledge about the period, which was to exist eighteen hundred years after he wrote, he would certainly have named Varus. But he was writing for readers who could as easily find out about Quirinius as about Varus, and he had no regard for us of the nineteenth century. Quirinius ruled for a shorter time than Varus, and he controlled the foreign relations of the province, hence he furnished the best means of dating."

Now, it is just the last sentence which is not quite satisfying. The foreign relations of Syria never enter into the New Testament. They have nothing to do with the Gospels or the readers of them. Or, if foreign relations were really needed to mark the period of time, a single mention of Varus would have sufficed. For the reader of early times could never forget that in the next three years Varus perished with his legions in the overwhelming defeat by Arminius near the Teutoburger Wald. This was the Calais of the aged emperor Augustus. What we do want is the internal relations, if we are to have any names of governors at all, if only Herods and Pilate. If Luke were a historian he would not drag in *the foreign relations* where there were no relevant foreign affairs. But even if he did, *the foreign relations* of the Homonadenses were nothing at all—a mere hill-tribe of Taurus—dangerous and troublesome to wayfarers, roadmakers, and neighbours, but not invaders, hardly marauders. As Ramsay

* *Was Christ Born at Bethlehem?*

points out, Quirinius as *legatus Divi Augusti Syriam obtinuit*—he was therefore *dux*,* as Vespasian was while Mucianus was governor of Syria. As *dux* Quirinius would be called ἡγεμών, as Luke calls him. But this does not explain why he, and not Varus, is mentioned in connection with the enrolment, with which Varus had to do and Quirinius nothing to do. The explanation must therefore be found in the associations of the name of Quirinius as seen in some other light, the light of prophecy.

The same question, in other words, has been asked from the opposite side to Ramsay, by Gardner : † " Why should a census in Judea be dated by Luke by the irrelevant fact of a campaign being at the time fought by Quirinius in Cilicia ? " When he further asks : " Even if an enrolment by tribes was carried out by Herod, would this be likely to involve a journey of all Jews to the native town of their family ? " The answer must be that, though unlikely, it is possible that there might have been some reason why the conscientious and scrupulous Joseph should have decided to go to Bethlehem. But when, finally, he asks : " How could the presence of Mary be required at Bethlehem, when it was a settled principle of all ancient law to treat the male head of a family as responsible for all its members ? " there is no answer provided so far by history, and the only answer provided by prophecy is akin to that given above.

Questions for Luke as a Historian.

It is an instance of Luke having followed carefully the parallels of prophecy and history, as he professes in his preface to have done. It is not a proof of his being a

---

* Tac., *Hist.* I¹⁰. *Syriam* et quattuor legiones *obtinebat Licinius Mucianus*. . . . Bellum Judaicum Flavius *Vespasianus* (*ducem* eum Nero *delegerat*) tribus legionibus administrabat.

† *Enc. Bib.*, Art. "Quirinius," 3996.

JOSEPH

historian. An artistic biographer he might be called, but the scientific historian has a totally different function.

However, without pursuing the question further, we may survey with advantage the conclusions which Schürer has reached on the question of the enrolment, and endeavour to find out what light is thrown upon the principal questions raised by Luke in connection with them. We have surrendered the claim for Luke to be a historian, as a claim that he never made, and we have also surrendered the hope of harmonizing him with Matthew, because Luke was not written in view of Matthew, whose subsequent writing Luke did not anticipate, and the divergences of the two are incessant. But perhaps in doing so we have avoided a mass of unnecessary difficulties and found a way of understanding Luke better than before. Had Luke given us any information concerning the character and antecedents of Joseph, for instance, he would have made the task easier for us. Three times he calls Joseph * the "father" of Jesus, and therefore his reticence about him is hardly consistent with the duty of a biographer—not that he professed to be such, though he comes nearer to the biographer than to the historian. One question that must certainly be asked is why Joseph came to leave Nazareth in order to be enrolled at Bethlehem-Judah. According to our proposed interpretation of Luke 2 he came for the purpose of the first enrolment, which is at least intelligible; according to the generally accepted view he came for a previous enrolment or sort of enrolment which was not effective but preliminary—a sort of false start, a sort of echo of what happened in Syria or in Egypt, so that it was certainly not "the first enrolment"; and that is not intelligible. The main point to be remembered is that Cæsar Augustus held a census of *Roman citizens* but not

* Luke $2^{33, 48}$, 4^{23}. The first of these passages by itself proves that Luke did not hold the virgin-birth.

of population, and it is not contended that Joseph was a Roman citizen.

But the whole question has been treated in an ample and masterly way by Schürer,* whose pages ought to be studied for the necessary historical information. He has laid down the following conclusions—

(1) Of a general imperial census in the time of Augustus history otherwise knows nothing.
(2) (a) Under a Roman census Joseph would not have been obliged to travel to Bethlehem, and (b) Mary would not have been required to accompany him thither.
(3) A Roman census could not have been made in Palestine in the time of King Herod.
(4) Josephus knows nothing of a Roman census in Palestine in the time of Herod, and speaks rather of the census of A.D. 6–7 as something new and previously unheard of.
(5) A census under Quirinius could not have taken place in the time of Herod, for Quirinius was never governor of Syria during Herod's lifetime.

These theses can hardly be shaken, in view of the very considerable knowledge on the part of historians concerning the early Roman Empire. The theory that a census was held in Syria by the Roman governor in 9–8 B.C. and that Herod then proposed a census for Palestine which was postponed and not carried out till A.D. 6–7 and then carried out on a different plan from the Roman census, is one that assumes too much and imports too many unnecessary difficulties to be seriously entertained. The argument from the analogy of a Roman census in Egypt or in Syria breaks down just because they were Roman

---

* *Hist. of Jewish People*, § 17. See also *Enc. Biblica*, articles on "Joseph," "Nazareth," "Quirinius," etc.

provinces, while Palestine was not. Herod, as an allied king, was dependent on Rome for permission to declare war and to execute his son, but not to remit or impose taxes. Even if he paid tribute to Rome, and there is no proof that he did, he was unrestricted in his own taxation.

But with these few and scanty observations—to add to them would prolong a discussion which would in any case be most effectually based upon Schürer and his authorities —the historical question must here be left in order to see what light is thrown by Luke's study of prophecy. With regard to (1) it will appear that so far as a *general* imperial census depends on " the whole world should be enrolled " this expression of Luke can be understood. With regard to (2a) we also discover something, but not as to (2b). (3) is beyond us. As to (4) Josephus confirms Luke entirely in saying that the Quirinian enrolment was *the first* in the only sense of the word. As to (5) Quirinius has been considered above.

Some Questions answered by Luke the Prophet.

Let us first take, to illustrate (1), the oracle—

> Isa. 10$^{19\,ff}$ And they that are left as a remnant from them (the Assyrians) shall be a cipher and [*the*] *little child shall write them*. And it shall be in that day that the remnant Israel shall no more *have to be added*, and they that are saved of Jacob shall no more trust in them that injured them, but they shall trust on God the holy one of Israel in truth. And there shall be the remnant of Jacob [trusting] in God in his strength. And [even] if the people of Israel become as the sand of the sea, [only] the remnant of them shall be saved: completing and cutting short an account in righteousness, for *a short account* will the Lord make *in the whole world*.

This shows rather that the period of Assyrian oppression under the Herods is over, and, so far, points to the time when the Jews obtained their prayer to Cæsar of nine years before, to be delivered from the wild beast of a Herod and placed under the administration of Roman praetors. On the other hand, the application of the prophecy to the end of Herod's tyranny, before Archelaus gave the Jews a taste of his own, is also possible. That *the little Child shall write them* (παιδίον γράψει αὐτούς) would be taken of the Nativity is certain. The word (προστεθήσεται) *have to be added* is virtually a translation of the name *Joseph*. So we might translate " the remnant shall no more be Joseph but be called after Jesus the Christ." *A short account* (λόγον συντετμημένον) suggests a list or catalogue (κατάλογον, for which LXX uses καταλογισμόν, —ίαν) or register such as enrolment implies. And, finally, *in the whole world* (ἐν τῇ οἰκουμένῃ ὅλῃ) seems to have provided Luke 2¹ with the expression (πᾶσαν τὴν οἰκουμένην) *all the world*, which has been found so troublesome.

Then we come to the question, (2) What induced Joseph to go up? on which one or two considerations can be offered from the side of the oracles. The somewhat tangled prophecy must be quoted from—

Isa. 9¹ *Make* this first, make quickly, O country of Zabulun, the land of Nephthalim, a sea-way : and [ye] the rest who inhabit the sea-coast and beyond Jordan, Galilee of the Gentiles—*the parts of Judea*. Ye people that sit (*or*, walk) in darkness, behold a great light . . . .

The Hebrew original is obscure and the Greek version not less so, while totally different from it. The first word, *Make*, is actually given by most MSS. as *Drink*, but it may be asserted with confidence that this is nothing but an early copyist's error (πίε for ποίει). Much depends on what verb is supplied before the conclusion—*the parts of Judea.* From the first part of the sentence, *make a sea-way,* it seems probable that we ought to supply *make a way to, go and inhabit,* the parts of Judea. The sea-coast refers to Gennesaret as naturally as not. In spite of the obscurity of sense, the effect is that dwellers in Zabulun, like Joseph of Nazareth, should turn their eyes towards the parts of Judea. It would be vain to distinguish between what Joseph would think and what Luke would attribute to him : the latter alone is recoverable, or may be. For Luke saw that this passage followed close upon the rout of the Assyrian (Isa. $7^{10\,ff}$), while it immediately precedes the oracle of the Nativity. Its position in Isaiah therefore guarantees its significance as an oracle.

The Rod from the Root of Jesse.

In confirmation of this opinion there is an adjacent text which has been combined with this, and which was certainly used as an oracle, in connection with Joseph.

> Isa. 11^1 And there shall come forth a rod from the root of Jesse, and a flower shall go up from the root. (Contrast 9^4, the rod [that was] upon their neck.) And * the Spirit of God shall rest upon him. . . .

This is a case where the use of an Old Testament passage can be conjectured from its later use in the Apocryphal Gospels. The Gospel of James (8) says, " And behold the angel of the Lord stood by, saying unto Zacharias, Zacharias, go forth and summon the widowers of the people, and let them take a rod apiece, and she (Mary) shall be the wife of him to whom the Lord shall show a sign. And the criers went out through all the region

* Dr. Abbott sees in this the origin of the Dove in the Baptism, [705].

round about Judea, and the trumpet of the Lord sounded and all ran together. Now Joseph cast down his axe and went out to meet them. And having assembled, they went away to the high priest, taking the rods; and he received the rods of all, and entered into the holy place and prayed; and when he had finished praying he took the rods and went out and delivered them to them; and there was no sign among them. But Joseph received the last rod, and behold a dove went out of the rod and flew upon the head of Joseph." The dove is explained by another form of the story in the *Nativity of Mary*: "While they all bowed down in prayer the chief priest went to consult God according to custom, nor was there any delay: for in the hearing of all there came a voice from the oracle and the place of the mercy-seat, that according to the prophecy of Isaiah inquiry must be made, to whom the virgin ought to be commended and espoused. For it is clear that Isaiah saith, *A rod*, etc. Thus he foretold that all of the house and family of David who were fit to be married but not married should bring their rods to the altar; and he whose rod when brought should *produce a flower*, while on its top the Spirit of the Lord sat in the form of a dove, was the man. Now among others was Joseph, an aged man . . ." The flower is here combined with the dove. In the *Sposalizio* at Milan, Raffaelle has represented the rod of Joseph sprouting into a lily at the top: but I have not discovered the dove in it. The disappointed suitor breaking his rod in the foreground is based upon—

Isa. 9^4 He hath shattered the rod of the suitors * (τῶν ἀπαιτούντων).

So that we have the four stages, first of Isa. 11^1, the

* This use of ἀπαιτῆσαι occurs in Judith 12^{16}, if the reading is correct.

flower; next of the *Nativity*, the flower and the dove; next of James, the dove only; lastly of Pseudo-Matthew, where the dove, instead of coming from heaven and perching, "*passed out from the top* of the rod, whiter than snow, very beautiful and, fluttering long among the temple pinnacles, *flew to the heavens.*" The stories, which are record-breaking in their own thaumaturgy, still betray the remnant of an idea of the oracles of God, but it has become hardened into the pagan notion of consulting the oracle.

The general basis of the story of the choice of Joseph by " the high priest Abiathar," as related in these Apocryphal books, is to be seen in Num. $17^{2\,ff}$—

> Speak unto the children of Israel, and take of them rods, one for each father's house, of all their princes according to their father's houses, twelve rods: *write* thou every man's name upon his rod . . . And thou shalt lay them up in the tent of meeting before the testimony, where I will meet with you. And it shall come to pass that the man whom I will choose, his rod shall bud.

(The brief and meaningless version of the story contained in *Joseph the Carpenter* happens to preserve a feature of this testimony to Aaron : " they *wrote the names* of the twelve tribes of Israel," though they had already gathered twelve aged men of the tribe of *Judah.* " Now the lot fell upon the pious old man Joseph the just.") A comparison of the scripture oracles seems to point to the idea that the " rod of Jesse " should have some name or names written upon it. Should they not be those of Joseph and Mary or the former alone ? If written, should they not be *written* by the Lord in the form of *the little child ?* The next passage will throw a further ray of light.

Ezek. $37^{19\,ff}$ Thus saith the Lord, Behold, I will take the *tribe of Joseph* through the hand of Ephraim, and the tribes of Israel which lie over against him, and I will put them to the tribe of Judah, and they shall be *one rod* for the hand of Judah. And the rods upon which thou wrotest (one "*Judah*," the other "*for Joseph*" 37[16]) shall be in thy hand in their presence, and thou shalt say unto them, Thus saith my Lord the Lord, Behold, I take *every* house of Israel out of *all the nations* where they have entered, and will gather them from all them that are round about them, and will bring them into the land of Israel, and I will make them to be one nation in my land and in *the mountains* (ὄρεσιν) of Israel, and one ruler shall there be of them . . . and *my servant David* (shall be) ruler in the midst of them; there shall be one shepherd of all.

Taken as a scripture this text simply declares in parable the union of Israel and Judah. But treated as an oracle, as St. Luke treated it, it speaks of the tribe of Joseph, meaning the tribe to which Joseph belongs. This, by hypothesis, was Judah, for Joseph was the father of Jesus of the house of David. The royal descent is through Joseph entirely: in Scripture there is no attempt to show that Mary was of the royal house. Therefore those of the tribe of Judah who were *left* living in Galilee were transported, in the evangelist's mind, *through the tribe of Ephraim* to the territory of Judah *in the hill country* (ὀρινή, Luke 1[39-65]), and placed there they become an access of strength to Judah. The same applied to the members of other tribes over against them, Issachar, Naphtali, Zabulon, etc. *Every* house of Israel was to be brought out of *all the nations*, for *Galilee of the nations* was so called because of the number of Gentiles included in its borders. This perhaps may serve to explain why Luke 2[3] has said

JOSEPH

that "*all* went to enrol themselves, every one to his own city." Then in the mountains of Israel *my servant David* was to be born, to unite them under *his shepherd's* sway together. For—

Isa. 9^7 Great is his rule, and of his peace there is no bound.

Thus if we revert to Isa. 10^{19}, *The little child shall write them* seems to mean that the birth of the Child, who is to be *my servant David*, shall be the cause, the final cause, of the enrolment or writing of Joseph and Mary at Bethlehem. The *rod of the root of Jesse* has actually become the *rod of Joseph*, "*for Joseph*" being written upon it (by the hand of the prophet) by the Lord, who further promises that His servant David shall rule over them in the mountains of Israel, to which Joseph, with others, is to repair.

Nazareth and Nazarene.

That Joseph *went up from the city of Nazareth* and belonged to it can hardly be considered one of the data of the Gospels. Matthew, who (4^{15}) quotes Isa. 9^1 from *the oracles*, that is with variations from Hebrew and from LXX, applies it to Jesus' leaving Nazareth. But then Matthew has never said that Joseph was a native of Nazareth; he is only a settler there after leaving Egypt, and in fact Matthew implies he was not a native (*a city called* Nazareth, εἰς πόλιν λεγομένην N. ὅπως πληρωθῇ, Matt. 2^{23}). We read also in Matt. 4^{12} "Now when he heard that John was delivered up he withdrew into Galilee. And leaving Nazareth he came and *dwelt* in Capernaum which is by the sea (τὴν παραθαλασσίαν) in the borders of Zabulon and Naphtali; that it might be fulfilled . . . ."

Dr Cheyne * has raised the question whether Nazareth

* *Enc. Bib.*, " Nazareth."

means anything more than Galilee, *Gen-nesareth*: if so he would translate Luke 2⁴ presumably *Joseph went up from a city of Galilee*. The fact that Nazareth is not mentioned either in the Old Testament or in Josephus would seem to show it was unimportant, but yet new places do, and did then, grow up, and the site is such that it ought to have possessed a town at any and every time.

A further question which Dr Cheyne puts concerning *He shall be called a Nazarene* may fitly be considered here. He says, "Most commentators have seen an allusion to the prophecy of the *shoot* (*nêtser*) in Isa. 11¹. It is hardly conceivable, however, that the synonymous word *branch* (*tsemah*), which had long been in possession of the field as a Messianic title, should have been displaced among the Christians by *nêtser*. It is rather an allusion to Isa. 9¹ . . . which was surely applied by the first Christians to His early ministry by the sea of Galilee—not to His residence at Capernaum nor to His earlier teaching at Nazareth, but to His Galilean ministry as a whole. In a word, Nazareth ought to mean Galilee, and Nazarene ought to mean Galilean." But may not the explanation be this? The *Branch* is clear enough in the Hebrew but has disappeared in the Greek Bible (see Ch. V., VII.), for *Anatolê* means Dayspring and does not mean Branch. And *Anatolê* in six places (Jer. 23⁵, 33¹⁵, Zech. 3⁸, 6¹², Ezek. 16⁷, 17¹⁰) is all that remains of *tsemah* in the Old Testament. Consequently the value of *The Branch* for fulfilment of prophecy was gone. There was gained instead the far more fruitful imagery of the Dayspring, and as regards the etymology of the synonymous Shoot, *nêtser*, it brought itself easily into connection with *Nazareth* without much detriment to the meaning of the established idea. On the other hand, the Hebrew word *nêtser* occurs only four times in the Old Testament: in Isa. 11¹ it is translated ἄνθος, *flower*; in Isa. 14¹⁹ νεκρός,

JOSEPH 173

corpse; in Isa. 60²¹ φύτευμα, *plantation*; and in Dan. 11⁷ φυτόν, *plant*. Thus *nêtser* would form a very narrow basis for any foundation whatever for the name *Nazarene*. This is only another instance of the fact that the Christian faith grows naturally out of the LXX Greek, but was not built and could not have been built upon the Hebrew Old Testament.

Joseph's Name and Circumstances.

But when we come to the character of Joseph we find an utter blank. We know not whether he was old or young at the Nativity—nothing of his inherited, political, ecclesiastical, devotional proclivities. The evidence for his having been a *carpenter* is found, strange to say, in—

> Ps. 78⁶⁷ He rejected *the tabernacle* of Joseph (σκήνωμα).
> Ps. 81⁶ᶠ A testimony in Joseph he made him when he came out of the land of Egypt : He heard a language that he knew not. He removed his back from *buildings* (ἄρσεων) : his hands wrought as slaves at the *basket* (κοφίνῳ).

Joseph, as a maker of tabernacles, buildings, and baskets, must have been a carpenter. Hence Joseph " cast down his *axe* ". (James 9 above). " He was busy making *tabernacles* " in Capernaum *by the sea* (Ps.-Matt. 10). " He made nothing of wood except yokes for oxen and ploughs and hoes and wooden bedsteads " (Ps.-Matt. 37). " He made ploughs and yokes " (G. of Thomas 13). Further evidence might be likewise found in—

> Gen. 49²² A stalwart son [is] Joseph; my stalwart son [thou art] envied : my youngest son, *turn thou unto me* again. Against whom they *contrived plots* and reviled him : the lords of arrows aimed at him : and he crushed their bows mightily together, and the strings of their strong arms were snapped, by reason

of the hand of the strong man of Jacob. *Thence is he who made Israel strong*, from God thy father.

In accordance with this we find that Joseph removed from Capernaum because of *the malice* of the men who were hostile to them (Ps.-Matt. 40).

The expression *turn thou to me again* takes us back to Isa. 10. Luke knew that the name of " Joseph " was translated into Greek " *He shall add* " (προσθήσει). He was therefore justified by his own principle of interpretation in understanding that the enrolment of Joseph in Judah was *an addition* of strength to the royal tribe, and particularly to the royal house of David, which had long been in extreme obscurity and near to extinction. Hegesippus related that Vespasian, after the destruction of Jerusalem, ordered search to be made for any descendants of the family of David in the hope that none should be *left* surviving (περιλειφθείη) of the royal tribe, at the cost of great persecution to the Jews. The statement seems to lack confirmation, but if it be true, and if we assume that St. Luke knew of the fewness of David's descendants, then additional force is given to the expressions in the oracles of Isa. 10[20], " the remnant Israel shall no more *have to be added* " (προστεθήσεται) [for *God will add* now *Joseph* to Judah]. But the same idea of strengthening the house of Judah by the addition of the house of Joseph derived a powerful confirmation from another passage, where Zechariah, after saying, " The Lord God Almighty will *visit* his flock the house of Judah," proceeds—

Zech. 10[6] And I will strengthen the house of Judah, and I will strengthen the *house of Joseph*, and will settle them anew (κατοικιῶ), because I loved them, and they shall be as though I had not turned away from them (or, them away from me).

JOSEPH

The Remnant or Residue.

Thus Matthew has Joseph settled or *resettled* at Capernaum (κατώκισεν). In the blessing of Jacob to Joseph (Gen. 49²²) the tribe addressed, indeed, was Joseph, but for ages past there had been no tribe corresponding to this name, and it would seem impossible to apply it to the tribe of Ephraim and the two half-tribes of Manasseh. Therefore that oracle must mean the tribe to which Joseph of Nazareth belonged, the tribe of Judah. But then, was it conceivable that the outlying members of the tribe should return unless the chief and royal family of the tribe, above all others, could return? Therefore Joseph, as one of the few remaining descendants of David, was bound in duty to return. Thus would be fulfilled the prediction, "The remnant of them shall be saved" (Isa. 10²²). This was confirmed by another, in which, speaking of *the day of the Lord*, which might well refer to the time of *His birth*—

> Isa. 13¹⁰. There shall be darkness when the sun is rising and the moon shall not give her light. And I will command *for the whole world* (Luke 2¹) evils, and for the ungodly their sins: and I will destroy the insolence of *the lawless*, and will humble the insolence of the overweening.

Again, this takes us back to the idea of the *lawless* King Herod, whether Archelaus or his father was meant.

> And they *that have been left behind* (οἱ καταλελιμ-μένοι, that is of the tribe of Judah " the residue ") shall be more precious than gold untouched by fire ... and they *that have been left behind* shall be as a little gazelle that fleeth and as a sheep that strayeth, and there shall not be one that gathereth [them], so that *a man shall turn away unto his people*, and a man shall hie swiftly unto his own country,

For whosoever is caught shall be defeated, and they that have gathered together shall fall by the sword.

Then there was a further promise in—

Isa. 37^{31} And [when] they that *had been left behind* shall be in Judea, they shall strike root downwards and bear seed upwards.

Meanwhile, the consciousness that the house of David had fallen from its high estate and needed restoration from obscurity was manifested in the more familiar oracle—it becomes less unintelligible when compared with those quoted above—quoted in Acts 15^{16} from—

Amos 9$^{11\,f}$ In that day I will set up again the tabernacle of David which had fallen, and I will build again the ruins thereof . . . that *the residue of men* may seek it out, and all the nations upon whom my name hath been called, saith the Lord who doeth these things.

The residue (οἱ κατάλοιποι) of men does not of necessity mean the Gentiles, but may be taken of Joseph *rebuilding the tabernacle of David* in the form of the Church of Christ, which the Gentiles enter. This remnant was already known in some sense as *the residue of Joseph* according to—

Amos 5^{15} Even as ye said, We have hated evil things and loved good things, so *restore* ye (ἀποκαταστήσατε) judgment in the gates, that the Lord God Almighty may have mercy on *the residue* (περιλοίπους) of *Joseph*.

The comparison of these oracles fails, however, to throw any further light upon the supposed or inferential character of the person of Joseph even as a "righteous" man. All that finally emerges from them is that he is to serve as the instrument of the restoration of things, the Messianic *apokatastasis* (p. 154), in the special regard of the restoration of the house of David to and with the tribe of Judah. This particular restoration had seemed to become necessary ever since the plaintive utterance of—

> Ps. 89[35 ff] I swore once for all by my holy One, that I will not fail David : his seed shall abide for ever, and his throne as the sun before me, and as the moon prepared for ever : and the witness is faithful in heaven. But thou hast abhorred and set [him] at naught, thou hast put off $(ἀνεβάλου)$ thy Christ. Thou hast overthrown the covenant of thy servant, thou hast defiled to the ground his holiness. ... How long, O Lord, wilt thou *turn him away* $(ἀποστρέψεις)$ to the end ? ... Blessed be the Lord for ever. So be it ! So be it !

The hope of this restoration came, therefore, with all the added force of disappointed centuries in which the house of David had dwindled and pined in darkness and disgrace, and Joseph of Nazareth was to be the prime agent in the fulfilment of the same magnificent psalm.

> Ps. 89[21 ff] I have found David my servant, *with holy oil* (or, *pity*), I have anointed him. . . . He shall invoke me, Thou art my father, my God, and the helper of my salvation, And I will make him *my firstborn* (Luke 2[7] : And she brought forth her son, *The firstborn*, $τὸν$ $υἱὸν$ $αὐτῆς$, $Τὸν$ $Πρωτότοκον$), higher than the kings of the earth.

And in the same sense of reliance upon the oath to David the psalmist has appealed to God—

> Ps. 132[10] For the sake of David thy servant *turn not away* the face of thy Christ.

The result of the above inquiries is not that we find St. Luke to be more of a historian than he was thought to be before or than he ever claimed to be, but we have perhaps demonstrated his dependence upon the oracles of prophecy as a prophet himself, versed in the ancient scriptures as no Gentile could have been, and deeply imbued with the spirit of them. The fact that he does not profess or attempt to exhibit the book-work of his problem is precisely in accordance with his practice in numerous other parts of Luke and Acts. Ponderous, ungainly, and inartistic would his work have been indeed, had he done so. He has left quite enough for the modern reader as well as for Theophilus, and yet it is a modern assumption that he even wrote for a modern reader. Who can prove that he contemplated such a possibility as that the world would last eighteen hundred years longer than his age? Whatever inspiration we attribute to him besides an artistic inspiration, we must attribute all the more when we find how much he has supplied, how much he has suggested to the reader and the critic, to the organizer and builder and worker in the cause of Christ's Church. In preserving for us the parable of the Prodigal Son he is perhaps to-day profoundly moving the native of Corea and the Moslem of North Africa as they have not been moved before. Why should we complain that he is not a modern historian? But let him be appreciated as a prophet, and we shall find in him a subject of no less intellectual than of devotional interest, while his power will be attested by the thousands who find in his brief work of a hundred and forty pages a treasury of thought and feeling hitherto unknown.

CHAPTER VII

JOHN THE BAPTIST

The Benedictus a Levitic Cradle-song.

WE shall now endeavour to determine whether the hymn of Zacharias, father of the Baptist—the canticle known familiarly as the Benedictus—is prechristian or not, and if not, to what date it can be assigned. That it is largely constructed out of the phraseology of the Old Testament is visible at a glance to those who have seen it in Westcott and Hort's text, in which some forty-one words of it are printed in uncials, as citations, leaving some ninety-six words as fresh composition. But of the latter there are many expressions which might also be printed uncially. Thus *in holiness and righteousness* is a citation from Wisd. 9^3, where it occurs in an address to "God of our fathers." Then Zech. 10^3, "The Lord God *shall visit* his flock the house of Judah" is a phrase which would justify the uncializing of *he hath visited* and *whereby* (there) *shall visit us*. Then again, in connection with this passage, we bear in mind that Zech. 3^8, 6^{12}, has twice spoken of the Dayspring ('Ἀνατολή, not meaning Branch* at all), and so it is clear that

---

*. The only places where 'Ἀνατολή could ever possibly mean Branch are Ezek. 16^7, where it certainly does mean the rising dawn over the country, and Ezek. 17^{10}, where it is better to translate "with its clod at the first dayspring shall it wither." Even if the Greek translator of Ezekiel used ἀνατολή for *bud* it would not follow that the translator of Zechariah did the same. But can it be maintained that "with the clod of its growth it shall wither" is as good a sense? Even so, *growth* is not *branch*. The context favours the other.

Dayspring (Luke 1⁷⁰) should also be uncialized. Then, although *the remission of sins* does not appear in the Old Testament as a substantival phrase, it appears as a sentence in Isa. 33²⁴, "for their *sin may be forgiven them:* " the words in Luke 1⁷⁷ might therefore be uncialized. Once more we read in Mal. 2⁶, "*in peace* he walked *straight* (ἐν εἰρήνῃ κατευθύνων ἐπορεύθη) with me," which differs very little from *making straight our feet into* the way of *peace* (κατευθῦναι εἰς ὁδὸν εἰρήνης), and therefore these words might also be uncialized. What then remains not uncialized of the original composition? Very little but such expressions as "Abraham our father," which occurs again and again in the Old Testament, and the necessary prepositions and conjunctions which connect the several parts. The whole of the Benedictus is a cento of Old Testament passages. And such a mode of composition was quite natural on the part of those who took the Old Testament as the Bible, and the Bible as a storehouse of texts, of Logia, of oracles; which only needed to be collected and arranged in order to furnish a complete Messianic picture. This was the prophetic position in the first Christian century, and the most signal example of its practice is to be seen in the Apocalypse with its five hundred and eighteen citations from the Old Testament on a moderate computation by Westcott and Hort.

A hymn, however, being an artistic composition, must possess a more striking unity than a vision, and follow a more definite line of thought. Its materials must be familiar to the readers of similar compositions. While, therefore, the substance of the hymn is entirely scriptural, its form is the form of a psalm of David and still more that of a psalm of Solomon * (about 47 B.C.), to which it made a very near approach in its date of composition. How closely the train of thought of the Benedictus re-

* *Psalms of Solomon*, Ryle and James.

JOHN THE BAPTIST

sembles that of Ps. Sol. 9, will appear from the following comparison—

BENEDICTUS (Luke i)	PS. SOL. VIII. 40; IX. 1-19
68. *Blessed be the Lord*	40. Praised *be the Lord* . . . and *blessed* be Israel of the Lord
the God of Israel for he hath *visited*	16. *The God of Israel* 8. thou *visitest* the sons of men.
and *redeemed his people*	1. which *redeemed* them. 16. we are *thy people*
71. salvation from our enemies and from all that hate us	2. cast away among every nation
72. to do *mercy with our fathers*	16. remove not thy *mercy* from us that they set not upon us
to remember his holy *covenant*	19. thou didst *covenant with our fathers* concerning us.
73. the oath which he sware unto *Abraham*	17. thou didst choose the seed of *Abraham*.
75. to serve him in *holiness* and *righteousness before him*	6. the *righteous* acts of *thy holy* ones *before thee* 7. to do *righteousness*
77. to give *knowledge* of salvation by *remission of their sins*	6. from the *knowledge* of thee 14. To whom will he *remit sins* but to them that have sinned?

These are remarkable correspondences between sixteen lines of St. Luke and twenty verses of the Psalms of Solomon. But the most important among them all is the last—the remission of sins. This doctrine is of course mentioned in the Old Testament, but, strange as it may seem, it is not at all common to find the two words *to forgive sins* outside the Pentateuch, and *forgiveness of sins* is actually unknown. Its occurrence in the same context with a dozen more coincidences seems to prove that the Benedictus owes this also to the Psalm of Solomon, though Ecclus. 2^{11} *forgiveth sins and saveth* may also be quoted for it.

And St. Luke, in order to show clearly that he understood and intended the Benedictus to be understood as a prophetic hymn, the composition of a prophet, has been careful to introduce it with the usual statement that Zacharias " was *filled with the Holy Spirit, and prophesied*, saying . . ."

The contents of the hymn are very simple. The first part praises God for raising up salvation for His people in the house of David, in fulfilment of the prophecies and of His oath to Abraham. The second part is addressed to the infant John as prophet, forerunner, and preacher of forgiveness of sins, thanks to the mercy of God, whereby a Dayspring shall visit His people, to enlighten the Gentiles and to guide the Jews.

The range of reference to the Old Testament is not very extensive, most of it being directed to the Psalms (105, 106, 107, 111, 132). Ps. 105 refers to the covenant that he made with Abraham and the oath which he sware unto Isaac, and " that they might keep his statutes and observe his laws." Ps. 106 furnishes the doxology, " Blessed be the Lord God of Israel," and " redemption from the hand of the enemy," and " He remembered his covenant." Ps. 111 furnishes the expression " He hath sent forth redemption unto his people." Ps. 132, " There will I make the horn of David to rise as a Dayspring ($\dot{\varepsilon}\xi\alpha\nu\alpha\tau\varepsilon\lambda\tilde{\omega}$)." These are the characteristic features of the first part of the Benedictus, and no other portions of the Old Testament need have been considered in the composition. We have seen elsewhere that Ps. 132 has been particularly made the subject of prophetic interpretation in connection with Bethlehem.

The second portion has a somewhat wider range, while it draws from Ps. 107 " them that sit in darkness and the shadow of death," meaning the Gentiles, in sharp contrast with " us," the Jews, in the following line. Then Mal. 3^1 is laid under contribution for the thought of the forerunner—

Mal. 3^1 Behold, I send forth my messenger and he shall look out for ($\dot{\varepsilon}\pi\iota\beta\lambda\dot{\varepsilon}\psi\varepsilon\tau\alpha\iota$) a way before me—

while Mal. 2⁶ has suggested the straightening of the feet of the Jews into the way of peace, and Mal. 4² the Dayspring—

> Then there shall *dawn* upon you that fear my name the sun of righteousness.

Then again, Zech. 10³ has suggested the visitation of His people by God, and has enlarged the idea of the Dayspring. But there is still one expression which causes some difficulty. "To dawn upon (ἐπιφᾶναι) them that are in darkness and the shadow of death" seems to mean to enlighten *the Gentiles*, not only because of the contrast which the sense of the verse requires, but also because of the parallel passage in the Nunc Dimittis, "a light to lighten the Gentiles," which is contrasted with "the glory of thy people Israel." It can hardly be maintained that the words refer only to the Jews as another expression for "us" (*shall visit us*) in the former line. Sense and rhythm combine to forbid such interpretation. It cannot be said that the people of God as a whole "sit in darkness and the shadow of death," especially when we have had immediately before this the rehearsal of the promises and the oath which God had given to them. The idea of the Jews being in darkness is not consistent with—

> Isa. 60² Darkness shall cover the earth and gross darkness the Gentiles, but the Lord shall appear upon *thee*.

The idea, on the other hand, of the Gentiles being brought out of darkness harmonizes well with—

> Isa. 42⁴ Upon his name the Gentiles shall trust,

along with

> Isa. 42⁷ To bring forth from prison them that sit in darkness,

and with Isa. 49^6 "for a light of the Gentiles" with 49^9 "bidding them that are in darkness to be uncovered." There is no passage in which the people of the covenant are said to be in the shadow of death: so the meaning of the words can only be the Gentiles. Consequently, we have here a promise that the infant John should be the immediate forerunner of one who should enlighten the Gentiles: but this promise is abundantly made in Mal. 1^{11} and does not affect the question, which is, Must this hymn put in the mouth of Zachariah have been composed after the event of Jesus being confessed as the Christ? Or could he have uttered it upon his infant as a current composition, expressing the pious wish of a father that his son should grow up to be a prophet, indeed *the* prophet, who was immediately to precede the Messiah? There is reason to think the latter is the true alternative. There was to be such a prophet. Every devout parent therefore would pray that his son would be he. I can see nothing in Mal. 2^6, 3^1 which could not be expected to occur in a hymn addressing any infant intended for a prophet's career years before the day of the Christ. Any and every prophet must be prepared to find in a Messianic time that—

Mal. 3^1, the Lord whom ye seek shall *suddenly come* to his temple—

and in this very expectation he would be prepared to find a stimulus of unwonted and unparalleled force. There is no reason why these verses and the whole of their context should not be the cradle-song upon any son of a prophet of that period as well as John, son of Zachariah.

John's Ministry based on Malachi.

The more we study the accounts of John's ministry, the clearer it becomes that they are all based upon the

JOHN THE BAPTIST

four chapters of the book that we call Malachi, which is really a portion of Zechariah which precedes it. The question is, what is the nature of the connexion? The following conspectus shows that John took this passage of scripture as the model of his teaching.

MALACHI III, IV	LUKE III
iv. 1. The day as it cometh shall *kindle* (ἀνάψει) them, and there shall not be left of them *root* or branch.	9. Already the axe is laid unto the *root* of the tree, every tree that bringeth not forth fruit is cut down and cast into the *fire*.
1. All they who do lawless shall be as straw.	7. Whose fan is in his hand to purge his floor, and the chaff will he burn (κατακαύσει).
1. The day cometh burning (καιομένη) as an oven and he shall burn (φλέξει) them.	16. He shall baptize you with the holy spirit and fire.
iii. 8. Wherein have we robbed thee? In tithes and offerings . . .	13. Exact no more than is appointed you.
10. And ye have brought all the produce into your treasuries.	
5. I will be a swift witness against them that swear falsely and	14 Neither accuse any man falsely.
5. Against them that oppress the widow	14. Do violence to no man.
5. And them that rob the hired servant of his hire.	14. Be content with your wages.
2. Who shall abide the day of his coming?	7. Who hath warned you to flee from the wrath to come?
3. He shall purify the sons of Levi. (And where is the God of righteousness? 2¹⁷)	8. God can raise out of these stones children to Abraham.
7. Turn ye unto me and I will turn unto you.	3. Repentance unto remission of sins.

Here are the ideas of Malachi, but very little of the language. The picture drawn by Luke is exceedingly graphic. One cannot easily suppose it is made up out of Malachi, even by one who knew that the tax-farmers were likely to address to John a question about their own class, and soldiers on service (στρατευόμενοι) likewise, apart from questions put by the multitude. These discriminating touches are just what prove the art of St. Luke. But no discovery of such art can impress us with the suspicion that the scene by Jordan bank is not a real scene, that it is artificially composed out of the prophecy of Malachi.

Josephus on the Baptist and the Son of Sirach on Elijah.

If any confirmation of the gospel account of John the Baptist were needed, one would expect it to be found in Josephus's account :* " a good man, who urged the Jews to practise virtue, with righteousness *towards one another*, and piety *towards God*, and to come to baptism (βαπτισμῷ συνιέναι). For thus, too, would their baptizing appear *acceptable* (ἀποδεκτήν) to him, when they employed it not for the *expiation* (παραιτήσει) of certain sins, but for cleanness (ἁγνείᾳ) of the body, inasmuch as the soul had been entirely purified beforehand (προεκκεκαθαρμένης) by righteousness. The people flocked to hear his discourses, and were roused to the highest pitch of excitement." The fact that John came forward in the spirit and power of Elias (Luke 1[17]) made him a formidable person. Who can say how widely current was the Wisdom of Sirach, which describes Elijah, and therefore John, in the following passage ?—

Ecclus. 48[1 ff] Then stood up Elijah the prophet as fire, and his word burned like a lamp (ὡς λαμπὰς ἐκαίετο, hence John 5[35], ἐκεῖνος ἦν ὁ λύχνος ὁ καιόμενος καὶ φαίνων) : he brought a sore famine upon them, and by his zeal he made them few; by the word of the Lord he shut up the heaven, he brought down fire also thrice. How wast thou honoured, Elijah, in thy wondrous deeds, and who may glory like unto

* *Antt.* 18, 5[2].

JOHN THE BAPTIST

thee ? Who didst raise up a dead man from death . . . who broughtest kings to destruction . . . who heardest in Horeb the judgments of vengeance, who anointedst kings to take revenge and prophets to succeed after him, who wast taken up in a whirlwind (but A reads *lamp, λαμπάδι*) of fire and in a chariot of fiery horses, who wast ordained for reproofs in their times, to pacify wrath before [the Lord's] anger, and to turn the heart of the father to the son (Mal. 4^5) and to restore the tribes of Jacob.

There is enough in this passage to justify Josephus in saying, "Herod feared that his great influence would lead his followers to a revolt, for they seemed ready for anything at his counsel, and he therefore thought it better to catch him before he gave rise to a revolution, and kill him, rather than repent too late in the midst of an upheaval." If Herod's fear was based on substantial grounds, for John was further said (Ecclus. 48^{12}) to be "protected by a whirlwind" (ἐν λαίλαπι ἐσκεπάσθη), how great in proportion must have been his disciples' disappointment when he was beheaded!

And yet we can clearly discern again in this picture by Josephus of John's teaching some of those features of Malachi which characterize it,—the stress upon the duty *towards God* (Mal. 3^8) and the duty towards *one's neighbour* (Mal. 3^5)—the *acceptable* (δεκτόν) offering to God (Mal. 2^{13})—the command to *entreat the favour of God* (Mal. 1^9), the *purification* (καθαρίσει, Mal. 3^3) of the sons of Levi. Indeed, there is a volume of religious passion contained in the fact that John, as the youngest of the sons of Levi, was trained by his father, the priest Zacharias, to fulfil the words of Malachi, "He shall purify the sons of Levi,"—trained by his father to prepare the way for the Christ in this work, if not in others too. And the lines which he should follow are thus laid down in terms of simple grandeur—

Mal. 2⁵ ᶠᶠ *My covenant was with him of life and of peace, and I gave them to him that he may fear me with a [right] fear and stand in awe before my name. The law of truth is in his mouth, and unrighteousness is not found upon his lips: in peace he walketh straight in his goings with me, and many he converteth from unrighteousness. For the life of the priest shall keep knowledge, and they shall seek out the law from his mouth, because* he is the Messenger of the Lord Almighty.

John's Charter and Mission to the Levites.

Such was the charter of John, corresponding in a measure to the profoundly moving passage in Zech. 3⁷ which we may imagine to have been the charter of the Saviour, as we shall see later (Ch. X). But in John's case there is no great margin for imagination; there is first of all the fact that Zacharias was conscious of the pressure of the prophet Malachi's words—if we only believe the Benedictus to be his actual utterance, whether it was his composition or not: then there is the fact that John modelled his own teaching on Malachi; then there is the fact that he and his father were of the tribe of Levi. And there is another fact. A later age delighted to teach that John * *was sitting* at the river Jordan when he shouted, " I baptize you with water unto repentance, but there shall come," etc. Here is one of the numerous cases where Justin has been found to diverge from the gospel narratives. We hardly know what precise meaning to place upon " sitting," whether literal or not. But the origin of Justin's expression is beyond a doubt. Either through the medium of Papias's *Exposition of the Oracles concerning the Lord*, or some other similar work, Justin drew it from the LXX of—

* Justin Martyr, *Dial.*, 49, 268 c, καθεζόμενος ἐβόα.

JOHN THE BAPTIST

Mal. 3³ *He shall sit* as a refiner and purifier of silver and gold.

Consequently all the context in Mal. 3³ is to be taken as a prediction, not of the Christ, but of the forerunner, at least according to the exegesis of the first decades A.D. And if so, it was probably so interpreted from the very first A.D., even by the Baptist himself. The fact that, as will be noticed in the above comparison of Mal. 3¹ and Luke 3¹⁶, the former is applied to the Christ by the Baptist as if he declined it for the Forerunner, so far from throwing any doubt upon the genuineness of Luke and Matthew in their report of the Baptist's address, exactly serves to confirm it. For the one person who would have naturally passed on the interpretation of Mal. 3³ to the majesty and power of another as the Christ was the Forerunner.

The important result of this consideration is that John was conscious that his mission was to the Levites and priests first of all; to them whose privilege it was not only to minister in the Temple, but on the great annual day of the Feast of Tabernacles to carry in their turns the golden tankard of water from the Siloam fount and pour it into the silver pipe beside the altar. It may be an exaggeration to see anything but a fortuitous correspondence to this solemn ceremony in the words of—

Mal. 3³ He shall purify the sons of Levi and shall *pour* (χεεῖ) them even as *the gold* and as *the silver*: and they shall be *bringing* (προσάγοντες) to the Lord an offering in righteousness, and (the) offering of *Judah and Jerusalem* shall please the Lord as the days of old and as the years that are past.

But yet the coincidences are worthy of notice. At any rate the duty of purity on the part of God's ministers above all other classes of His people seems to be inculcated by Malachi more than any other prophet, and the general proposition that he announces a mission to the priests is beyond dispute. This mission fell upon the shoulders of the last of the Old Testament prophets, John the Baptist. Consequently we can now understand how the Fourth Gospel represents that *priests and Levites* came *from Jerusalem* to ask him, Who art thou ? " The object of " the Jews " who dispatched them (John 1[19]) was to ascertain, on this as another occasion, by what authority he held a mission to the sons of Levi in particular. Nor would it be surprising if the reason why a great multitude of the priests were obedient to the faith (Acts 6[7]) was that the blessing of God had previously rested upon the mission of John to the sons of Levi.

The Sadducees and the Pharisees.

One more observation may here be made before we pass from the Baptist to one greater than he. The resemblance of his mode of life to that of Elijah was due, not to any fancy of his, but to his conviction that he was called to become that " Elijah the Tishbite " whom God would " send as his apostle (ἀποστέλλω, Mal. 4[5]) before the Lord's day, the great and illustrious day, came; who should restore (ἀποκαταστήσει) the heart of the father to the son and the heart of a man to his neighbour, lest he come and smite the earth utterly." He lived like Elijah—" a hairy man and girt about with a leathern apron "— because it was part of his divine instruction (and may we not also say his parental training ?) so to live. And yet when asked the questions, " Art thou Elijah ? Art thou the prophet ? " he answered No. This is at first perplexing to those who know that he had undertaken the position of Elijah who was the prophet, even if some people entertained the belief that Elijah and the prophet were destined to prove two distinct persons. The reason of his denial may, however, be seen if we consider how these priests and Levites came to be sent. The Sadducee

JOHN THE BAPTIST

party chiefly belonged to the priesthood.* John's mission was originally to the Sadducee party, the class which had for a century, indeed for the greater part of several centuries, furnished the rulers of the State, the wealthy aristocratic well-to-do class, who drew their name Sadducee from Zadok the priest. In politics, their tendency was to temporize, for the maintenance of the Jewish State; in religion, to uphold the law and ritual regardless of the "tradition of the elders;" in morality to maintain private opinion, individual liberty, and modern adjustments. The Pharisees, on the other hand, had the bulk of the nation at their back, and swayed the masses, so that a Herod who found the Sadducees compliant would be forced to come to terms with the Pharisees. The Pharisees had more religion on their side in spite of the derision they drew from the Sadducees for their strict distinctions of clean and unclean. To politics they were comparatively indifferent.

Now let us see what would be the effect of John's mission to the Sadducees on the assumption that Malachi was his basis. Professional religion in all times and places is beset with inevitable dangers, and the Sadducees presided over the professional religion of the Jews. A little consideration will show that though to the modern mind the Pharisee has become the type of the religious professor, the ordinary Jew would have attributed that character rather to the Sadducee, whose party included most of the Levites, and was practically invested with the rule of Church and State, holding the monopoly of public religious ceremonial. Where formality was entrenched as a privilege, formalism was the chronic danger, and this danger was the Sadducees' and not the Pharisees'. The parable of the Pharisee and the Publican stands in no particular relation to the public religion: the lesson of it is directed generally to the state of the

* Schürer, *Jewish People*, § 26.

heart, and applies to the Sadducee and to the Pharisee with an equal force, though the latter was more given to prayer than the former. Now John's teaching was addressed first of all to conventionalism, formalism, and officialism, and his preaching of repentance sounded a note of personal religion. John would find the duty of personal religion declared by Malachi. When Mal. 2^7 said: "The priest's lips should keep knowledge, and they should seek the law at his mouth; for he is the messenger of the Lord of hosts," what did he mean but the duty of the priest to be a teacher of the law as well as an official of the ceremony of Moses? The prophetic order had become broken and enfeebled when Malachi wrote in the age of Nehemiah; it was broken and enfeebled still more when John preached; it was disorganized and nearly extinct. Its resurrection under a new organization for half a century could not have been foreseen by John, much less the issue of that organization in the catholic Church of Christ.

The basis of John's reform then was, we may suppose, the spiritual life of the individual priest and his responsibility as a teacher. There was the written word in Malachi before them, and he would urge it home with all the passion and earnestness of an ascetic Levite himself. "Take heed to your spirit, that ye deal not treacherously" (Mal. 2^{16}), was the direct appeal for a spiritual reformation. But not only must renewal take place within: there were also external points of observance, which he could urge from Malachi upon the Greek-reading and generally hellenized Sadducees. For where the Hebrew of Mal. 3^{11} said, "And I will rebuke the devourer for your sakes," the Greek translated—

Mal. 3^{11} And I will make a distinction for you in regard to food :

the very ground on which the Sadducee was fain to taunt

JOHN THE BAPTIST

the Pharisee was cut from under his feet by that Greek text in which the Sadducee took pride. John's own language of teaching was probably Aramaic, as we infer from the play of words in what would be the Hebrew of Luke 3^8, where there is no such play of words in the Greek: but this is no reason for supposing that John was illiterate as regards the Greek Bible.

John's Message out of Malachi.

Again, if we pass from personal responsibility to the treatment of the law by the Sadducees, we can see with what force John could employ a text from—

> Mal. 1^{11} For from sunrise unto sunset my name is great among the Gentiles: and in every place incense is offered unto my name, and a pure offering: for my name is great among the Gentiles, saith the Lord of Hosts. But ye profane it in that ye say the table of the Lord is polluted, and the fruit thereof, even his meat, is contemptible. Ye say also, Behold, what a weariness is it! and ye have sniffed at it.

Here is all the carelessness, the boredom, the *accidia*, as Dante would call it, of monotony and routine-work, condemned in anticipation by Malachi. Other abuses of the powers entrusted to the Levites by law there may well have been, like those denounced in—

> Mal. 3^8 But ye say, wherein have we robbed thee? In tithes and offerings.

But the main thread of the four chapters of the prophecy is the offering to the Lord of hosts made by the tribe of Levi for the whole house of Israel, and the prophet admonishes those who offer while he denounces the blemishes of their offering.

> Mal. 2^{10} Why did they profane the covenant of their fathers? Mal. 2^{13} The Lord regardeth not the offering any more?

194 ORACLES IN THE NEW TESTAMENT

Thus he is led from the injury to the law back to moral vice and abomination. Witchcraft was rife in Malachi's time (3^5), and it was one of the crying evils of that Hellenism which the Sadducees condoned and promoted. How could they reconcile their action with the worship of Him who said—

> Mal. 1^{14} I am a great king, saith the Lord Almighty, and my name is terrible [but LXX " illustrious "] among the Gentiles?

Then, too, mixed marriages, whether figurative or literal, were another source of sin.

> Mal. 2^{11} Judah hath profaned the sanctuary of the Lord which he loveth, and hath married the daughter of a strange god [or, LXX, loved and done worship to foreign gods].

Here was the opening of a wide range of denunciation of the invading paganism. And in the Greek of Mal. 3^{15} there is a much more pointed text than in our version—

> Mal. 3^{15} And now we felicitate foreigners [ἀλλοτρίους, *i. e.* Greeks, as the Sadducees who read the LXX in their hands would have to admit was the meaning] and they are all being built up in doing deeds against the law (of Moses), and they oppose God and come safely through.

Then follows that remarkable verse which has so often proved the encouragement of a small committee of reformers secretly gathered in some obscure place.

> Thus said they that feared the Lord, each one to his neighbour: and the Lord gave ear and heard, and he wrote a book of memorial before him for them that feared the Lord and thought upon his name. And they shall be mine, saith the Lord Almighty, unto the day which I appoint for redemption, and I will choose them as a man chooseth his son who serveth (δουλεύοντα) him.

JOHN THE BAPTIST

In the last words there would be some who would discern a special reference to John the prophet, the successor of the great prophet, *Moses the servant* (Mal. 4⁶) of the Lord. And the successors of these would be Christian prophets, and they themselves would become followers of John and afterwards perhaps Christians. To such—

> Mal. 4² ᶠ, to those who feared his name, the Dayspring should arise, the Sun of Righteousness, and they should tread under foot the lawless heathen.

The answer of John to the priests and Levites that he was not Elijah, not the prophet, is an ironical answer in the truest sense of irony which belongs to the man who is, like Socrates, dissembling his true value, and whom Horace describes in memorable words—

> "Dissimulator opis propriæ."

The priests and Levites had been sent in consequence of (ἐκ) the Pharisees, says John 1²⁴, which probably means not by (ὑπό) the Pharisees, but by the Sadducees in consequence of a discussion with the Pharisees. Neither party was able as yet to understand anything but a mere bodily re-creation and return of Elijah the Tishbite as he appeared before Ahab and ascended from beside Elisha. In such, if he came, these parties would see nothing but an unintelligible and useless phenomenon, the precursor of a mechanical and idle Christ. John answered them according to their own sense of the words that they used, and in that sense a negative was the only possible answer. But the cause of the discussion which led to the deputation was the mission of John to the sons of Levi.

The Locality of John's Witness.

And now, perhaps, we can see what was the dominant thought of John's mind when he uttered the memorable words which frame the first declaration of Jesus as the Christ. There seems to be a certain harshness of transition between the section John 1^{19-28} and that which follows close upon it. He has just said that he is not Elijah, not the prophet, and then forthwith he says, " Behold, the Lamb of God." What, we ask, has led up to this declaration? What in John's mind, what in Jesus, what in the outward world of both? What in the thoughts of bystanders, if we could only suppose they were the same on the two successive days? It is plain that the one common factor of the two statements of John must be found in his mind and his only. But we have seen that his mind was occupied by the main theme of Malachi, " His Messenger," as the LXX entitles the book (Mal. 1^1, see R.V. margin). And the main theme is the offering to the Lord of Judah and Jerusalem. The offering, and those who make it, and the covenant under which it is made, run through every second verse of the book. Therefore the offering of a blameless and sinless life, such as John beheld in his own kinsman Jesus, was a thought, long cherished, we may suppose, which rushed to his lips when *he saw Him coming towards him in that place beyond Jordan* where he was baptizing. "Behold, the Lamb of God, which taketh away the sin of the world."

How remarkable it is that this first intimation of Christ Jesus is delivered not at Nazareth, not at Jerusalem, not in the holy land at all, but beyond Jordan! And yet here is the prediction of it in—

Mal. 1^5 And your eyes *shall see*, and ye shall say, Magnified is *the Lord beyond the borders of Israel*.

Let any one account for the circumstances as he thinks fit, by the presence of sufficient waters, by the neighbourhood of Nazareth, by the previous appointment that the two kinsmen should meet somewhere at the time, or otherwise; it is nevertheless conceivable that John $1^{28\,f}$

JOHN THE BAPTIST

is a narrative constructed directly out of the desire to show in this particular way a fulfilment of Mal. 1^5. So—

> Mal. 1^{10} Oh that there were one among you that would shut the doors, that ye might not kindle mine altar in vain! I have no pleasure in you, saith the Lord of hosts, neither will I accept an offering at your hand . . . for my name is great among the Gentiles.

The words may naturally have predisposed John to seek for the true and only offering not among the sons of Levi, not even in some sense among the Jews, on Jewish soil, but " among the Gentiles." Nor can he have been ignorant of—

> Isa. 9^1 In the latter time he hath made it glorious, by the way of the sea, *beyond Jordan*, the district of the Gentiles (Heb.).

Out of the hated "Edom," out of the Idumæa which in the person of Herod had already produced Antichrist, out of " the borders of lawlessness " (Mal. 1^4) comes the first declaration that here is the Christ. How far John was acquainted with the identity of Herod with Antichrist it does not seem possible to say, but if we assume the general accuracy of St. Luke's statement (1^{80}) that " he was in the deserts until the time of his shewing unto Israel " we are not therefore to assume that even before this he remained in total ignorance of the course of thought in Jerusalem. But, on the other hand, there is no trace of John's desire or resolution to hurl the Christ against the Antichrist if the latter was in his mind. In no such way did he conceive of his Chief ($\pi\varrho\tilde{\omega}\tau\acute{o}\varsigma\ \mu o\nu$, John 1^{30}).

> Mal. 3^1 The Lord whom ye seek shall suddenly come to his temple

was the formal way in which his Master should come. The " offering (sacrifice, $\theta\upsilon\sigma\acute{\iota}a$) pure " (Mal. 1^{11}), was the figurative way, in accordance with universal usage; for no less could be offered in Jerusalem and in the Temple than was offered " in every place " from sunrise to sunset. " The Lamb of God taketh away," said John, not the sin of Israel, but " the sin *of the world* " (John 1^{29}). And Mal. 1^{14} has a special curse upon him that is powerful (LXX, but Hebrew " deceiver "), which hath *in his flock* a male, and then voweth upon it, and *sacrificeth unto the Lord* a blemished thing [instead thereof]. Thus, without overstepping the limits of Malachi, it is possible to see that John was supplied with the thought of his momentous declaration.

"*Behold, the Lamb of God.*"

And one more consideration connected with Malachi may here be added. John felt that he was charged " to sit as a refiner and purifier " (Mal. 3^3), in other metaphorical words, to sift the grain from the chaff,

> Mal. 3^{18} To discern between him that serveth God and him that serveth him not.

He performed his duty as thus defined when he said —certainly to himself, but not to any man, for the imperative is used in the singular.* number—" Lo, here is before me the lamb that is God's, that taketh away the sin of the world." As if in contrast to the blemished offerings of which Malachi complained (1^8), the blind, the lame, and the sick, he might say of this one perfect life—

> Mal. 1^9 And now atone ye ($\dot{\varepsilon}\xi\iota\lambda\dot{\alpha}\sigma\varkappa\varepsilon\sigma\theta\varepsilon$) the face of your God and intreat him—in your hands these things have taken place—verily I will not accept of *you* your persons, saith the Lord of hosts.

But this he did not say aloud : the soliloquy continues until John 1^{32} where the open speech begins, " and John bare witness saying (testified and said)." Not only does

* But ἴδε is sometimes used by John of plural interjections like ἄγε, also, Jas. 4^{13}, 5^1.

JOHN THE BAPTIST

literal translation require the soliloquy,* but the relation of John 1^{29-31} to what follows also requires it. For the incident of the baptism of Jesus by John in $1^{32\,f}$ must have preceded the soliloquy, and took place in the course of his baptizing, as mentioned in 1^{28}. There is no other supposition upon which we can possibly explain the difficult words (1^{31}), "And I knew him not," any more than they (or, you)—this is the force of κἀγώ and the only possible meaning of it. Κἀγὼ οὐκ ᾔδειν αὐτόν is true in the sense "knew not by intuition that this my own cousin is my Chief." It would not have been true to say ἔγνων here for ᾔδειν, for that would have meant "I recognized him not," and this is hardly a conceivable position. Mary and Elizabeth were most intimate, and even if we suppose that Elizabeth had long been dead and John far away in the desert—and the desert was not far away by any means—it would be strange that the two cousins should have been so completely isolated from each other as not to recognize one another. Mary probably kept in some sort of touch, in affectionate touch, with John. Jesus must have been known to John.

Two Trances of John.

Is not what happened this? In the course of baptizing John fell into a state of trance, a state which his fasting condition of life or a particular fast at the time would naturally induce. His trance is described in precisely the same language which describes other trances, for instance, those of the seer of Ephesus in the Apocalypse (Rev. 4^1), "After this I saw and behold a door had been opened in heaven"; (Rev. 19^{11}), "And I saw the heaven opened, and behold a white horse"; and of St. Peter (Acts 10^{10}), "There came upon him a trance, and he

* See John $1^{36\,ff}$, where ἤκουσαν could not have been used unless the words before it, ἴδε, etc., had been a soliloquy. They *overheard* John. When A and B converse together, it is never said that A *heard* B; it is assumed.

beholdeth the heaven opened and a certain vessel descending": and St. Stephen (Acts 7^{56}), "Lo, I behold the heavens opened and the Son of man standing at the right hand of God"; and St. Paul (2 Cor. 12^2), "I know a man in Christ fourteen years ago . . . caught up to the third heaven." The state of trance in John's case is beyond the possibility of doubt, nor is it to be doubted that the evangelists meant their readers to understand that it was such, for St. Luke employs the regular formula (Luke 3^{21}), "It came to pass that the heaven was opened and the Holy Ghost descended in bodily form as it were a dove upon him (Jesus)." (Mark 1^9) "And straightway while coming up out of the water, (John) saw the heavens being cleft asunder and the spirit as a dove descending upon (Jesus)." (Matt. 3^{16}) "And behold the heavens were opened and (John) saw God's spirit descending as it were * a dove, coming upon (Jesus)." In all these cases the psalmist's immemorial Messianic declaration as a voice from heaven, "Thou art my beloved son . . ." (Ps. 2^7) is heard by John in the trance.

It will be contended by many that these accounts, or some of them, imply that Jesus saw the vision, whether John saw it or not. Perhaps Mark is that which comes nearest to this view, which however is, I contend, incorrect. In Mark 1^{9f} the last person mentioned before "And immediately" is John. And the whole of Mark 1^{2-8} has dealt with John, who is the first and most prominent person in the narrative so far. Jesus is brought on to the scene in 1^9, but we have been immediately brought back to John in the same verse, and John is still, therefore, the main subject of thought. Moreover, as Mark knows the use of ἑαυτόν, he would have used it instead of αὐτόν, had he wished to say that Jesus saw the spirit descending upon Himself. The same applies to Matt. 3^{16}, where, however,

* For further illustration of the prophetic use of "as it were," see *St. Luke the Prophet*, p. 301.

JOHN THE BAPTIST 201

the persons are more mixed, and yet it is clear that
" then he (John) *suffers* Him (Jesus) " because Jesus had
just said " *Suffer* (Me) so far (to come to thee for baptism)."
Then there is a parenthesis, as I contend, of one line, of
which Jesus is the subject, and then follows the remark
he saw, meaning John. It must be admitted that
Matthew has made Jesus ascend out of the water as if
he understood Mark to mean that, whereas Mark meant
John ascended. But I think Matthew intended to leave
the door open, being himself uncertain. Luke, too,
avoids deciding the question. John, while avoiding to
say that *John baptized Jesus*, is quite clear that John
saw the vision. Nothing can be inferred on this point
from the address, " Thou art my Son, etc.," simply because
it is a citation of Ps. 2.

But the hour of the trance is not wont to be the hour
of its declaration. Nor is it likely that the first discovery
by the Baptist that his instructions were now crowned
with fulfilment, his hopes realized; his expected Chief
identified, would be followed by the instantaneous outburst of his testimony in public. The discovery was a
revelation in the fullest and truest and most technical
sense of the word. It was a divine revelation on the one
side, and it was the beginning of a mighty drama, and, he
could not doubt, of a world-wide tragedy, on the other.
Raw haste were here unseemly. He pondered a day and
a night. No other prophets were there to whom his
apocalypse could be submitted, even if he could find a
single member of his order: but, in fact, he supposed
himself the last of the prophets, born at the brink and
shoal of the prophetic time. He mused in prayer over
the instructions of a previous trance in which he had
heard the voice, " Upon whomsoever thou shalt see the
spirit descending and abiding upon him, the same is he
who baptizeth with the spirit, with the holy spirit and
fire." For the words " He who sent me said to me "

(John 1^{33}) are distinctly words that imply a previous trance, and have their parallels in almost every page of the Apocalypse of St. John of Ephesus* (Rev. 10^4, 21^5, etc.). We can imagine that in this trance the Baptist might have heard the voice saying, as it said to Isaiah, " Whom shall I send ? and who will go for us ? " and that he answered, " Here am I : send me " : and that this was the origin of " *He that sent me* to baptize." But it does not appear that he was instructed as to the special form in which the holy Spirit should descend upon the chosen Chief. The dove was not hitherto the symbol of the Spirit. The dove had never yet been associated with the Spirit. When, then, he saw in the trance a dove descending and abiding upon Him, we can understand that the process of thought would be an inquiry whether the dove was indeed a symbol, not so much of the descending Spirit,† but of *Him who was to baptize with the holy spirit.* Now let us try to see how the thought would develop in the Baptist's mind.

The Covenant of Noah.

He was the " messenger of the covenant " (Mal. 3^1). He had his charter, as we have seen, in Mal. 2$^{5\,11}$: " My covenant was with him of life and of peace "—this is the same covenant mentioned, only more generally, as made " with the Levites " in the preceding verse. To this divine promise John would loyally and absolutely hold, and he would be persuaded that God would deal with him and guide him according to the terms of it. But the line of his guidance in the future must be that of guidance in the far past, for the covenant was not new, it was " the covenant of our fathers " (Mal. 2^{10}), and the offering, which was the guarantee of the covenant, " was to be pleasant

---

* See *The Christian Prophets*, p. 85.
† See *Expositor*, Nov. 1910, " The Carefulness of Luke ; Peter's Conversion."

JOHN THE BAPTIST

unto the Lord *as in the days of old* and as in ancient years " (Mal. 3⁴). To what ancient years did the covenant go back but to those of Noah himself, with whom the first covenant was made that ever was made? That, too, was a " covenant of *life* and of *peace*," for it was made " between me and you and every living creature of all flesh; and the waters shall no more become a flood to destroy all flesh." And John was charged with the solemn duty of seeing this covenant of Noah performed in every act, for the waters that had been destructive were used by him for the saving purpose of " turning many from unrighteousness " (Mal. 2⁶). And here he would remember the words of—

Isa. 54⁸ In overflowing wrath I hid my face from thee for a moment; but with everlasting kindness will I have mercy on thee, saith the Lord thy redeemer. For this is as the waters of Noah unto me; for as I have sworn that the waters of Noah should no more go over the earth, so have I sworn that I would not be wroth with thee, nor rebuke thee.

We speak rightly of the baptismal covenant of Christ, but the first baptismal covenant in the world's history is that of Noah, only the baptism there intended is a baptism of the whole world for destruction and of Noah and his crew for salvation. This is the teaching which 1 Peter 3 developed more fully afterwards. But John, when he saw the dove and pondered upon its meaning, could hardly come to any conclusion but that it was the dove of Noah, that it symbolized a baptismal covenant such as Noah's, only far greater, and that it belonged to Him who should baptize with a fuller and more perfect baptism than his own. When, therefore, he saw in the trance on Jordan the spirit descending as a dove and abiding upon Jesus, he knew by this guidance, though he knew not by intuition before, that Jesus was his Chief, He who baptizeth with the holy spirit. And now, said he, I *have* seen, and have borne witness that He is the chosen of God.

The Purgation of the Temple.

This inquiry was not undertaken with any purpose of throwing light upon the structure of the Fourth Gospel, but it seems to have been the means of bringing a sidelight upon a portion of John 1. And it is, further, just possible that we may see some light upon a very difficult question which arises in John 2, the purgation of the Temple. Why does John place this event at the very commencement of the Ministry when the Synoptics place it at the end? Historically, it is improbable that the Lord was supported thus early in his career with such a force of popular enthusiasm as to make it possible to overpower the Temple authorities who were charged with the maintenance of order or, at the best, of the *status quo*. At the later time it is conceivable. The reason why John thought the date was early and not late may perhaps have been that he was considering Malachi through the mind of the Baptist, and when he read there—

Mal. 3^1 And *there shall suddenly* (ἐξέφνης) *come to his temple* the Lord whom ye seek, and (even) the messenger of the covenant whom ye desire—

he thought that this prophecy must have had its fulfilment in a time as early as possible. Bacon well says in his powerful work,* "There is no consideration given (in John) to the fact that the purging of the Temple, a huge fortress, with its 'captain of the temple' and garrison of organized Levitical police, could not be carried out before Jesus had reached the zenith of His popularity with the masses, nor to the fact that, when carried out, all its consequences, including those of the saying on 'destroying the temple,' could not be quiescent for a period of two or three years, awaiting Jesus' return to Jerusalem."

* *The Fourth Gospel in Research and Debate*, 1910.

JOHN THE BAPTIST

Here, however, a difficulty is presented which perhaps has been already present to the reader in what was said before concerning the interpretation of the prophetic sense of Mal. 3^{1-3}. It was observed (p. 188) that at least as early as Justin the person who "shall sit" (Mal. 3^3) was understood to be the Baptist: whereas the English reader is disposed to understand the Christ to be here described. And, in Mal. 3^2, the majesty of the person coming seems to belong to the Lord rather than to His Messenger. But this must, however, be somewhat doubtful, for Mal. 3^1 is certainly concerned first of all with the Messenger, and only next to him is the Lord mentioned, and then, in the third place, the Messenger of the covenant is mentioned again. It is clear that the comings are much interlaced. What is difficult for us was also difficult for the apostles. There were probably two traditions, that of Justin mentioned just now, which interpreted Mal. 3^3 of the Baptist, and another which interpreted it of the Lord, so that He, the Lord, "shall purify the sons of Levi," and the fulfilment of this interpretation was found in the purging of the Temple where the Levites were.

When we examine the fulfilment as presupposed in John $2^{14\,\text{ff}}$, what do we find? We find that He did not "sit," whereas the money-changers *sat*. "Refining and purifying" He did completely, by act and word. "As the gold and as the silver" is a comparison. "And he shall purify the sons of Levi," the responsible Temple guardians, morally and spiritually, as thoroughly as He shall remove the money-changers whom they have permitted to desecrate the Temple. "And he shall *pour them* ($\chi\epsilon\epsilon\bar{\iota}$) as their gold and as their silver" (and if any proof were needed that the Malachi passage is fulfilled, it is here) as He "*poured out* ($\dot{\epsilon}\xi\acute{\epsilon}\chi\epsilon\epsilon\nu$) the small coins of the money-changers." The fact that the description is much more detailed in John than in the Synoptists seems to show not the presence of an eyewitness so much as the author's sense of the relative importance of the action. But relative to what? To the completion of the mental picture sketched by Malachi and converted into reality by the Forerunner so far as he went, and by the Lord, the greater than he, after his chief work of witnessing to the Christ was fulfilled. For the Forerunner is not allowed by John to remain in the foreground of the picture for a moment longer than the necessary introduction. His mission was to the Levites, and the importance of it was that in course of it he unfolded the infinitely greater mission of his Chief. There John considers that it ended : " This my joy therefore is fulfilled. He must increase and I must decrease." These are the terms describing his wholly subordinate position after the first, in John, where we must observe a sharp contrast to the position attributed to him by the Synoptics. " He hath borne witness to the light," and there is no more for him to do. Even his mission to the Levites is not carried into practice by him, but by his Chief in His own person, " coming suddenly to His temple," so that, in spite of the authorities set for the purpose, no one " endures the day of his entering, no one withstands at his appearing " (Mal. 3^2).

Is Justin's Tradition earlier than one in the Fourth Gospel?

That this gospel tradition of interpretation of Malachi is later than that of Justin is perhaps not beyond a sort of indication, though the balance of probabilities is here decidedly delicate. The striking feature of the narrative in the Synoptics is that it is connected by them with two ancient prophecies—

Is. 56^7 For my house shall be called a house of prayer for all the nations (saith the Lord who gathereth the dispersed of Israel),

and

Jer. 7^{11} Shall my house be a den of robbers ?

JOHN THE BAPTIST

The first question to be answered is what connection, if any, these prophecies have with Mal. 3^3? And surely it is not difficult to answer. For Mal. 3^{3c} proceeds thus—

> And there shall be (*some*) bringing to the Lord a sacrifice in righteousness, and (also) *the sacrifice* of Judah and Jerusalem shall *please the Lord* as the days of old and as the years that are past.

But this is merely a reassertion in regard to (*some*) of the passage in—

> Isa. 56^{1-6} (concerning the influx of foreigners, including eunuchs, as proselytes into the Jewish Church)— Their whole burnt offerings and *their sacrifices shall be acceptable* upon my altar.

In other words, the course of thought on the part of Mark has been from Mal. 3^3 to Isa. 56^7, and he has represented our Lord as embodying the latter passage in his " teaching " on the occasion, in which particular Matthew and Luke have not followed him, but are content to write " he saith to them, It is written." In John 2^{17} this is all changed into " And his disciples remembered that it was written, The zeal of thine house shall eat me up " (Ps. 69^9), which quotation is presented as if the parallel were an afterthought of some long consideration and not as part of the occurrence at the time; at least the close vicinity of the expression in 2^{22}, " When he was risen from the dead his disciples remembered that he had said this unto them and they believed the scripture," suggests a much later date for the discovery of the parallel. Therefore Ps. 69^9 may be left aside for the present purpose, and it is clear that the Johannine narrative is not intended to supplant the Synoptic in regard to the use of the prophecies applying to this particular occasion.

We have, therefore, three separate considerations: first, that of the Lord's action, which appears to be described as a fulfilment of Mal. 3^3; next, His teaching on the occasion, which fulfils Isa. 56^7 and Jer. 7^{11}; lastly, the parallel suggested afterwards by the action with Ps. 69^9.

The first of these prophetic passages has provided the train of thought which in the mind of John (as we have seen at length) connects the event with the work of the Baptist which immediately precedes it (save for the interruption of the miracle at Cana); it has also provided some of the phraseology; it has also, perhaps, accounted for the strange and incomprehensible position of the event in the Johannine narrative. While it is easy to imagine that Mal. 3 is the starting-point of thought which arrives later at Isa. 56^7, it is anything but easy to imagine the converse course. And Mal. 3 has been the source of the Baptist's inspiration and of John's understanding of it from the first; only in the later part of the narrative (2^{14-17}) John has followed a tradition which saw prefigured in Mal. 3^3 the action of Jesus, where the earlier tradition which Justin follows had seen the action of the Baptist.

If this is so, then we have an instance of the encroachment on prophetic property, *i.e.* a context of Malachi first applied to John has been afterwards claimed in application to Jesus. (See Ch. V. p. 139.)

The Chananæans.

So far, however, we have not found that the prophecy of Mal. 3 exhausts the particulars of the narrative in John 2. Nothing is said of the buying and selling of oxen, sheep, and doves, nor of the scourge of small cords, though the main features of the visit to the Temple have been found. We have, therefore, to look further into ancient prophecy, but yet not far. For the last verse of Zechariah immediately precedes Malachi, which indeed belongs to it, as we have seen, and is never mentioned in scripture under a name of its own : it is part and parcel of Zechariah. Now Zech. 14^{21} ends with the words, " And there shall not be a Chananæan any more in the house of the Lord Almighty in that day." Who is meant by the Chananæan? When we turn back to Zech. 11⁴ we begin to see several elements which strike us as bearing on the question before us. The sellers of sheep come here into view.

> Zech. 11⁴ Thus saith the Lord Almighty, Shepherd the sheep for slaughter, which they that had gotten them slaughtered and repented not, and *they that sold them* said, Blessed be the Lord and we have become rich.

Evidently, then, there were some sheep used for a sacrifice unaccompanied by repentance, and sold at a profit by those who blessed the Lord. Presently we read—

> And I will shepherd the sheep for slaughter into the Chanaanite country—

an obscure expression, like many of Zechariah's. It continues—

> And I will take to myself two rods ($ῥάβδους$), the one I call Beauty and the other Rushbound ($σχοίνισμα$), and I will shepherd the sheep.

The Greek means *an implement of rushes;* but this is unmistakably the foundation of the term in John 2¹⁵, "*a scourge (of small cords)*" *of twisted rush* ($φραγέλλιον$ $ἐκ\ σχοινίων$), which, as Westcott observes, was a symbol of authority and not a weapon of offence. The twisted rush would be easily made into a rod, which would soon assume the form of a scourge. "Small cords" is a misleading term. After a verse the prophecy continues, "And I said I will not shepherd *you*," addressing, perhaps, the Chananæans, and perhaps the Jews. And presently—

> Zech. 11¹¹ And *the Chananæans shall be scattered abroad in that day*, and shall know the sheep that are being

kept; because it is the word of the Lord.* And I will say unto them, If it be good in your sight, give my wage or else forgo it : and they weighed my wage, thirty silver pieces. And the Lord said unto me, Put them into the refinery, and see if it be proof, even as I was proven on their behalf. And I took the thirty silver pieces and I cast them into the house of the Lord for the refinery. And I threw away the second rod, the Rushbound, to scatter abroad the covenant in the midst of Judah and in the midst of Israel (or, between Judah and Israel).

It is evident to readers of Matt. 27 that we have come upon the source of a second fulfilment before we have quite done with the first. To this we shall return in the next chapter. Meanwhile the conviction is forced upon one that the Chananæans are somehow in possession of the house of the Lord, that they are the sellers of sheep for sacrifice, that they reap a profit thereby, and that they are to be scattered by the bearer of the Rushbound implement who penetrates into the Chanaanite country for the purpose. Thus we have advanced to the two principal elements lacking in Mal. 3, in the narrative of John 2, the sellers of sheep and the whip of small cords.

But why, it may well be asked, are the sellers the Chananæans ? What conceivable connexion is there between the characters and this name ? The answer to this question will be easy to any observant reader of Edersheim's *Life and Times of Jesus the Messiah ;* the wonder is that neither he nor Westcott has pointed it out, and it is one that carries with it a demonstration far more extensive than any which its own little problem demands. " There can be little doubt," says Edersheim,†

---

* This is the reading of the Alexandrine MS., which is usually that which the apostles followed. Another reading makes the sheep to be scattered instead of the Chananæans.

† *L.c.,* p. 371 (III. v.).

JOHN THE BAPTIST

" that the Temple-market was what in Rabbinic writings is styled ' the Bazaars of the sons of Annas ' * (*Chanuyoth beney Chanan*), the sons of that High-Priest Annas (Chanan), who is so infamous in New Testament history. . . . From the unrighteousness of the traffic carried on in these bazaars and the greed of their owners, the Temple-market was at the time most unpopular. . . . Popular indignation (in A.D. 67) swept away the bazaars . . . on account of the sinful greed which characterized their dealings. . . . Josephus describes Annas, the son of the above-mentioned, as a great hoarder of money, very rich, and despoiling by open violence the common priests of their official revenues. . . . The Talmud also records the curse which a distinguished Rabbi of Jerusalem (Saul) pronounced upon the high-priestly families, who were themselves high priests, their sons treasurers, their sons-in-law assistant treasurers, while their servants beat the people with sticks ? " What a comment this passage offers on the bearing of Jesus, as He made a scourge to drive out the very servants who " beat the people with sticks," and upset their unholy traffic ! The last sentence of Edersheim is, as we have seen, to be taken with caution, for though John 2^{15} says he cast them all out from the Temple, it does not say that the " whip of small cords " was a means of offence. The learned Talmudist has not observed either the composition or the precise bearing of the *rush-whip*, and when he adds, " even this not without significance; and *with it* drove out, etc.," he seems to refer to the idea of Jewish tradition that the Messiah should come with a scourge for the chastisement of evildoers, rather than to the exact facts of the case.

The LXX has got Χαναναῖοι, Chananæans, here (Zech. 11^{11}) where the Hebrew has no proper name. It is easy to see how the difference of reading arose. And it

* חֲנֻיוֹת Jer. 37^{16}, *cabins, cells.*

is quite likely that the LXX represents the original and the Hebrew misrepresents it. For כנעני is genuine in Zech. 14^{21}, and it is altogether unlikely that the name should not have been mentioned till this last line but one of the whole prophecy, where there is no clue whatever to its meaning. The mere addition of a *yodh* has given the present Masoretic readings of 11$^{7, 11}$, making the divergence from the LXX, which I submit has the true sense. Remove the intrusive *yodh* and then we have good sense in the Hebrew, so that before we reach the last verse of Zechariah we do know some part of its meaning.

The LXX translation of the word has brought a most astonishing coincidence into the range of probability. The χαν. represents the original כנ׳ of Zechariah, but then, when retranslated into Hebrew of the first century A.D., it is represented by חנ׳, חנה, whence חנות, *tavern*, *shop*, or *inn*, κατάλυμα; *khan* Arabic. That this current name for the shops of the Temple-vendors forced itself into the interpretation of Zech. 11–14 at that time and when the Gospels were written seems highly probable. Here is an example of the effect of the Greek. At the same time, חנן (*Annas*) belongs to a different root, whence *Hannah, John*, etc. (*grace*). And this latter name is the true origin of Χαναναῖοι (*Chananæans*), though the word for *shops* contributed something to the interpretation. The Annas in question is he who was high priest A.D. 6–15.

In other words, we may express the probable history of Zech. 11^{11}, etc., thus—

(1) The prophet Zechariah wrote כנ׳ both in Zech. 11$^{7, 11}$ and in 14^{21}.

(2) LXX has translated this correctly *Chananæans* Χαναναῖοι Χανανῖτιν.

(3) The *Chananæans* are understood by all readers of LXX about A.D. 30–70 as the Temple-vendors.

JOHN THE BAPTIST

(4) [We may suppose that " Matthew," in his " collection of the Oracles in Hebrew," turned the *Chananæans* into 'חנ if, as is possible, he included Zech. 11 in it. And one is inclined to suppose that the author of John had seen this, or at least knew the traditional identity.]

(5) The authors of the Hebrew text represented by our Masoretic Hebrew (intentionally, as I believe, at the Synod of Jamnia, A.D. 90, where some of " the sons of Annas " were present) altered the reading, at the cost of making almost nonsense, by inserting a *yodh* or *jot*, and away go the *Chananæans!* Nothing in the Hebrew text is left but the innocuous because unintelligible reference to the *Canaanite* (R.V. margin *trafficker*) in Zech. 14^{21}. After which the Purgation of the Temple is at any rate no longer a prophecy fulfilled by Jesus for readers of the Hebrew of Zechariah.

CHAPTER VIII

JUDAS

A Trace of a List of the Oracles.

WE have seen that the track of the Chananæans was intersected by another, which we have now to pursue—the connection of this same prophecy of Zech. 11 with the wages of guilt of Judas Iscariot. The application of it is found in Matt. 27, and nowhere else, though there is some kind of veiled reference to it in Acts 1[18]. We notice first of all the extreme freedom which this prophecy has received at the hands of Matthew. In the original the verb is in the first person, " And I took the thirty silver pieces," in obedience to the Lord's command: but in Matt. 27[9] the evangelist has indubitably changed the verb into the plural " they took," so that the singular would leave the action of the chief priests without any support. In no case, however, would there be any true analogy between the action of the prophet Zechariah and either of the parties understood by the evangelist. The attribution by Matthew of the prophecy to Jeremiah, when it is Zechariah's and not Jeremiah's, is another mistake to notice : the most probable explanation being that the words were first placed in a list of oracles of the Old Testament concerning the Lord,* even that very list which " Matthew compiled in a Hebrew language " according to Papias ($Ματθαῖος\ μὲν\ οὖν\ ‘Εβραΐδι\ διαλέκτῳ\ τὰ\ λόγια\ συνεγράψατο$), and which Papias himself probably followed very closely in his Greek book, *The Exposition*

* See Ch. XIII below.

JUDAS 215

of the Oracles concerning the Lord. Here it was placed next after some oracle from Jeremiah, and following down the list the eye of the evangelist passed rapidly from the one oracle to the other without noticing that the second was taken from a different prophet.

The Potter's Field in Matthew.

It is possible to conjecture what the Jeremiah oracle was, and it has been conjectured, in fact, that it was an oracle also concerning Judas. Such an oracle may be seen in Jer. 18 or 19. For instance—

Jer. 18³ Then I went down to the potter's house:

of which prophecy we may conjecture that the fulfilment ran, " Judas went down thither to kill himself." However, we are not left to conjecture concerning other points in the somewhat confused tangle of stories which attend the subsequent fate of the traitor. There is no *potter's field* at all in the Bible except in Matt. 27¹⁰, for the words in Zech. 11¹³ are *unto the potter* (Heb.) and "into the refinery" (LXX); the *field* is supplied by the tradition of the age of Matthew. The earlier part of the Zechariah passage quoted above has been employed at an earlier stage of the history by Matt. 26¹⁵, " What are ye willing to give me, [and I will deliver him unto you?] And they weighed unto him thirty pieces of silver." That the expression of Matthew is really directly due to Zech. 11¹² is clear from the word *weighed;* since it would not be at all likely that Judas had his thirty pieces *weighed* by the Sanhedrin authorities. But the passage which supplies the greater part of the particulars after the making of the bargain and the price is to be found in Jer. 19, and it has supplied not only Matthew, but also some other accounts of the awful end of the life of Judas. First let us take these which have been taken up into Matthew.

Jer. 19¹ Then said the Lord unto me, Go and *obtain* a potter's earthen bottle and [thou shalt bring it (Gk., but the Heb. leaves it blank)] from *the elders of the people and* from *the elders of the priests.* (Now Matt. 27³ says that Judas returned the thirty pieces of silver to *the high priests and elders.*)

And come forth unto the cemetery (πολυάνδριον) of the sons of their children which is at the entry of the gate of *potsherds.* (This is the right reading of Heb. and of the Alexandrine MS. of the Greek, which is, as usual, to be trusted, and " the gate of Tharsis " is pure error. But Matt. 27⁷ tells us that the high priests bought with the money " the Potter's Field *to bury* strangers in," εἰς ταφὴν τοῖς ξένοις.)

The kings of Judah [or, *of Judas*] filled this place *with innocent blood* (αἱμάτων ἀθῴων). (But Matt. 27³ says that Judas " said to the high priests and elders, I have sinned in betraying *innocent blood* " (ἥμαρτον παραδοὺς αἷμα ἀθῷον). This is the right reading which the Revised Version has preserved, as the four best MSS. overwhelmingly prove, together with other strong evidence.)

⁶ *Wherefore* behold the days come, saith the Lord, when *this place shall no more be called Falling asunder* and Cemetery of the son of Hinnom, but *Cemetery of the Slaughter.* (But Matt. 27⁸ says, " *Wherefore* that field *was called the Field of Blood* unto this day." The evangelist has followed his original so closely as to preserve even the *wherefore* of it, though indeed the circumstances of the reason were in the two cases not identical. At the same time, though between *Cemetery of the Slaughter* and *Field of Blood* (Ḥagal Dema, Akeldama, Acts 1¹⁹), the difference of meaning is small, the latter retranslates the former back into Hebrew but not the Hebrew of Jeremiah. Is it not probable that Akeldama was in the list of

JUDAS

oracles which Matthew collected in Hebrew, and that Acts[18,19] were written by one who had read the list?

[7] And I will slaughter (Heb. empty out) *the counsel of Judah* [or, *Judas*] *and the counsel of Jerusalem* in this place, and I will *cast them down*. . . . (With this we may compare Luke 23[51]: Joseph of Arimathea " had not consented to *the counsel* and deed *of them*," while the corresponding verb is used more than once elsewhere of the Sanhedrin. But Matt. 27[5] says " And he *cast down* the pieces of silver into the sanctuary and departed; and he went away and hanged himself.")

Thus, while the passage in Jeremiah has nothing to do with the traitor and the betrayal, it has very much to do with Judas, with innocent blood, with a consequent change of name of a place close to Jerusalem by the gate of potsherds, used as a burial-place, formerly known as *Falling asunder* (Διάπτωσις, a quaint play of words in translation by the LXX of the familiar name of *Tophet*) and thenceforward as *Field of Blood*, with the counsel of Judas and the counsel of Jerusalem as represented by the elders of the people and the priests, which is destroyed by violence. What other particulars of the narrative in Matthew remain, after those which Jeremiah supplies have been utilized, up to the point of Judas's violent death?

Then we come to the circumstances of the death, concerning which the early Christian imagination was allowed to enjoy a considerable and horrible indulgence, ranging far in the wilds of exaggeration which opened out beyond the modest gate of ancient prophecy. First of all we have the moderate statement of Matthew given above—he went and hanged himself. This by no means wanders away from the path of prophecy, but instead of following Jeremiah it follows—

2 Sam. 17²³ Ahitophel (the arch-traitor) saw that *his counsel* had not taken place, and saddled his ass and rose up *and went away* to his house unto his city, and he gave charge to his house, and *he hanged himself* (ἀπήγξατο) and died, and he was buried in the tomb of his father.

It has been usual generally to identify Judas with the "familiar friend whom I trusted, who did eat of my bread," and yet "laid great wait for me." Those who are familiar with this identity will be interested to observe one of the features of the Greek version of this—

Ps. 41¹⁰ For the man of *my peace*, on whom I hoped, who eateth my loaves, hath made great scorn upon me.

We shall see later how the type of Judas in covenanting with the elders of Israel promises that "to all the people," that is, to the disciples, "there shall be *peace*."

The Falling-asunder in Acts.

Then we come to the Lucan account, Acts 1¹⁸: "Now this man obtained a field with the reward of his iniquity; and falling headlong he burst asunder in the midst, and all his bowels gushed out. And it became known to all the dwellers at Jerusalem; insomuch that in their language that field was called Aceldama, that is, the field of blood. For it is written in the Book of Psalms—

Let his habitation be made desolate, and let no man dwell therein,
And, His office let another take.

These citations are from Ps. 69²⁵ and Ps. 109⁸, and if we look, as usual, into the contexts we shall easily see what right the apostolic writers claimed in virtue of the Argument from Prophecy to find what seemed to them evidence for the circumstances of the end of Judas,—

JUDAS

exactly the same right as that which entitled Luke to quote the lines quoted. Let us observe that the former psalm has already provided John 2[17] with the fulfilment which "the disciples remembered" afterwards—

> The zeal of thine house shall eat me up,

and St. Paul (Rom. 15[3]) with the illustration of Christ pleasing not himself, " but, as it is written—

> The reproaches of them that reproached, thee are fallen upon me "—

and the fourth Gospel with the words of John 19[28], "After this Jesus, knowing that all things are now finished ($\tau\varepsilon\lambda\acute{\varepsilon}\lambda\varepsilon\sigma\tau\alpha\iota$), that the scripture may be accomplished ($\tau\varepsilon\lambda\varepsilon\iota\omega\theta\tilde{\eta}$), saith, I thirst," and St. Paul, again, with the illustration of the wickedness of Israel in Rom. 11[9], "And David saith—

> Let their table be made a snare, and a trap, and a stumbingblock, and a recompense unto them: let their eyes be darkened that they may not see, and bow down their back alway."

Besides this considerable total of actual quotation, Ps. 69 has furnished a verse in Matthew, Mark, and John, almost without any change in its wording and without the mark of quotation—

> *They gave me gall* for my meat, and *in my thirst they gave me vinegar to drink* (Ps. 69[22]).

We are therefore to expect that this psalm which has produced so many recognized illustrations for the apostles' guidance has produced others which are less recognized, but can yet be discovered. The same is true of Ps. 109, which, however, is seldom quoted in the New Testament.

We observe that according to Acts 1[18], " Judas had obtained a field ($\dot{\varepsilon}\kappa\tau\acute{\eta}\sigma\alpha\tau o\ \chi\omega\varrho\acute{\iota}o\nu$) with the reward of iniquity," whereas Matt. 27[7] says that " the chief priests bought the potter's field." Next Acts 1¹⁹ says that the name, Field of Blood, was due to the suicide of Judas, while Matthew attributes the name to the death of Jesus. A third discrepancy in the accounts is in the mode of death, for hanging is quite different from the falling headlong and bursting asunder. There is no object in harmonizing the two accounts, which obviously represent two different traditions. The Lucan tradition, in which there are three points, the headlong fall—the bursting asunder—the bowels gushing out—appears to take its rise in the name *Falling asunder* ($\Delta\iota\acute{a}\pi\tau\omega\sigma\iota\varsigma$) of Jer. 19⁶, when we take it in connection with Luke's remark that " this became known ($\gamma\nu\omega\sigma\tau\grave{o}\nu\ \grave{\varepsilon}\gamma\acute{\varepsilon}\nu\varepsilon\tau o$) to all the dwellers in Jerusalem." The reasoning would be this: the plot of ground was once known as *Falling asunder* because of Jer. 19⁶. This name was given because Judas was to fall, and did fall, asunder in it. This name was then changed to *Field of Blood*. It is highly probable that the falling asunder was found to be further explained by—

> Ps. 109¹⁸. He clothed himself with cursing as with a garment, and it came like water *into his bowels*.

But this would hardly suffice to justify the clearer statement in Acts 1. For this we must refer again to—

> Jer. 19⁴ *The kings of Judah* [*or, of Judas*] filled this place *with innocent blood*.

Now the kings of Judah in order to be *kings of Judas* must be kings who prefigured Judas. History knows but one such, Jehoram the unworthy son of Jehoshaphat, who did evil in the sight of the Lord, and slew all his brethren with the sword. In one respect he was like Judas, for—

> 2 Chron. 21⁹ *He went with the rulers*, and all the horsemen with him, and it came to pass that he arose *by night*.

For his wickedness he was smitten with an incurable plague so that *his stomach (κοιλία) fell out.** Therefore it seemed that Jehoram, who slew his brethren though he was himself the firstborn (πρωτότοκος), and was therefore a traitor to his own father's house, and who, moreover, *went with the rulers* on an expedition *by night*, provided the fulfilment of the prophecy in Jer. 19⁴ which spoke of "the kings of Judas who filled this place with *innocent blood."* Therefore, as he prefigured Judas in three particulars, this was evidence that he prefigured him in the fourth, the manner of his death.

The third point of the Lucan tradition is the headlong fall, which we consider last because the other two points, though they follow it in the resulting composition in Acts 1¹⁸, have preceded it in the order of thought in the evangelist's mind, connected as they were with the main thread of the prophetic theme. The scene is now changed to a beautiful passage in Wisd. 4¹⁵ ff, where the writer, after saying that "God created man on the scale of immortality," proceeds to draw out the contrast between the elect and the wicked—

> Wisd. 4¹⁵ For grace and mercy are among his elect and overseership (ἐπισκοπή) among his holy ones. (This reference to overseership, "bishopric," is just the link between Wisdom and Ps. 109⁸ quoted in Acts 1¹⁹, which proves that the passage in question was present to the writer of Acts.) And the righteous in his trouble (καμών, which is just not θανών) shall condemn the ungodly which are living, and youth which is soon finished the old age of the unrighteous of many years. For they shall see the end of the wise and shall not understand what God designed

---

* The same fate was said to have befallen the heretic Arius in A.D. 336 (see Hefele, *History of the Councils*, ii. 34 and references). "Athanasius related that after this incident very many Arians became converted."

for him and to what end the Lord set him in safety: they shall see him and set him at naught, but the Lord shall laugh them to scorn: and they shall after this be *a vile carcase* (πτῶμα ἄτιμον) and *a reproach among the corpses of old time*.* For *he shall rend* (ῥήξει) *them speechless, headlong* (πρηνεῖς), *and he shall shake them from the foundations; and they shall be utterly laid waste* (χερσωθήσονται) *and be in pain, and their memorial shall perish.*

The same word *headlong* is adopted by Luke, and it occurs nowhere else in the Bible or Apocrypha. The whole passage is most instructive when read in the light of the betrayal as narrated in the Gospels. But here, too, the reference to the vile carcase being a reproach among the corpses of old time takes us back to Jer. 19^2, where the burial-place near the Potsherd Gate becomes the burial-place of the Bloody Deed (Πολυάνδριον τῆς σφαγῆς).

This disposes of the Lucan tradition of Judas's death in Acts, though it would be interesting to show how the immediate sequel to the passage in Wisdom is also further taken up by the immediate sequel in Acts, where one of the features of the narrative is the *confidence* (παρρησία πολλή) of the apostles. This word for confidence is very rare in the Old Testament (six times in the Old Testament and Apocrypha), and it occurs in Wisd. 5^1, " Then shall there stand *in great confidence* the righteous man in front of them that afflicted him," etc.

We may remark that though the Lucan account is fuller in regard to the actual circumstances of the death of Judas, this is no reason for concluding that it is of later origin than Matthew. The two traditions would be concurrent, and Luke is much simpler than Matthew in regard to the confusion of the " Potter's Field."

* The reading translated above is that of the Alexandrine MS., which omits διὰ before αἰῶνος, and is undoubtedly right; the reading with διὰ would mean " for ever " and would be insipid.

JUDAS

Postscriptural Accounts of Judas. The Bag, the Bursting, the Curse, the Crushing.

Next we come to the extra-canonical accounts of Judas's death, though one of these, Papias, is not many years later than Luke and Matthew. We have Apollinarius (about A.D. 160) writing thus—

" Judas did not die in the halter but survived, having been taken down before he was strangled; and this the Acts of the Apostles show, that falling headlong he burst asunder in the midst and his bowels gushed out; and this Papias, the disciple of John, relates more plainly, saying thus in the fourth book of the Exposition of the Words of the Lord (τῆς ἐξηγήσεως τῶν κυριακῶν λόγων) : But Judas walked about in this world, a great example of *impiety* [ἀσεβείας, so Wisd. 4^{16} above], *his flesh blown out* so much that he was *not able to pass where* a wagon passes easily, nay, not even the bulk only of his head. The lids of his eyes, they say, were swollen so much that he *did not see* the light at all, that *his eyes could not even be seen* by a physician with an instrument ([διὰ] διόπτρας), they were so much below the outward surface. Other organs were distorted to an unnatural size, and he suffered from foul *discharges* of matter and worms *for reproach*, but after many torments and retributions having died, they say, on his own *estate* (ἐν ἰδίῳ χωρίῳ), the estate became deserted and uninhabited *to this day* from the smell, and not even to this day *can any one pass by* that place unless *he stop his nose* with his hands, so great a discharge was excreted upon the earth through his flesh."

The harmonizer has been at work again here, but has only made matters worse, besides giving us a far more nauseous story. Let us see how far he has been faithful to originals according to his lights—whether his originals or the originals of his tradition. It was said above that

Ps. 69 and Ps. 109, two especially imprecatory psalms, would be found perhaps to provide more material on this subject, besides the verses which Luke in Acts has actually quoted from them. And so it proves. Judas was regarded as the curser on whom his own curses recoiled.

> Ps. 109[19] He loved cursing, and it shall come unto him: and he chose not blessing, and it shall be far removed from him. And he put on cursing as a garment, and it came *like water into his inward parts* and like oil into his bones. Let it be unto him as the garment that he throweth about him, and as *the girdle that he is alway girded withal.* (ζώνη ᾗ διὰ παντὸς ζώννυται).

Here we can hardly mistake a reference to the bag which Judas kept in *his girdle*, if this did not actually serve as his purse: girdle and purse are the same thing in Mark 6[8] = Matt. 10[9]. The bag of Judas, which is only mentioned in John 12[6], 13[29], and is there called γλωσσόκομον, was at least theoretically a box, and in 2 Chron. 24[8] the same word is translated box. Moreover, John says clearly that it was a box into which contributions were *cast* rather than a purse in which they would be put. The fact rather seems to show that John's statement is not manufactured out of Ps. 109[19], and yet it is almost certain that the box was kept in a fold of the girdle, which was an outer garment, and most unlike what we should call a girdle. The Greek ζώνη is used to express both the inner (now become outer) garment ('ēzōr) and the outside waistband (hăgōr) referred to in John 21.

But what is the explanation of "cursing coming like water into his inward parts"? If nothing more than common drinking is intended, the expression is simple enough, and doubtless the psalmist meant it simply so: "let cursing be drunk by him with his drink and put on with his clothes!" But in the application these

JUDAS

words appeared to bear a more subtle meaning. Assuming that Jer. 19¹ applies to Judas, he is to be taken *like an earthen bottle* and *dashed in pieces* publicly (Jer. 19¹⁰) *before the eyes of the elders of the people and the priests* who come out with Jeremiah, "and thou shalt say, Thus saith the Lord, Thus will I dash in pieces this people and this city, even as an *earthen vessel* is dashed, *which cannot be healed.*" This is just like what Matthew records when, instead of making Judas dashed in pieces after his hanging or instead of it, he makes him come *before the high priests and elders* and make public confession of his sin: he is figuratively dashed in pieces by their answer, "What is that to us?" Again, the concluding words in Jer. 19¹¹ form a link with the passage in 2 Chron. 21¹⁸, where "the king of Judas" is smitten with a plague *that cannot be healed.*

But what is very strange is that the mention of an *earthen vessel* takes us to a passage in Num. 5¹⁷ ᶠᶠ declaring the law of jealousy. One part of the ceremony was that the priest should take pure water in an *earthen vessel*, and in his hand the water becomes a cause of the curse, in the Hebrew, but in the Greek, "the water of conviction of this cursed man," and it is mentioned seven times in a few verses. The only verses that we need notice here are—

> Num. 5²¹ ᶠ May the Lord give thee in curse, and an oath in the midst of thy people, in that the Lord maketh thy thigh to have *fallen asunder* and *thy belly blown out;* and *this water of the curse* shall *come into thy stomach, to blow out thy stomach* and for thy thigh *to fall asunder* (διαπεσεῖν).

What is this but the origin of Papias's account of Judas? "He loved cursing, and it came like *this water of the curse* into *his stomach.*"

Then again, this writer found evidence for the other

features of Judas's punishment in the imprecations of Ps. 69^{24} " Let *their eyes* be blinded that they see not : " therefore he reasoned that the traitor became blind : " and do thou bow together their back continually "; therefore some others have pictured him as a hunchback. The mode of his blindness as given by Papias or his elder is not so easy to account for. There is a verse in—

Ps. 17^{10} They have *closed together* their own fat—

which may have suggested it; for two reasons in the context. Just before this we have had " Guard me as the pupil of an eye . . . from the face of the ungodly who afflict me. Mine enemies compass my life." And just afterwards we have " They surprise me *as a lion* ready for prey, and *as a whelp* lurking in secret places." Would not this be likely to receive a further interpretation from the blessing of Jacob ?—

Gen. 49^{9} *Whelp of a lion*, Judas . . . thou stoopest and couchest *as a lion* and *as a whelp*.

Naturally, if we consider that Christ was of the tribe of Judah we are reluctant to think that any part of his blessing by Jacob could be tinged with an adverse meaning; and yet the adverse meaning is not only a tinge in the opening verses of this poem, it is a thorough strong-coloured condemnation of all the three patriarchs Reuben, Simeon and Levi, who have been named before Judah. And Judah is not very favourably described at the outset : he is a dangerous animal to stir. In any case we have to suppose that Judas was of the royal tribe of Judah from the fact of his name being the same.

But, after all, it is quite likely that Papias, so far from following any original in the Old Testament, was merely exaggerating on the lines of Ps. 69^{24}. The foul discharges and worms may be drawn from the picture of—

JUDAS

Job 2⁸,⁹ *The devil smote Job with a grievous sore from feet to head.* And he took a potsherd to scrape *the discharge*, and he sat upon the dunghill *outside the city*. . . . *And thou sittest alone in corruption of worms*, passing all night in the open air.

The expression in Papias *for reproach* (εἰς ὕβριν) reminds us once more of Wisd. 4¹⁸ above. The *estate* (χωρίον) is simply *the place* Aceldama. Then the description of those who pass by it is drawn from—

Jer. 19⁸ *Every one who passeth by* towards it (the city) *shall make a wry face* (σκυθρωπάσει) *and hiss for all its plague.*

Lastly, the conjecture is propounded with hardly less confidence that there is also a reference to the passage which is quoted in Rom. 2—

Ps. 14³ *Their throat is an open tomb* (because) with their tongues they were treacherous (ἐδολιοῦσαν); poison of asps is under their lips; whose *mouth* is full of *cursing* and bitterness. Their feet were swift to shed blood: *crushing* and misery are *in their roads* . . . they that devour my people *in eating of bread.*

The last words may well have been taken to refer to the Last Supper, where " he that *eateth bread* with me hath lifted up his heel against me " (Ps. 41⁹ = John 13¹⁸). If so, the rest of the context may have been taken in a literal sense and craving for a fulfilment, which was found for it in the latter end of Judas. Here, then, is the reference to the *burial-place* again: the poisoned *orifices of the body;* the *cursing;* and the *crushing in the road* where a wagon could easily pass.

There is finally a later reference to Papias by Œcumenius * which represents him as having said that

* Routh, *Reliquiæ Sacræ*, i, p. 26.

Judas was actually crushed by a wagon so that his bowels were poured out. This is the exaggeration of an exaggeration or of more than one.

Thus we have three traditions concerning Judas's death, for the harmonizing Apollinarius prolongs his life in order to insert his torments, and these are such as to be inconsistent with either of the other two accounts. It would not be impossible for the traitor to have survived the time of the Ascension and of Peter's speech in Acts 1, for the account in that chapter is a parenthesis by St. Luke, who makes Peter in his speech confine his remarks to the fact of the vacant apostleship. But he also makes him say that Judas "transgressed to go unto his own place" (Acts 1^{25}, πορευθῆναι εἰς τὸν τόπον τὸν ἴδιον). On the assumption of survival this is a hint of prescience on Peter's part. Or are we to suppose that Peter's speech ends at "Judas transgressed" and the following words are Luke's own parenthesis? They would not have been spoken, one would think, by Peter at the time if Judas had merely disappeared for the time, alive but ashamed. If he had taken his own life they would be appropriate enough. Certainly the traitor's death is made impressive by the rapidity with which it follows on the betrayal. But the theory of a parenthesis here is altogether a subterfuge. Luke implies, as Matthew implies, a speedy end. Therefore Apollinarius is altogether wrong, and only interests the student by showing once more how in the second century all that the Old Testament contained, whether poetry or history or prophecy, was supposed to be evidence of what befell the characters of the New Testament, when once the eye was set upon a line of reference by an idea of resemblance and parallelism. The present instance is valuable as a proof of Luke and Matthew being independent of each other, and Papias independent of both.

There is still another oracle of Judas, somewhat of a

JUDAS

more general nature, which deserves to be mentioned in connection with his supposed avarice. This is—

Mal. 2¹¹ Judas [Judah] was left behind in [? the city] and became an abomination in Israel and in Jerusalem, because Judas profaned the holy things (τὰ ἅγια) of the Lord, in that he loved and practised unto strange gods. The Lord shall utterly destroy the man that doeth these things, until he is brought low out of the tabernacles of Jacob and out of them that bring sacrifice to the Lord Almighty.

Here Judas is represented as an idolater, but idolatry is covetousness (Col. 3⁵, Eph. 5⁵), and "no unclean person nor covetous man, which is an idolater, hath any inheritance in the kingdom of Christ and God." Is the traitor referred to here? Why is his name not found in New Testament after Acts 1? Several types of wickedness are mentioned—Cain, Balaam, Corah, why not Judas? Such a notorious example of treason would have carried weight. But he had not become an example when the books of the Canon were composed. This is a strange fact and suggestive. But Eph. 5 looks rather like a reference to Mal. 2¹².

CHAPTER IX

PETER AND PAUL

Christ the Rock.

AN instructive piece of biblical exposition by St. Paul is given in 1 Cor. 10^{1-6}—

"I would not have you ignorant, brethren, how that our fathers were all under the cloud and all passed through the sea, and were all baptized unto Moses in the cloud and in the sea, and did all eat the same spiritual meat, and did all drink the same spiritual drink: for they drank of a spiritual rock that followed them; and *the rock was Christ* . . . Now in these things they became figures [types] for us."

He seems at first sight to speak as if there was no time since the Jews were a people when the spiritual life was not begun by baptism and sustained by the spiritual meat and drink. That the baptism was wholesale and not individual, nor imparted to those who were born in the desert, and that the meat and the drink were not of the same kind as those of the Eucharist, are noteworthy limitations to the view that he represents the baptism and the eating and drinking as sacraments. Though they were figures or types of sacraments, even this cannot be said without an understanding of his use of the term *spiritual*, which differs from our use of it when we speak of *the spiritual life* in Christ. He uses *spiritual* to mean *prophetic*, as a matter of interpretation. The same use occurs in Rev. 11^8, "the great city which is called *spiritually* Sodom and Egypt, where also their

Lord was crucified." For we find that Jerusalem is called Sodom by the prophet Isaiah (1^{10}) and Egypt by the prophet Jeremiah (24^8). The *spiritual* interpretation of the Bible is that which is inspired by the Holy Spirit " which spake by the prophets." That the baptism of the children of Israel unto Moses did not produce a spiritual life in them is proved by their subsequent idolatry and rebellion, on which St. Paul proceeds to comment : they were carnal, sold under sin. But just as they ate of the prophetically interpreted meat, the manna, so they drank of the prophetically interpreted drink, the water, which poured from the prophetically interpreted rock.

The Smitten Rock.

The origin of the spiritual interpretation " the rock was Christ " may be found in—

2 Sam. 22^2 O Lord my rock (πέτρα) and my stronghold.

The Lord Christ was therefore the rock. But what is meant by the *spiritual* rock which *followed them ?* For this also has a meaning which is not to be found in any idea of Christ's omnipresence or of His particular presence with the idolatrous and rebellious people who had never heard of Him even as a type. The explanation lies in—

Ps. 105^{41} He smote asunder the rock and waters flowed : they journeyed among desert rivers.

This is the reading of the Alexandrine MS., supported by two good authorities, the Verona and the Zurich psalters. The common reading would, however, justify the same inference on St. Paul's part : " rivers journeyed in the deserts." The cardinal word is *journeyed.* The children of Israel journeyed, and wheresoever they journeyed waters were with them : in other words, " they drank of a spiritual following rock," that is, of water which followed them in a prophetic sense from the smitten rock.

The source of this thought is to be traced to the second Isaiah, celebrating the return from Babylon—

> Isa. 48[20] Come thou forth out of Babylon, fleeing from the Chaldeans : proclaim ye a voice of gladness and let this be heard, proclaim it to the end of the earth; say ye, the Lord hath rescued his servant Jacob : and if they thirst, across the desert he will bring them water, out of the rock he will bring it forth for them, the rock shall be cleft and water shall flow, and my people shall drink.

The same promise is represented in the adjoining chapters—

> Isa. 44[8] For I will give water in time of thirst to them that *journey* in the desert.
>
> Isa. 43[19] And I will make in the wilderness a way, and in the desert rivers . . . to make my race the elect to drink.
>
> Isa. 41[18] But I will open rivers upon the mountains and springs in the midst of the plains.

How could the apostles read these verses without taking them as copious evidences for Christian baptism?* They would say inevitably with the prophet,

> Isa. 55[1] Ye that are thirsty, journey to the water.

The striking of the rock by Moses twice (Num. 20[11]) has received an interpretation from very early times which arrests our attention. The Targum of Jonathan on the Pentateuch says upon this passage, "Moses smote the rock twice, and first it gushed out blood, then water." How early this tradition is, none can say. It is not to be believed that it was adopted from St. John, who says

---

* See " Philip and the Eunuch," *Expositor*, March 1911, and "The Epiphany," in the *Journal of Theol. Studies*, Oct. 1911.

(John 19³⁴) "one of the soldiers with a spear pierced his side, and forthwith came there out blood and water." On the other hand, it is fairly certain that John 19³⁴ itself adopts that ancient Jewish tradition. When it is once established that the Lord Christ is the Rock, the apostles have every right to expect that what was said concerning Him in the Pentateuch will be fulfilled in the Gospel, upon the assumption which they have invariably made. Therefore the emphasis laid upon this particular declaration by the author of John in its present form * has a particular force, for it is joined to that of 1 John 5⁵ ᶠ, which involves no less than the conquest of the world: "who is he that conquereth the world but he that believeth that Jesus is the son of God? This is *he that came* by water and blood, Jesus Christ; not by the water alone but by the water and by the blood: and the spirit is that which witnesseth, for the spirit is the truth." Is it not clear from this that *the Spirit* is that *which spake by the prophets?* that whose guidance has led to the prophetic and figurative or typical interpretation of the Old Testament? that which caused the explanation in Rev. 11⁸ of the great city as *spiritually* called Sodom and Egypt? The issue of blood and water from the pierced side was proof that Jesus was the Rock who was the Lord Christ, and herein lay the importance of the eyewitness to whose testimony the editor of the Gospel, in writing John 21, refers as "the other" ($\dot{\varepsilon}\kappa\varepsilon\tilde{\imath}\nu o\varsigma$) who wrote John 1–20, believing that "the other" was an eyewitness of the crucifixion. Thus the reference in John 19³⁴ to Christian baptism (not the baptism of Jesus by John) is not fully intelligible without going back to the rock in the wilderness which Moses smote twice and to the *spiritual* water and blood which flowed from it. The train of thought which is presupposed is that which is expressed in John 5⁴⁶, "For if ye had believed Moses, ye would have

* See Bacon, *The Fourth Gospel*, etc.

believed me, for he wrote *concerning me.*" That *He came by water* does not mean that Jesus opened His ministry by being baptized of John, but that He was proved to be the Christ " that *was to come* " by the water that poured from Him as the Rock.

Peter's Confession.

From this idea of the Rock that was smitten we pass easily to that of the solid rock, which cannot be moved.

> Isa. 51[1] Hearken to me ye that follow that which is righteous *and seek the Lord*, look ye unto *the solid rock* whence ye were hewn . . .

as if he said, " and there in the solid rock ye shall find him, for he is the Rock." May we not, perhaps, in the light of this thought, understand the Oxyrhynchus saying, [4] " Raise the stone and there "—in the solid rock on which the stone lay—" thou shalt find me : cleave the wood and there am I," for the two pieces of cleft wood compose the cross ? And what, then, is the explanation of the promise to Peter which these conclusions force upon us ? Matt. 16[15 ff] " But who say ye that I am ? And Simon Peter answered and said, Thou art the Christ, the Son of the living God. And Jesus answered and said unto him, Blessed art thou, Simon son of John; for flesh and blood hath not revealed it unto thee, but my Father which is in heaven. And *I also* say unto *thee*, that thou art a boulder of rock, and upon this rock I will build my church " . . . ? (This passage should be kept in close comparison with John 1[13], "Them that believe on his name, who were born, not *of blood*, nor of *the will of the flesh*, nor of the will of men [at all], but of God.") The rock on which He will build His Church is *His Name*, Himself, the Rock, and nothing but a deeply seated prejudice would ever suggest any other meaning. Peter is a boulder, a block ($πέτρος$) of rock ($πέτρα$), the steadfastness and solidity here attributed to him being the qualities which he ideally possessed but really lacked at that point in his lifetime. But there is also another implication in the words: "And I *also* say unto thee, Thou art Petros," imply that Peter had previously said to Jesus, "Thou art Petra." The actual word was perhaps used, but instead of being so reported we have the sense of it in "Thou art the Christ."

But Peter added to this confession, according to Matt. 16^{16}, but not Mark 8^{29} nor Luke 9^{20}, "the Son of the living God." The words are from the Old Testament, and it can hardly be doubted that they bore a meaning appropriate to the occasion as well as of everlasting and general import. Which passage of scripture was in his mind? The place where he spoke was Cæsarea Philippi, or rather the parts about it, and we can readily understand that, as travellers have said, the impressive scenery has helped to shape the promise to build upon the rock. There in contrast stood the heathen worship of Augustus, formerly of Pan, earlier still of Baal-Hermon, on the high cliff of limestone above the source of Jordan, just outside* the boundary of the twelve tribes. This fact gives us the clue to the passage quoted—

Hos. 1^{10} And it shall be that *in the place where* it was said to them, *Ye are not my people*, they shall be called there *Sons of the living God*.

This was taken by Matthew to mean that *The Son* of the living God was at any rate to receive that title at Cæsarea Philippi from the lips of Peter. Nor is it incredible that the words of Matthew were used at this time, as we shall see in the next chapter (p. 284). The verse of Hosea is employed by St. Paul, Rom. 9^{26}, where he is illustrating the free purpose of God in calling not only Jews but Gentiles. The first reference, therefore, to the *living*

* *Enc. Bib.*, "Dan," 997.

God is in contrast to the idolatry of the neighbouring high place, in Matthew as in Hosea. To Matthew we may add John $6^{66\,\text{ff}}$, though there Cæsarea is not mentioned, and the scene of action is apparently distant by two days, though still in " Galilee of the Gentiles." In this passage the words " we have believed and known that thou art the holy one of God " are to be taken along with John 1^{12}, " he gave them power to become *children of God*, them that believe on *his name*," and thus it is probable that John has Hos. 1^{10} in view.

Peter and Eliakim.

The continuation of the promise to Peter conveys the power of the keys. " And the gates of Hades shall not prevail against it. *I will give unto* thee *the keys of* the kingdom of heaven : and whatsoever thou shalt bind on earth shall be bound in heaven ; and whatsoever thou shalt loose on earth shalt be loosed in heaven " (Matt. $16^{18\,\text{f}}$). The enormous importance which has become attached to this passage is out of proportion to its original meaning, and yet the latter requires that we should not diminish aught from it. It takes us back to the days of Hezekiah (Isa. 22) and to a crisis in his reign which can best be described in the words of Stanley—

" Up to this point Hezekiah had been firm in maintaining the independence of his country. But now even he gave way. The show of resistance which he had assumed on the death of Sargon he could sustain no longer. He paid the tribute required. The gold with which he had covered the cedar gates and the brazen pillars of the Temple, he stripped off to propitiate the invader. Peace was concluded. Both at Nineveh and Jerusalem we are able to read the effects. Sennacherib spoke as follows : ' From those places (of Hezekiah) I captured 200,150 people old and young. . . . And

PETER AND PAUL

Hezekiah himself, I shut up in Jerusalem his capital city, like a bird in a cage, building towers round the city to hem him in, and raising banks of earth against the gates to prevent his escape. . . . Then upon Hezekiah there fell the fear of the power of my arms, and he sent out to me the chiefs and the elders of Jerusalem with thirty talents of gold and eight hundred talents of silver and divers treasures and rich and immense booty . . . as a token of his submission to my power.'

" But instead of regarding this as a day of humiliation, the whole city was astir with joy. . . Whatever evil might be in store, they were satisfied to live for a day. ' Let us eat and drink, for to-morrow we die ' (Isa. 22^{31}, the source of 1 Cor. 15^{32}). Isaiah was there and looked on with unutterable grief. ' Look away from me, I will weep bitterly. Labour not to comfort me.' In the midst of the revelry an awful noise sounded in his ears, ' that this was an iniquity that could never be forgiven on this side the grave ' (Isa. 22$^{4-14}$).

" Amongst the advisers of the king in this act of submission there was one who attained a fatal eminence. It was Shebna, the chief minister ($\gamma\varrho\alpha\mu\mu\alpha\tau\varepsilon\acute{v}\varsigma$, $\tau\alpha\mu\acute{\iota}\alpha\varsigma$, $o\grave{\iota}\varkappa o\nu\acute{o}\mu o\varsigma$, Isa. 22^{21}), who was over the household and bore the key of state. On him the prophet poured forth a malediction—

> Behold the Lord shall sling and sling, and pack and pack, and toss and toss thee away like a ball into a distant land, and there thou shalt die.

Eliakim was to assume the insignia of the key of state, the mantle and the girdle."

> And I will give unto him the glory of David, and he shall rule and none shall gainsay him, and *I will put the key* of David upon his shoulder, and he shall open and none shall shut, and he shall shut and none shall open. And I will set him as ruler in a trusty

place, and he shall be for a throne of glory in the house of his father. And every one that is glorious in his father's house shall have trust in him, from small unto great, and they shall hang upon him [as a large house-peg] in that day.

The Porter and the Keys.

There can be no doubt that the language reported in Matthew as spoken to Peter represents that of Isaiah concerning Eliakim. *The keys* are the keys of *gates* as well as of treasuries, and Matthew has preserved *the gates.* But Mark 13³⁴ has a significant hint in a brief parable, "As a man sojourning in another country . . . commanded *also the porter* to watch." Now in oriental phrase the gates, as in the Ottomon *Porte,* represent not merely the palace but the kingdom. The kingdom of Hades shall not *prevail* against the Church of Christ. The term *prevail* (κατισχύσουσιν) is also present radically in—

Isa. 22²¹. And I will clothe him with thy robe, and thy crown will I give him and the might [*or,* mightily (κατὰ κράτος)], and thy stewardship will I give into his hands; and he shall be as a father to them that dwell in Jerusalem and to them that dwell in Judah.

But what is perhaps more clearly apparent than the reproduction in Matthew is the fulfilment of Isa. 22 in Acts 12, where Peter is released from prison. First, we bear in mind what is shown elsewhere that *the gates of Hades* in Isaiah can hardly be dissociated from the king that goes—

Isa. 14¹¹,¹⁵ Down to Hades with his glory and all his gladness.

This is shown to be the king of Babylon, whose fall is—

Isa. 14²⁵ To destroy the Assyrians upon the land that is mine and upon my mountains:

in other words, precisely the king of Rome whose fall entails that of the Herodians: that is to say, Herod Agrippa I (see p. 103). The gates of Hades, therefore, mean naturally the government of Agrippa, who had *imprisoned* Peter, one *of those from the church* (Acts 12¹). (The expression *from the church* is somewhat strange: it is perhaps only the second time that Luke has used it in this sense, but he may mean it even here only for the Jerusalem congregation.) A remarkable feature of the story is that the *robe* and *girdle* of Isa. 22²¹ (Heb.) are both present in Acts 12⁸ (ζῶσαι . . . ἱμάτιον). The second *gate* (πύλη ἡ σιδηρᾶ), the iron gate, opened to them of its own accord. Very different was the door of Mary's house, which did not open, while Peter had to continue knocking. Perhaps we may add that here, too, is the explanation of another strange expression in Acts 12¹⁷, " he came forth and journeyed to another *place*," which recalls—

Isa. 22²³ I will set him as ruler in a trusty *place*.

The immediate sequel in Acts is the death of the Babylonian-Assyrian.

The story of Peter's release from the prison *which he opened and no man shut* would naturally be current when Matthew wrote, and it is no great assumption, therefore, that he had it in view when he composed Matt. 16. But whereas St. Luke, in Acts 12, had treated the material and practical side of the fulfilment of the prophecy, Matt. 16 translates it on the spiritual side and gives it a general importance which it has never since lost, while again it has been retranslated into a most material and far-reaching article of teaching. Between opening and shutting on the one hand and binding and loosing on the other there is but a step of metaphor, from a door which is locked to a dispatch which is tied, and yet there is all the difference in the world between a release from prison and a world-wide power of absolution. Such is the popular exposition of scripture. Where is the sober voice of understanding in it?

The Power of the Keys put in Commission.

Before considering further the application of Isa. 22 to Peter, it is important to notice the sequel in Isaiah and to compare it with the sequel in Matthew.

> Isa. 22[25] Thus saith the Lord of hosts, The person that hath been established in the trusty place shall be moved, and he shall be taken away and shall fall, and the glory that is upon him shall be destroyed utterly, for the Lord hath spoken it.

So Matt. 16[20-23] "Then charged he the disciples. . . . And he turned and said to Peter, Get thee behind me, Satan; thou art an offence to me, for thou mindest not the things of God, but the things of men." Any lingering doubt whether the one passage depended on the other is quickly removed by the observation that the new steward or minister is quickly set down from his place by the same authority which set him up, in Matthew as in Isaiah. The reader is likely to miss a particular point in Isa. 22[25] that *he that hath been established* is precisely a translation of the name *Eliakim*, " whom God establishes." And just in the same way *Petros* the boulder is he to whom *Petra* the Rock has given the promise to stand firm, endowing him ideally with the quality on which He will build His Church, while He by no means builds it upon the individual Peter. The parallel could hardly be closer than it is. No sooner is the promise given and the appointment made than it is unmade for a sufficient reason. In terms, indeed, it is not unmade, but it is modified severely. The position of steward or minister or deputy was that of the "king's friend" ($\dot{\varepsilon}\tau\alpha\tilde{\iota}\varrho o\varsigma$, Hushai, 2 Sam. 16[37]; Zabud, 1 Kings 4[5], but *steward*, οἰκονόμος, 1 Kings 4⁶), but instead of walking with the King the steward is commanded now to get behind Him, and he is called an offence and an adversary and Satan. "Can two walk together except they be agreed?" And since to walk behind is to follow, the King instructs him what following Him really means. Thus the Roman claims for the supremacy of Peter based upon this text are destined to be perpetually overthrown by the witness of a repugnant context, all the more repugnant when its origin has been discovered.

But it would seem that Matthew intends the reader to see that the power of the keys was actually put in commission to the twelve by what he says two chapters later (Matt. 18¹⁸). "Whatsoever *ye* bind on earth" . . . This text marks a further stage from the Isaiah passage, but not further from the Hosea, which asserts the plural, "Ye are sons of the living God," and thus completely agrees with—

> Ps. 82⁶ I have said, Ye are gods, and *all children of the Highest* (both on its positive and on its negative side), but ye shall die like men and fall like one of the princes.

This is a passage which, as addressed to judges, covered the power of binding and loosing, and conveyed the absolute power of establishing and disestablishing which resided in the Judge of all the earth, and it is quoted (John 10³⁴ ᶠᶠ) by Jesus to repel the charge of blasphemy. Probably the Lord adopted* a current mode of speech when he said to the disciples that whatever they bound (forbad) or loosed (allowed) on earth (in expounding the new law) should be bound or loosed in heaven. The idea of their being judges in spiritual courts becomes distinctly more prominent as the cognate passages are examined, and the plurality of judges takes the place of the individual judge, Peter.

* *Enc. Bib.*, col. 574.

The third stage is visible in John 20^{23}, "Receive ye the Holy Ghost: whosoever sins ye let go, they are let go for them; whosoever sins ye hold fast, they are held fast." The less Judaic form of speech is here employed, while the heavenly relation of the judicial function of the disciples is still implicit. The two texts used here and in LXX are the two simplest and commonest correlatives, which the English *remit* (*forgive*) and *retain* are not: these are therefore here unsatisfactory. Whether the words are addressed to the apostles as such or as the whole Church at that time, is a question which will never receive a definite solution for all Christians. Meanwhile, the position of Peter is more and more lost in that of the apostles as we read further in the Gospels until we come to John 21, which is an appendix to the fourth Gospel, and while recognizing the fact of his crucifixion* (John 21^{18f}), emphasizes not his judicial but his pastoral office, and in doing this it does not reinstate his character entirely favourably. In comparison with this passage Luke 22^{31} is in a way more favourable: "Simon, Simon, behold Satan obtained you (plural) by asking, that he might sift you as wheat, but I made supplication for thee (sing) that thy faith fail not; and thou, when once thou hast turned again (*converted*), *stablish* thy brethren." *Stablish* takes us back to Eliakim, whom *God stablished*. But on the whole Peter is left by the four Gospels in a double character: first, that of an unconverted man, whose conversion we are to expect, and we have to wait till Acts 10 for it, and secondly, that of a future martyr. Now both these characters are to be discerned in Isa. 22, the former in—

> He shall be moved and shall fall, and the glory that is upon him shall be taken away—

(the Alexandrine reading of Isa. 22^{25}, which is very much gentler than the Vulgate), and the latter in—

* Bacon, *The Fourth Gospel*, etc.

PETER AND PAUL

Isa. 22^{21} And I will give him thy crown and the might [*or,* mightily].

The crown of martyrdom would here be understood in spite of the unworthiness of Shebna. This, then, is the earliest mention of Peter's martyrdom.

The Martyr's Crown.

But the martyrdom itself is not without an illustration from the same passage of Isaiah which was quoted just now (p. 232). It is woven of legend, and the most popular and touching of the legends is the *Quo vadis.* When the persecution began, the Christians at Rome, anxious to preserve their great teacher, persuaded him to flee, a course which they had scriptural warrant to recommend and he to follow—

Jer. 51^{45} Come ye forth out of Babylon, my people, and save ye each his own life from the wrath of the Lord.

But at the gate he met the Lord and asked Him, Lord, whither goest thou? I go to Rome, was the answer, there once more to be crucified. St. Peter understood, returned, and was crucified. Let Isa. 48$^{20\text{ ff}}$ be read again from Peter's point of view. Babylon is Rome, as we know from 1 Peter 5: no other interpretation of the verse is even probable, to any one who will read Rev. 18 with care. The Chaldeans are the idolatrous heathen of Rome, of whom Juvenal speaks as leaders of society in Rome. "Fly thou from Rome, from these heathen astrologers," is therefore the advice to Peter of his Christian friends, who further urge that he and his fellow-apostles—the plural is used—shall go and preach the gospel elsewhere. He prepares to go, but then a higher truth is borne in upon him that the suffering of the Lord, the Rock, is the secret of the world's life.

Isa. 48^{21} Out of the Rock he will bring forth water for them: *the Rock shall be cleft*—

as it was cleft before. "The Lord goes to Rome to be crucified again : further, therefore, I cannot go." Petros, the boulder of rock, must obey the nature of Petra, the Rock.

The Precious Test and the Precious Word.

When we pass from Peter himself to 1 Peter, the authenticity of which has been much impugned of late, though quite unjustly, we find some features in it which are in close accordance with those of the Pauline Epistles. The first that will here be noticed is the *test* (δοκίμιον), 1 Pet. 1[7], "that the test which (embodies) your faith, a more precious thing (this test) than gold that is perishable, though gold too has to be tried by fire, may be found to result in praise (from God) and glory (to God) and honour (among men) by the (gradual) revelation of Jesus as Christ."

At first this passage would seem to imply that martyrdom by burning had commenced for Christians, and therefore that 1 Peter was as late as the second century. This inference, however, comes to nothing when we consider that the writer was full of ideas from the Old Testament and was here reproducing the fiery test which proved *the oracles of God.*

> Ps. 12[6] *The oracles* (λόγια) of the Lord are pure oracles, silver *tried in the fire* (πεπυρωμένον), a *test* (δοκίμιον) for the earth, purified seven times.
>
> Ps. 18[30] *The oracles* of the Lord are *tried in the fire.* So Ps. 119[140], Prov. 30[5].

This shows that the test is of the nature of the oracles of God, which were living and indestructible.*

---

* Before the conclusion of the *Didachê* was written, *the fire of testing* (ἡ πύρωσις τῆς δοκιμασίας) has been extended to the whole *creation of man* and has been placed in the last days. This is due to the effect of the tradition set forth in Rev. 20[9]. "There came down fire from heaven and devoured them." But the same passage is seen at work in the same portion of the

The revelation of Jesus as Christ here mentioned, though usually considered to be the final revelation at the last Day, and though one comes slowly to any other interpretation, may be confidently understood differently, in the continuous sense, because the same expression occurs six verses later in what must be the continuous sense (1^{13} φερομένην, *being borne*). As Hort says, "it may be a long and varying process, though ending in a climax." But until the climax arrives the revelation can only be by means of successive revelations or apocalypses conveyed to the prophets in trance, whose reports were delivered according to rule and issued, if accepted by the criticizing board, in what may fairly and accurately be called dogma; if rejected, in suspense of judgment or else in that form of teaching which St. Paul gives " by way of permission " (1 Cor. 7^6, 2 Cor. 8^8) contrasted with the command of the Lord (1 Cor. 7^{10}), and the confidence of " This we say unto you by the word of the Lord " (1 Thess. 4^{15}). At the same time, in order to understand 1 Peter $1^{6, 13}$ more fully, we have the benefit of a running commentary upon it in Eph. $1^{17\,\mathrm{ff}}$, " that God may give you a spirit of wisdom and revelation in the further knowledge of him "—to mention one of the hundred striking parallels between these two brief Epistles.* This comment, together with its context, serves to show once more how the gift of prophecy was at that time a living gift, a continual means of grace in the Church, and that every term in the Epistle is instinct with vivid meaning which only the narrowness of imagination and the lack of sympathy on the part of

---

Didachê where the third sign of the truth is *the resurrection of the dead but not of all*, only of the saints. So Rev. 20^5 *This is the first resurrection*, which precedes the 1000 years. The same conclusion is forced upon us by the compound term *world-deceiver* (*Did*. 16), which is based upon Rev. 20^8.

* See *St. Luke the Prophet*, p. 185, where the double origin of the two epistles, Ephesians and Peter, on a single momentous occasion is considered at length, in connection with the reconciliation of the two leading apostles.

expositors has impaired and enfeebled. "A spirit of wisdom and revelation in the further knowledge of him" implies certainly a gradual process of growth. But if *the test* is of the nature of a precious saying *of your faith*, it cannot do anything but embody that faith in words. This justifies us in supplying *which embodies* in the translation given above. The test is of the nature of a precious saying *which embodies your faith*. This cannot be anything else but the formula commonly used, the briefest possible, *Jesus is Lord*, or *Jesus is Christ*. This is proved by—

> Rom. 10⁹ If thou shalt confess *the word* (λόγον) with thy mouth, *Jesus is Lord*, and shalt believe in thy heart that God raised him from the dead, thou shalt be saved.
>
> 1 Cor. 12³ I give you to understand that no man speaking in the spirit of God saith *Jesus is accursed*, and no man can say *Jesus is Lord* but in the holy spirit.

This is illustrated by the fact that Polycarp, before his martyrdom, was invited to recant in the formula *Cæsar is Lord*. The utterance of the words would have saved him from the subsequent pressure of the proconsul to "revile Christ." He then passed actually to the fiery ordeal. We thus find that *the test* meaning *Jesus is Lord*, as a dogmatic confession of hearty belief, gives a clear point to the passage.

We have another reference to the same meaning in 1 Cor. 11²⁸ Let a man continually *test* himself (δοκιμαζέτω) by the use of the heartfelt confession which is specified nine verses later—*Lord Jesus :* the object being to discern the Body and concurrently to discern ourselves (11²⁹, ³¹).

The test, however, in 1 Peter is compared with gold and not with silver, as in the Psalms, and if that were an objection to the origination it might be sufficient to reply that all the oracles of the Old Testament together only served to point to the one great fact which was their end, that Jesus was Christ. But there is, further, a passage in Zechariah which underlies much of 1 Pet. 1, 2.

> Zech. 13$^{7\,\text{ff}}$ O sword, awake against my shepherd and against *a fellow-citizen of mine*, saith the Lord Almighty : smite the shepherd, and *the sheep of the flock* shall be scattered abroad, and I will bring my hand upon *the little ones*. And it shall be in all the earth, saith the Lord, that two-thirds of it shall be utterly destroyed and fail, and one-third shall be left in it; and I will bring the third part through fire, and will *refine* them with fire as silver is refined, and *I will test* them *as gold is tested :* he shall invoke *my name*, and I will hear him and will say, *This is my people*, and he shall say, *The Lord* (is) my God.

Here, then, is the source of the contrast *with gold* that has to be tested by fire. And there are several more ideas which 1 Pet. 2 has worked upon. *As newborn babes* (2^2) recalls *the little ones*. Then *Ye were as sheep going astray*, but are now returned to *the shepherd* (2^{25}); which in time past were no people but *are now God's people* (2^{10}); are other products. Likewise, Sanctify in your hearts Christ as *Lord* (3^{14}) and Glorify God *in this name* (4^{16}), and *Shepherd the flock of God* (5^2).

St. Paul and St. Peter at Babylon.

But it is impossible to pass by Zech. 13^7 without further reflections. First of all, we know that 1 Peter was written in Babylon (5^{13}), and it becomes more and more certain to every patient student of the New Testament that Babylon was the common equivalent (Rev. 17^5) on the apostle's lips for Rome. Next, we inquire what indications there are in Zechariah of God's purposes of guidance for His prophets in regard to Babylon, where St. Peter and

St. Paul had in the fulness of time arrived. We find a passage that cannot fail to have been present to the mind of Luke when he wrote the last verses of Acts concerning St. Paul's dwelling at Rome.

> Zech. 5[11] And he said unto me, Build him an house in the land of Babylon, and prepare it, and they shall set it (the measure) there for his preparation (ἑτοιμασίαν). Acts 28[30 f] "He abode in his own hired dwelling " . . .

We note that from this very house was written the Epistle to the Ephesians, the parallel letter to 1 Peter, in which St. Paul uses the words, " your feet shod with the preparation (ἑτοιμασίᾳ) of the gospel of peace " : perhaps he had this text (Zech. 5[11]) in his mind. However, it might very well seem to the apostles there to be the sequel of—

> Isa. 43[12-14] Ye shall be my witnesses (martyrs) . . . for your sakes I will send apostles (ἀποστελῶ) unto Babylon.

Let us place ourselves in thought beside the two chief apostles and St. Luke in Babylon, where they met after some years of a separation that was more than geographical. It is fair to suppose that Isa. 43[11] was at least one reason why St. Paul desired to go to Rome : he must, like his Master, fulfil prophecy. But there had been a moral separation, a breach between Peter and Paul which nothing but the charity that is not provoked and takes no account of evil could have prevented from widening week by week. It originated in the language of undue severity which Paul had used concerning Peter's action at Antioch. A colleague cannot in writing accuse a colleague of " standing condemned," of " fearing " a party, of " withdrawing " (like an unbeliever, Heb. 10[38 f]), of " walking not uprightly according to the truth of the gospel," of " living as the Gentiles " (Gal. 2[11 ff]), without a reconciliation being needed between them and without a declaration also in writing of a joint and definite character to pacify and close the dissension between their several adherents arising out of the accusation.* What, then, we may ask, would a friend of St. Paul reply to a friend of St. Peter who drew the former's attention to Zech. 13^7, " O sword, awake against my shepherd and against a fellow-citizen of mine " in Babylon ? The prophecy would surely seem to be pointed at the very case of St. Paul, the " fellow-citizen of the saints " and the citizen of Babylon. The reading is either *shepherd* or *shepherds*. Both apostles were shepherds, and by their dissension being perpetuated in Paul's writing—he could not have dreamed how it would be immortalized—the flocks of both suffered. If the prophecy was brought into discussion, the plural reading would indicate that both were at fault, the singular that one was, and that must be Paul. Such application might very well serve as a golden bridge over which either party might pass to a reconciliation as between " men of good-will " (Luke 2^{14}).

The doctrine of Kenôsis, emptying.

That St. Paul would swiftly respond to any appeal that was firmly based on ancient prophecy cannot be doubted for a moment, for every page of his writings proves it. But it may be appropriate to show here how a passage in Isaiah had impressed him and inspired him to unstinted labour in the Lord. But before doing this it is to be observed that the same passage is a source of revelation to him of the work of Christ Jesus, who made Himself empty of His equality with God, taking the form of a servant, being made in the likeness of men, and (then) being found in fashion as a man, He humbled Himself, becoming obedient unto death. This great doctrine of the Kenôsis is developed out of—

* See *St. Luke the Prophet*, p. 151 ff, where it is shown how St. Luke reconciled his seniors.

Isa. 49¹ From my mother's womb (the Lord) called my *name* . . . And he set me as a dart elect. And he said unto me, Thou art my *servant*, Israel, and *in* thee will *I be glorified*. ⁴ And I said, in *empty* wise (κενῶς) I labour, for vanity and for nothing I give my strength : therefore my judgment is with the Lord, and my toil before my God. And now, thus saith the Lord who formed me from the womb [to be] his *servant* to gather Jacob unto him and Israel, I will be gathered and glorified before the Lord, and God shall be my strength.

Is not this passage the basis of Phil. 2⁶⁻¹¹, containing as it does the ideas of the *name, servant, glory*, and *emptiness* of labour on the servant's part ? The *name* of the servant *in* whom God will be glorified is reproduced by St. Paul in the words so often misunderstood, " that *in* the *name* of Jesus every knee shall bow (to God)." The words " he *humbled* himself " are partly drawn by St. Paul from the same context, Isa. 49¹³, " the *humble* ones (ταπεινοὺς) of his people he encourageth," which repeats the idea of 49⁷ᶜ " Sanctify him that belittleth his life " (φαυλίζοντα τὴν ψυχὴν αὐτοῦ). Though the Lord is never apparently addressed as Israel elsewhere, it does not seem improbable that He, as " King of Israel," should be addressed as such in Isaiah in St. Paul's interpretation. That the actual word δοῦλος for *servant* should be found in the Greek Old Testament for the basis of *the form of a servant* (without the article) is almost a necessity : and where if not here ? In Isa. 52¹³ the word is παῖς. There is no justification whatever for supposing that St. Paul meant *the form of a slave*. His meaning must have been *the form of a prophet*, since every prophet was the servant of God, and this is what St. Paul, like James and Jude, meant to express in calling himself the *servant of Jesus Christ*, though he seems to press the meaning of *slave* in Gal. 6¹⁷. In Tit. 1¹ he is the *servant of God*.

We now pass to the parallels which he finds between the same Isa. 49 and his own case, and the correspondence illustrates his own *imitatio Christi* (1 Cor. 11¹).

ISAIAH XLIX	ST. PAUL
1. Give heed, ye *Gentiles* . . . *From my mother's womb he called my* name,	Gal. 1¹⁵ *from my mother's womb* and *called me* through his grace, to reveal his Son in me, that I might preach him among *the Gentiles*.
2. and he set *my mouth* as a sharp sword . . .	Eph. 6¹⁹ that utterance may be given to me, in opening my *mouth* with boldness.
	Acts 9¹⁵ Saul is an *elect* vessel unto me.
he set me as a dart . . . *elect* and *hid me in his* quiver.	Col. 3³ Your life is *hid* with Christ *in God*.
4. And I said, I *labour* uselessly *unto vanity* and for naught I give my strength: wherefore *my judgment is* with *the Lord* and my *toil* before my God.	1 Cor. 15⁵⁸ Your *labour* is not *in vain* in the Lord.
	Gal. 4¹¹ I am afraid of you, lest I have bestowed *labour* upon you *in vain*.
	1 Cor. 4⁴ *He that judgeth me is the Lord*.
5. I will be *glorified* before the Lord, and *God* shall be my *strength*.	Eph. 1⁶ unto the praise of the *glory* of his grace.
	1 Cor. 1²⁵ the weakness *of God* is *stronger* than men.
	2 Cor. 11²⁹ Who is weak and I am not weak ? and 12⁹.
6. Behold, I have given thee for *a covenant of the* [*Jewish*] *race*, for a *light of the Gentiles*, that thou shouldest be for salvation unto the end of the earth.	Rom. 9³ I could wish myself cut off from Christ for my brethren's sake, my *kinsmen* whose are . . . *the covenants*.
	Acts 26¹⁸ To turn *the Gentiles* from darkness *to light*.
	Rom. 15²⁸ I will depart through you unto Spain.
	Acts 20²⁴ I count not *my life* dear unto me.
7. Sanctify him that belittleth *his life*, that is abhorred by the Gentiles the servants of the *rulers : kings shall see him*, and there shall stand up *rulers* and worship him for (ἕνεκεν) *the Lord's sake*.	1 Cor. 4¹³ We are made as the filth of the world, the offscouring of all things.
	Luke 21¹²,¹⁷ brought before *kings and rulers for* (ἕνεκεν) *my name's sake*.
8. *In an acceptable time*, etc.	2 Cor. 6² *In an acceptable time* etc.

This passage of Isa. 49 might be illustrated from St. Paul's Epistles at much greater length : the spirit of it permeated his being. But the point which now concerns us is that the prophecy refers to Babylon (47^1, $48^{14, 20}$).

> Isa. 48^{14} In love of thee I do thy will upon Babylon to take away the seed of the Chaldeans.
> Isa. 48^{20} Come thou forth out of Babylon fleeing from the Chaldeans.

Babylon to St. Paul was certainly Rome, and where should it be possible for " kings to see him " if not in the imperial city, to which as Babylon the oracle applies—

> Isa. 49^{12} These shall come from far, these from the north, and the sea, and others from the land of the Persians.

The Chaldeans the Enemy.

He formed, therefore, the design of going to Rome, and it is very remarkable that the time at which St. Luke records the expression of that design by St. Paul (Acts 19^{21}) is precisely the time when he was at Ephesus about to pen the portion of 2 Corinthians which contains the quotation from Isaiah. Acts 19^{21} says, " Paul purposed in the spirit " : and the words imply a revelation in the state of trance in which scriptural texts were sought and found for application. Assuming that the passage prominent in his mind was that from which he has quoted, let us see what guidance was yielded for him from the adjacent chapters.

When a faithful Israelite came to deal with mention of the Chaldeans in connection with Babylon-Rome, he was faced with the most urgent and overwhelming difficulty of the time. The Chaldeans were the Jews' worst enemies, the embodiment of all idolatry; and at the same time they ruled the world, for they ruled its rulers. From Brutus to Marius, Pompeius, Crassus, Cæsar, Tiberius, the leaders of the Roman state had all been closely and

PETER AND PAUL 253

inevitably associated with augury and divination. But the Chaldeans were now superinduced to the Roman system. They were the astrologers and fortune-tellers of Rome.* The fatalist emperor, Tiberius, had studied astrology under them in Rhodes before his accession to the throne. Afterwards jealous of their influence on others while he cultivated their arts on the rock of Capri, he honoured and advertised them, as the emperor Claudius honoured † the Jews later by expulsion from the city, from which they had twice been expelled before. Tiberius's own astrologer Thrasyllus, who had predicted for him the throne, had made him so expert that he foretold ‡ to Servius Galba, "Thou, Galba, too, one day shalt empire taste"— a brief day in the far future.

The Chaldeans were the bloodhounds of the imperial palace in the case of Lepida : § the promoters and the wreckers of imperial ambition in the case of Libo Drusus.¶ One of them by his predictions was a primary cause of Otho's insurrection against Galba. But against the Chaldeans and their clients the punishments of prison and of exile were in vain, for they were a race, says Tacitus, " that in our city will always be prohibited and always kept." ‖ A century later Julia Domna, the Syrian wife of the emperor Septimius Severus, never forgot that she owed her crown to her horoscope, and never lost her passion for the mysteries of divination and astrology. There was no single action of life, no hour of the day, that was not regulated in Roman society by the Chaldeans and their " numbers," which not even Horace could laugh to naught, and their calendars that were in every lady's hand as often as her ambers. Even the poorest must have the stars read for them.

* Mayor on Juv., 10[4], 94. Tac., *Ann.*, 6[20].
† Inde fides arti sonuit si dextera ferro.—Juv., 6, 560.
‡ But Suet., *Galba*, 4, gives another version of the story.
§ Tac., *Ann.*, 3[22]. ¶ *Ann.*, 2[27].
‖ *Hist.*, i. 22. Juv., vi. 574 foll.

254 ORACLES IN THE NEW TESTAMENT

The copious references to the Chaldeans or *mathematici* in the silver-age literature of Rome prove sufficiently that neither Isis-worship, nor Mithras-worship, nor state-worship, nor any other was the religion of the people, but astrology was their only substitute for it. The "Chaldeans" stood for the paramount falsehood of the age in its religious sphere.

But here was the serious contradiction of the divine purpose : thousands of Jews in Rome and elsewhere had sold themselves into the bondage of Satan, like Simon the Magian at Samaria, to rival the Chaldeans in the practice of the black art. The sons of the covenant were leagued with their immemorial foes and oppressors of ancient Babylon,

"Qui saepius exsul
cujus amicitia conducendaque [hireling] tabella
magnus civis [Galba] obit et formidatus Othoni."
Juv., vi. 557.

An outside observer like Juvenal saw in the begging and fortune-telling Jews, whose whole chattels were a basket for broken bits and a wisp of hay to sleep on, the alternative resource of the superstitious Roman to the Chaldeans whom they undersold even in soothsaying. Each beneath his tree* which he rented outside the city by the Appian aqueduct, they interpreted with trembling caution the will of high heaven, the dreams of their clients, under the guise and subterfuge of the Mosaic law. They were by the side of other oriental quacks and impostors from Armenia, Commagênê, and Chaldea. The renegade Jew was hand in hand with the false prophet in Rome and all the world over.

Now the rulers of the world, to St. Paul's mind, would be comprehended in the term " kings." And the older prophets frequently refer to the action of kings in connection with the spread of the gospel. Thus the con-

* Juv., iii. 11, vi. 542.

PETER AND PAUL

demnation of false prophecy in Isa. 59 is immediately followed by—

60^3 Kings shall journey at thy light, and Gentiles at thy brightness, O Jerusalem.

60^{11} To bring in unto thee the power of the Gentiles and their kings brought [captive]. For the Gentiles and the kings who shall not serve thee shall perish.

60^{10} And foreigners shall build thy walls, and their kings shall stand beside thee.

60^{16} And thou shalt suck the milk of Gentiles and eat the wealth of kings. . . . And I will set thy rulers in peace and thy overseers (*or*, bishops) in righteousness.

62^2 And Gentiles shall see thy righteousness and kings thy glory.

What inference could the apostle draw from the perusal of these promises in prophecy but an encouragement to his devout belief that the earth should be full of the knowledge of the Lord, and the rulers of the earth, the proconsul Sergius Paulus among them, should lead the way?

The Chaldean Elymas or Hetoimas.

This being so, the duty of the prophet was clear enough, to advance against the false prophet, to overthrow him by the power of God, and " to destroy utterly the seed out of Babylon " (Jer. 50^{16}). The very first of the *islands* (Isa. 49^1, see above) to which St. Paul's first missionary journey after his solemn separation had brought him produced a specimen of this *false prophet* (Acts 13^6) in the renegade *Jew* and " magian," which is to say Chaldean, Elymas or Hetoimos, whom the apostle rebukes in language of ancient prophetic force recalling that of Micah, Ezekiel, and Isaiah, against the false prophets. His language and behaviour will surprise none but those who forget that there was a treatment prescribed of old for the false prophet in the writings of those three prophets, which St. Paul as a member of their order could do nothing but perform. First we observe Ezekiel—

EZEK. XIII. 9	ACTS XIII
9. I will stretch out *my hand against the prophets* who see *false* visions and utter vain things.	6. They found a certain magian, *a false prophet*, a Jew.
17. *Prophesy* against them and say, Thus saith the Lord...	11. Behold, *the hand of the Lord is against* thee.
18. *To pervert* souls.	9. Saul, *being filled with the holy spirit.*
22. Because *ye were perverting* the heart of the righteous.	8. Seeking *to pervert* the proconsul,
23. Ye *shall not see* [your] falsehoods, and ye shall not divine divinations any more.	7. Sergius Paulus, a man of understanding.
	11. Thou *shalt be blind*, not seeing *the sun* for a season.

But the judgment of Ezekiel on the false prophets was but a re-enaction of—

> Mic. 3$^{5\,\text{ff}}$ Thus saith the Lord against the prophets who make my people to err, who bite with their teeth and proclaim upon them, Peace (cp. Ezek. 13^{10}), when it was not given into their mouth—they [do but] raise against him war—therefore *night shall be unto you in place of sight,* and *darkness* in place of divination, and *the sun* shall set upon the prophets, and daylight shall *close in darkness* upon them, and they that see dreams shall be put to shame, and the diviners to ridicule. . . . Hear ye this . . . ye who *pervert* all that is *straight.*

We compare St. Paul's expression here, "Wilt thou not cease to *pervert the straight ways* of the Lord?"

A third passage of scripture which St. Paul followed is hardly less discernible than the other two beneath the narrative of Acts 13^6, and it is this—

> Isa. 59$^{7\,\text{ff}}$ Detriment and wretchedness is in their ways, and the way of peace they know not, and there is no judgment in their ways: for their paths are perverted which they travel, and they know not peace. Wherefore judgment is departed from them, and righteous-

ness shall in no wise overtake them : because they persist, light is turned into *darkness* for them, after expecting *daylight* (αὐγὴν) they shall *walk about* in twilight (ἀωρίᾳ). *They shall grope as blind men* for a wall, and as though they had not eyes they shall grope : they shall *fall* in midday as if in midnight. Here we are struck by the close parallel to St. Luke's account—*not seeing the sun*, there *fell* a *mist* and *darkness* (ἀχλύς is not far from ἀωρία, "creeping glimmer and the poring dark," *nox intempesta*, which it causes), going *about*, he *sought for guidance*. Thus the parallel is there beyond all dispute. And considering that the three earlier prophets speak of a figurative blindness, the question must arise whether St. Luke's language, if carefully scrutinized, asserts that St. Paul's sentence on Elymas * was followed by material blindness. No doubt the words "not seeing *the sun* for *a season*" appear *prima facie* to bear the material meaning. Still, this is not necessary, and the subsequent language of the narrator is consistent with the idea that Elymas pretended to suffer the sentence passed upon him and so to close the interview. As a Jew he was certainly acquainted with the narrative of Ex. 8^{19}, where the magicians † "Jannes and Jambres," who withstood Moses "the servant of the Lord" (we compare the words of the Philippian girl, Acts 16, "These are *the servants of the most high God*") closed their interview with Pharaoh with the words, "This is the finger of God." After which we might have expected that Pharaoh would have been "astonished,"

---

* A remarkable fulfilment is here to be noticed. The original type and presumed fount of false prophecy being Balaam, at the close of the narrative in Num. 24^{23} we read, "Ah, ah, who shall live when God doeth these things? They [*i. e.*, perhaps, 'the fledglings of villainy' (or it)] shall come forth out of the hand of them of *Kitium*"—a city near Paphos in *Cyprus*, where Elymas was.

† Tertullian classes the Egyptian sorcerers with Elymas, *De Idol.*, 9.

if not converted like Sergius Paulus, but his stony heart was incapable of admiration and even of wonder.

The English reader of Isa. 59, R.V., might fail to discover that the class of persons there concerned is that of sorcerers and false prophets. So the LXX takes it. The Hebrew is rather more figurative than the Greek version, especially in verse 5, where the translators living in Egypt possibly had in their mind some local kind of jugglery or magic. They interpret the Hebrew in a very literal sense, as if the sorcerers took viper's eggs, hatched them, and enclosed the young in a ball of spiders'-web (which does in fact harden with years to a semi-transparent ball), which they present as an egg, " and he that is about to eat of their eggs, when he hath broken it, findeth it a wind-egg, and therein is a basilisk viper " (Isa. 59^5). In the next verse but one " their thoughts are of murders," and the LXX treated the above as an instance, but the instance is one of which only sorcerers would hold the keys. The spider * appears in folklore and in sorcery as an emblem and a means both of luck and ill-luck. Moreover, false prophecy is combined with idolatry generally in—

Hos. 12^1 Ephraim is an evil spirit, . . . he multiplies empty things and vanities.

And still more closely we have false prophecy expressed by the uncommon word "empty talking" (κενολογεῖν) in—

Isa. 8^{19} The talkers of falsehood who call out of their stomach,

ventriloquists,† as they are termed in the previous line, " who call out of the ground." So, too, Isa. 19^3, " those who call out of the ground and the ventriloquists."

* See Leland, *Etrusco-Roman Remains*, 1892, p. 261, where spells are quoted.
† See *Enc. Bib.*—Art. " Divination," 4.

Elymas has been bisected into two persons and his story into two stories by Schmiedel in *Enc. Bib.*, but he does not mention what seems a very simple explanation of the name Elymas, from the Assyrian god of magic, Alamu.* This explanation of Elymas is etymologically the best, for it accounts for the presence of the vowel *u* in the name. But almost equally probable is Dalman's derivation from Elamitês, shortened normally into Elamas, the Elamite, a term connected with Babylon, the great fountain of all magic, in Isa. 11^{11} and $21^{2, 9}$, Ezek. $32^{11, 24}$. And Strabo and Diodorus are competent authorities for the spelling Elymæus, a native of Elymaïs or Elam, which would equally become Elymas for short.

Whatever be the true translation of the name Elymas, there is another *crux* in the name Etœma or Hetœmas or Hetœmus, for which we might suggest the equivalent "Readyman," and which is maintained by Blass † to be the original mode of writing of the name by St. Luke's hand in Acts 13^8, instead of Elymas. I suggest that what St. Luke wrote is, "But they were withstood by Elymas the sorcerer—for thus by interpretation *of prophecy* is meant the name of the man Hetoima." Hetoima is from Deut. 32^{35}. The words in brackets represent the first draft of Acts, οὕτως γὰρ μεθερμ. λέγεται τὸ ὄνομα τοῦ ἕτοιμα. This reading is still preserved for us by the Stockholm MS. as regards Elymas in this order, and as regards the longer expression "by interpretation said," in which Lucifer (A.D. 350) agrees; but no extant authority has *Hetœma*

* A certain exorcist is said to have had statues of the Gods Lugalgira and Alamu put one on each side of the main entrance to his house, and in consequence he felt perfectly impregnable against all evil spirits. Tallquist, *Ass. Beschw.* 22 (1895). *Enc. Bib.*, Art. "Magic."

† Blass's remarkable theory of the original draft of Acts, which I respectfully hold to be made good in spite of some objections not yet entirely removed, though wishing that Blass had been directed to the view of prophecy maintained in these pages, has contributed more than anything else in recent years to the interest of Acts. See *St. Luke the Prophet,* index.

where I place it. The reason is that no copyist understood the reference to Deut. 32³⁵. As the copyists did not understand Etœma, which they saw resembled Elymas, they either thought that it was a correction for Elymas, and substituted it accordingly as the Bezan does and Lucifer with him : or that it was a dittography from the previous line

ανθιστατο δε αυτοις ελυμας
λεγεταιτο ονοματον ετοιμα.

The name ετοιμα was therefore likely to drop out of its original place in the first draft in the course of copying. But it is quite easy to see why, as Blass thinks, St. Luke himself struck out the word in his second draft. The use of the name required a reference, but as, in fact, it is not a proper name at all, and only a common adjective, no reference could be given, and since the quotation of the whole verse would occupy space, he omitted it, merely altering ονοματον ετοιμα into ονομααυτου—a change of two letters. The bracketed words then make perfectly good sense, " for thus by interpretation is his name called," *i. e.* Elymas's name is translated as " the magician " from *Alamu*, the name of the Assyrian god who presides over magic.

The passage in Deut. 32³⁵ is a part of Moses' song which deals with idolatry and false prophecy. The context (32³²) has been applied by St. Peter in his condemnation of Simon Magus, the magician corresponding to Elymas (Acts 8), " Their grapes are grapes of *gall*, a cluster of *bitterness* is theirs," and it continues—

Deut. 32³⁵ For the day of vengeance I will recompense when their foot slippeth, for near is the day of destruction unto them, and (πάρεστιν ἕτοιμα ὑμῖν) there are at hand *things ready* for you.

The latter words are as they stand a truism amounting to nonsense. Therefore, readers of St. Paul's time would naturally consider that ἕτοιμα here meant not "things ready," but a personal name of some sort, and so they would translate, There is at hand Etoimas for you. The very next verse would guide them on the road to *Cyprus* where Elymas was, for it runs—

For God will judge his people, and will be *exhorted* (or comforted) upon His *servants*.

And there beside him was the servant or prophet of God, Bar-Nabas, *Son* of *Exhortation* (or *Comfort*), himself a native of Cyprus, confronted with the sorcerer Bar-Jesus! The series of coincidences of names was remarkable enough—Saul with Sergius Paulus, Barnabas with Barjesus, Elymas with Etœmas—so much so that the author of Acts wished at first to include all three in his narrative : eventually he was content with less.

One more remark upon the same context, which gives us—

Deut. 32^{30} How shall one man pursue a thousand, and two move ten thousand from their place, unless . . .

The declaration implied in the question is also given in the context which follows after the Rout of Idolatry in

Isa. 60^{22} The *least one* shall be for thousands.

We are reminded once more of him who spake of himself as "*the least* of the apostles " (1 Cor. 15^9, Eph. 3^8)—and in a similar context to a similar judgment (Isa. 30^{17} following 30$^{6-10}$), "thousands shall fly because of the voice of one."

From these ancient prophecies it would rather seem that the sentence of blindness which the apostles pronounced was intended to be one of spiritual and moral blindness, however material its effect was, or was pretended by Elymas to be.

Other Chaldeans.

The encounter of St. Paul with Elymas was to be followed by many more of the same sort in other cities, of which we have instances in the ventriloquist girl of Philippi and the sons of Sceva the Jew at Ephesus. On the latter occasion he was about to take his pen, as we have seen, in order to write 2 Cor. 1-9, when his mind was actively running upon the Babylonian thoughts and expressions of Isa. 49. But to return for a moment to Philippi, could he have read Isa. 47 without recognizing in the poor enslaved hireling girl at Philippi a veritable " daughter of Babylon " (47^1), a daughter of the Chaldeans? without saying to her, in thought if not aloud, the very words of Isaiah ?—

> Isa. $47^{3\,\text{ff}}$ That which is righteous I will take from thee, I will not hand it over [like thy wages to men]. He that rescueth thee is the Lord of hosts, his name is the Holy One of Israel. Sit down, astonied one (she was probably subject to states of trance—$\kappa\alpha\tau\alpha\nu\varepsilon\nu\nu\gamma\mu\acute{\varepsilon}\nu\eta$), enter into darkness, O daughter of the Chaldeans, thou shalt no more be called the strength of the kingdom (she had followed Paul and Silas, crying out and saying, "These men are the servants of the Most High God, who declare unto you the way of salvation.") . . . Now it shall come suddenly upon thee in thy sorcery, in the strength of thy enchantments exceedingly, the prospect of thy wickedness. . . . . Stand now in thy enchantments and thy much sorcery, things which thou learnedst from thy youth, if thou shalt be able to profit. Thou hast laboured in thy counsels : let them stand and save thee, the astrologers of heaven, let them that see the stars announce to thee what is to come upon thee.

The Philippian girl, however, was but an example,

Her release from the bondage of Satan by the direct charge of the apostle was but an example and a foretaste of that wholesale though gradual release of the world from the same spiritual slavery which he was inspired by the Spirit of God to commence. He certainly knew that the " daughter " of Babylon meant not an individual but the " people " of Babylon ; nothing less than a whole population was the object of his mission. He read further—

> Isa. 48[12] Hear me, O Jacob, and Israel whom I call : I am the first and I am for ever . . . I will call them, and they . . . shall hear. Who announceth unto them these things ? *In love for thee I do thy will unto Babylon to take away the seed of the Chaldæans.* I speak, I call, and lead him, and prosper his way. Draw near unto me and hear these things. I have not spoken from the first in secret : when it took place, there was I, and now the Lord my Lord sendeth me as an apostle, and his spirit . . . I have shown thee that thou shouldest find the way on which thou shalt journey in it.

There is something so penetrating and personal in this appeal of the Lord that a less faithful servant, a less responsive listener than St. Paul, could hardly fail to be moved by it to a missionary campaign against the Chaldeans in the conditions given. And this campaign would have to be undertaken at Babylon itself, the second home of the Chaldeans and the haunt of renegade Jews. The end of its destined seventy years was approaching when, saith the Lord—

> Jer. 29[10] I will visit you (ἐπισκέψομαι) and set my words upon you to turn away your people unto this place.

There, then, before its destruction there would be time to unfold the banner of the cross, to perform the twofold duty, the purgation of the Jews and the conversion of the Gentiles. The same Isaiah which stirred the apostle to answer the Lord's question—

> Isa. 6^8 Whom shall I send as an apostle, and who will journey unto this people? Here am I, send me. And he said, Journey and say to this people, Hearing ye shall hear, etc.—

the passage which St. Paul quotes at Rome (Acts 28), had said just before—

> Isa. 5^{25} The Lord of Hosts was sore wroth against his people, . . . Therefore he will lift up a standard among the Gentiles who are afar off, and will hiss unto them from the end of the earth, and beheld they come quickly—

and he was to say in a counterstrain later—

> Isa. 62^{10} Lift up a standard unto the Gentiles: for behold, the Lord makes it heard unto the end of the earth. Say ye to the daughter of Sion, Behold, thy Saviour hath come with his own reward and his work before his face. And he shall call it a holy people.

The criticism which has at length distinguished for us the first and the second Isaiah enables us to understand these contrasted and opposing judgments, which to St. Paul must have presented in the pages of one and the same prophet an opposition, an " antinomy " indeed. One injunction, however, they contained in common, to unfurl the standard among the Gentiles who were afar off, in Rome and in Spain and unto the ends of the earth.

CHAPTER X

THE TRANSFIGURATION

The Bases of the Narrative.

IN passing to the Transfiguration, we come to a question of the greatest perplexity on which there is very little agreement among different leaders of the same host, whether conservative or critical. How far we are to admit the presence of prescriptural or extra-scriptural and cosmic ideas, how long we are to think of sitting down, or kneeling, before a mystery, how far we must be material or allegorical, literal or ideal, subjective or objective, are questions which the same reader will probably answer differently at different times in his life. " Is it truth or falsehood; was it reality or vision—or part of both, this Transfiguration scene on Hermon ? " says Edersheim. " One thing, at least, must be evident : if it be a true narrative, it cannot possibly describe a merely subjective vision without objective reality." The introduction of this distinction between subjective and objective is somewhat paralyzing at the outset, but like most dangers it vanishes if disregarded. Every man's experience is subjective and yet it is a fact. The narrative, though not without difficulties, is one of the most certain of all the evangelic accounts. It occurs in all three synoptists, and Professor Bacon has observed that the whole of the fourth Gospel is a substitute for it. Let us first attempt to discover the meaning as interpreted by the underlying passages of the Old Testament.

These main substructures are three, Exod. 24, Ps. 2, and Zech. 2–3.

Exod. 24¹ ᶠᶠ. And he said unto Moses, Go up unto the Lord, thou and Aaron and Nadab and Abihu and seventy of the elders of Israel, and they shall worship the Lord afar off. And Moses alone shall draw nigh unto God, and they shall not draw nigh, and the people shall not go up with them. . . . And Moses took the book of the testament and read it in the ears of the people, and they said, All that the Lord hath spoken we will do and hear. . . . ⁹ And Moses went up and Aaron and Nadab and Abihu and seventy of the seniors of Israel, and they saw the place where the God of Israel stood, and under his feet as it were a work of sapphire stone, and as the appearance of the firmament of heaven for clearness. And of the chosen ones of Israel none uttered a dissonant voice, and they *were seen* in the place of God, and did eat and drink. And the Lord said to Moses, Come up unto me to the mount and be there: and I will give thee the tables of stone, the law and the commandments which I have written to legislate for them. And Moses arose *and Jesus* who stood beside him, and they went up into the mount of God, and they said to the elders, Tarry ye here until we return to you. . . . ⁵¹ And *the cloud* covered the mount. And the glory of God came down upon Mount Sinai, and the cloud covered it *six days;* and the Lord called Moses on the seventh day from the midst of the cloud. And the appearance of the glory of the Lord was *as it were fire* burning upon the top of the mount before the children of Israel. And Moses came into the midst of the cloud and went up into the mount. . . . Exod. 34³⁰: The outward sight of *his face had been glorified.*

Owing to the triple account (PJE) in the Hebrew, the exact sequence of events is far from clear, but it is evident that Moses, Jesus, and the three, are apart from the

THE TRANSFIGURATION

rest. So Mark 9^2, "*After six days*, Jesus taketh Peter and James and John and bringeth them up into a high *mountain by themselves alone.* And he was transfigured before them. And his raiment became glittering white exceedingly, so as no fuller on the earth can whiten them. And there was seen by them Elias with Moses, and they were conversing with Jesus. ... And there came *a cloud overshadowing them*." Luke 9^{29} is somewhat closer to the appearance of *fire;* " and his raiment white flashing forth " (ἐξαστράπτων), and Matt. 17^2, " and his face shone as the sun and his raiment became white as the light." The phrase in Mark 9^4, " Elijah *with* Moses," clearly shows the presence of Moses as more original in some sense than that of Elijah.*

The next passage will strike the reader as of doubtful application, but not so doubtful perhaps when its sequel has been considered in connection with the sequel to the Transfiguration in all the three Gospels, and when *Sion* has explained itself.

> Zech. 2^5 And I will be unto Jerusalem, saith the Lord, a wall of *fire* round about, and for glory will I be in the midst of them. Ho, ho, flee ye from the north, saith the Lord, for I will gather you from the four winds of heaven. *Unto Sion* come ye up and be saved, ye that inhabit the daughter of Babylon. Therefore thus saith the Lord, *After* [the] *glory* he hath sent me to *the Gentiles* that spoiled you, because *he that toucheth you* toucheth the apple of his eye. For, behold, I bring my hand upon them, and they shall be spoil to them that did serve them, and *ye shall know that the Lord Almighty hath sent me.* Rejoice and be glad, O daughter of Sion, for, behold, I come and will *tabernacle in the midst of thee*, saith the Lord. And many nations shall flee to the Lord

---

* J. Lightfoot calls Elijah " the first prophet of the Gentiles,"

for refuge in that day, and they shall be to him a people and shall *tabernacle* in the midst of thee. . . . 3¹ And the Lord showed me Jesus the priest, the great priest, standing before the angel of the Lord, and the devil stood at his right hand to be his adversary. And *the Lord said unto the devil*, the Lord *rebuke thee* (ἐπιτιμήσαι ἐν σοί), devil . . . Is not this, behold, a brand plucked out of *the fire*? And Jesus was clothed in soiled raiment. . . . And they clothed him with *raiment*. . . . And the angel said, *If thou walk in my ways* and keep thee in my commandments (προστάγμασιν), thou shalt judge (διακρινεῖς) my house: and if thou keep my fold [or court, αὐλήν, John 10¹⁶], then I will give thee men who converse *in the midst of these who stand* [*here*] (ἀναστρεφομένους ἐν μέσῳ τῶν ἑστηκότων τούτων). Hear now, O Jesus the great priest, thou and ye who are near thee and ye who sit in the presence, for they are *watchers of wonders* (τερατοσκόποι), for, behold, I bring my servant the Dayspring.*

This passage of Zechariah, which conveys obscurely the recovery of Jerusalem and the victory of the Lord's people over the hitherto oppressive Gentiles, ending with the triumph of Jesus over Satan, is quite appropriate

* J. Lightfoot says, on Matt. 17², "In this transfiguration he is sealed for the high priest. When Christ was baptized, being now ready to enter upon his evangelical priesthood, he is sealed by a heavenly voice for the high priest, and is anointed with the Holy Spirit, as the high priests were wont to be with holy oil." But while Lightfoot shows that He is marked as "the greatest Prophet," he fails to show the high priest. Now Lightfoot has no idea of the connection of Zech. 3¹·⁸ with the Transfiguration. Had he had this, he would have thereby justified his observation. Presumably Ps. 110 is in Lightfoot's mind. If so, he might well have claimed that it also takes us to Hermon, Ps. 110², "The Lord shall send the rod of thy power out of *Sion*. Be thou ruler in the midst of thine enemies." The whole psalm, indeed, is very close to Zech. 2, 3.

THE TRANSFIGURATION 269

to the train of thought in Matt. 16[13] and onwards from the confession at Cæsarea Philippi.

We must remember that Cæsarea Philippi was a sort of Mecca of paganism. All the coins of Philip bear the image of a temple—the splendid temple of Augustus, built by Herod the Great near the grotto of Pan at the source of the Jordan, as if to claim the river throughout its course for pagan tutelage, and consequently for what would seem to a scrupulous Jew something like pollution.* The words of Zech. 2, " Ye that inhabit the daughter of Babylon," would be interpreted to mean the inhabitants of Cæsarea Philippi long before Babylon was found to be Rome, which could hardly be before A.D. 60. The " daughter of Babylon wasted with misery " not only stood in A.D. 30 for the oppressor, but for the idolatry of Greece and Rome. As Jesus did not go to Cæsarea itself, but only to the neighbourhood of it, it was necessary for the population to come to Him.

In Matt. 17[7], therefore, *after* the vision on the mount, " Jesus came near and *touched them* (Zech. 2[8] above), and said, Arise and be not afraid," while Luke 9[30] preserves the idea of *glory*, " who *being seen in glory* " : *being seen* is from Exod. 24. The *voice from the cloud*, This is my beloved Son, is anticipated in " Ye shall know that the Lord hath sent me." The reference to the *raiment* in the Transfiguration is perhaps connected with this passage also. But the encounter with the power of Satan immediately following on the descent from the mountain (*after the glory*, Zech. 2[7]) is especially remarkable, for the three Gospels agree in treating the *rebuke* of the devil as part of the Transfiguration. On coming to the disciples they saw a great multitude (*in the midst of those*, etc., Zech. 2[7]) *round about them* (Mark 9[14]). Not only the crowd but the disciples are the *wonder-watchers*

---

* Since writing the above I find the waters were held impure. See Neubauer in Abbott, *From Letter to Spirit*, 615a.

who *tried to cast out* the devil and could not. The *walking in my ways* reappears in the answer of Jesus, " This kind can come out by nothing save by prayer [and fasting] " (Mark). For the last words Matt. 17[20] substitutes the more comprehensive, " Because of your little faith . . . if ye have faith . . . " considering that faith represents both *walking* and *keeping*. Although in Mark *prayer* corresponds to faith and *fasting* to keeping, the correspondence hardly suffices to determine the reading in dispute in Mark. The demoniac boy, whose symptoms are less fully described by Luke " the physician " than by Matthew and Mark, was one who had often been cast into *the fire*: he was therefore a " brand snatched *out of fire*," as Zechariah describes him. But the most significant of all the parallels here is the repeated term *tabernacle* which has suggested the reply of Peter in the Transfiguration.

Sion is Hermon.

The third source of the gospel account is—

Ps. 2[6] But I was established by him upon *Sion his holy mountain*, proclaiming the *commandment* ($\pi\varrho o\sigma\tau\acute{a}\gamma\mu a$) of the Lord. The Lord said unto me, *Thou art my Son*, this day have I begotten thee. Ask of me and I shall give thee the nations for thine inheritance, and thy possession the ends of the earth. Thou shalt shepherd them with a rod of iron, as a potter's vessel thou shalt dash them in pieces.

The connection of this text with the Transfiguration might have been questioned, since this is not the only possible base for the form of testimony, " This is my beloved [chosen] Son, in whom I am well pleased, hear ye him," Matt., Mark, Luke) : but it is placed beyond all doubt by the mention in 2 Pet. 1[18], " And this voice we heard borne from heaven when we were with him *in the*

THE TRANSFIGURATION 271

holy mountain." The author of 2 Peter, whatever his date, was not so far removed in time from the Gospels that we need to suppose that he imported Ps. 2^6 into the criticism when it was new in that connection. And as soon as we see this, we see that there are other points of contact. In Zech. 2^7 the mention of Sion must have seemed altogether inappropriate to the occasion of Hermon or whatever the high mountain may be.* And yet Ps. 2^6 mentions Sion again as if it stood for the Transfiguration. How is this? The explanation is simple. But the fact was clear to me before the simple explanation appeared. It is just the clear statement of—

Deut. 4^{48} Mount Sion which is Hermon—

which is apt to be overlooked. Also—

Ps. 133^3 Like as the dew of Hermon which falleth on the mountains of Sion—

a passage which may have perplexed the thoughtful reader. The name is said to be short for Sirion, but Sion simply means the high mountain, Hermon, which dominates Palestine. *The commandment of the Lord*, in Ps. 2, is taken as delivered in the very next words, *Thou art my Son*. And again, the immediate sequel is the promise of victory over the heathen—" the nations for thine

* Mount Hermon (9166 feet) owes its name, " of a sanctuary," or of " devotion " (ἀνάθεμα), to the two hundred wicked angels who swore an oath (ἀνάθεμα) upon it, according to the Book of Enoch, of which the disciples had probably some knowledge. See Charles, *The Book of Enoch*, p. 49. If the mount of the wicked Oath was the scene on this occasion of the divine Assurance, their terror and their relief were both indebted to this Book, supposed to belong to the remotest antiquity, that of " the seventh from Adam " (Jude 14). It uses the term " The Elect One " to mean Messiah. But Joshua (Jesus) is the chosen (ὁ ἐκλεκτὸς) long before the Book of Enoch in Num. 11^{28}, " he that standeth beside Moses " (ὁ παρεστηκώς) twice. Lightfoot wrote two hundred and fifty years ago : " Now your pardon, reader. I know it will be laughed at, if I should doubt, whether Christ were transfigured upon Mount Tabor; for who ever doubted of this thing ? " Such is the tenacity of church tradition. " Mt. Tabor was at that time crowned by a fortified city " (Robinson).

inheritance." But this is the very same thought as in Zech. 2 and in Matt. 16 = Mark 8, about Cæsarea Philippi. Meanwhile the connection of Ps. 2 and Zech. 3[7] is quite clear: for the latter says, *If thou keep* thyself in *my commandments* (προστάγμασιν).

The Trance of Peter on Hermon.

But if we have secured these three passages as the basis of the narrative, we are still very far from understanding its construction in its present form. We require to know how much of it is vision, and whose vision it is, and what preparation there has been for a vision of this kind at this point in the gospel history.

That there is a vision seems to be quite evident. A vision is preceded by the conditions of prayer and fasting. Prayer was present here (Luke 9[28]). Fasting (see Mark 9[29]) is easily assumed, especially as Hermon is only reached by an exhausting walk of many hours. Luke 9[30] has preserved one of the most certain indications of an ecstatic vision in the words, "And behold," though it is not added that the heavens were opened, nor who saw the vision. St. Luke is misrepresented in the Revised Version; what he really says is, "Now Peter and those with him *had been* heavy with sleep." R.V. leaves the reader with the impression that the vision was in a dream. This it was not, for a vision is of a different order from a dream, and St. Matthew, who speaks elsewhere of dreams, agrees here with Luke and calls this clearly enough a *vision* (ὄραμα, Matt. 17[9]). The ecstatic vision took place after the three awakened from their drowsiness, and since ecstasy is transmissible as dreams are not, it seems quite possible that "*they saw* his glory and the two men that stood by him." The difficulty of supposing a joint ecstasy is not great, for we know that "the spirit of God leapt upon Saul and he prophesied in the midst of them"

THE TRANSFIGURATION 273

(1 Sam. 10¹⁰) : thus there is no objection to the supposition of Peter seeing the vision and impressing it vividly on his companions. The question would be set at rest if instead of (Luke 9³²) διαγρηγορήσαντες . . . είδαν, we found any support in MSS. for διαγρηγορήσας είδεν [having kept awake (R.V. marg.) *he* saw], but we do not, slight as the change would have been. The original use here of the singular number, however, is implied in the words that follow, "as they parted *from him, Peter said* to Jesus." . . . "As they parted from him" (ἐν τῷ διαχωρίζεσθαι) is a phrase which implies of necessity a vision, it is hardly intelligible of a dream : and it so happens that 2 Cor. 12³ uses the root of this word *apart from the body* (χωρὶς τοῦ σώματος) of a vision, which is there appearing and here is disappearing. There is nothing in Matthew and Mark to oppose this supposition, but there seems to be something lost in their reports which should account for Peter *answering* (Matt., Mark) and saying to Jesus, "Lord, it is good. . . ." This we shall see later.

The recipient, or the chief recipient, of the vision is probably Peter. In favour of this conclusion is, first, the previous context in which Peter has prominently figured, the other two disciples being always relatively in the background, and having, indeed, scarcely any several identity, and very little joint identity, anywhere in the three Gospels. Next there is the tradition, which Tertullian * (A.D. 200) follows in the well-known passage

---

* *Adv. Marcion.*, 4²². Lightfoot well observes, "Whence Peter should know them to be (the) prophets it is vain to seek, because it is nowhere to be found." The inference is irresistible that the vision was subjective, seen in trance. But Godet's four explanations may be mentioned here, even at the cost of a smile. "Perhaps Jesus addressed them by name, or indicated who they were unmistakably. Or is it not rather true that the glorified bear upon their form . . . their new name (Rev. 3¹²) ? Could we behold St. John or St. Paul in their heavenly glory for any length of time without giving them their name ? "

T

where he says, " How could Peter at the Transfiguration have recognized Moses and Elias except in a state of ecstasy ? " And this is a very telling remark. Lastly, it is not conceivable that the vision should be that of the Lord Himself, reported to the three chosen disciples. " He was transfigured *before them :* " " there was seen by them Elias with Moses."

General Conditions of a Vision.

But if we have cleared some difficulties so far, we are only brought up to the grand difficulty of all the three Gospels—When did the Messiahship become a resolution of Jesus and known to the disciples ? This is the problem of all problems which now occupy thinking minds. Did Jesus resolve to be the Christ at the Baptism or at an earlier moment ? Is it even a right question to ask whether others knew that He would be the Messiah at Capernaum, at Nazareth, or at the cradle ? The fourth Gospel has no hesitation on this point, and it answers, He knew Himself from all eternity, and was known from the lips of the Baptist at the Baptism, though, as Prof. Bacon has shown, he does not say that John baptized Jesus. But this is not the voice of the Synoptics. The portion of the problem which concerns us just now is whether the Transfiguration is a result of causes that we can trace or not : and we may add the question whether we are to infer that it was a revelation to the Lord which marked an epoch in his resolution or a revelation only to the disciples.

A vision implies pre-existing elements of knowledge composed in a new form. It would be incredible, as it is inconsistent with all the scriptural records of visions, that one of those whom Peter saw in the Transfiguration should have been, for instance, St. Paul. Thus when Ananias saw Saul in a vision, we find him saying, " Lord, I have heard from many concerning this man." When

THE TRANSFIGURATION

Saul saw a man in a vision, Ananias by name, we are constrained either to strike out the verse, with Blass and with the Fleury MS., or to end the speech of the Lord with the previous verse and consider this (Acts 9^{12}) a Lucan parenthesis, " Now he had seen in a vision a man—to wit, Ananias, but his name was unknown to him then—coming in. . . ." Nothing can occur in a vision which is entirely unknown to the seer : what is seen is previously known, but it appears in a fresh combination, and just this combination results in new knowledge which is called revelation. If the Transfiguration contained only new elements it would not fulfil the conditions of a vision. If it contains only old elements in their usual setting, to whom is it a revelation ? *

The elements are what we have seen. Moses, the first prophet of all, the servant of the Lord, represents the law, Elijah the prophets who foretell the Christ, and particularly Elijah is the Forerunner. Does, then, his appearance supersede or confirm or correct the appearance and ministry of the Baptist who was Elijah in a figure, if indeed Elijah was not rather the Baptist in a figure ?

Particular Conditions of this Vision.

For in dealing with the elements we must remember the conditions of time : the biographical requirements, if we may so call them, must be kept in view. Briefly, they turn upon the death of John the Baptist, who, as we have seen (Ch. VII. p. 187), was identified so completely with Elijah that he was expected by his disciples to be taken up to heaven in a chariot of fire. When, then, instead of this, he was beheaded, the revulsion of feeling must have been overwhelming. It was then seen that he was, after all, not Elijah. Therefore his witness was not the Forerunner's witness. But he had borne witness, the

* See Abbott, *From Letter to Spirit*, 904.

first witness, to Jesus as the Christ. Therefore, perhaps, this witness was not true; its credit was shaken. A very grievous shock at least was thus dealt to the belief in Him as Messiah which was to come. Could this be the Christ, whose Forerunner had now been so swiftly cut off? The popular belief had been running on false lines, or had at least outrun the true lines. Could it be restored? The three Gospels are directed to showing that it could be restored. This fact by no means implies that the Lord Himself was desirous of such restoration.

But, again, let us consider whether any light is thrown upon the popular belief by John's own later belief, for it is clear that John when he delivered his testimony was not conscious of infallibility—the term has only to be mentioned to show how little it applies to the conditions, which forbid whatever is mechanical. The two evangelists, Luke and Matthew, agree that John when he was in prison sent two of his disciples to ask Jesus, Art thou he that cometh (ὁ ἐρχόμενος), or look we for another? Let it be supposed that Jesus was the Christ by a resolution of his will inwardly and by John's testimony outwardly, then it is clear that the inward fact and the outward testimony were mutually interdependent, for the purpose of fulfilling prophecy, in what must by hypothesis be a public and visible fulfilment. Now the inward fact might hold good, by the resolution lasting unchanged, but if so there must be a public proof of this from time to time; and there must be a confirmation of testimony from the lips of a person in authority, or from visible guidance; where was this confirmation to come from? John, the previous testator, was in prison and therefore unable to act as a personal witness. The guidance of events was imperfect if it rested solely on works of healing, for the Jews themselves cast out devils, and this power at least was by itself no proof that the possessor of it was Messiah.

THE TRANSFIGURATION

The growing of the belief in Jesus as the Christ was certainly a kind of confirmation, but John had no means of being informed in his prison whether the belief was growing. What was he to do except to ask for the information at the source itself? And this is what he did. He virtually asks, Is Thy will strong to-day as yesterday? Is God's power with Thee still within, without? During this time of imprisonment Jesus must bear his own witness (John 5^{31}).

Thus it must never be supposed that the Lord's answer to John's disciples conveyed a disparagement of the question. The question was not and is not either obscure or theatrical. It is profoundly solemn. The context of John 5^{35} bears a direct reference to Ecclus. $48^{1\,ff}$, which deals with Elias (see Chapter VII). And that the belief concerning John was based upon that scripture is assumed by the fourth Gospel. This belief is a measure of the corresponding shock produced by his death. Then, however, the confession of Peter at Caesarea came as a guarantee that the seed had struck. And close upon it followed the Transfiguration as the rehabilitation of the witness of John who had been Elias. The question which the imprisoned Baptist was most fully entitled to ask was set at rest again by the vision in which he was seen as Elias once more.

Meanwhile, the Fourth Gospel has not encountered this difficulty. By avoiding the death of John, it has avoided the necessity of a makeweight to it. It takes us to the point of John's imprisonment or nearly so (John 3^{24}), but it veils the sequel under a slow and gradual decline of his position (John 3^{30}, ἐλαττοῦσθαι). How entirely this view is at variance with the earlier tradition is only to be realized by a thoughtful consideration of the facts. And more than this, the very testimony of John is relatively disparaged by the words of the Lord himself in—

John 5³³ Ye have sent unto John, and he hath borne witness to the truth. . . . But the witness that I have is greater than that of John, for the works, etc., . . . and the Father that sent me he hath borne witness of me.

The Fourth Gospel takes up the expression of Ecclus. 48 concerning Elijah, and while maintaining the truth of John's witness (1⁷⁻¹⁵, etc.) draws the strongest possible contrast between the *lamp* and the *light*. Later still, on a touching occasion when the Saviour revisits the place of John's baptism, men come to him and say, "John did no miracle, but his witness was true" (John 10⁴¹). This implies that there had been a time shortly before when the same speakers had not been so sure that his witness concerning Jesus was true. And it is added, as if in proof of the recovery of belief in John's witness from the overthrow, that many believed on Him there. The Fourth Gospel is careful to preserve all the strength of John's witness with a minimum of notice of his person after the great scene at Jordan bank. The baptism at Ænon near to Salim was made to contribute to the same end.

The treatment of John's death by John serves to check the treatment of it by Matthew, Mark and Luke. They do not refer to the greatness of the disappointment, but they assume it, not only in describing the Transfiguration where they do, shortly after John's death (in Luke 9⁹ it is a bare mention), but in giving the opinion of some that Jesus was "John risen from the dead," as if it were impossible for John to be extinguished by death.

We must of necessity suppose that the disciples knew the scriptures concerning Mount Sinai and Moses and Mount Horeb and Elijah. That they should appear together and converse with their own Master-prophet Jesus, on Hermon, was the new combination. That they

THE TRANSFIGURATION 279

should speak of the exodus that he was to accomplish at Jerusalem was new. Yet this, if we may venture to say so, is quite in accord with other visions. All three Gospels have placed the forecast of these sufferings just before the Transfiguration. Also Matthew and Luke have previously recorded the delivery of the new law from a mountain (Matt. 5, Luke $6^{12, 17}$). Mark seems to be drawn away from this record by perpetual digressions, but its preceding position is not necessary to the understanding of the vision. At least in Mark 3^{13} He had gone up into a mountain and called whom He would, and He had ordained the twelve that He might send them forth to preach.

When once the character of Jesus as the Prophet of Nazareth and of the world, and the successor of Moses, is strongly understood, the difficulties of the Transfiguration are greatly diminished, and it appears as a confirmation of previous knowledge possessed by the disciples, if hardly yet realized by them. But that the sufferings were to be an *exodus*, and to take place at Jerusalem, was not previously known. The Masterprophet is seen as he was not before, lifted in their estimation to a level with Moses, whose glory He shares to the uttermost of all possible brightness, while He converses with Moses and Elijah, whose departures were both mysterious and grand, as their lives had been divine, solitary and unique. Their names had long ago been coupled together in the last verses of Malachi (Mal. 4^{2-6}). In this fact lies one of the strongest predispositions of the Transfiguration.

There is, however, more than this in the declaration of the voice out of the cloud, " This is my Son, my chosen [Son], *hear ye him.*" Tertullian scornfully derides Marcion for saying that "hear ye *him*" is so emphatic as to exclude the hearing of Moses and Elijah, whom henceforward they were forsooth to cease hearing. At the same time he points out what is undoubtedly true, that the passage of scripture to which the voice refers is—

> Deut. 18$^{15, 18, 19}$ A prophet from among thy brethren like unto me shall the Lord thy God raise up unto thee: *him shall ye hear*, . . . and I will put my words in his mouth, . . . and whosoever will not hearken . . . I will require it of him.

This is the text of Peter in Acts 3^{22}, and again of Stephen in Acts 7^{37}, who quote it, and Philip refers to it also in John 1^{45}. Moses in this text claims a hearing and obedience from the Israelites to his successor Jesus * of Nauê. But if there is anything clear in this narrative at all it is that Moses is understood to have claimed in those very words obedience to his successor the second Jesus, of Nazareth, an obedience which the children of Israel heartily accorded him in the terms in which they were asked, to the extent of vowing death to the rebel (Josh. 1^{17}). There is no misquotation by Peter. And it was one of the fundamental beliefs of the apostles that Moses meant this. No voice from heaven was needed to proclaim or to reiterate it. No scorn of Tertullian was needed to diminish its importance. Hence we have the first part of the Hermon testimony from Elijah at the Baptism; the second part from Moses, *Hear ye him.*

The Voice from the Cloud.

But neither are we told, except in 2 Pet. 1$^{17\,f}$, that there was a voice from heaven: there was a *voice from the cloud*, as all three Gospels agree in saying, as also they agree in using the rare word *overshadowing*.

---

* For the connection between Jesus of Nauê and Jesus of Nazareth, see *St. Luke the Prophet*, p. 60. Later Rabbinic explanations do not count. See Abbott, *l.c.*, 845 ff. They use the last and feeblest subterfuge of defeat in war with Christian argument, when they generalize *a prophet* into any prophet of all his successors.

THE TRANSFIGURATION 281

And while Peter said these things, there came a (bright) *cloud* and *overshadowed* them : and they feared as they entered into the cloud. And a voice came out of the cloud, saying, This is my Son, my chosen [my beloved Son], hear ye him (Luke).

This takes us at once to—

Exod. 40$^{34 f}$ And *the cloud* covered the tabernacle of witness, and the tabernacle was filled with the glory of the Lord. And Moses was not able to enter into the tabernacle of witness, because the cloud *overshadowed it*.

The ecstatic vision is already past, and the bewildered Peter has uttered the words which seemed to be at random then, but ere many moments were proved to be significant. A mountain cloud passed over them, as it were with a baptismal effect. They were for an instant like the children of Israel who, as St. Paul said (1 Cor. 10^2) "were baptized unto Moses in the cloud." Peter had spoken of *tabernacles*, thinking of Zech. 2, but the cloud succeeding the vision of Moses recalled the Mosaic *cloud* which had covered the *tabernacle of witness* (or, tent of meeting, R.V.), where the Lord would " appoint for the sons of Israel, and would be sanctified in his glory, and would sanctify the *tabernacle of witness* " * (Exod. 29$^{43 f}$). The disciples then were entering the awful presence of God in the tabernacle of witness, whence the Lord would

* " And thou shalt anoint it (χρίσεις, Ex. 30$^{23, 24, 26}$) with a holy unction of oil and myrrh, after the art of the apothecary " (μύρον μυρεψικὸν τέχνῃ μυρεψοῦ) : it was to contain " sweet spices, stacte, onycha, galbanum and pure frankincense or spices, myrrh, cinnamon, calamus, cassia and oil "; and what is John 19$^{39 f}$ with its " mixture of myrrh and aloes and spices " for the burial of the body in which Jesus had *tabernacled* (John 1^{14}) but a fulfilment of this charge ? The clue to the difficult expression " pistic nard " (Mark 14^3, John 12^3) is in these verses of Ex. 30, " Πιστικὴ is Syriac, from Pistaka (Talmud) = βάλανος, mast, myrobalanon " (Lightfoot on Mark 14^3). " Nardin consists of omphacium, balaninum, bulrush, nard, amomum, myrrh, balsam, etc."—Pliny, *N. H.*, 13^1.

" be *made known* unto thee *so as to speak to thee* " (ἐν οἷς γνωσθήσομαί σοι ἐκεῖθεν ὥστε λαλῆσαί σοι, Exod. 29⁴²). And yet how great their privilege! Moses excluded by the cloud which they entered! Marcion was not far wrong. " And they feared as they entered the cloud."

For they are thus brought to the moment of expectation of the witness that God would speak to them. That if He spoke, He would speak to them in accents of scripture was a foreordained conviction. But " did ever people hear the voice of the living God speaking out of the midst of the fire, as Israel had heard it, and lived ? " Hence their fear. But then why blend with the imagination the whisper of the wind in the distant forest ? The voice of Jesus Himself repeating aloud the language of Deuteronomy, repeating the second Psalm as it was framed* in the vision of the Baptist, even as on the cross he repeated Ps. 22 in soliloquy, was here the " voice from the cloud." They looked up to find none but Jesus there.

Peter's Study of Holy Scripture.

To attribute to Peter so much scriptural knowledge is not to attribute much. How much ought one to attribute to him or to the other disciples ? This is a question that one ponders over. The intelligence of the other disciples we have no data for determining. It seems from various passages to have been very small. Whatever John may have become in later years, in old age, if he lived to be old, he was now little more than a stripling and very immature. " Aside from the two rebukes " (Mark 9³⁸, Luke 9⁵⁰), says Prof. Bacon,† " we

---

* The opening words, *This is*, undoubtedly take us back to the vision of John by the Jordan, which was also the scene of Elijah's ascent to heaven. Yet the agreement of Matthew, Mark and Luke in the Transfiguration in the actual words is limited to *This is my Son, hear him*,—the two last being the emphatic words.

† *The Fourth Gospel*, etc., p. 330.

THE TRANSFIGURATION 283

have absolutely nothing in Synoptic tradition to distinguish John from the rest of the group of fishermen first called to discipleship at the sea of Galilee, save the grouping with Peter and James in three Markan scenes, and the faint traces in Luke and Acts of his appearance as a satellite of Peter." The impression grows upon the reader that the only member of the circle who was qualified to stand up as a witness " of all that Jesus began both to do and to teach," was in the early days Peter. But he was a fisherman ! But he was infirm of purpose ! But he was not the speaker and the theologian that Acts represents him to be, and Luke has composed his speeches for him ! The first two objections may be granted, without admitting that his study of scripture and his intelligence are any the less on that account. Let us look at the third.

According to the evidence, within a month or two of the Transfiguration Peter stands up as the speaker and theologian that we see in Acts, and the denial of the Lord has occurred in the interval. The denial, however, is no reflection upon his intelligence. The two are entirely consistent. How often do we see the greatest eagerness, intellectual and practical, united with infirmity and instability of purpose and lack of moral courage ! The denial had not prevented him from being trusted as a leader of the infant Church, if only because intellectually he was head and shoulders above the rest of the twelve. The early chapters of Acts are far too consistent a record and all counter-hypotheses far too doubtful for us to reject them as a whole. If we reject them, we must admit they assume that Peter had read his Bible well — and the assumption on Luke's part is worth much. If we keep them, they prove it.

But if he was a reader of the Bible he must also, as the disciple of a prophet, have studied the book of

Zechariah and Malachi, which is part of Zechariah, the former because it is one of the very few books after Jesus (Joshua) which mention Jesus * by name, the latter if only because it announces the Forerunner of the Christ. He therefore knew already, before the Transfiguration, by experience of the many expulsions of devils which he had witnessed in the ministry of Jesus, the application of Zech. 3^2, " And the Lord said unto the devil, The Lord rebuke thee," as a prophecy abundantly fulfilled. From this it was but a step to the preceding verses in which occur twice the words, " I will *tabernacle* in the midst of thee." Does not this account for " Peter said . . . Let us make three *tabernacles* . . . for he knew not what he said [what to answer] ? " That something here has been omitted to account for the word " answer " on Peter's part, was observed just now. But perhaps we can account for the omission by looking once more not in the Gospel but in—

> Zech. 2^{13} Ye shall know that the Lord Almighty hath sent me. Rejoice and be glad, O daughter of Sion : *for, behold, I come, and will tabernacle in the midst of thee, saith the Lord.* And many nations shall flee for refuge to the Lord in that day, and they shall be his people, and shall *tabernacle* in the midst of thee. . . . And the Lord shall inherit Judah, and *shall yet choose Jerusalem.* Let all flesh be silent before the face of the Lord; for he hath awaked *out of the clouds of his saints.*

If Peter has seen the vision of the two prophets talking with Jesus and heard the discourse concerning His exodus which He was about to fulfil, as was written in the prophets (*e.g.* Zech. 2^{12}), at Jerusalem—*seeing* and *hearing* are

* There are four Joshuas mentioned : (1) 1 Chron. 7^{27}; (2) 1 Sam. $6^{14\text{ ff}}$; (3) 2 Kings 23^8; (4) Ezra $3^{2\text{ ff}}$, 4^3, Hag. 1, 2, Zech. 3, 6^{11}.

THE TRANSFIGURATION

necessary parts of most visions as described in Acts, 2 Corinthians and Revelation—then the last traces of the parting vision may well have been the words of Zechariah, " I will tabernacle in the midst of thee, saith the Lord," which Peter received as an address to himself, and to which he made the answer which the Gospels have reported. The fact that the answer is reported at all shows that it was believed to be not entirely without sense by those who reported it.*

A reference to Zech. 2 will show that this process of identification advances in reverse order from *Jesus* in Zech. 3 to *tabernacle* in Zech. $2^{11,10}$; thence to *Ye shall know that the Lord hath sent me*, Zech. 2^9; and we observe that this is the very order of events recorded in the Gospels, only that they give the declaration in the form *This is my Son*, etc. The next item should be *he that toucheth you*, etc., and so it is in Matt. 17^7, " Jesus *touched them*, and said, *Arise*, and be not afraid." (In *Arise*, however, are we to trace a reference to " he hath *arisen* from the clouds of his saints," Zech. 2^{13}? If so, there is a slight retrogression here. The *cloud*, if drawn from this passage at all, and not from Exod. 24, where it is very prominent, has been already mentioned after the *tabernacles* and the conclusion of the vision). The next item is, " *After [the] glory* he hath sent me *to the nations* that spoiled you "; and so it is that after the Transfiguration in the descent from the mount He expels the devil (Matthew, Mark, Luke). The last item is the command to flee to Sion for the salvation to come, and leave *the north*, where they were, for Jerusalem.

* They had before them a verse in Wisd. 9^8 which they would apply to this event : " Thou hast bidden me to build a temple upon thy *holy mount*, even an altar in the city of *thy tabernacling*, a copy of *the holy tabernacle* which thou hast prepared from the beginning."

The Expulsion of the Dumb Spirit.

In the account of the sequel, which is obviously intrinsically united with the Transfiguration by all three Gospels, we note that Zech. 3^1 represents the devil as "standing at his right hand to resist him," but *not uttering a word*. Does not this account for Mark $9^{17, 25}$ calling the spirit *dumb*, and then *deaf and dumb?* That the father of the patient belonged to *the nations* of those parts and was not a Jew but a Gentile, seems to be proved by his saying, " Lord, I believe; help thou mine unbelief." In the devil that possessed his son the spoiler of the Israel of God was himself to be spoiled. At the end of this event Luke uses a very uncommon expression—*the majesty* (μεγαλειότητι) *of God*. This is repeated in 2 Pet. 1^{16} of the Transfiguration, with (or without) its sequel, this triumph over the spoiler. To the modern reader of the Gospels this expulsion does not seem to be pre-eminent above many more : but to Luke it evidently did : " And they were all astonished at *the majesty of God*. And while all were marvelling at all the things which he did. . . ." But this is accounted for by the fact of Zech. 3 being in some way or other behind the Gospel. The majesty is that of " Jesus the priest,* the great priest, who is transfigured as to his *raiment* in this chapter also, after his triumph over the devil.

The Raising of the Widow's Son.

Though the Transfiguration and the expulsion are inseparable, some verses are inserted both by Matthew and Mark between the two accounts. He charged them to tell no man till the Son of man be risen from the dead. Mark adds that this last expression conveyed a doubtful meaning to them. This is quite credible. There is singu-

* Moses in scripture is "among the priests " in Ps. 99^6 ; as " the great priest " Jesus surpasses him.

THE TRANSFIGURATION 287

larly little in the scriptures to justify an expectation that any one should ever rise from the dead. Moses had not risen. Elias was to come, but not to rise from the dead, for he had not died. The saying that the Baptist had risen from the dead was uttered as a popular belief by irresponsible retainers of Herod. But in Luke, who does not here record the perplexity about the resurrection, nor the question of Elias coming which follows it, we have previously had the story of the raising of the widow's son at Nain. Had Mark recorded this, it would be incredible that the one question should not have been connected with the other as an illustration. Mark, therefore, has deliberately omitted the widow's son at Nain, or was ignorant of it. This leads to the inquiry whether Luke had some account behind his record of this remarkable miracle, which he alone describes.

There can be little doubt that he had, and that it was the account of Elijah and the woman of Sarepta. This story has been shown elsewhere to lie behind the narrative in Acts 20^7 of Eutychus* at Troas, and the remarkable thing is that it should be also behind this narrative in Luke 7^{11}. That one original should produce two gospel narratives is a case which finds a partial parallel in another raising to life, that of Dorcas (Acts 9^{40}) with the words Tabitha kumi, compared with the raising of Jairus' daughter with the words Talitha kumi (Mark 5^{41}).† But there we have two writers, whereas here is one evangelist using the same original (1 Kings 17$^{8\ \text{ff}}$) first in the Gospel and then in the Acts. Observation shows that, apart from the main subject, he has used some of the circumstances in Luke and others in Acts.

* *St. Luke the Prophet*, p. 59.
† J. Kreyenbühl (*Zeitschr. neut. Wiss.*, Preuschen, 1909, 4) explains the Tabitha-Talitha miracle as originating in the preaching of Peter at Joppa. But I cannot agree with him that Luke has not recognized the connection of the miracle of Jairus' daughter with that of Joppa (*l.c.*, p. 276).

There are seven or eight particulars of the story of Sarepta repeated at Nain.

1 Kings XVII	Luke VII
10 He journeyed (ἐπορεύθη) to Sarepta to the gate (πυλῶνα) of the city.	11. He journeyed (ἐπορεύθη) to a city called Nain, and as he approached the gate (πύλη) of the city.
10. And behold, there	12. and behold . . . (and is here ungrammatical and is plainly imported from elsewhere)
10. a widow woman	12. and she was a widow
19. In which he (Elijah) sat (ἐκάθητο)	15. and the dead sat (ἐκάθισεν)
22. and the boy cried out	15. and he began to speak
23. and he gave him to his mother.	15. and he gave him to his mother.
24. Behold, I know that thou art a man of God.	16. A great prophet is raised up amongst us.

In the above comparison, besides the trace of the extraneous narrative in *and behold*, another trace is to be noticed in *city*. Now Nain was in no sense ever *a city*: * it is called so here only because Sarepta was in the original and was *a city*. Luke frequently uses the term "village," which would have been appropriate here. In order to meet the difficulty, it has been suggested † that, instead of Nain, Luke wrote the name *Shunem* (συνημ); the last syllable of which was misread by the copyist as *Ναιμ* and the first syllable lost through a possible confusion with the next word but one (καὶ συνεπορεύοντο). But this would not help us at all: there is no trace of any connection between Luke's miracle and that of Elisha at Shunem. What is clear is that Luke had in his mind the comparison of Jesus and Elijah which has been instituted shortly before in Luke 4^{25f},

---

* "There are numerous traces of ruins extending beyond the modern hamlet to the north, but these ruins have a modern appearance. There is a small spring north of the village: a second exists on the west, and beside it are rock-cut tombs. No remains of walls or of very ancient buildings were noticed." —*Survey of Western Palestine* (Conder), II. p. 86.

† Cheyne in *Enc. Bibl.*, "Nain."

THE TRANSFIGURATION

" There were many widows in the days of Elijah in Israel . . . and to none of them was Elijah sent, but only to Sarepta, in the land of Sidon, to a widow woman." And as soon as the two miracles at Sarepta and at Nain are contrasted the latter is seen to be on the greater scale. The Lord is attended by one "great multitude" (Luke $7^{11\,f}$) and the funeral procession by another "considerable multitude," in sharp contrast to the quiet isolation of the figures at Sarepta. Then the death at Nain was of longer standing than the other. Thirdly, it appears that the youth at Nain was the only son ($\mu ονογενὴς\ τῇ\ μητρί$), the boy at Sarepta was not. Next, the command "I say unto thee, Arise," is short and absolute, while Elijah's action is prolonged. Lastly, the miracle at Nain is followed by "fear taking hold on all; and they glorified God."

" *Elijah restoreth all things.*"

Enough has been said to show that Luke could not have placed in $9^{36\,f}$ the account which we read in Mark of the disciples' perplexity about the resurrection from the dead, and on the other hand that Mark knew nothing of the raising of the youth at Nain. The case of Jairus' daughter had been pronounced by the Lord Himself to be one of sleep. But we return to Mark and Matthew in their account of the descent from the mountain, and we see that Elijah is there under discussion again: "Why do the Pharisees and scribes say that Elias must first come?" The answer is, "Elijah cometh first and (you will read in Malachi) restoreth *all* things." This is a citation of—

Mal. $4^{4\,f}$ And he shall restore the father's heart to the son, and a man's heart to his neighbour.

" Elijah, I say unto you, hath come already, and they have done unto him all that they chose." This is the explanation of Elijah's coming, that he has come in the person of the Baptist. And so, says Matthew, the disciples then understood the fulfilment. "And so it is written of the Son of man, that he must suffer many things. . . ." The discussion reminds us of the fact that the context of Mal. $4^{4\,f}$ was one of the strongest predispositions of the Transfiguration. That Peter had been studying Zechariah-Malachi before the Transfiguration took place is an opinion which this discussion following it only confirms. The question is not why must Elias first come—which would seem to admit of a very simple answer, "Because it is written,"—but why the scribes say so. Perhaps because the disciples (or Mark) knew the tradition that the Baptist's mission had been to the Sadducees (see Ch. VII), and knew that the [Pharisees and] scribes had said that his mission was not that of Elijah because of its very limitation to the Sadducees, so that the disciples saw that there was a discrepancy. This theory would further account for the Lord's answer, "Elias restoreth *all* things," for the emphasis must be somewhere, and this is the one word in the answer that is common to both the reports. "Elijah's mission, that is the Baptist's, was a comprehensive mission and not limited to a class." We may also note that while Matthew made the Pharisees come to the baptism of John (Matt. 3^7), he did not mention the scribes as coming too; while here (Matt. 17^{10}) he does not mention the Pharisees, but only the scribes; the scribes, therefore, are made to speak as if conscious that the Baptist's mission had not been to them. Mark, on the other hand, has mentioned neither before as coming to the baptism, but mentions the scribes here.

However this may be, Zechariah-Malachi is under discussion among the little group: and yet the fruitful train of ideas connected with restoration or the restitution of all things, which was to be understood later (see above,

THE TRANSFIGURATION

p. 154) is not here pursued further. The lesson emphasized is that the prophecy of Elijah's coming has been fulfilled : Elijah has been unrecognized by the people of Israel as a whole, and put to death : and as the Lord's Forerunner has suffered, so the Lord, the Son of Man, in a sense certainly no less comprehensive and unlimited, must also suffer.

The Result of the Transfiguration.

Perhaps it is possible now to gather some conclusions from the above observations. The vision of Peter on the mount is a fact, and it implies the previous study of scripture passages by him. Some of these passages were the subject of study by the disciples and the Lord. They served to focus and to reflect the thoughts of the Forerunner John in relation to the Christ, and of his prototype Elijah in relation to Moses, and so of Christ to Moses. All revelation comes to the disciples through the study of scripture in the light of events, and of events in the light of scripture. This is only to say that they are the disciples of a great Prophet, learning from Him the more excellent method of prophecy and, what is much more, of life. The Transfiguration is the first vision recorded of any one of these disciples. To Peter, and so to the others, it was a revelation that the impending suffering of the Son of man was glorious, with the glory of Moses and that of Elijah, for at present they were not capable of imagining a greater glory. And it sent them back to the light of scripture with renewed zeal.

To the Lord Himself it was no sort of revelation, for He was conscious of nothing but of the prayer for which He had gone up into the mountain. His purpose was formed long before, and this time of prayer to Him was like other times of prayer, renewing, reviving, sanctifying, inspiring we know not what of power and mercy, of grace and truth, but inspiring purpose, resolution to be Messiah, rather than a consciousness that He was Messiah. But the Transfiguration was for the disciples' sake and not for His. Only because it was for theirs, to make them prophets more worthy of their Lord, the Masterprophet, honoured of Moses and of Elias, was it possible for St. Paul to write about Transfiguration as he did (2 Cor. 3^{18}, Rom. 12^2)—that we, the prophets, have had the Jewish veil removed from our hearts, and so are able to* reflect the glory of God, the same image (εἰκόνα) which He was,† while we pass in form from one glory to another in our varying reflections of the same theme, even as the Lord's interpretation of prophecy tells us that Jesus is Lord.

"Transfiguration" in St. Paul's View.

Possibly if we examine St. Paul on Transfiguration we may be helped to understand the construction of the gospel narrative on the subject. There are only these two passages in which he refers to Transfiguration, and we may take them in the order of their composition, 2 Cor. 3 and Rom. 12. In the former passage he is urging the argument from prophecy with its utmost force,

---

* Compare Wisd. 2^{23} " God made the man the image (εἰκόνα) of his own ownness " (τῆς ἰδίας ἰδιότητος). This was in St. Paul's mind, as the parallelism of the two contexts Wisd. 2^{21} = 2 Cor. 3^4 shows.

† Reflection here is everything, and seeing in a mirror is very little indeed. The key to the meaning is in *our gospel*, which we apostles preach as we are charged, that *Jesus is Lord Christ*, to make *the radiance of the gospel to reach* all but those who are blinded. This is the immediate context in 2 Cor. 4. The cosmic doctrine of a light-body, lost at the Fall, and a skin-body, which J. Lightfoot mentions, is confirmed by the newly-discovered Odes of Solomon (see Harris, *Odes and Psalms of Solomon*, 1910, p. 68). " I was clothed with the covering of thy spirit," Ode 25; " I clothed myself with light," Ode 21; " the Lord *renewed* me in His raiment," Ode 11. This is itself a good instance of the Restitution.

THE TRANSFIGURATION 293

and deploring the failure of it to move the mass of Jews. On the one side are the Jews whose " faculties of thought are callous " (2 Cor. 3^{14}), " a veil remaineth upon them to this day at the reading of the Old Testament " in the synagogue, and it is not withdrawn nor " being withdrawn," and they are unable to see that " in the idea of Christ it begins to be abolished "; they cannot see that the temporary character of the law of Moses is prefigured in Exodus, which says that Moses veiled his face in order that the fading of his glory should not be visible, which means, to wit, that his glory was intended to fade, and now it is fading before the glory of Christ. The veil to-day, says St. Paul, is not so much upon the face of Moses as upon the heart of the Jews (3^{15}), whose mental faculties have been blinded by the god of this world (4^{4}); they are " unbelievers," and " our gospel is hidden from them."

On the other hand, we who cherish hope in Christ (3^{12}) enjoy much boldness of speech and freedom (3^{17}). We can see that the time has come when the veil is being withdrawn from Moses' face. Exodus (34^{34}) says—

> But when Moses went in before the Lord to speak with him, he took the veil off until he came out.

Although LXX here agrees with Hebrew, St. Paul has given a different and loose paraphrase of his own, " But whensoever he shall turn unto the Lord the veil is removed." And he adds that the spiritual construction that we place upon the words is that the veil was and is removable, and we say it is being removed to-day, when " Moses turneth to the Lord," that is, when *the Mosaic dispensation turns to face Messiah* : in other words, when *the believers in Moses fairly face the argument from prophecy.*

This spiritual construction of the Old Testament is

the spirit (2 Cor. 3¹⁷), the prophetical interpretation of this and any and every other passage of the Old Testament to which we can discover the application. The application, when discovered and made, abolishes the Old Testament so far as it was temporary, removes the veil which concealed that temporary nature of it, enables us to look undazzled upon (ἀτενίσαι 3¹³) the fuller glory which Moses in privileged moments was enabled to see, and which, when he did see it, illumined and glorified his face. When he turned to the Lord he had a glimpse of " the spiritual meaning " of the law, which " is the Lord " (3¹⁷). Where we get the spiritual meaning (or inspiration) of the Lord Christ, or where the spiritual meaning is sovran or paramount (for the alternative readings τὸ πνεῦμα κυρίου and τὸ πνεῦμα κύριον amount to the same sense in 3¹⁷), there is freedom. Our face is unveiled, we behold the glory of the Lord; we are illumined by it, and we reflect as a mirror one and the same image, Messiah the image of God, though we have varying revelations of Him in our trances which we variously report; they are various glories; so we are *transformed* in passing from glory to glory, as we must be in receiving them from a sovran inspiration. The key to this inspiration is that *Jesus is Lord*, and " we " throughout the passage means " his apostles and prophets." The result of it is " our gospel " (4³) whose " illumination we reflect and radiate " as best we can into " the faculties of the unbelievers," because it is " the gospel of the glory of Christ who is the image of God." " The illumination consists in the experience of the glory of God in the face of Messiah " (4⁶). Our method, so far from being " craftiness or a deceitful handling of the word of God," as the Jews accuse it of being, is " the manifestation of the truth whereby we commend ourselves to every man's conscience in the sight of God " (4²).

The other passage in which " transfigured " is used by

THE TRANSFIGURATION 295

St. Paul (Rom. 12²) is one where he exhorts his readers to "let themselves be transformed by the renewal of their mental faculty instead of following merely the superficial fashion of this world "—to be thorough instead of conventional, where, however, the convention intended is largely a Jewish standard of conventional doctrine, because "this world" here must in the main agree in meaning with the "god of this world" in 2 Cor. 4⁴ who "blinded the faculties ($νοήματα$, so here $τοῦ νοός$) of the unbelievers." The two Epistles, belonging to the same period of writing, have very much common meaning. In both passages the Revised Version has followed the Authorised Version in translating *transformed*, and doubtless the Revised Version would fain have altered the term in Matthew and Mark likewise had this been possible in modern times.

Did St. Paul know the Transfiguration Narrative?

Now let us ask whether St. Paul had before him anything like our gospel story of the Transfiguration. That he goes back to Exodus is not a conclusive consideration, for Exodus must in any case be the basis of any parallel between a glory of Moses and a glory of Christ. But does St. Paul speak of the glory *of Christ*, or *of Jesus?* Does he refer to "the fashion of Jesus' countenance being altered"? To his raiment? To Moses appearing with Him? or Elijah? To tabernacles? To a testimony? To an *exodus?* To a cloud? To all these questions the answer has to be in the negative. He is as far from the Lucan narrative as from Matthew and Mark. But a little later we seem at first to discover possible traces of St. Paul having had Zech. 2, 3 in his mind. He says (4¹⁴) "he will raise us with Jesus." And Zech. 2¹³ says, "He hath been raised from clouds of his saints" (LXX) or "out of his holy habitation." Again (2 Cor. 5¹), "if the earthly house of our tabernacle be dissolved " rather seems to recall Zech. 2^{11}, " they shall tabernacle in the midst of thee." And lastly, 2 Cor. 5^2, " desiring to be clothed upon with our habitation which is in heaven, if so be that being clothed we shall not be found naked," may suggest Zech. 3^4, " Clothe [Jesus] in a long robe down to his feet." But all three references, though consecutive and parallel to a consecutive prophecy, are nugatory. They all rest upon other foundations beside Zechariah, and none of them possesses a feature characteristic of Zechariah. They must therefore be dismissed, and nothing is then left to show that St. Paul had in view anything like our gospel narratives of the Transfiguration when he wrote 2 Cor. and 2 Rom. The only conclusion possible is that he knew nothing of them, though we know that he had conversed with Peter, James and John, " who were reputed to be pillars " and two of whom were witnesses of the Transfiguration long before he wrote in the later fifties.

But again, is it conceivable that St. Paul, in deploring the callousness and blindness of the Jews to the new Testament, should have failed to use one of the strongest available arguments in the testimony of Moses himself in the vision of St. Peter on the holy mount of Sion, had he known of it? " Moses . . . appeared in glory and spake of His decease (departure, exodus) which He was about to fulfil." This train of thought, *Moses—glory —exodus—fulfil*, is precisely one that would have suited St. Paul's argument, which has actually included the first two ideas but stops short of the two last. Moses, in Luke 9, appears in order to "seal Jesus for the Great" Prophet. He there repeats the words "hear ye Him" that he said in Deuteronomy. Could there possibly be a stronger proof of the old " ministration of condemnation being abolished " ? And yet no sort of reference to it in the argument of 2 Cor. 3^1 !

THE TRANSFIGURATION

Is another Explanation of the Origin of the Gospel Narrative possible?

Further consideration, therefore, compels us to reconstruct the genesis of the gospel Transfiguration. We find in it a most marvellous fulfilment of Zech. 2, 3, so that what the gospels give as the events of one night followed by those of the morrow exactly coincide with what Zechariah prophesies in the self-same order—the Transfiguration dimly involved in Zech. 2 followed by the expulsion of the devil in Zech. 3. This fulfilment is so marvellous that if it happened it must have been one of the strongest cases of fulfilment ever known up to that time. Yet not a word is said about it! Why not? The only reason we can at first suppose is that the original Old Testament has been taken as evidence of the events narrated in the New Testament. Dr. Abbott has pointed out that Mark "*never quotes prophecy as being fulfilled*, not even in the entry to Jerusalem, where Matthew and John quote Zechariah, nor in the 'parting of the garments,' where John quotes from Psalms. Yet it is highly probable that Mark wrote these two descriptions (and many others) with prophecies in his mind." (*From Letter*, etc., 703.) The reader of the following pages will see to what extent Mark has taken Zech. 2, 3 as evidence.

> Zech. 2^6 Ho! flee ye from the land of the north, saith the Lord: for I will gather you from (Hebrew, I have spread you abroad as) the four winds of the heaven, saith the Lord.

Therefore the Lord Jesus went at one time on a missionary journey to the north of the Holy Land, and indeed also went west and east and south, since the four winds of the heaven are mentioned, from which He gathered or drew with Him (or to which He had spread) His disciples. The conditions are met by His going from Capernaum first west to Tyre and north to Sidon, after John's death—it has been suggested on purpose to avoid Herod Antipas * (Mark 7[24]). He then returns (through Sidon, or possibly the place may have been originally Bethsaida, as Wellhausen says) *east* and *south* to the south-east of the Sea of Galilee; then He visits Bethsaida on the north of the sea. Then another journey is made to the north to Cæsarea Philippi, thence to Sion (Hermon) near it. These journeys follow all points of the compass—the four winds of the heaven—more than once. What is further remarkable is that on two occasions there is an encounter with the devil and on two occasions with a "deaf and dumb spirit." The four winds of the heaven from which "ye shall be drawn" might almost have suggested, concurrently with Exod. 24, the number four for the mount of transfiguration, Jesus and the three. But we shall presently see a better explanation.

Again, the prophet had said—

Zech. 2[7] Unto Sion come up and be saved (ἀνασώζεσθε), ye that inhabit Babylon's daughter.

Therefore Sion (Hermon) was in some sense a point of salvation, of healing, to which the inhabitants of Cæsarea Philippi, with its pagan Roman temple of Augustus, were to come up. This condition was met by the crowd meeting the four on the way down, and a work of healing being performed there. The crowd was presumably of the inhabitants of that pagan region; a "faithless generation" (Mark 9[19]) means pagan people, outside the *Jewish* faith, and could not mean anything else (ἄπιστος is like ἄνομος, *outside the* Jewish *law*) at that time and place. "How long shall I be with you? How long shall I endure you?" is explained by—

* Burkitt, *The Gospel History and Transmission*, p. 92. He quotes Celsus, "You run off with your disciples hither and thither." But we shall see that fear of Antipas was not the motive.

THE TRANSFIGURATION 299

> Zech. 2¹⁰ I will come and tabernacle in the midst of thee, O daughter of Sion—

which is only the Hebrew way of expressing "of you inhabitants of Hermon." The question is most graphic. But, in fact, no sooner do we come to it than we see that it provides the key to the whole situation. The key is this: The Master was obeying the prophecy of Zechariah and was uncertain of the length of time foreshadowed.

> Zech. 2⁸ For thus saith the Lord of hosts, *After the glory* he hath sent me unto *the nations which spoiled you*, for he that *toucheth* you *toucheth* the apple of his eye.

Therefore the glory was the actual Transfiguration to be described at length, and then to be followed by a mission of some kind to the heathen (or possibly even Jewish) spoilers. This is what we have seen. And we saw above how Matthew represented the touching of the three by Jesus. Mark introduces some scribes among the heathen crowd, disputing with the disciples. But Mark had just before (7¹ ᶠᶠ) told how the Lord scornfully rebuked the scribes for their false doctrine of defilement. He had thus represented them in one sense as spoilers of the Jews. And Luke was about to record the Lord's word, that they devoured widow's houses (Luke 20⁴⁷).

> Zech. 2⁹ For, behold, I bring my hand upon them, and they shall be a spoil to their servants, and ye shall know that the Lord hath sent me.

Therefore the testimony to Jesus as sent by His Father is at this time to be delivered. And if so, it is to be delivered, as before, at the Baptism, or even more clearly. This condition is met by placing it in the account of the Transfiguration.

> Zech. 2¹² The Lord shall yet choose Jerusalem.

Therefore Luke 9³¹ has clearly marked "his exodus which he should fulfil at Jerusalem." The sequel in Zech. 3 of " Jesus the great priest " need not occupy us again in connection with the sequel of the Transfiguration, but we have seen that there is another encounter with a deaf and partly dumb ($\mu o\gamma\iota\lambda\acute{a}\lambda o\nu$) spirit in Mark 7³¹, and another with the devil that possessed the Greek-speaking Syrian woman's daughter (Mark 7²⁵). But these narratives fail to satisfy the condition of " Jesus rebuking the devil " who answers not a word in Zech. 3, for two reasons— there is no "rebuke" recorded in them and they do not follow closely " after a glory "; rather the reverse, for He had " wondered at their unbelief " (Mark 6⁶).

Deliberate Fulfilment of Zechariah by Jesus is the True Solution of the Coincidences.

The view was mentioned two pages before that these coincidences of the gospel with the prophecy of Zechariah were astonishing, and yet Mark makes no reference to them, and it has rather been implied from other statements that the reason why he does not is that he simply took statements in Zechariah as evidence of what the Lord did. But now we have seen that there is another way of explaining the fact, and the competing theory is that the Lord was deliberately fulfilling the passage in Zechariah. When once we have begun to see that a deliberate purpose of fulfilling the Old Testament dominates His mind, there is no reason for astonishment either in us or in the evangelist. This is the true explanation, as we shall see later, of several passages in the narrative of the Betrayal, and it is the true explanation here.

The details of *the glory* have next to be considered. The place is given, " Sion, which is Hermon." A reason for Him to go there is seen in—

THE TRANSFIGURATION

Ps. 89^{14} Tabor and Hermon shall rejoice in Thy name.

The glory took place on Sion. The Great Priest and Prophet must be like Moses, for Moses also was glorified on the Mount of God. The parallel between Moses and Jesus, his successor of whom he spake, was known as early as (Acts 2) Pentecost, if we may believe St. Luke in what he says of Peter: and the assumption is reasonable.* The parallel is worked out into greater length in Heb. 3^f; where the *Venite* which refers to Moses is claimed to refer more surely to Christ Jesus (Joshua). Then come in the biographical requirements given above.

Peter is the natural agency of the vision and was its reporter.

Yet here, once more, the opinion asserts itself that Peter did have the vision as it is described, but not there and not then, not till some years after the Ascension. How else can we account for the remarkably simple and graphic touches which mark it? That it did not belong there and then seems at first rather a necessary inference from Ps. 2 as applied. That it *was* applied to the Transfiguration by 2 Peter 1 is a certainty. The date of 2 Peter 1 is greatly disputed still, but those who oppose its authenticity will admit that it contains very much more sound doctrine than 2 Peter 2, which certainly is written in a different and later style. It is quite tenable that St. Peter in his lifetime applied Ps. 2 to the Transfiguration. If so, then the Sion of Ps. 2^6 was then understood to be Hermon. But this can hardly have been till years after the Ascension, the first and natural sense of Sion in Ps. 2 being Mount Zion. And Ps. 2^{1f} was interpreted of Herod and Pilate by the disciples (Acts 4^{27}), while Ps. 2^1 was applied to the resurrection ten years

---

* It underlies the very important question affecting the credibility of Acts raised by Acts 16^3, Timothy's circumcision, on which see *St. Luke the Prophet*, pp. 60^{ff}.

later by St. Paul (Acts 13^{33}), as if Sion were still Jerusalem. Then we have seen that the non-existence of the narrative is probable till about 60, and we are disposed to think that at that time the Sion of Ps. 2 began to be Hermon. In agreement with this view is the fact that soon after that date Rev. 19^{15} adopts the warlike verse, Ps. 2^9, "Thou shalt shepherd them with a rod of iron," which wears an aspect of Zech. 2^9, "the Gentiles that spoiled thee shall be a spoil to their servants"—the passage in which Sion is certainly, for the Transfiguration purpose, Hermon. If Peter had not had the vision before 50 or 51 we can see why St. Paul did not know of it in writing several years later, for he had not seen Peter for years. If he had it about that time, the presence in the vision of all the characters described is conceivable, though James was dead. There is, however, one fatal objection—the confusion of date between the lifetime of Jesus and twenty years later. This is insuperable. The theory falls to the ground.

All this time there is one very simple explanation which has never been taken into account. We have observed above that Peter must have been a student of the Bible. But who was the inspiring motive of his study and his thought? Of course, the Master Himself. He was the stimulus, and Peter was the apt learner, and his learning was to bear its chief fruit after the denial, the death, and the resurrection. The Master-prophet was led by His own interpretation of Zech. 2 to go to Hermon, ignorant of what precisely should befall Him there, but only trusting the purpose of God to be in some way fulfilled. And it was fulfilled in the way that we have seen.

The Lord's Movements governed by Prophecy.

It behoves us to trace, if we can, the movement of the Master's thoughts in this eventful journey with all reverence, with no prejudice, and with as little other sentiment as is possible. I do not remember to have seen any

THE TRANSFIGURATION 303

attempt hitherto made to trace His movements on the principle here stated, that He studied the prophecies and was guided by them in His movements from place to place. And yet this is undoubtedly what was done, for instance, by St. Paul in Acts 16, St. Peter in Acts 10, St. Philip in Acts 8. How shortsighted, then, are theologians not to have seen this principle at work in Him ! He must have studied more than most the books which contained His name Jesus (p. 284). Most of these are by no means Messianic books. First of all is the Pentateuch, containing, indeed, several Messianic passages here and there, but these are particularly obscure. Though He had resolved before He was at Hermon to be Messiah, the Pentateuch and Joshua would throw no light upon Him that we can see, except—and it is a fundamental exception—as Jesus the successor of Moses. Then the other historical books, Judges, 1 Samuel, 1, 2 Kings, Chronicles, are particularly devoid of Messianic passages. Then the last group, Haggai and Zechariah—the former exceedingly brief—are books which both contain the name Jesus and are strongly Messianic. These, then, would have been His especial study. Edersheim has given a very careful list of Old Testament passages applied to the Messiah or to Messianic times in the most ancient Jewish writings. They amount in all to four hundred and fifty-six : seventy-five from the Pentateuch, none from Joshua (this we might infer), four from the group mentioned next above, twenty-eight from the last group, including Malachi, as we must include it.

We must suppose that the death of John was an event which came upon Jesus with an almost overpowering shock, and yet we can hardly wonder that the effect is not described in the Gospels. His subsequent retirement is plain. But Mark is so full of the works of healing and of the apostles' report of their doings and teachings that he puts the retirement on the need of rest (Mark 6^3).

To be out of the reach of Antipas may have been a reason for part of His absence from Galilee, but the Gospels do not say so, and clearly before He journeys to Tyre and Sidon He does not shun publicity, for He feeds the five thousand; He is beset by patients in crowds at Gennesaret; He discusses the question of defilement with the Pharisees and scribes. This shows no fear of Antipas. Why not admit, then, another motive for His movements? There had been much to encourage, and also much to discourage His great resolution. The position is fairly expressed by John $5^{33\,f}$, that the works of healing were a testimony greater in one way than that of John.

But nothing, perhaps, could compensate just yet for the shock, unless it was found in the fulfilment of prophecy, and this must be done by Himself. The very obscure prophecies were before Him: " Flee ye from the north." Had He gone to the north? Yes. First, He had tried to do so after feeding the five thousand, but the ship was blown west. North, then, He must go, and He goes. The first journey is very uncertain in its extent (Mark 7^{24-31}), for the boundaries of Tyre [and Sidon] might only mean some twenty miles from Capernaum. The healing works upon the heathen demoniac daughter of the Syrophenician and upon the heathen deaf and dumb Decapolitan resulted. But no fulfilment of Zech. 2, 3! He could say with Zech. 2^8, " He hath sent me (and I have now gone) to the nations that spoiled you in Decapolis." He could say, too, that this was " After the glory " ($\delta \acute{o} \xi \eta \varsigma$), for it followed upon the renown ($\delta \acute{o} \xi a$) which was certainly His since the feeding of the five thousand. But there was still no guidance. He was now again back from the heathen Decapolis (to the south-east of the lake) at Magdala Bay, ($\lambda \iota \mu \acute{\eta} \nu$, d-limin-utha *) in its north-west corner. Here He is pressed for a sign from heaven.

* Edersheim seems rightly to have solved this riddling name Dalmanutha thus.

THE TRANSFIGURATION

The request appeared to be conveyed in the words of an ancient Psalm where the *generation* (or, *kinsfolk*, ἡ συγγενία αὐτῶν) is taken as saying—

> Ps. 74^{8f} We see not our *signs*: there is no prophet more, and [He] shall not recognize us any more.

This follows in the Psalm immediately after the plaintive lament—

> Ps. 74^6 Together *with axe* and stonecutter's tool they brake it down (the porch),

where the axe was most appropriate to the recent beheading of the Baptist, who was one of those *who had been smitten with the axe* for the testimony of Jesus (Rev. 20^4). This again follows closely on the reference to Hermon—

> Ps. 74^2 Mount *Sion* here, wherein thou dost *tabernacle*.

But, once more, the Psalm continues—

> Ps. 74^{13} Thou didst make the sea strong in thy power: thou bruisedst the heads of the dragons on the water.

The reference appears to be satisfied by the narrative of the stilling of the wind (Mark 6^{51}); but, what is more remarkable, the following verse is—

> Ps. 74^{14} Thou gavest him [for] meat to peoples, the Ethiopians. (What can be made out of *the Ethiopians* is far from clear, the more so that in this portion of the Psalter we lack the invaluable aid of the Alexandrine MS. Perhaps it would here have agreed with the Hebrew " in the *desert*." In any case we observe that the Synoptists all specify that " the place was *desert*," Luke 9^{12}, Mark 6^{35}, Matt. 14^{15}).

Though He gave them the answer that no sign should be given to their generation (them), He may have felt that the guidance of Providence was far from clear. The testimony of the Baptist rang incessantly in His ears, the

x

more so since his death—Thou art my beloved Son, in whom I am well pleased—and the words were like Ps. 2. Now they sustained Him, more even than before. They were the words of the Lord. But in that Psalm what was the context ?

> Ps. 2⁶ But I was stationed by him upon *Sion* his holy mountain, proclaiming *the command of the Lord*.

Had He done this ? Had He gone to mount Sion ? Then go He must, and He goes once more north by Bethsaida and thence by the villages of Cæsarea Philippi. Here takes place the confession of Peter, and, strange to say, a rebuke of him as *Satan*, as if His mind was moving on the lines of—

> Zech. 3² The Lord rebuke thee, O devil, the Lord who chooseth Jerusalem—

as the scene of My passion. For what was *the command* ($\pi\varrho\acute{o}\sigma\tau\alpha\gamma\mu\alpha$) *of the Lord ?* It was now understood by Jesus to mean His own impending decease which He must fulfil at Jerusalem, as had now become only too certain. The life must be laid down that He might take it again. The duty of the compensation ($\dot{\alpha}\nu\tau\acute{a}\lambda\lambda\alpha\gamma\mu\alpha$), had come home.

The Compensation, The Sons of Men, and The Man.

For, once more it is clear that, whether recalled by the chance expression of the Syrophenician woman, "Lord, son of David," or by his own thoughts, He was pondering the latter part of—

> Ps. 89³⁹⁻⁵¹ But thou hast thrust away and brought to nought, *thou hast put off thy Christ !*

Thou hast overthrown the covenant of *thy servant** and defiled in the dust his holiness.

---

* John, *i. e.* Elijah, is "thy servant" in 1 Kings 18³⁶. "Let it be known this day that thou art God . . . and that I am thy servant."

THE TRANSFIGURATION 307

> Thou hast exalted the right hand of his oppressors—
> made all his foes to rejoice.

How all this passage suits the dejected mind that pondered upon John's death!

> Thou hast undone him *from purification*, and dashed *his throne* to the earth.

What is *purification* in this place but John's baptism? and what is *his throne* but the chariot of fire that should have been his?

> Thou hast shortened the days of his time ($\chi\rho\acute{o}\nu o\upsilon$, A, etc.) and covered him with shame.
> How long, Lord, dost thou turn away, for ever? Shall thy wrath be burnt up as a fire?
> Remember what my condition is! Hast thou made in vain indeed *all the sons of men?*
> Who is THE MAN who shall live and shall not see *death?* He *shall deliver his life from the hand of hell*.

Is it presumptuous to think that we look into the Lord's mind here, and touch the very springs of His thought? Peter having said "the Christ of God," we next, in Luke 9[21] have the rebuke, above-mentioned, in a different form and not addressed to Peter, but as part of the command of silence, and he adds—

> *The Son of man* must suffer many things . . . and be put *to death* and . . . *be raised again.*

It seems an exceedingly simple supposition that *the Son of man* is precisely the person, that One of *the sons of men* of Ps. 89[48] *who shall live* because God *shall deliver his life from the hand of hell*. This was now one of His sustaining convictions, sustaining in the face of the great ordeal which awaited Him. The concluding lines of Ps. 89 contain an expression which serves to prove the foregoing statements—

x 2

> Where are thy mercies, thy ancient mercies, Lord, which thou swarest unto David in thy truth?
> Remember, Lord, the reproach of thy servants, which I bear in my bosom from many nations,
> Wherewith thine enemies reproach, O Lord, wherewith they reproach *the compensation* (τὸ ἀντάλλαγμα) *of thy Christ*.

Here is the second use within a few verses (39, 52) of *thy Christ*. If the words are adopted by Jesus, then it follows that He had realized—let us rather say *resolved*—ere this that He was the Christ. Now it is a certainty that He was at this time using the psalm as His own from the fact that in the narrative of Mark 8^{37} Matt. 16^{26} this very strange word *compensation* (ἀντάλλαγμα) is used. Nowhere else in the New Testament does it occur, and hardly ever outside LXX, where it occurs eight times and here. Euripides used it once, and this fact ought to have made it popular, and yet it did not.* The occurrence of so remarkable a term is conclusive, considering its connection —losing *life*—gaining *life*—saving *life*—*compensation* for *life*—*Christ*, that He was applying Ps. 89 to Himself. He was discoursing on the value of a life laid down, and certainly it was Christ's life, and almost as certainly His life. He saw from it that He, as the seed of David, and as God's Holy One, was the Son of Man, and that He must suffer many things, and be put to death, and be raised again. But when we ask whether He saw further that the suffering must be at the hands of the Jewish authorities, the answer is not so clear. The Greek has *from* [or, *on the part of*] *many nations, wherewith thine enemies* reproach thee. But the Hebrew has only—

* In the other eight places in the LXX it means *exchange*, and so it may here, but it was probably meant by the LXX translator for the *heels* or *alternating footsteps*. How few of the disputants of the Atonement-doctrine throughout the ages have thought of looking to this text, which is probably its basis more than any other text!

THE TRANSFIGURATION 309

The reproach of thy servants—how I bear in my bosom all (these) many peoples—wherewith thine enemies have reproached.

And Dr. E. G. King says, "the words are strange and possibly not altogether correct." Have they ever been tampered with? Since, however, it is clear that Jesus here used the LXX as the evangelists did, the Hebrew is of less importance and use. He may have taken *the reproach from (of) many nations* to refer to the journeys he was now making among the Gentile parts of the country, while He foresaw the Jewish authorities were, after all, more certain to overthrow Him than Antipas or the Romans.

Lastly, there is no trace in Ps. 89 of anything to justify the rising *on the third day*. But in connection with the idea of *compensation* there is a passage which can hardly fail to have been present to the Lord—

Zech. 9[11 f] And thou by the blood of thy covenant didst send forth as apostles thy prisoners from a pool (λάκκου) that hath no water. And [the] prisoners of the synagogue shall set themselves in a stronghold: and instead (ἀντὶ) of *one day* of thy sojourn (παροικεσίας) I will *recompense* thee double (διπλᾶ ἀνταποδώσω σοι).

This is seen easily after the event to be applicable to the descent into hell followed by the resurrection of Jesus after one whole day in the tomb. It is not so easy to imagine that it would have suggested such an expectation to Him at Cæsarea. There was also—

Hos. 6[2] He will make us whole after two days: on the third day we shall set ourselves up (ἀναστησόμεθα) and shall live before him.

This comes much nearer to the expression in Mark 8[31] (ἀναστῆναι), and either this was the cause of it or it is supplied here by the Gospels automatically.

But there are two oracles that must not be forgotten in this same connexion, one that has been before us already in—

> Isa. 8⁸ A MAN that shall be able to lift up [his] head or powerful to accomplish something [great],

and another that combines *the Man* with the idea of Resurrection—

> Num. 24¹⁷ᶠ There shall arise (ἀνατελεῖ) a star out of Jacob, and there shall rise up (ἀναστήσεται, as if from the dead) A MAN (ἄνθρωπος) out of Israel, and he shall crush the rulers of *Moab* and shall plunder all the sons of Seth. And *Edom* shall be his inheritance, and his inheritance shall be Esau his foe, and he maketh Israel to be strong.

Edom here again stands for the Idumæan house of Herod, and *Moab* represents the stronghold of Antipas at Machærus, where the Baptist had been beheaded. It has been observed above that the Old Testament contains few references to the Resurrection. But this passage must be accounted one of the most important of them all, being referred to the Messiah in the *Targum of Onkelos* and the *Mishna* (see Edersheim, *Life and Times*, etc., App. ix). It is therefore entirely credible that the Lord, having resolved to be THE MAN, did at Cæsarea predict on Scriptural grounds His own Resurrection.

Further Guidance of Ps. 89.

We must not leave Psalm 89 without observing that in its earlier portion it has provided not a little geographical guidance—how much, indeed?—to the Prophet of Nazareth—

> Ps. 89¹² Thou hast made *the north* and *the sea* (of Galilee):

THE TRANSFIGURATION 311

Tabor (in view from Nazareth) *and Hermon* shall rejoice in thy name.

Thine arm is with power (the mighty works performed in Galilee).

Let thine hand be strengthened, thy right hand be exalted.

This passage would at first suggest that the *north* was identical with *the sea of Galilee*, but what if it were rather the Mediterranean Sea, in sight from Nazareth hill? If the doubt possessed Jesus thus, we can forthwith account for the strange journey to the borders of Tyre [and Sidon], which is still involved in so much obscurity that we do not know whether Matthew and Mark make Him go to the Mediterranean or not. Luke is silent on the whole period, as if he were equally uncertain.

The conclusion of this discourse, which is impressively solemn, is (Mark 8^{38})—

For *whosoever* shall be *ashamed* of me and of my words . . . the *Son of man shall be ashamed* of him, when he cometh in the glory of *his father* with the holy *angels*. Verily I say unto you, There are some here *of them that stand* which shall not taste of death until they see the kingdom of God come with power.

We ask how much of this passage also is inspired by Ps. 89. *The shame* of *the son of David* (either directly or indirectly through the Forerunner) has been mentioned (89^{45}) and is implied in *the reproach*. And the reproach is *of many nations:* hence *whosoever*. But the *Remember, Lord* implies a visitation of this reproach on those who make it; hence *the Son of man shall be ashamed*. This he cannot do unless empowered by the Lord: hence *when he cometh*, etc. Earlier we have had the references to *the angels* in 89^{6-8}. Also we have had (89^{26}) he shall call me *Thou art my father:* hence *his father*. The concluding *Verily*, etc., is the inference of the Master-prophet

Himself. And yet here, again, how sternly and closely scriptural He is! For Ps. 89^2 opened with—

> For thou saidst, For ever shall mercy be built up, in the heavens shall be prepared thy truth—

and it went on to say—

> $89^{8\,ff}$ Lord God of the powers, who is like unto thee? Mighty art thou, Lord, and thy truth round about thee. . . . Righteousness and judgment are the preparation of thy throne, mercy and truth shall go before thy face. Then thou spakest *in a vision* to thy sons and saidst, I lay help upon a mighty one, I exalt *the Elect one* out of my people. I have found *David my servant*, with the oil *of my holiness* I have anointed him. For my hand shall assist him, and my arm shall strengthen him. The enemy shall find no profit in him, and *the son of lawlessness* shall not proceed to hurt him. And I will cut down his foes before him, and will rout them that hate him. And my truth and my mercy are with him, and in my name shall his horn be exalted.

The Psalm almost insists on being quoted, for every line is capable of a fresh and vivid meaning drawn from the situation at Cæsarea Philippi. *The son of lawlessness* is Herod Antipas, as we know. Hence, another reason why He need not fear or flee. *I exalt the Elect one* confirms the testimony of John: " Thou art my beloved Son, in thee I am well pleased "; but also increases it, for the title *The Elect* has not hitherto been used. The *visions of thy sons* in the past had been matched by His visions in the wilderness at the Temptation. That He was of the house of David—did He not know this from His father's tradition? One supposes that He did. Yet the cardinal and indeed fundamental importance of this one supposition must be fully considered, although it

THE TRANSFIGURATION 313

does not seem possible to treat it as anything else. If this be a datum, the resolution of His Messiahship follows intelligibly—easily or naturally are not adverbs that could be used of this subject, but intelligibly—from Ps. 89. If it be not a datum, then much if not all of the difficulty is overcome by—

> Ps. 89^{27} I will adopt him [as] my Firstborn (πρωτότοκον θήσομαι αὐτόν).

The Charter of the Lord.

But in any case with how much searching of heart and how much searching of Scripture must He have come to the resolution to be the Christ of God! All youthful aspiration, imagination, ambition, must have been put away with childish things, absorbed and swallowed up in the mighty determination. Others have written and talked of the Christ—I will be the Christ, and God help me! And so far from anointing with oil, He had but *the oil of my holiness*, like Jesus the great priest in—

> Zech. 3^7 Thus saith the Lord Almighty, If thou walk in my ways and keep thee in my *commands* (προστάγμασιν), then thou shalt judge my house : and if thou guard my fold, then will I give thee some that converse in the midst *of these which stand* [here].

We note in passing how προστάγμασιν is one more link with τὸ πρόσταγμα of Ps. 2 (see p. 306). Can any words of Scripture have possessed His soul more strongly than these? The whole strength of Messiahship turns upon the *If*. The sinlessness of Christ turns on His resolution. Yes, for any other theory would reduce His office to a mere piece of mechanism, and His example as representative of man (and the Son of man is precisely *man's representative*) would be for ever lost and gone. Thus the closing expression of Cæsarea in Luke 9^{27} = Mark 9^1 = Matt. 16^{28}

reproduces Zech. 3. Mark 9^1 gives a strange arrangement of words : " there are *some here of them which stand,*" which by itself is quite unnatural, and *by* has to be added. Matthew and Luke have corrected accordingly. But in fact Mark has preserved two of the words of Zech. 3^7, τῶν ἑστηκότων τούτων, *these which stand.* This is a minute point that speaks volumes; for the expression is anything but justified by one or two only apparent parallels.

The inference is that when He says *the kingdom of God come with power* we are to fill up the content of the expression, battered and broken as it is with the age-long commentary of men, of churches, and of events, by such an idea as we may be able to draw from the source, which is Ps. 89.

Finally, a word must be said upon St. Paul's ignorance of the Transfiguration. It is of a part with his ignorance how Jesus resolved upon Messiahship. The subject is not treated by him in writing. He closed his paper, if not his eyes, to the whole question, and this he almost implies in saying (2 Cor. 5^{16}), " Though it is true we have known Christ in the ordinary way in which men know him, we now dismiss the knowledge." This, of course, has nothing to do with the question whether St. Paul had ever met Jesus, and throws no light upon it. He is speaking of Messiah, and of the popular notion of Messiah that most men entertained. The self-realization as the Christ by Jesus is a question that would involve the popular notions of Messiah, if only or chiefly by contrast, and these notions he does not wish to enter upon at all. Thus the Transfiguration vision he has left to Peter as his own property, helpful as it would have been to his argument. This, however, he felt was sufficiently strong without it.

The interpretation of Sion as Hermon in Ps. 2^6 may have been concurrent with Sion as Jerusalem. We know that Jerusalem was called Sodom and Egypt, but that did not prevent the concurrent meaning of those

THE TRANSFIGURATION

names. Again, while the Gospel of Peter is quoting Zech. 11[13], "At this price let us apprize the Son of God," and applying it to the mockery, Matt. 27[9] was applying the same verse to the bargain of Judas.

The Messiah-secret.

There is another question which of necessity arises out of the confession at Cæsarea, and to which an answer has been indicated in Ch. II (p. 49)—if He had resolved to be the Messiah of the kingdom, why conceal the fact first from His disciples, and, when revealed to them, from the world? The answer is to be found in the fulfilment, deliberate on His part, of the prophecy—

> Isa. 31[9], 32[1 ff] Thus saith the Lord, *Blessed* (Μακάριος) is he who hath *in Sion* a seed and *men of his house* (οἰκείους) in Jerusalem. For, behold, a king, a righteous king, shall reign, and rulers with judgment shall rule. And THE MAN (ὁ ἄνθρωπος) *shall hide* his words [or, *these words*], and *he shall be hidden* as from rushing water (ὡς ἀφ' ὕδατος φερομένου), and he shall appear in Sion as a river rushing glorious (φερόμενος ἔνδοξος) in a thirsty land. And they shall no more trust in men, but they shall give their ears to hear. . . .

After Cæsarea, Sion which is Hermon. We are to understand that at Cæsarea He contemplated the visit to Hermon, not knowing what should befall Him there, but convinced that this prophecy was one that ordered Him to go there. We note in passing that the reply to Peter at Cæsarea contains two marks of resemblance to this passage, *Blessed* art thou (Μακάριος εἶ), and Thou art Peter, and upon *this rock I will build* (Πέτρος . . . πέτρα οἰκοδομήσω), for a *Rock* is *of the house of rock* (οἰκεῖος τῇ πέτρᾳ, *akin* to it), and " the House of the Great King," as said the book of Enoch (91[13]), " shall be builded for evermore " upon this rock—where the Great King is the *Righteous king* of Isa. 32. When we come to *The man shall hide these words*, in Isa. 32, and *he shall be hidden*, we recollect how *the Man* has been marked in Ps. 89[49] immediately after *the sons of men* as He *who shall live and not see death*, as, in fact, *the Son of Man*. Jesus, therefore, was commanded here *to hide these words* which in Peter's mouth gave Him the kingdom of David by Ps. 89, apart from the command to use parabolic teaching, and Himself *should be hidden* as from the Assyrian Antipas —the violent river, which, as we saw (Ps. 89[23]), should be powerless to hurt him. He was further bidden (Isa. 31[9], 32[2]) to repair to Sion Hermon, where He should appear as a river rushing gloriously in a thirsty land, presumably a land barren otherwise of living water. He went there and was not Himself conscious of a glory ($\check{\epsilon}\nu\delta o\xi o\varsigma$), but his disciple Peter saw Him there in glory ($\dot{\epsilon}\nu\ \delta\acute{o}\xi\eta$), and thus he was enabled to see that Isa. 32[1] was partially fulfilled. For Peter's vision of His Transfiguration was a proof to Him that He had a spiritual son, a *seed in Sion*, Hermon, and a pledge that He should have a *kindred* spirit in him *in Jerusalem*. Nevertheless, it was also a fulfilment so partial that He must look forward to the other Sion, Jerusalem, as the place where He must appear as a river rushing glorious : and that was, indeed, a more thirsty land where Siloam was the only fountain. The eventual fulfilment of *the river* was found in Christian baptism.

To say that the Cæsarean confession was the greatest encouragement that the Lord received in the course of His ministry is a statement which has considerable truth in it, but the truth can perhaps be appreciated best in the light of Isa. 32[1] and Ps. 89. For the seed of David there mentioned is capable of two meanings, first, the Son of David who was Himself, and next, the spiritual descendants of the Son. The latter seed was to be everlasting, no less

THE TRANSFIGURATION 317

than the former (Ps. 89⁵, ³⁰, ³⁷), even as God would "*build up* His throne to all *generations*." Therefore when afterwards He beheld that Peter had seen Him transfigured, He knew that He possessed the blessing which He had pronounced upon Peter *as Peter upon Him* (κἀγὼ δὲ, Matt. 16¹⁸) : *Blessed* was He that had in Sion Hermon a seed. The blessing in Matt. 15¹⁷ presupposes the blessing in Isa. 31⁹.

Now comes the crowning fulfilment of this Isaian prediction in an unexpected place of the fourth Gospel, John 7³⁷ ᶠᶠ. " On the last day, the great day of the feast (of Tabernacles, Sept. 21) Jesus stood and cried [with the prophet's cry] saying, If any one *thirst*, let him come unto me and drink. He that *believeth* on me, as *the scripture* * *saith*, out of his belly shall flow *rivers* of living water." This is His exact and deliberate fulfilment of what *the scripture saith* in Isa. 32². He had been *hidden* in the northern borders, he now *appeared in* Sion (Jerusalem). He appealed to *the men of His own house in Jerusalem*, to whoso *believed on Him*, for *they shall no more trust* in men, but *they shall give ears to hear*, and the prophetic cry, *Whoso hath ears to hear, let him hear*, which is common in the Synoptics, is represented here in John by *Jesus cried and said*. The *rivers of living water* which *shall flow* reproduces Isaiah's *river rushing gloriously*, and *if any man thirst* reproduces Isaiah's *thirsty land* (see below p. 375). The occasion has already been mentioned as that of the water-bearing from Siloam, when Isa. 12³ was sung : With joy shall ye draw water out of the wells of salvation.

It follows from this that John's tradition placed the Hermon visit, if at all, before Sept. 15, but John does not recognize the visit. The place for it seems to be between John 6 and John 7. For at John 6⁶⁶⁻⁷¹ we have what is obviously the confession at Cæsarea, though the place is

---
* The passages mentioned by Westcott suit for baptism in a later age but not for this occasion.

not mentioned by name. When Simon Peter says, " We have believed and learned by *experience* (ἐγνώκαμεν) that thou art *the holy one of God*," he makes the Cæsarean confession in other terms. The *experience* is consistent with the experience of the vision on Hermon : and it represents it. Ps. 89^{36} says, " I sware once for all by [or in the case of] *my holy one* * that I will not fail David." And Ps. 2^7 says even more. But there is in John 6^{70} a significant turn of meaning away from the Synoptics, for where they record the rebuke to Simon Peter as Satan, the saying *one of you is a devil* in John is taken to refer to Judas *son of Simon* Iscariot.

If any one were to urge that here is a trace of *ex post facto* reasoning by the evangelists direct from the Old Testament to the proceedings of Jesus, and that whereas the Synoptics had taken Sion to mean Hermon and John took it only of Jerusalem, the answer would appear to be this. The original Zech. 2 speaks of the Hermon visit as first and the exodus at Jerusalem as afterwards : " the Lord will yet choose Jerusalem." The identity of Sion with Hermon did not prevent Sion being in other places Jerusalem. Thus in Isa. 31^9 Sion, where He hath a seed, may be first Hermon and then Jerusalem, while Isa. 32^2, which follows immediately, is certainly Jerusalem. The question of the itinerary is one upon which very much might be written if space permitted. All that can here be said is that Jesus is evidently guided in John 7^4 by considerations of hiding, which, however, His brethren do not understand : " No man doeth anything in secret and himself seeketh to be known openly." He is still in hiding when later He goes up to the feast (John 7^{11}). Has any satisfactory explanation ever been given of this hiding ? The sole and simple explanation of it consists

---

* The various readings for *the holy one of God*, the son of God, the Christ the son of the living God, etc. (and A is defective), may probably be due to *supposed* parallel influences, as Westcott says, but may possibly be due to various traditions older than our MSS.

THE TRANSFIGURATION 319

in the understanding of the oracle of Isa. 32, which guided His movements because He was resolved to fulfil it. Whether there is a contrast intended in *his brethren who did not believe in him* and *his own kindred in Jerusalem* (Isa. 31^9) may be doubtful, but in every respect this narrative in John seems to wear the appearance of being genuine and anything but a fiction of the evangelist. The case would have been different had it been said that *the disciples* objected to the hiding, for we should expect that He had ere this acquainted them above all others with the meaning of Isa. 31, 32, and that therefore they understood His movements, having believed on Him.

The Synoptics, however, are equally clear in showing the fulfilment of this same oracle by means of the secrecy enjoined by Him on the disciples and those whom He cured. But the discrepancy of the seasons indicated by them and by John is a question which cannot here be discussed.

CHAPTER XI

THE OLIVET DISCOURSE

False Attribution of Discourses to a Genius.

WE have now reached a point in our inquiry at which the habit of finding scripture at the back of the gospel-events has disposed us to expect to find it behind the discourses. Here it must be said, therefore, that there is a vast difference between the record in the New Testament of a discourse and that of an event. When narratives of the Lord's life, such as that of Nain, are eventually found to resemble Old Testament narratives, the simplest explanation of them for our time is that they were constructed by the evangelist in the belief that the Antitype fulfilled what was written of the type, so that to him the evidence of the type's action was evidence of that of the Antitype. There were, in fact, a number of cases in which the Antitype not only fulfilled, but had set Himself to fulfil, the words and also the actions of the type, as we shall see in the case of the Betrayal. There were other cases where the evangelist outran the range of fulfilment. But, quite apart from fulfilment, it is possible from given data of time and place to construct a certain number of minor events to adorn the biography in default of evidence. There have been men of genius, not of action—Shakespeare is one—whose biographies have been eked out upon probabilities superinduced upon scanty evidence.

And yet, given a genius of thought, though antecedently there may be little to show what things, or even what sort of things, he would suffer and do, there is incomparably less to show what he would be likely to say. Socrates and the Saviour were alike in one point, that

THE OLIVET DISCOURSE 321

they wrote nothing; in another that their lives perhaps were less remarkable than their deaths; in a third, that in Plato and in St. Paul they had each a disciple who carried on his master's work in his name.* The life of Socrates is, on the whole, uneventful. But his thoughts are epoch-making. Knowing the date of his life we could construct an imaginary life for him which would not be very wide of the mark. But could any subsequent writer, even if himself a genius, possibly invent the method of Socrates? His great disciple possessed the master's method, and by developing and applying it he was able to invent some words and some thoughts which we so far accept as Socrates' own that we do not care to raise the question whether this or that dialogue of Plato represents or misrepresents Socrates. We say of Plato's account, " This is good "; and of Xenophon's account we say, " This also is good." Any disharmony in the two accounts we leave specialists to determine, and the specialists do not in this case of Socrates startle the public ear. The only way to do so would be to discover a third contemporary account of the genius, which should exhibit him in a fresh light.

While therefore events in the life of a genius can be constructed out of probabilities, the discourses of a genius cannot. Every attempt to place words in the mouth of Jesus—and here, of course, St. Paul bears no analogy at all to Plato—is attended by the danger that if He was a Genius the words attributed to Him may betray their bastard origin. Since nobody disputes the fact that the Lord was a Spiritual Genius—to use a common term—the apostles ran that danger if they attributed words to His lips which He did not use. For even in the case of a genius we are able to fall back upon the negative faculty which is common to all intelligence, of

* No reader, learned or unlearned, can fail to profit by reading Stanley, *Jewish Church*, III, Sec. 46 on Socrates.

Y

being able to pronounce on what he did not say. For instance, certain kinds of contradictory propositions, especially if attributed to him in the same breath where irony or paradox or humour has no place, may be disowned. Again, a detailed number of statements, each drawn from a pre-existing context to which it belongs and in which it makes good sense, but strung together in no visible order or mutual relation, so as to produce no intelligible sense in the new juxtaposition, may be disowned. And at the same time it is a matter of some interest, if not also a bounden duty, to account for the facts. That the attempt to explain these phenomena will contribute to the discovery and explanation of them and of others is the faith-venture of him who makes it.

But here again we must distinguish. A citation of scripture was often on the lips of One of the most scriptural of men, without His being expected to give chapter, verse or author. On the other hand, whenever, for instance, He is reported to use words which are used in the Old Testament in the course of a conversation by David the King, we cannot dismiss the suspicion that they may have been put into the mouth of David's greater Son, the King of the Jews. The occasion of the speech, the opportunity of the reporters, the fitness of things, so far as we can judge of it—and that is sometimes not far,—and also other considerations, have to be taken into account. Each separate discourse must be judged upon its merits as reported. But what can be done is to prepare and arrange the evidence of the facts.

The Form of the Olivet Discourse.

In form the Olivet discourse is an apocalypse[*] which in very tiny compass follows the usual lines of an apoca-

[*] " A veritable Apocalypse lacking nothing essential to this species of composition "—Colani, *Jesus Christ*, 140; *Enc. Bib.*, 4721—but this apocalyptic form is entirely due to the evangelists, not at all to Jesus.

THE OLIVET DISCOURSE

lypse, with the exception that it does not, as most apocalypses, begin with a retrospect of history to the date of composition. It has one stage after another approaching the climax, and it leaves the climax undetermined though approaching. Thus in Matt. 24 = Mark 13 = Luke 21 we observe the stages, six in number: first, of approach, "and the end is not yet"; next, of the beginning, "these things are the beginning of pangs"; next, or "before all these things," the affliction, "and then shall come the end"; next, the signs of "great affliction," "when the desolation of Jerusalem hath drawn nigh," "these are the days of vengeance," "which are shortened for the elect's sake"; next, signs which shall come "immediately after the affliction of those days"; next, and finally, the statement that "concerning that day and hour knoweth no man, but the Father only."* Several writers think that Mark 13 contains an apocalypse of three parts (13^{7f}, 13^{14-20}, 13^{24-27}) interwoven with the words of Jesus. Many combinations are possible, and perhaps none of these is much better than another. The total effect of the discourse is far from clear as to the question whether it deals with the end of the world or the end of Jerusalem only. It starts with Jerusalem and it proceeds with it, but at two intervening points, if not more, it must refer to a cosmic catastrophe.

The Matter of the Discourse.

It is well known that in point of language the discourse is largely based on the Old Testament, especially on the Book of Daniel. But it is not well known how

* For the whole question the reader must refer to the valuable and comprehensive article "Eschatology" in the *Encyclopædia Biblica*, by Dr. R. H. Charles, who is the acknowledged master of this subject in England, and whose editions of the apocalyptic books are of great importance. See especially col. 1374. The present chapter, however, is not indebted to that article.

much, how nearly all, is Old Testament phraseology. Let us see what light can be thrown by examining the sources. It originates with the prospect of the Temple. "Seest thou these great buildings? There shall not be left one stone upon another that shall not be destroyed." The prediction, as we shall see, bears a striking resemblance to the remark of Ahitophel on a similar occasion, from the record of which many features of the night of Gethsemane have been drawn. That leads to the questions on the disciples' part, When shall these things be? and what is the sign (to show) when they shall be consummated (of thy coming and of the consummation of the age)? The answer is one of mingled admonition and prediction but entirely indefinite, and let it be said at once that, after discovering the fact that all the predictions in this discourse are already made in the Old Testament, the first impression is that it is purely a composition of the evangelists, while the conclusion alone has any title to be considered a saying of Jesus, "the Father only knoweth." First let us examine the indebtedness which causes the impression.

Of the two passages which constitute the main theme of the discourse, the first and the chief is the latter portion of the Book of Daniel, out of which the question of the disciples takes its rise, "the sign when these things shall be consummated" (Mark), "the sign of thy coming and of the *consummation* of the age," συντελείας τοῦ αἰῶνος " (Matt.). This follows—

Dan. 12[4] Cover the injunctions and seal the book until the time of *the consummation*.

But not only is the term which excites curiosity there used, the very question is there raised as the disciples raise it: Luke repeats even the *therefore* of the original Daniel.

THE OLIVET DISCOURSE 325

Dan. 12⁶ And I said to the man clothed in linen, who was above the water of the river, *When, therefore, is the consummation* of the wonders which thou hast told me ?

The answer was given to Daniel, but in such a form as not to allay curiosity; the curiosity continued and increased during the two hundred years between the composition of the book and A.D. 30. The puzzle remains one of the chief questions which apocalyptists looked to one another to solve. The "time, times, and half a time," lent themselves to every kind of solution and received nearly every kind. In a problem where every prophet and apocalyptist had even in those days tried his 'prentice hand, what would the Master-prophet do ? The only possible supposition is that He would say from the first, "No man knoweth, save the Father only." That He should be a competitor with the herd in a question that was neither ethics nor science, neither mathematics nor history, and that His solution should outstrip the rest, is an intolerable imagination. In solemn guessing He never could have taken part. Consequently the whole discourse, if from beginning to end it is a cento of Old Testament passages, either proves itself to be constructed and interpolated by the evangelists, or else must needs be treated neither from the traditional nor yet from the literary-apocalyptic point of view, but from some other.

I. The Daniel passages which have been employed further are these—

DANIEL	MATT. 24, MARK 13, LUKE 21
11⁴⁴ *Rumours (of wars)* shall trouble him.	Mark ⁷ When ye hear of wars and *rumours of wars* be not afraid.
2²⁸ *Things which must needs come to pass* in the last days.	*Ibid.* These things *must needs come to pass*, but the end is not yet.

326   ORACLES IN THE NEW TESTAMENT

11⁴⁰ At the time of the consummation the *kings* of the south shall push at him, and the *king* of the north shall rage *against* him with chariots, etc.

11¹⁴ And in those days many shall rise up (ἐπαναστήσονται) ... and the sons of the tyrants of the people shall rise up.

12¹ That is the day of *affliction*.

Isa. 26¹⁶ᶠ Lord, in affliction I remember thee, in small *affliction* [is] thine instruction for us. And as she that is *in pangs* draweth near to delivery ... so have we been to thy beloved [son].

11⁴¹ And many shall be made to stumble.

11¹¹ And the multitude *shall be delivered up* into his hands.

12¹⁰ And *the lawless do lawlessly*.

12¹² Blessed is *he that endureth* (ὑπομείνας εἰς) ...

12¹¹ The *abomination of desolation be set up*.

11³¹ They shall defile *the holy place* of awe and set up *the abomination of desolation*.

12¹ The day of *affliction such as never was since they were made till that day*.

7²⁵ He shall wear down (Deut. 13⁵ *deceive*) the saints of the Most High.

7¹³ Behold, *upon the clouds of heaven there came one like the Son of man*.

11¹³ At the end ... there shall come in entrances in great *power* and in much substance.

12¹ On that day all thy people shall be saved whose names are written in the book.

12⁷ Unto a time and *times* and half a time ... *all these things* shall be consummated.

Mark ⁸ Nation shall rise against nation, and *kingdom against kingdom*.

Mark ¹² And children *shall rise up* (ἐπαναστήσονται) against parents.

Matt. ⁸,⁹ the beginning *of pangs*. Then they shall deliver you *to affliction*.
(This seems to show a distinction from the *greater* affliction to follow, such as never was.)

Matt. ¹⁰ *And* then *shall many be made to stumble*.

Ibid. And they *shall deliver up* one another.

Matt. ¹² 'Because *lawlessness shall be multiplied*.

Mark ¹³ He that endureth (ὑπομείνας εἰς) to the end shall be saved.

Matt. ¹⁵ When then ye see *the abomination of desolation* spoken of by Daniel the prophet *standing in the holy place*.

Matt. ²¹ There shall be great *affliction such as never was from* the beginning of the world *till then*.

Matt. ²⁴ So as to *deceive*, if possible, even the elect.

Matt. ³⁰ They shall *see the Son of man coming upon the clouds of heaven*.

Matt. ³⁰ With *power* and great glory.

Luke ²⁸ Lift up your heads, for your redemption draweth nigh.

Luke ²⁴ Until the *times* (καιροί) of the Gentiles be fulfilled.

Mark ³⁰ Until *all these things* take place.

THE OLIVET DISCOURSE

II. The next group of passages is from the concluding chapters of Zechariah—

ZECHARIAH	MATT. 24, MARK 13, LUKE 21.
Zech. 13² And it shall be in that day that I will remove *the false prophets* (LXX).	Matt. ¹¹ And many *false prophets* shall arise.
13³ *His father* and his mother shall say unto him, Thou shalt not live.	Mark ¹² And *the father* shall deliver up the child to death.
13⁶ The wounds with which I was wounded in the house *of my beloved friend* (τοῦ ἀγαπητοῦ μου).	Matt. ¹² The *love* (ἀγάπη) of many shall wax cold.

It is clear that Matthew here follows the Greek of Zechariah, for the Hebrew has *prophets* where the Greek has *false prophets*. It seems to be clear that Matthew knew that the original of Mark was in Zech. 13, and turned to the passage again in Greek to draw further ideas from it. He has drawn the *false prophets* and the *love waxing cold*.

12⁶ Jerusalem shall dwell by itself in Jerusalem.	Luke ²¹ Let them that live in the country places not enter into her.
14² But the rest [half] of my people shall not be destroyed out of the city.	Mark ²⁰ For the elect's sake he hath shortened the days.
14² I will gather *all the nations* against Jerusalem to war, and the city shall be taken, and the half of the city *shall go into captivity*.	Luke ²⁴ And they shall *go into captivity* to *all the nations*.
12³ And I will make Jerusalem a stone *trodden down by all the nations*.	Luke ²⁴ *And Jerusalem shall be trodden down by the nations.*
12¹² In that day . . . *the earth shall mourn, tribe by tribe*.	Matt. ³⁰ *Then shall all the tribes of the earth mourn.*
2⁶ Ho! flee ye from the north, for I *will gather* (συνάξω) you *from the four winds of heaven*.	Matt. ³¹ And *shall gather* (ἐπισυνάξει) his elect *from the four winds*
[Deut. 30⁴ *from the end of the heaven to the end of the heaven*]	*from the ends of heavens to the ends of them.*
14⁷ And *that day* is known unto the Lord.	Matt. ³⁶ Concerning *that day* knoweth no man but the Father only. So Mark.

The last correspondence is very remarkable, as a proof of one unswerving eye in exposition of scripture.

III. The next is a group of passages from other books—

Isa. 10²³ The remnant of them shall be saved ... for a concise account will the Lord make in the whole world.	Mark ²⁰ for the elect's sake he hath shortened the days.
Isa. 65⁸ for thy servant's sake (*elect* 65 ¹), I will not destroy all.	Matt. ²² for the *elect's* sake those days shall be shortened.
Is. 55⁶ (gospel in Gentiles) *for the sake of* (ἕνεκεν) the Lord.	Luke ¹² *for my name's sake* (ἕνεκεν, διά,¹⁷ Mark ⁹,¹³; Matt. ⁹).
Isa. 13⁶, ¹⁰ *The day* of the Lord is at hand... *the sun shall be darkened, and the moon shall not give her light.*	Mark ²⁴ In those *days* ... *the sun shall be darkened, and the moon shall not give her light.*
Isa. 13⁸ *pangs* shall take hold of them.	Mark ⁸ These are the beginning of *the pangs*.
Isa. 34⁴ *The powers of the heavens* shalt melt ... *and all the stars shall fall.*	Matt. ²⁹ *the powers of the heavens shall be shaken and the stars shall fall* from heaven.
Ecclus. 16¹⁸ heaven and earth *shall be shaken* at his *visitation*.	(Luke 19⁴⁴ the time of thy *visitation*).
Isa. 27¹³ in that day they shall blow *with* the *great trumpet*.	Matt. ³¹ and he will send his angels *with a great trumpet*.
Isa. 34⁴ as *the leaves* fall from *the fig tree*.	Matt. ³² When *the fig tree* putteth forth *leaves*.
Isa. 13⁷ every man's heart shall be a coward.	Luke ²⁶ men's hearts failing them from fear.
Isa. 59²¹ This is my covenant with them ... *my spirit* which is upon thee and the words which I put into thy *mouth* shall never fail.	Luke ¹⁵ I will give you a *mouth* and a wisdom which etc. Mark ¹¹ It is not ye which speak, but *the Holy Spirit*.
Hos. 9⁷ *the days of vengeance* have come.	Luke ²² these are *the days of vengeance*.
Isa. 9¹⁹ a man shall not pity his *brother*.	Mark ¹² *brother* shall deliver up *brother* to death.
Isa. 24¹⁷ fear and a pit and *a snare upon you who dwell on the earth*.	Luke ³⁵ that day .. as *a snare*, for it shall come *upon* all that dwell on the face of all the earth.
Ezek. 34¹³ I will lead my sheep out of the Gentiles ... and will feed them *upon the mountains* of Israel.	Matt. ¹⁶ Then let them that are in Judea flee *upon the mountains* (ἐπὶ τὰ ὄρη), Mark, Luke εἰς.
Gen. 19¹⁷ Look not *back* (εἰς τὰ ὀπίσω) nor stay in all the country.	Mark ¹⁶ He that is in the field let him not turn *back* (εἰς τὰ ὀπίσω).
Isa. 13¹ff *a man shall be pursued* into his own country.	Luke ¹² and they *shall pursue* you.

Isa. 49⁷ Sanctify . . . him that is hated *of the Gentiles*. . . .	Matt. ⁹ Ye shall be hated of all *the Gentiles for my name sake*. (Luke ¹⁷=Mark¹³ omits *Gentiles*.)
Isa. 49⁷ *Kings* shall see him and *rulers* . . . shall worship him *for the Lord's sake* (ἕνεκεν).	Mark ⁹ Ye shall stand before *rulers and kings for my sake* (ἕνεκεν).
Isa. 55¹ ff Ho! ye that are thirsty come ye to the water . . . and I will make an everlasting covenant with you, the holy and sure [blessings] of David. Behold, I make him a *testimony* (μαρτύριον) among *the Gentiles*, a ruler and commander to the Gentiles.	Matt. ¹⁴ And this gospel of the kingdom shall be preached in all the world for a *testimony* unto all *the Gentiles*. Mark ⁹ ye shall stand before rulers and kings for my sake for *a testimony* to *them*. Luke ¹³ it shall turn into you for *a testimony*.

" *The blessings of David.*"

The last is the most remarkable of these parallels and requires further attention. Where Isaiah says *David*, the evangelists put the Son of David, as they have done elsewhere. And the next stage of exposition is to say that *the [blessings]* mean the resurrection of the Son of David; this is the stage that is shown in Acts 13³⁴ by St. Paul at Antioch, who quotes " the holy and sure [blessing] of David " in that sense. The next stage is to say that *David* means the preachers and preaching of the resurrection who are to be not only delivered up to sanhedrins and synagogues and prisons, but arrested and made to stand before Gentile rulers and kings. The fact that *David* stands for the preaching is proved by our having here the expression, " the gospel of the kingdom,"* *i.e.*, the gospel of the kingdom *of David*. Consequently we find " the *everlasting covenant*, the holy things of David, the *faithful* things " is used from very early times to mean the resurrection. How is this? The answer is to be found by reference to Ps. 89²⁸ ᶠ—

* For the only places where this term occurs are Matt. 4²³, 9³⁵. In the first of these it is preceded by the citation of Isa. 9¹ which declares Him the regal offspring of the house of David. In the second He has just before been saluted as the Son of David.

And I will make him my Firstborn, higher than the kings of the earth.

For ever (εἰς τὸν αἰῶνα) will I keep my mercy for him, and my *covenant* is *faithful* to him.

We then look onwards twenty verses, and we find the culmination of this promise—

Who is the man that shall live and shall not *see death* ? *He will deliver* his soul from the hand of Hades.

In Acts 13[34 ff] this is supported by—

Ps. 16[10]. Thou wilt not suffer thy *holy* one (ὅσιον) to *see corruption*—

which is very close to the other text, but being, in fact, a rather stronger and more pointed expression, has caused it to drop out of sight, so that the modern mind fails to see any logical connection between *the holy and sure blessings of David* and the *resurrection of Christ* to which it is supposed to point.

If it should be objected that Isa. 55[4] is not here behind the evangelists at all, it may be well to observe that there is yet another reference to the same context of Isaiah in this very discourse—

Isa. 55[9 ff] For as *the heavens* are higher than the *earth* . . . Thus shall be *my word*, whatsoever proceedeth out of my mouth, *it shall not* return *until all* that I please shall be accomplished.	Matt. 24[34 f] . . . *until all these things shall* take place. Heaven and *earth* shall pass away, but *my words shall not* pass away.

Assuming, then, that the evangelists are working upon Isa. 55, let us try to see how they have dealt with the passage. They took the appeal " Come ye to *the water* " as an invitation to baptism. Justin Martyr (A.D. 140, *Dial.* 14) quotes Isa. 55[3-13] in full, and presses it home as a strong appeal to the Jews to be baptized with the laver of repentance and the knowledge of God. The Lord's own words in John 7[37f], " If any man thirst, . . ." which are

THE OLIVET DISCOURSE

almost a verbal citation, take us back about a generation earlier still. Baptism, therefore, was found in Isaiah as a sign of the covenant with David mentioned in Ps. 89, where there is no reference to baptism. The gospel of the kingdom, therefore, is the tidings of this new covenant or *fresh testament*—for to this meaning the term *covenant* perpetually tended from the very first.* Hence Justin is sometimes found putting *testator*, *martyr* (μάρτυρα) for *testimony*, and Tertullian *testament*, But Justin and Tertullian do but exhibit in a later stage the developments of the meanings that were less fully expressed in the earlier. Therefore, when the evangelists wrote, the *testimony* had already the meaning of *martyrdom* strongly associated with it. Luke shows this more clearly than the other two, " It will turn *unto you* for martyrdom." Matthew, after following Mark more closely in saying that the preaching must be *to* the Gentiles, then gives a dramatic turn to its effect by the sudden addition, " *and then* shall come the end." But this was because he read the words next following in Mark, " The gospel must first [of all] be preached unto all the Gentiles," as if Mark had meant that *the end* should be an instantaneous consequence † of the universal preaching. But Mark never mentions *the end* until three verses later, when he says, " He that endureth unto the end (εἰς τέλος, not εἰς τὸ τέλος) shall be saved." Now Matthew has given these very words on a previous occasion (Matt. 10^{22}) with the whole passage of six verses which are here read in Mark —sanhedrins, synagogues, rulers, kings, premeditation of speeches, family treasons, hatred of all for the name.

* But every reference to the testament implies a reference to the testator, or at least to the witness of the will, and this is identical with the witness of Ps. 89$^{37\,\text{ff}}$, " And the witness in heaven is faithful." After His exaltation, the martyr Christ was *the witness in heaven, faithful*—to whom Rev. 1^5, 3^{14} refer. No valid distinction can be maintained between μαρτύριον and μαρτυρία in the New Testament or elsewhere.

† The analogy of δεῖ πρῶτον in Mark 9^{11} is obviously imperfect.

332 ORACLES IN THE NEW TESTAMENT

Plainly then Matthew, to avoid repetition, was compelled to vary his version of the discourse here. But he has done so by first confusing the subjective end ($εἰς\ τέλος$) with the objective ($εἰς\ τὸ\ τέλος$), and then adding the latter to the former (Matt. 24$^{14,\,13}$) with the dramatic words, *And then*. For this he had no authority, either in Isaiah or even in Daniel.

The Fig Tree.

One of the strangest things in this discourse is the sudden turn from the dispatch of the angels in order to gather the elect from the four winds of heaven, to " Now from the fig tree learn her parable," which parable is of the extremely simple kind, presenting an astonishing contrast with the signs in its immediate context. The fig tree putting forth leaves, as every peasant knows, betokens summer approaching. But no patristic or other interpretation in the world can show what analogy there is between this gradual normal growth and the signs showing that " he [it] is near [even] at the doors."* The words " *Even so ye also, know ye,*" in Matthew, Mark and Luke, become false by reason of this want of analogy. It is not conceivable that the Lord ever used such language. Various attempts have been made to escape from this difficulty, but none are at all successful. The fig tree is referred, for instance, to the Jewish people which it " emblematizes "; if so, then the position of the parable in the discourse is very strange, for it ought as it stands to refer to the cosmic portion which has immediately preceded it and not to the Jerusalem portion. Moreover a parable, in the usual limited sense in which it is understood in the synoptic gospels, is designed to illustrate the moral and spiritual abstract by the visible and natural concrete. This emblematizing, however, would replace

* "At the doors." See Nestle in *Preuschen*, 1909.

THE OLIVET DISCOURSE

the easy by the difficult. Most commentators refuse to notice the difficulty. Now the reason of the parable being placed here is apparent as soon as we refer to the original in—

> Isa. 34⁴ And all the powers of the heavens shall melt, and the heaven shall roll up like a scroll, and all the stars shall fall as leaves from a vine, *and as leaves fall from a fig tree.*

Here is the simile, *And as*, here are the *leaves*, here is the *fig tree*. The similitude in Isaiah is poetical as always—the stars fall as autumnal leaves drive through the air. There is no thought of a sign, such as the " wicked and adulterous generation sought after," and such as the disciples also sought after, yielding as they did to the ineradicable curiosity of mankind, whether for themselves or for their readers. But are we to infer from this that they manufactured the poetic simile of Isaiah into a parable of Jesus ? Let us see presently. Meanwhile the moral that one draws from this discourse is that whatever else has been unlawfully attributed to Him, one portion of His teaching is undoubtedly His,—that in which He has prohibited all sign-seeking under all conditions, whether of Messianic intimations or " judgments " by inference from the event. It is a striking fact that one of these occasions on which He condemned sign-seeking (Luke 13$^{1-5}$) is immediately followed by another parable of the fig tree, which we may call the original parable, as this is the derived—derived from Isaiah. If we are to recognize and remove the attributions to the Master which so grievously disparage His teaching and His Person, the first thing to be done is to understand the mechanism which has caused them.

" *Not a hair of your head.*"

There is an obvious difficulty in Luke 21^{18}: " And not a hair of your head shall perish." This promise, following closely on "they shall put some of you to death," seems to contradict it if taken in the physical and natural sense. Therefore some have decided to take it in a "spiritual" sense of the soul being saved. Now, had the words been "not a head of you," this might have been possible. But how can it be meant by "not a hair of your head"? The "spiritual" meaning breaks down. Again, St. Luke has used this expression of the occasion before the shipwreck, at which he was present (Acts 27^{34}). He heard St. Paul say, "I beseech you to take food: for it is for your saving, for not a hair of your head shall perish." Here, though *saving* ($\sigma\omega\tau\eta\rho\iota a$) is mentioned, no one will take the words in any but the natural sense. But we observe that this we-passage* of Acts was not only in Luke's mind but on his paper before Luke 21 was written, because it was in his diary. Now is it likely that he would write the words in his Gospel in a different sense from that which he had borne in mind all those years? But again, if we retain the obvious and physical meaning, what can we make of the contradiction? For Luke has gone beyond Mark, who said vaguely that *some* should be delivered up, without saying whether they should be some friends or some foes, thus perpetuating the obscurity of his original in Zech. 13^3. Luke has said, "You must be confident: you must face martyrdom: you need not premeditate speeches, for which you shall have eloquence and wisdom from on high. And you shall be delivered up and some of you killed, and you shall be hated." But he adds, "You shall be scatheless." There is quite a different tone here, a tone of confidence, which Matthew and Mark do not exhibit. The words in question do not seem to have been textually imported into the gospel from Acts. Neither do they seem to be due to the story of the Three

* Prof. Burkitt says (*Gospel History*, 117), "He had already interpolated it into the eschatological Discourse, now he puts it into St. Paul's mouth." Rather, he had it from St. Paul's lips *and then* put it into the Discourse.

THE OLIVET DISCOURSE 335

Children (Dan. 3^{27}). They seem to be written here by Luke, but it must at the same time be doubtful if he had any warrant for them but St. Paul, whose use of them he must have remembered well and whom he may have questioned concerning their authenticity. As to the meaning, it is to be taken with the aforesaid deductions in the natural and concrete sense, that " though some of you will be put to death you are still to be confident, and you shall be surprised to find how by that confidence you will again and again save your lives." St. Luke's experience of his own and St. Paul's hairbreadth escapes due to the grace of God and presence of mind is really visible in the verse.

Was the Discourse constructed by the Evangelists with a Predictory Purpose?

What then, it must now be asked, are we to make of the facts? The Olivet discourse is a cento of Old Testament passages, mostly predictions concerning *the last thing, those days, that day,* a crisis itself most indefinite and capricious, of which we can safely say that it is an abstraction of many different crises foreseen or reviewed by several prophets of several ages. If a master-prophet took these texts and picked them out and pasted them together he would for whatever purpose be certain to classify them according to some order. But can any one say in what order they are now placed? The attempt has been made often, with the poorest result, and can any one confidently say that he believes in their having an order which he cannot yet see? If so, is this a fruitful spiritual or scientific belief? It forfeits the rightful duty of the understanding, and on every ground is evil, if indeed it really exists. Are we then to be content, on the other hand, to wipe out the discourse as simply unhistorical? Are we to say it was constructed by the evangelists, and if so, for what purpose ? Was it the purpose of proving that Jesus was a true prophet because, about A.D. 30, He foretold exactly what happened in A.D. 70 ?

This seems at first to be an intelligible purpose, though discreditable to its authors. It obviously assumes that the discourse was published after A.D. 70. But that implies that most of it was constructed also after that date, for, as was observed above, it starts with Jerusalem, in the middle is Jerusalem, and at the end is the prediction that this generation shall see it *all* fulfilled : the cosmic portions are intervening, possibly interpolated. Certainly on the whole it deals with Jerusalem. But if it was after A.D. 70 why was it not written much more to the point ? Why was not Jeremiah employed again to say, " This city shall be delivered into the hand of the King of Babylon by the sword and by the pestilence " (Jer. 32^{36}) ? If precision was wanted, Jeremiah was more precise. By the year 70 it was very well known that Babylon was Rome, and Jeremiah had named Babylon; he had named the valley of the dead bodies unto the brook of Kidron : he had foretold the king of Babylon setting fire to this city and burning it with the houses. He had described in Lamentations many a ghastly picture of the siege of Nebuchadnezzar which was re-enacted in the siege of Titus. Why are not these utilized by the evangelists ? If that was their object, they could so easily have attained it far more effectually. That they have not done so is a proof that it was not. They had ready to their hand a number of coincidences great and small between the two sieges, and have made no use of them, thus throwing away the weapon of all others that they knew so well how to use—the argument from prophecy. This, therefore, is not a credible proposition.

THE OLIVET DISCOURSE

Certain Features of the Discourse and an attempted Reconstruction.

And what remains? It seems only possible to suppose that the Master did quote the passages in the discourse, with doubtless many more, as scripture proofs that there had been predicted again and again a coming crisis, but still more as topics for meditation and prayer. He did not imply by any means that the crisis in each prophet's mouth was one and the same, but as it had been the duty of every prophet to foretell a crisis, so He too, without giving them such a sign, as they expected of Him, would give them His warning, to be sober and watch unto prayer. The crisis, when it came, would be like many another, and would bring its own signs, if they were not asleep, but awake and watching.

Before we attempt an analysis of the discourse in order to test this theory about its construction, we may observe a few of its more salient features in the three separate forms of it. (1) Its hortatory or imperative form is best represented in Mark, who delivers an imperative mood rather more than once in every four lines. Next to him is Luke, who does the same rather less than once in four lines. Matthew, however, has lost very much of this character, his imperatives being less than one in five lines; they are fewer while his signs of the end are longer. And it is true that if Luke had included in the discourse all that passage in 17^{24-35} which corresponds to Matt. 24, the proportions of Luke would resemble those of Matthew. Now this fact is of some importance for the understanding of the discourse as a practical matter. The curiosity of the disciples was checked, in fact, at every turn, and a strong, robust moral and practical bent was the main feature of the original discourse. Who can doubt it? But there are many who say that while this was so, we have none of

338 ORACLES IN THE NEW TESTAMENT

the true original discourse before us, and the question is —what is the nature and origin of this report of it ? The answer is—that we are enabled to arrive at it by observation of the fact that the further we go back the more traces we find of some feature that we assume to be original. We assume this to be original because it fits the case. The furthest of the three accounts from the original, the most popular, is that of Matthew, and it has merged the exhortation in the description of the future, still on the basis of ancient prophecy, in order to gratify the reader's curiosity.

(2) The present form of the discourse is certainly damaging to the current idea of what the Christian faith is, not only from its chaotic obscurity but because it represents the Lord as predicting with emphasis what was not fulfilled. Indeed, the Bishop of Birmingham told the Church Congress at Cambridge, in 1910, that the late Henry Sidgwick became an agnostic because Christ foretold things which had not happened. It may be conjectured that the verse which is nearly identical in the three Gospels is as responsible as any for this result : " Verily I say unto you, that this generation shall not pass away *till all [these] things be fulfilled.*" No toning down of *this generation* is possible. It must bear the same meaning as the verse spoken at Cæsarea : " But I tell you of a truth, there be some of them that stand here that shall in no wise taste of death, till they see the kingdom of God" (Luke 9[27], Mark 9[1], Matt. 16[28]. See above, Ch. X, p. 314). The Lord's expectation was the same at Olivet as it was six months before at Cæsarea—that the crisis would take place within the next forty years. The then generation of men would see it, but the day and the hour He could not foresee and knew that He could not. He was not deceived in His prediction of the future : He did not prophesy falsely. Even the overcharged anticipation of the Olivet discourse was fulfilled in most of its

THE OLIVET DISCOURSE

details actually, but in some only figuratively—those which concern the heavenly bodies. Hence Luke, misled into the quagmire of the Olivet discourse, has modified Mark by the cautionary omission, as it seems, of *these*, and has written *till all things happen*,* by which he means all things that are destined to happen. For it must be admitted that Luke is somewhat unrestricted in his use of the word *all*; in fact, he employs it to excess in Luke and Acts, leaving the reader to make the necessary deduction again and again. It is not too much to suppose that when he wrote 9^{27} and 21^{32} he was reserving the cautionary and express statement for a later and not less important occasion—the very last sentence that Jesus was to speak upon earth (Acts 1^7) : " It is not for you to know times or seasons which the Father hath appointed by his own authority." This latter saying, which is the oracle of—

Zech. 14^7 That day is known to the Lord—

is plainly far more general than either of the two earlier; and Luke had lived to see its paramount force. For in the interval between Cæsarea and (say) A.D. 75 the greater part of even the Olivet discourse had been fulfilled, while there was no limit that might not be too narrow for the rest.

(3) Comparing the three forms of the discourse together we find Matthew very closely follows Mark, but has added to the height of the colours as usual. He has also added a third prediction of false prophets to the two contained in Mark, which Luke, on the other hand, with a truer literary sense, has reduced to one. The use by Matthew of *then* nine times has rather a heavy if solemn effect : it occurs but four times in Mark, and thrice in Luke. Luke 21^{10} betrays a trace of previous argument

* Luke 21^{32} γένηται. How can this be translated, " be fulfilled " A.V., " be accomplished " R.V. ? It can only mean *happen, come to pass*, take place. There is a great difference. See also p. 330.

concerning the texts in Daniel : *Then he said unto them.* In Luke 21[12] *before all these things* does not point to a categorical order of signs in answer to the disciples' question, but rather to the greater stress laid by the Lord upon their conduct in persecution, as if He said : *But what is more important is,* that *you* will be arrested. Again, Luke definitely says that the abomination of desolation is not to be a profanation of the temple * as in the time of Antiochus Epiphanes, but something different— a desolation by armies. This should fulfil the predictions of Daniel. There is nothing in Luke 21[20-24] which could not have been uttered in A.D. 30. *The times of the Gentiles* have a reference to the three times and a half of Daniel, and yet the expression is too wide to be limited to arithmetic computations. Luke is also more alive to the encouragements provided by ancient prophecy. He says, *Look up, for your redemption draweth nigh*, just as he said, *Not a hair of your head shall perish.* In saying the fig tree *and all the trees* he draws nearer to the original of Isa. 34[4] : " *as leaves from the vine, and* as leaves fall from the fig tree," though, perhaps, at some cost of literary sense.

And this consideration enables us to answer the question propounded above, concerning the *parable* to be learned from the fig-tree. The *parable* is to be understood in the sense in which the word is used frequently in the Old Testament, of a dark saying that needs an effort of thought. There is not a deliberate manufacture of a poetical phrase of Isaiah into a parable of the Lord, but the evangelists, instead of representing Him as drawing a moral lesson from an ancient text, have introduced the words without much regard to their original in Isaiah, and without full regard to their true position in the

---

* For the identification of St. Paul with Antichrist by the Ephesian Jews on his last visit to the Temple at Jerusalem and the considerable evidence for it, see *St. Luke the Prophet*, p. 70.

Olivet discourse. It is safe to assert that He used Isa. 34⁴ to draw the disciples away from particular vaticinations based upon the texts of the Old Testament to the observation of the unfailing course and constitution of nature as a sure guide to their future action. And *emblematizing* is an inappropriate term. There is not only a pause before the mention of the fig-tree and its parable, there ought to be marks of a total contrast and conversion of thought. These marks the Evangelists have not supplied to the modern reader, who is unversed in the imagery of Isaiah in the passage which was under discussion with the disciples and from which the lesson was drawn.

The last verse of the discourse in Luke is one that presents some difficulty: "that ye may prevail to escape ... and to stand before the Son of man." To *escape* strikes with a strange sound, for "to withstand in the evil day" is rather what we should expect. And then to *prevail to escape* is still more strange. Lastly, to *stand before* the Son of man is also uncommon. This last, however, is of those who "only stand and wait, as members of His staff ready to do His bidding, while He sits enthroned." An observation of the aorist *to stand* (σταθῆναι) in Luke shows that there is identity between it and the perfect * tense. But the perfect is just that which we have seen used in Zech. 3³ ᶠᶠ, ⁷ ᶠ, where *to stand before the face*, πρὸ προσώπου, is only expressed more briefly by ἔμπροσθεν here. We infer that Zech. 3 is still in Luke's mind, and even in the Lord's also, in this passage. But that is just the passage where Jesus is the Great Priest, to whom it is said, "If thou walk in my ways ... I will give thee [some] of them *that stand* here." Now it is natural to look for illustration in another passage where the Great Priest is receiving his charge.

* See esp. Luke 18¹¹, ¹³ of the Pharisee and the publican.

Hag. 2⁴ And now *prevail* (κατίσχυε), Zorobabel, and *prevail*, Jesus, son of Josedek, *the Great Priest*, and *prevail*, all *ye people* of the land, and be doing . . .

Thus, though the construction is still rough and awkward in Luke 21³⁶, the term *prevail* seems to be clearly and duly traced, and its connection with sleepless watchfulness is maintained from its origin in Zech. 3⁹, which mentions " the stone with seven eyes," that it may never sleep. But meanwhile the same text, Zech. 3⁹, provides the idea which conclusively proves the explanation of *to escape*. For Luke has just used the term *snare* from Isa. 24¹⁷ to convey the sudden complete capture of the earth's inhabitants. A snare (παγίς), however, was commonly made by means of a pit skilfully covered, into which the beast was made to fall, and this kind of *pit* is mentioned in the same—

Zech. 3⁹ Behold, I dig a *pit*, saith the Lord, and I will touch all the iniquity of the earth yonder in one day.

Therefore *to escape* this form of capture does not involve flight before the foe or failure to withstand in the evil day, but simply a watchfulness against the snare into which the world at large falls and is captured. Once more, it is clear that Zech. 3 is present to Luke, and, for all that can be said, to the Lord also in this passage : but it does not follow that He uses it for any other purpose than moral exhortation.

May we not, then, arrive at something like the actual discourse, not by reconstructing so much as repunctuating and perhaps also interpunctuating the present form of it? In Mark it would be something like this : " Ye have asked me the question in Daniel the prophet; I answer with a warning that is older still, Be not deceived from the way that I command you (Deut. 11²⁸). You know what I have told you before of false prophets who shall come saying, in the words of the law, See ye, see ye

THE OLIVET DISCOURSE 343

that *I am* (Deut. 32^{39}). Daniel, ye say, also spoke of wars and rumours of wars. True, but be ye not afraid. Daniel himself said, It must needs be. It doth not follow from this that the end is yet. Not with wars, nor with earthquakes, nor with famines : for ' oft the teeming earth is with a kind of colic pinch'd and vex'd.' This, as Isaiah saith, is your instruction. Take heed to yourselves. Have ye not also read Isaiah, how he saith, Behold, I make David a testimony among the Gentiles ? This is your gospel, which ye shall preach. And when they arrest you, remember what he saith also, This is my covenant with them, My spirit which is upon thee, and the words which I put into thy mouth, shall never fail. If they deliver you, they shall also deliver one another, to death. Have ye not read Daniel concerning endurance ? But ye say, Daniel spake also of the abomination of desolation standing where it ought not. And this may come again, though in a different shape. What will ye ? Is not flight a counsel that Ezekiel predicted for the flock ? Flight, and farewell to home and happiness ? Yea, for this is affliction, the affliction that hath been foretold by Daniel, such as never was. But have ye not read what Isaiah and Zechariah said, how ye, the elect, are the cause of the shortening thereof ? Yet take ye heed, for even the elect may be led astray by false prophets. Believe it not, O men. But ye say, It hath been foretold that the sun and moon shall be dark and and the stars shall fall. Yea, and hath it not been said, that the Son of man shall come with clouds, and will gather his elect, scattered though they be ? I counsel you to learn of nature, which in the growth of the fig tree from birth to fertility and decay, as saith Isaiah, teacheth the lesson of the world that reneweth itself. I predict no more than nature's own law : I predict no sign but this, as did Isaiah : but there be of them that stand here who shall see all these natural stages of development—growth, full-blooded life, withering decay,—before they pass themselves; there shall be a new heaven and a new earth, but my counsel is eternal: from the great deep to the great deep it moves. The day and the hour are known to the Father only: your duty is to be sober, prayerful, awake."

The Lord without Eschatology.

And now, if the above account of the Olivet discourse, or anything like it, be admitted, what inference may be drawn in regard to the eschatological question, in which the discourse is not a secondary but a primary factor? The eschatological question does not exist for the Prophet of Nazareth. He quoted scripture again and again, but He has not lent His authority to the idea of its literal vaticination whenever he quoted it. He gave the disciples no revelation of His own on eschatology. If this is a bold statement, it is not greatly qualified by saying that a high and holy sense of duty must and can be reconciled with a string of old sayings imperfectly reported and ill-punctuated and jumbled together. When this string is construed aright we shall have the reconciliation. To assert omniscience in Jesus would be to reject St. Paul's doctrine of His self-limitation or Kenôsis. If the discourse were printed so as to show His use of the contents, it would appear a mass of inverted commas with not a few notes of interrogation. It would read less like a discourse than like a dialogue. Clear of commas and interrogations the hortatory sentences would stand out, as Mark and Luke were aware that they stood out and were fain to represent them, as the *verba Magistri*. That these evangelists understood the discourse aright would be perhaps too much to say, but they misunderstood it less than Matthew, and infinitely less than those who came after them for many centuries.

To assert this partial understanding on the part of the

THE OLIVET DISCOURSE 345

evangelists is not to assert any new principle: it is but to claim that the Prophet of Nazareth was not always limited to the conditions of a prophet; that He could employ ironical conversation (Luke $22^{36, 30}$; see below, p. 383); that He could employ dialectic in His teaching in the temple; that He could employ paradox (Luke 16^{17}, " It is easier for heaven and earth . . . "); that He could convert to moral purpose the current ideas of the age though He could not eradicate them then (Luke 17^{20}, " The kingdom of God cometh not with observation . . .").

The above treatment of the Olivet discourse, imperfect and inadequate as it is, will not have been wholly in vain if it serves to draw attention to a point of view which shows it as a non-committal on the part of our Lord to some of those crude and contradictory statements which are usually considered to be as much His words as any that we possess as such : if it serves to show that a statement within inverted commas (a thing unknown to the Bible) is not the same as without them, and that the invisible commas have often to be supplied by the reader's own vigilance. To those who suppose that the trust in God through Christ which lies at the base of the gospel message is identical with the Christian faith as commonly understood, and that the former can be injured by a question of commas, this humble attempt will be of no avail. But it is offered in the hope that even now one portion of Christendom may be the better able to understand another portion, and that where agreement is not possible the voices of scorn and pitiful condescension may be assuaged and controlled.

CHAPTER XII

THE BETRAYAL

One Day of David's Life.

"THERE is no single day in the Jewish history of which so elaborate an account remains as that which describes this memorable flight. There is none that combines so many of David's characteristics." So writes Stanley of David's flight from Jerusalem in the picturesque pages of his *History of the Jewish Church*, a work which is still unsurpassed for its vivid and moving style, its graphic and suggestive grouping of characters and events, its luminous literary illustration and swift historical comparison. He adds that it is "strange that it should have been reserved for Ewald to have first brought out the singular interest of this day," and acknowledges his indebtedness to him. Stanley's History should be in the hands of every one who cares at all for the Old Testament, whether as a student or not; it cannot fail to awaken an interest in it where there was none before. It is an everlasting possession.* The whole story of the conspiracy of Absalom should be read in Stanley as a companion to the Bible—how he courted and gained popularity, how he went to Hebron and claimed the throne, how he was supported by the renowned Ahithophel, wisest of all the Israelite statesmen, how he rejected his counsel at the crisis with fatal results to both counsellor and prince.

* For the present purpose it may be added that it contains some of the many passages in the Greek Bible which do not exist in the Hebrew nor consequently in the English.

THE BETRAYAL 347

We shall be content here to give first of all the narrative as it occurs in the Greek, omitting a few lines here and there and italicizing passages that offer striking parallels to the action of the Son of David.

The Greek Narrative of David's Flight.

2 Sam. 15[14 ff] And David said to all his servants (παισίν) that were with him in Jerusalem, *Rise and let us flee* (ἀνάστητε καὶ φύγωμεν), for we have no safety from before Absalom : hasten to journey *lest* he hasten and overtake us, and thrust his evil upon us and *smite* the city *with the* edge of the *sword*. And the king's servants said unto the king, *According to all that our lord the king chooseth, here are thy servants.* And the king and all his house *went out* on foot, and stood at the Far House . . . *at the olive* in the wilderness, and all the people journeyed close beside him . . . and all the warriors . . . the six hundred men who had come on foot *to Geth* . . . And the king said to Ittai of Geth, Wherefore goest thou also with us ? Return and abide with the king . . . Yesterday was thy coming out and to-day shall I remove thee with us to journey . . . And *I shall journey whither I may journey* (καὶ ἐγὼ πορεύσομαι ἐφ' οὗ ἂν ἐγὼ πορευθῶ). *Turn thou about and turn thy brethren* (ἐπιστρέφου καὶ ἐπίστρεψον τοὺς ἀδελφούς σου) with thee, and the Lord shall do with thee mercy and truth. And Ittai answered the king and said, As the Lord liveth and as my lord the king liveth, wheresoever my lord the king is, *whether unto death* or unto life, *there shall thy servant be* . . . And all the land wept with a loud voice : and all the people journeyed with him *over the brook Kedron*, and the king went *over the brook Kedron* . . . *And behold* Zadok and all the Levites with him bearing the ark of the covenant of the Lord . . . And the king said to Zadok, Turn back the ark of God into the city : if I find favour in the sight of the Lord, then he will turn me and shew it unto me and the comeliness thereof :

but if he say, I have no delight in thee (οὐκ ἠθέληκα ἐν σοί), behold, here am I, *let him do to me as seemeth good in his eyes* (ἰδοὺ ἐγώ εἰμι, ποιείτω μοι κατὰ τὸ ἀγαθὸν ἐν ὀφθαλμοῖς αὐτοῦ) ... And David ascended from the ascent of [the mount of] Olives, going up and weeping, and he had his head covered, and he journeyed barefoot, and all the people that were with him covered every man his head, going up and weeping. And they told David saying, Ahithophel is with the conspirators with Absalom, and David said, Do thou shatter the counsel of Ahithophel, O Lord my God. And David was coming to the place Roōsh (ἕως τοῦ ῾Ροώς) where *he worshipped God* (οὗ προσεκύνησεν ἐκεῖ τῷ θεῷ), and behold there came to meet him Hushai, David's chief comrade, with his coat rent and earth upon his head ...

2 Sam. 16 And David *passed on a little* (βραχύ τι) from Roōsh, and behold Ziba the servant of Mephibosheth came to meet him ... And King David came to Bahurim, and behold there came out thence a man of the kindred of the house of Saul, whose name was Shimei son of Gera, and he came out and cursed still as he came, and he stoned David with stones ... And Abishai, son of Zeruiah, said to the king, Why doth this dead dog curse my lord the king? Now I will go over and take off his head. And the king said, *What have I to do with you, ye sons of Zeruiah?* Let him alone (τί ἐμοὶ καὶ ὑμῖν υἱοὶ Σαρουίας; καὶ ἄφετε αὐτόν) ... It may be that the Lord will look upon my humiliation and will turn for me good instead of his cursing this day ... Now the counsel of Ahithophel that he counselled in the days at the first was as if one inquired at the oracle (word) of God: thus was all the counsel of Ahithophel both with David and with Absalom.

2 Sam. 17 And Ahithophel said to Absalom, Let me now choose me out *twelve thousand* men, and I will rise up and pursue after David *in the night*. And I will come upon him when he is *weary and weak-handed*, and I will surprise

THE BETRAYAL

(ἐκστήσω) him, and all the people that is with him shall flee, and *I will smite* the king only, and I will turn all the people back unto thee *even as the bride turneth to her husband* (ὃν τρόπον ἐπιστρέφει ἡ νύμφη πρὸς τὸν ἄνδρα αὐτῆς) : *but the life of one man thou seekest, and to all the people there shall be peace.* And the saying was right in the eyes of Absalom and in the eyes of *all the elders of Israel.* And Absalom said, Call now Hushai the Archite also and let us hear likewise what he saith . . . And Hushai said, The counsel of Ahithophel that he hath counselled this time is not good . . . And thy father is a man of war . . . Behold he is now hidden in one of the hills . . . and it shall come to pass when he falleth upon them at the first that he shall verily hear saying, There is a slaughter among the people that follow Absalom. And even he that is a son of might, whose heart is as the heart of a *lion* (tribe of Judah) shall utterly melt . . . I counsel that all Israel be gathered unto thee from Dan even to Beersheba, as the sand that is by the sea in multitude, and thy face going in the midst of them. And we will come upon him in some place where he shall be found, and we *will encamp* (παρεμβαλοῦμεν) *against* him as the dew falleth on the ground, and we will not leave of him and of all the men that are with him so much as one. And if he draw together unto the [a] city, then shall all Israel take ropes to that city, and we will draw it even into the river, that there may *not be left there so much as a stone* (ὅπως μὴ καταλειφθῇ ἐκεῖ μηδὲ λίθος).

Points of Identity in the Gospel Narrative.

A reader of these chapters in the Greek can hardly fail to be impressed with the astounding resemblance of the scenes here described to those of the Gospels. David, the Elect and Anointed of the Lord, the promised seed who shall inherit the earth, together with his faithful few, has

350 ORACLES IN THE NEW TESTAMENT

left the city which has revolted from his rule. His chief counsellor has deserted to the rebels and proposes a plan for securing the person of the king without loss of life. The plan is to be carried out by night. The king's followers will forsake him and join the rebel force as readily as a bride turns to the caress of her husband. The plan is rejected and the traitor hangs himself. The king goes out, stops at *Geth* by the olive (olive-oil, *shemen*), crosses over the brook of Kedron, where, having uttered his resignation to the will of God, he passes on from the Mount of Olives with weeping and the signs of woe. At Roōsh, the summit, he worships God. The incidents of his meeting with Ittai, with Zadok and Abiathar, with Hushai, with Ziba, with Shimei distinguish various points of the road. Hushai, pretending friendship with Absalom and thus playing a part somewhat analogous to that of the traitor Ahithophel, carries his counter-proposal, sends warning to the king, and so secures the defeat of Absalom. This is the baldest analysis of a graphic and touching narrative, much of which is incorporated in the Gospels, though not in the same order and not always in the same portion of the history. We shall find the resemblance in phraseology rather less, perhaps, than in matter.

Rise up and let us flee is very close to *Rise, let us be going* (Matt. 26^{46} = Mark 14^{42} = John 14^{31}, ἐγείρεσθε ἄγωμεν), while Luke 22^{46} has *Rise up* and pray, ἀναστάντες προσεύχεσθε. As Bacon * has well demonstrated, John 14–16 are misplaced, and this verse should immediately precede 17, which prayer is said all standing. The subjoined clause *lest* he hasten . . . has its parallel in Luke, *lest* ye enter into temptation.

Smite the city *with the* edge of the *sword* has perhaps suggested (Luke 22^{49}) the question, Lord, shall we *smite with the sword ?*

According to all that our Lord the king chooseth, here

* *The Fourth Gospel in Research and Debate*, p. 488.

THE BETRAYAL

are thy servants. The corresponding profession is in Mark =Matthew, " Even if I must die with thee I will not deny thee. *Likewise also said they all."*

And *the king and all* his house *came out* on foot (1 Sam. 15[16, 17]). This appears in Matthew, Mark : " (They) *came out* to the mount of Olives " = Luke : " *He came out* and went his way to . . ." They *stayed at the olive* . . . they had come to *Geth* (*press*). The LXX of 2 Samuel represents these places as one and the same. The Hebrew for the composite name is none other than Gethshemen, and the Grecized form of this is *Gethsemane* or *Gethsemanei* (plural), press of olive or olives, *oil-press.* (Mark= Matthew.) In both passages it is a *place,* $\chi\omega\varrho\iota\sigma v$, but John speaks of a *garden*, which again is not inconsistent with 2 Sam. 15[17], for it is there the same place as the " Far House " and it is " in the wilderness," so that it might have something of an enclosure or garden about it : thus John has not departed from ancient prophecy here. The " wilderness " begins as soon as one steps outside the wall of Jerusalem. Obviously the place in 2 Samuel is on the west of the brook Kedron, whereas tradition since the fourth century has placed Gethsemane for the purposes of pilgrims on the east of it. The Synoptics do not make the Saviour pass over the brook Kedron, as John does.

I shall journey whither I may journey ($\pi o \varrho \varepsilon v \theta \tilde{\omega}$) is strikingly suggestive of John 13[33], " Whither I go ($\dot{v}\pi\acute{a}\gamma\omega$) ye cannot come." 13[36], " Whither I go thou canst not follow me now." 16[28], " I *journey* ($\pi o \varrho \varepsilon \acute{v} o \mu \alpha \iota$) unto the father." 14[3 f], " I *journey* to prepare a place for you." " The son of man *journeyeth* as it hath been determined of him " (Luke 22[22]).

Turn thou about and turn thy brethren. This is the foundation of " *Thou, when once thou art turned about* ($\dot{\varepsilon}\pi\iota\sigma\tau\varrho\dot{\varepsilon}\psi\alpha\varsigma$), stablish *thy brethren,*" said by the Lord to Peter (Luke 22[32]). We have already seen in Ch. IX why

Turn thy brethren has been altered into *stablish*, for Peter was *Eliakim, "whom God established."*

Unto the place wheresoever *my lord the king is, whether unto death*, or unto life, *there shall thy servant be.* This is the foundation of Peter's * reply to the Lord as of Ittai's reply to the king, " And he said unto him, *Lord, I am ready to journey with thee both to* prison *and to death."* Whatever parts of these chapters of 2 Samuel may seem to offer merely striking parallels or coincidences to the New Testament, one hesitates to class this passage of dialogue with them. The first impression is natural and strong, that the gospel account has been constructed upon the basis of this ancient narrative. The name of a place may offer a remarkable resemblance to the name of another place, and the present writer has shown † that the names of Macedonian cities in St. Paul's time offered astonishing resemblances to the names of places in Benjamin's territory in the Greek book of Joshua : in which case no manufacture of a narrative was possible. The Macedonian cities had their history, which we can follow in the Greek historians; the names in the LXX of Joshua were translated long before Christianity appeared and were themselves in Greek and in Hebrew even more ancient than some of those Macedonian cities. Their names had nothing whatever to do with Hebrew or Hellenized Hebrew names. Yet they largely coincide. The coincidences being in a successive chain in regard to the one tribe of Benjamin, and no other tribe, are quite astounding : and the events recorded as occurring at them bear just enough resemblance to the ancient history of Israel to warrant a fair and full sense of a fulfilment of prophecy upon the given conditions of that phenomenon, while it is beyond supposition that any ingenuity

---

* Ittai means *nearness of the Lord*. The name has, therefore, an obvious fitness as a parallel to Peter's position.
† *St. Luke the Prophet*, pp. 54 ff.

THE BETRAYAL

of a later historian could have invented such natural or even preternatural occurrences as those which are described in Acts 16-17.

Here, however, the case is different. A conversation in which both interlocutors utter such characteristic words as David and Ittai does not repeat itself centuries after in the mouths of the Lord and Peter *except on paper*. If it should be urged that Peter, on hearing the Master say, *When thou art turned again* . . . recognized instantly the word of King David, in 2 Sam. 15, and deliberately replied in appropriate terms as he knew that Ittai had answered the king, then it would seem that we credit Peter with a very complete knowledge of the Bible and a swiftness and smartness of reply which is at least a new feature in his character. If so, he deserves the more credit for the answer because he had not at this moment the events of Gethsemane to guide him: for while the discourse with Ittai took place at Geth, the discourse with Peter preceded the arrival at Gethsemane. Nevertheless we are to see whether even this is not explained.

All the people journeyed with him and *the king passed over the brook Kedron*. So *Jesus went forth with his* disciples *over the brook Kedron*.

Behold, here am I. So (John 18^5) Jesus saith unto them, *Here am I.*

I have no delight (ἠθέληκα) *in thee, let him do to me as seemeth good in his eyes.* "Father, if thou be willing remove this cup from me: nevertheless *not my will* (θέλημα) *but thine be done*" (Luke, Mark = Matthew similarly).

Now comes a very remarkable passage. The king goes barefoot, his head covered, all the people likewise, going up the Mount of Olives and weeping. At length *he was coming as far as Roōsh, where he worshipped God*. We look to see whether here, perhaps, some part of the Agony may not have taken place. "Having gone forward a little *he fell upon his face, praying*" (Matt.). "*He kneeled and prayed*" (Luke). These passages bear out the worship, but is it not possible that ἕως τοῦ ʿΡοώς contains more than this ?—that in it was found support for the ἰδρώς of Luke 22⁴⁴, " his *sweat* became as it were drops of blood descending to the earth "—as if it had been, Now David was entering in as far as the sweat of the place where he worshipped God ?

David passed on *a little* (παρῆλθεν βραχύ τι) from Roōsh. Jesus went forward *a little* (προελθών).*

What have I to do with you, ye sons of Zeruiah ? Luke records (9⁵⁴) an incident on the last journey towards Jerusalem, how James and John said, " Lord, wilt thou that we call fire to come down from heaven and consume them ? And he turned and rebuked them. And they journeyed to another village."

Let him alone reminds us of Mark 14⁶, *Let* her *alone*, "Ἄφετε αὐτήν (αὐτόν).

Twelve thousand men. This suggests the words that Jesus speaks (Matthew) to the disciple who smote Malchus. " Or thinkest thou that I cannot entreat my father and he will give me now *more than twelve legions* of angels." The superlative is in Matthew's manner.

When he is weary and weak-handed. " He began to be sorrowful and sore troubled " (Matthew); " Greatly amazed and sore troubled " (Mark).

Even as a bride turneth to her husband. " He that betrayed him gave them a sign saying, Whomsoever I shall kiss, that is he, take him " (Matthew). The ὅν τρόπον of 2 Sam. 17 means *as easily* as a bride turneth with a kiss, but in the gospel application it is taken to mean the precise *manner* (τρόπος) of the sign. Ahithophel means that the king's followers will gladly welcome an opportunity to come to their own again. The prearrangement

---

* But does not the strongly attested reading προσελθών here prove that it was once παρελθών actually, which, being found difficult, was modified into the easier πρos ?

THE BETRAYAL

of the kiss is in Matthew, Mark, not in Luke, John. The kiss is in Matthew, Mark, Luke, not in John. The words *even . . . husband* are not in the Hebrew (see above, p. x). Since writing this I find that both Dr Driver and Dr Budde (*ad l.*) say that the Hebrew *is mutilated here.* The reason for this mutilation may be conjecturally that which is stated in the preface and not merely that which Dr. Swete assigns (*Introduction to Old Testament in Greek*, p. 443). He has observed (p. 434) : "It represents a text, and, to some extent, an interpretation earlier than any which can be obtained from other sources."

And all the people that is with him shall flee, and I will smite the king quite alone ($\mu o\nu \omega \tau a\tau o\nu$). It must have occurred to many that the quotation of the prophecy " *I will smite* ($\pi a\tau \acute{a}\xi \omega$) the shepherd," etc. (Zech. 13^7) in Matt. 26^{31} = Mark 14^{27} (but Hebrew *smite*, imperative, instead of *I will smite*) is strangely inopportune to all human appearance, because, so far from encouraging the " little flock " to " fear not," it would dispose them to flee and to scatter. The time to which it is assigned is when " they had sung an hymn and went out to the mount of Olives." The corresponding time is marked in the plan of Ahithophel, and the same word is used for *smite*. Perhaps the remark of the false counsellor accounts for the insertion of the prophecy here. It is conveyed in a different form in John 16^{32}, " Do you now believe ? Behold, the hour cometh, and hath come, that *ye should be scattered* every one to his own home, and leave *me alone* ($\mu \acute{o}\nu o\nu$); and [yet] I am not alone, for the father is with me."

Except the life of one man thou seekest. " Jesus said, I told you that I am he : if therefore *ye seek me*, let these men go : that the word which he spake might be fulfilled, Of those whom thou hast given me I lose not one " (John $18^{8\,f}$).

And to all the people there shall be peace. This simple turn of speech is a pointed illustration of one of the features of Judas's character in prophecy : he was a *man of peace*. This was shown above by Ps. 41^9, which is familiar as a reference to Judas : "*For the man of my peace*, on whom I hoped, who eateth my loaves, hath made great scorn upon me." The term is just one of those links which bind together two prophecies which appear to be unrelated but probably are not. *The man of my peace* in Hebrew means only *my friend*.

In the eyes of all the elders of Israel. Judas "came with a great multitude from the high priests and *elders of the people*," which latter expression occurs four times in the concluding portion of Matthew. Moreover, the addition *and elders* occurs six times where it does not seem always to be necessary, and adds to the length, if also somewhat to the solemnity, of the narrative. It is fair to suppose that this verse partly accounts for the fact.

" We will *encamp* against the place as the dew falleth on the ground . . . and we will not leave in it and his men that are with him, so much as one : and if he draw together *into the city*, then shall all Israel take ropes against that city, and we shall draw it into the river, that *there shall not be left there so much as a stone*." Does not this remind us of Luke 19$^{43\ f}$: " For the days shall come upon thee when thine enemies shall *cast up* ($\pi\alpha\varrho\varepsilon\mu\beta\alpha\lambda o\tilde{v}\sigma\iota\nu$ the same verb) a bank about thee and shall compass thee round and keep thee in on every side and dash thee to the ground and thy children within thee, and they *shall not leave in thee one stone* upon another " ? The prediction of wholesale destruction is the same in either case, but the terms are different : Ahithophel was speaking of a city away from Jerusalem.

Tell ye David, saying, Lodge not ($\mu\grave{\eta}\ \alpha\grave{v}\lambda\iota\sigma\theta\tilde{\eta}\varsigma$) *to-night in the plains of the wilderness*. This word *lodged* occurs only here in the New Testament, Luke 21^{37} = Matt. 21^{17}, " Every night he went out and *lodged* in the mount that

THE BETRAYAL 357

is called the mount of Olives (Luke). That Luke and Matthew had 2 Sam. 17[16] before them and adopted this term from it is beyond a doubt. And it is lawful to suppose further that counsels of human wisdom were offered to the Lord to avoid what David avoided, the exposure of his life by continuing in one place, though the place of David was farther off near the Jordan.

The Agony in the Garden.

We now endeavour to find a point in the Davidic narrative where any event analogous to the Agony in the Garden may have taken place. The occurrence at Roōsh has been mentioned and some traces of the gospel account have been pointed out, but nothing at all definite can be concluded from them. The king was weeping till he came there: he worshipped God there. But the Lucan account (22[39]) is full of detail—

" And he came out and journeyed, as his custom was, unto the mount of Olives: and his disciples followed him. [49] And when he was *at the place*, he said unto them, Pray, that ye enter not into temptation. [41] And he was parted from them about a stone's cast; and he kneeled down and prayed . . . [[43] And there appeared unto him an angel from heaven, strengthening him. [44] And being in an agony he prayed more earnestly: and his sweat became as it were great drops of blood falling down upon the ground]."

Strengthening ($\dot{\varepsilon}\nu\iota\sigma\chi\dot{\upsilon}\sigma o\upsilon\sigma\iota\nu$) does occur in 2 Sam. 16[21] but in a neuter sense, and in a wholly inconsistent connection. When he had passed on *a little* from Roōs, Ziba met him and *strengthened* him and his people in the physical sense, but Ziba was not a messenger or angel. The passsage in 2 Sam. yields no support. We have to refer to a widely different passage—

Hos. 12[2] And the Lord [had] judgments ($\varkappa\rho\iota\sigma\varepsilon\iota\varsigma$) against *Judas* [to punish Jacob according to his ways, and according to his doings will he recompense him. In the womb he took his brother *by the heel*.] And in his agonies (κόποις) *he waxed strong* (ἐνίσχυσεν) towards God, and *he waxed strong by aid of an angel* (μετὰ ἀγγέλου) and prevailed (ἠδυνάσθη).

In order to make sufficient sense to apply this to the Agony, it seems at first sight to be necessary to overlook the parenthesized words. But that is not a reason for objecting to the reference: many other cases of such overlooking have been seen already. And we notice that the best MS. in the Greek (A, πρὸς τὸν 'Ιούδαν) gives the definite article which naturally emphasizes the individual person of Judas. *Jacob*, then, is put for Israel, and Israel here is understood by Luke or the Lucan tradition to be represented by the rebellious people and their rulers, the priests and elders. How much, then, of this verse is now to be bracketed? Only the second portion, *In the womb . . . heel*. But that is a mere explanation of the name *Jacob* (Gen. 25[28]), *one that takes by the heel*, or *supplants*. All the rest of the passage can, grammatically speaking, be taken of *the Lord*, although obviously Hosea was still speaking of Jacob's wrestling with the angel, and only a forced exegesis would think of applying the words to *the Lord*. The passage is now clearly prepared for the purpose of Christian fulfilment.

But this is, after all, but a small portion of the outward mechanism for expressing the crisis of a vast, world-wide, overwhelming purpose, which it was felt that no language could adequately convey. The retreat of the king from the holy city was to the Christian prophet not so entirely the retreat of Jesus as to be free of all reference to the historical David, quit of Ziba's tangible assistance and Hushai's allied stratagem, however pathetic his weeping unsandalled figure, outcast from his own city. The

THE BETRAYAL 359

besetting danger of all theology, whether positive or negative, whether offensive or defensive, is always a certain inertia of the sense of life. Theology implies study, and study seclusion, and the recluse is apt to lose touch with life. Theology involves the treatment of language, and language, especially when tied by previous scripture, is apt to become symbolic and lose the freshness of life. Theology, in so far as it is science—and even in the hands of the Christian prophets it possessed a certain scientific element, of research, of induction, of comparison—involves mechanical processes which are apt to retard the current of life. Theology, aiming to interpret the life of the world throughout time, is apt to be entangled in its own details, and so to miss the grander issues of the heart. The apostles were theologians, and it was conceivable that they might have missed their opportunity at the very crisis of the world's history. From such a miss the grace of God preserved them in Christ. The noisy centuries raged on, the waves came about to devour them, and in the very midst of the storm before its crisis they were enabled to discern a moment of mysterious calm at the brink of the engulphing whirlpool: the silence of man, the silence also of God.

In this moment they were enabled to place the final struggle of the will of man with the will of God and to fix the last act of resignation which was for ever to reconcile the human race to the Father. Then took place, as Ignatius says,* " the three mysteries of loud crying, that were wrought in the silence of God." The sinfulness of the whole world was unloaded upon that heavy-laden soul. But having fixed the moment, their language was unable to describe it, and ours, which is far richer, will fail to describe it too. " Language," says a great master of language and thought, " occupies the mid-region of our life, between the wants that ground us on the earth,

* See *The Christian Prophets*, pp. 8, 9.

and the affections that lift us to the skies. If we were all animal, we could not use it; if we were as God, we should give it up, and lapse, like Him, into eternal silence. It is the instrument of business, of learning, of mutual understanding, of common action; the tool of the Intellect and the Will; the glory of a nature more than brutal, the mark of one less than the divine; as truly the characteristic of labour in the mind, as the sweat of the brow of the body's toil; emblem at once of blessing and of curse; recalling an Eden half remembered, while we work in the desert that can never be forgot. When we try to raise it to higher functions, it only spoils the thing it cannot speak; which becomes, like an uttered secret, a treasure killed and gone. Religion in the soul is like a spirit hiding in enshadowed forests : call it into the staring light, it is exhaled and seen no more; or as the whispering of God among the trees: peer about behind the leaves, and it is not there. Men in deep reverence do not talk to one another, but remain with hushed mind side by side. Each one feels, though he cannot tell how it is, that words limit what faith declares unlimited; that they divide and break into pieces what it comprehends and embraces as a whole; that they distribute into dead members what it discerns as a life of beauty indivisible; that they reduce to successive propositions what it adores as a simultaneous and everlasting reality." *

The Bloody Sweat.

And it can hardly be doubted that the good taste of Luke passed over the moment of the silence of God in silence. The record of the Bloody Sweat, which is found in Luke only, is not his original writing; for, as Hort says, "the documentary evidence clearly designates it as an early Western interpolation." Its first appear-

* Martineau, *Endeavours after the Christian Life*, xlii.

THE BETRAYAL 361

ance before us is in Justin,* who says, "For in the memoirs, which I submit to have been composed by the apostles and those who followed with them, it is written that sweat poured from His body like heavy drops (ἱδρὼς ὡσεὶ θρόμβοι κατεχεῖτο) while He prayed and said, If it be possible, let this cup pass away—inasmuch as His heart was trembling and His bones likewise, and His heart was like melting wax in His bowels, that we may know that the Father hath willed for us His own Son to have become truly [a sharer] even in such sufferings as these, instead of saying that He, being the Son of God, did not take part in the things that came and befel Him." Here in Justin we notice the absence of the words *of blood* which have so deeply tinged the whole account. But what makes the passage in Justin especially interesting is that he is led to introduce it by the discussion of Ps. 22, from which so much illustration of the crucifixion is drawn.

He says—" Ps. 22[14] Like water all my bones are poured out and scattered abroad: my heart becomes like melting wax in the midst of my bowels—the thing that hath befallen him that night when they went forth against him to the Mount of Olives to take him, was a prediction (προαγγελία). For in the memoirs, etc." *A previous announcement*, however, would be a more accurate term than *a prediction* to express Justin's exact meaning. For to him, as to "those who followed along with the apostles," † the statements of the Old Testament were actually evidence of what happened to Jesus, as we shall presently see by

---

* *Dial.* c. Try., 331 D.

† Here is one of the rare uses of παρακολουθεῖν which we have in Luke 1[3], and it may seem as if Justin had not known the true prophetic meaning which it bore a few years earlier: he seems to take it to mean " followed (the Lord) along with *them* (the Apostles)." But even this is doubtful, for Justin says not αὐτοῖς but ἐκείνοις, and this is best taken to mean the writers of the Old Testament, including the author of Ps. 2, which he has quoted. In any case Justin is referring to St. Luke and to his preface.

an examination of Justin's own expressions concerning the relation of fulfilments to their prophecies.

Rejection of the Agony in the Fourth Gospel.

We must not be led away from the consideration of the Agony and its place in prophecy by the subsidiary elements—for such they are really—which Justin unfolds to view. The main idea of this cardinal event is rightly regarded by the Synoptics. John seems to concentrate all its meaning into the cross, and, so far from allowing it in Gethsemane, is determined to place the details of it elsewhere. Let any one read John 12^{27-33} without prejudice and he will say that this passage records the Agony in a different form and place and occasion. After saying to the Greeks . . . " If any one serve me, let him follow me, and where I am there shall also my servant be," which is the saying of Ittai mentioned above (p. 352). Jesus says in John, " Now is my soul troubled " (Ps. 42 in identical words, ἡ ψυχή μου ἐταράχθη) which is essentially the same as the citation of Mark = Matthew at Gethsemane; and the next verse to it is similar—

Ps. 42^6 Why art thou *exceeding sorrowful, my soul?*

Then He goes on to say, " And why * should I say, Father, save me from this hour? Nay, for this cause came I unto this hour "—which is essentially, " Father, *not my will*, but *thine be done.*" (see p.353), in the Agony in the three Gospels. Then occurs the voice from heaven, and some said, *An angel hath spoken to him;* this takes the place of Luke 22^{43}, " There appeared to him *an angel from heaven, strengthening him.*" Then He continues . . . " Now is [the] *judgment* (κρίσις) of this world, now shall the ruler of this world be cast out," which strongly recalls the text in Hos. 12^2, " The Lord had *judgments* (κρίσεις) against Judas,"

* Abbott, 933.

THE BETRAYAL 363

and is expressed by Luke's phrase, *being in an agony*. Then He proceeds to say, "I, if I be lifted up from the earth, will draw all men unto Me," to which John adds the comment, "Now this he said signifying by what death he was going to die." (The comment,* let it be said, is probably by the author of John 21^{19}, where the same words occur. It might be disputed whether the comment be actually and precisely just.) But however, after reading this passage, can it be maintained that in the opinion of John any room was left for the Agony in the Garden at all? He has placed the five successive stages of the story, all in order due, at a previous occasion (with a slight change in regard to the presence of the angel), and yet how actually different is the converse with the Greeks from the retirement of the garden! No other conclusion can be drawn than that John not only deliberately omitted the Agony in the Garden—the "garden" is John's own name for it—but deliberately transferred the occurrences of it to another place, apparently a public place in Jerusalem, where the interview with the Greeks is made the concluding scene of His public ministry. And yet John is consciously overthrowing the Synoptists, whose origins in the Old Testament he knows, for he has used Ittai's saying, and Ps. 42, and David's resignation, and Hos. 12, which have all been employed by them, and in other parts of his account of the Betrayal-night he follows the lines of 2 Sam. 15^f.

The Ode of Moses, and Ps. 92 concerning Malchus' Ear.

Another passage of scripture lies behind the story of Malchus. John, who uses the words "*I am* [*he*]" three times in the account of the capture in Gethsemane (John 18^{5,6,8}), shows us that the original of the passage is to be found in the Ode of Moses (Deut. 32^{39}) which has been fruitful of so many other suggestions—

* See Bacon, *The Fourth Gospel in Research and Debate*, p. 472.

See ye, see ye, that *I am* [*he*] and there is no God beside me. I will put to death and will make to live: I *will smite and I will heal, and there is none that shall take out of my hands.* For I will *lift up my hand* unto heaven and swear by my right hand and say I live for everlasting: for I will sharpen as lightning my *sword*, and my hand shall lay hold of judgment, and I will repay justice to my enemies and will requite them that hate me.

The close resemblance here of the four Gospels to the Ode is unmistakable. John has the *I am* [he], *the sword*, and the sense of *there is none*, etc. (John 18⁹). Luke has *the sword*, the verb *smite* ($\pi\alpha\tau\acute{\alpha}\xi o\mu\varepsilon\nu$) and its tense, and the *healing;* he alone has the last. Mark has *the sword*. Matthew has *the sword*, the verb *smite*, and in sense *I will lift up my hand unto heaven* (Matt. 26⁵³, " or thinkest thou that I cannot beseech my Father?") And he adds significantly the words, which we may suppose to be the evangelist's rather than the Lord's, "Now all this is come to pass, *that the scriptures of the prophets might be fulfilled,*" the particular scripture being the Ode of Moses. In Mark 14⁴⁹ this fulfilment is certainly put in the Lord's mouth, and Luke and John imply the same sense here of fulfilment, "this is your hour . . ." (Luke 22⁵³), "the cup which my Father . . ." (John 18¹¹). All three Synoptics have also a reference in some form or other to *lifting up* or stretching forth *the hand* in this scene.

Whether we can discover the origin of the wounded ear will appear later (p. 379). But there is a possible source of it in—

Ps. 92¹⁰ And my horn shall be exalted like the horn of an unicorn, and my *old age* in (*i.e.* like) *fat olive-oil*: and mine eye overlooked among mine enemies, and among them that rose against me to do evil *the ear* shall hear me ($\varepsilon\iota\sigma\alpha\varkappa o\acute{v}\sigma\varepsilon\tau\alpha\iota\ \tau\grave{o}\ o\tilde{v}\varsigma\ \mu ov$).

THE BETRAYAL

There is no doubt that the natural meaning of the latter words is " my ear shall ear," but the other translation is possible, especially if "the ear" has been emphasized and particularized by becoming the object of careful thought, " the ear [that has been wounded] shall be made to hear my voice forbidding retaliation on those who so unjustly assail me." In support of such a view we may suppose that the *fat olive-oil* is that of *Gethsemane, the oil-press*. The *old age* may be taken in support of the belief that the Lord's ministry was much prolonged: we know that Irenæus * not only positively stated that the Lord attained the age of fifty, but that it is an inference from John 8^{57}, and that it was the testimony of the Ephesian elders delivered to them by John the Lord's disciple. Also the next verse (Ps. 92^{12}) contains a reference to *the cedar* (ἡ κέδρος) which might be thought to be a parallel to the brook *Kedron* (τοῦ Κέδρου, or τῶν Κέδρων, John). Lastly, that the *high priest's* servant should bear the name of *Malchus* is perhaps not unconnected with the fact that Malchus is the name in Neh. 12^2 of one of the *Levites* who " went up with . . . Jesus."

The " Agony " connected with Hosea.

Once more we return to Hos. 12^2, which has gathered some fresh light from the digression. The crisis was of the same kind whether the moment of it be fixed at Gethsemane or at Calvary, and yet if Luke has suffered by his interpolator adding the Sweat of Blood, how much more has John suffered by his elimination of the Agony

* Iren. II, 22^5 " But that the age of thirty years is the prime of a young man's ability, and that it reaches even to the fortieth year, every one will allow : but after the fortieth and fiftieth year it begins to verge towards elder age; which was our Lord's when he taught, as the Gospel and all the Elders witness, who in Asia conferred with John the Lord's disciple, to the effect that John had delivered these things unto them; for he abode with them until the times of Trajan."

altogether! For the thought of the Synoptists was one that at any rate went back to the primal eldest curse upon man at the Fall and bore the accumulated appeal of all the ages as apprehended by scripture. The curse upon the first Adam passed of old in the Paradise of Eden, or *License* (τρυφή), was grasped and overthrown by the second Adam in the estate of Gethsemane (the oil-press). And so it came to pass that here "the Lord reigned from the tree" (ἀπὸ τοῦ ξύλου). This is the Pauline gospel of Rom. 5$^{12\,f}$, "Just as through one man sin entered into the world and death through sin,* much more the grace of God and the gift in grace by the one man Jesus Christ abounded unto all." Here is the plain symmetrical thought of the great Restitution, harbinger and pledge of the restitution of all things (Acts 3^{21})—a thought which is dominant by the fact of its primæval source and cosmic by its relation to the first man.

Turning then to Genesis, we find that the curse to the serpent reads—

Gen. 3^{15} He shall watch thy head and thou shalt watch his *heel*.

This is what Hos. 12^3 suggests: Jacob "in the womb took his brother by the heel." We have only to refer to the birth of Esau and Jacob to see that what the Lord said to Rebecca—

Two nations are in thy womb ... the elder shall be slave to the younger—

was a prediction which the Pauline gospel saw to be cancelled in the reconciling sacrifice of Christ (Rom. 9$^{10-31}$), etc., as everything else that was inconsistent with the purpose of God was overruled. The punishment of the nation of Jacob was now, therefore, in store from the Lord, for Jacob had enslaved the Gentiles, and henceforward

* Wisd. 2^{24} "*Through* envy of the devil *death entered into the world*" is the source of St. Paul's expression.

THE BETRAYAL

should enslave them no more. And here we cannot fail to observe once more that John is fully conscious of this fact when John 12[20 ff] brings the Gentile Greeks into the presence of Jesus, whom they " desire to see," and He " *answers them*, saying, The hour is come that the Son of man should be glorified "—through death alone. It is not easy to see that the Greeks could possibly understand the half of His words, which we can only suppose were addressed to Andrew and Philip, and not to the Greeks at all. But perhaps by tracing the thought in John's mind in some such way as is here indicated we may arrive at the meaning of the episode. For if it had no relation to the Greeks, with their desire *to see* Him, it has at least a relation to cosmic thought in connection with the Pauline teaching of the purpose of God. Henceforward there was to be " neither Jew nor Gentile, who were both one in Christ Jesus."

" *The Lord reigned from the Tree.*"

Thus one part of the curse was removed, and another part was also indicated as removed, the curse upon " *the ground* in the works of *Adam* " (Gen. 3[19]). " *In the sweat of thy face* shalt thou *eat thy bread.*" Now *the bread* of the Last Supper had been eaten just before the scene in which " *his sweat was* as it were great drops *falling to the ground.*" The great Restitution was here again performed by Him who was the son of Adam and brought *by His obedience* the grace that so much superabounded.

We shall now be in a position to understand how " the Lord reigned *from the tree.*" It is not necessary to discuss here whether Justin was entitled to accuse the Jews of having removed the words *from the tree* from—

Ps. 96[10] Tell ye among the Gentiles the Lord reigneth [*from the tree*].

The expression first appears in the Epistle of Barnabas 8, "*The reign* [kingdom] of Jesus *from the tree*": he is explaining in his extraordinary fashion, "the type of placing the scarlet wool on a tree"; which in due course he explains by the cross. But when we consider the Restitution of the Fall by the Exaltation, and when we read of the curse at the Fall being overcome by Him who conquered the last temptation of the devil in Gethsemane, taking Gen. 3 for its record of the cosmic fact, we cannot fail to observe that *from the tree* occurs in that chapter repeatedly as the immediate cause of the Fall. The same notion must therefore be the immediate cause of the Restitution. The meaning is that *the reign of Christ is the Restitution of the Fall of man*. We know what use St. Paul made of " Cursed is every one that hangeth on a tree " (Deut. 21^{23}, Gal. 3^{13}), where he shows that Christ did not shrink from being made a curse for us to redeem us from the curse of the law, and there again he adds that the object was the inclusion *of the Gentiles* by faith in Christ. Justin has not succeeded in persuading many persons of the truth of his assertion that the Jews had tampered with Ps. 96^{10}, and yet it is just as easy to hold it true as to hold it untrue; he wrote within half-a-century of the Synod of Jamnia. Elsewhere he is able to find that "the tree" (that is "the wood ") is capable of meaning the ark of Noah, and the idea is capable of much extension. As to Ps. 96^{10} it is probable that Justin had seen the words *from the tree* not in its proper place in the Psalter but as a separate verse in a collection, by Papias or some other, of *oracles concerning the Lord*, where they were supplied from some other passage and compounded with this verse. When it was once established that the supreme contest with evil took place not on Calvary but in Gethsemane, then Hos. 12^2 was introduced as fulfilment, but at the same time, instead of stopping there,

THE BETRAYAL

12⁴ was also introduced, and this brought *the angel* upon the scene as we find in Luke 22⁴³ f. This was seen in early times to be objectionable, and John in particular is so much opposed to it that he not only omits it but is determined that the Agony is not connected with Gethsemane at all and does belong to another place and time.

Justin on the Argument from Prophecy.

When we come to inquire what was the precise relation which Justin thought to exist between the Old Testament scriptures and the New Testament events—whether he considered that a statement in the Psalms was evidence of an event in the Gospels—we are met with a certain caution of expression which covers an intensity of conviction. The milder class of statement is represented by such phrases as : " it has been prophesied," " it has been said with regard to," " it points to," " it is symbolic of," " indicative of," " parabolically and covertly." The stronger class presents us with the forms : " declarative of," " proves " (ἀποδεικνύει), (Isaiah) " as impersonating the apostles " (ὡς ἀπὸ προσώπου τῶν ἀπ.), " Jesus Christ cries through Isaiah " (βοᾷ διὰ 'Η.), " Jesus Christ circumcises all those who choose, as was proclaimed of old, *with knives of flint* (Josh. 5²), that there may be made *a righteous nation,*" etc. (Isa. 26²), " we have demonstrated (ἀπεδείξαμεν) that all ointment whatsoever belongs to Christ, because the word says, Wherefore God thy God hath anointed thee with the oil of gladness beyond thy fellows." The only way to put Justin's attitude in plain English is to say that he treated the Old Testament statements as evidence of New Testament events. But can any one maintain that Justin had made a revolution in the method of exegesis hitherto usual in the Church ? No writer could be more determined than Justin to assert his own close following of tradition.*

* *Dial.*, 69, 296 A. etc.

B B

If Justin was not the first revolutionary expositor, who was before him? who was before A.D. 140? None can be found. The apostolic fathers exhibit no better taste or judgment than Justin in this exegesis; Barnabas, in fact, who was possibly a generation earlier, is considerably worse. We thus come back to the canonical writers, whose taste and judgment are much superior. But can we say that their principle is different? Affection says Yes, and reason says No.

Is the Betrayal Narrative manufactured, or does it describe Deliberate Fulfilment?

The time has now come to form some conclusion upon the prophetic phenomena concerning the Betrayal. At first they seem to point, in several cases, to a wholesale transfer of the pages of 2 Sam. to the pages of the four Gospels, as if what had happened to David of old happened also to David's son by a sort of automatic reproduction of scripture. So it had seemed to the writer of this book, and the discovery caused him very great concern. He then saw, however, in further study of the narrative of Cæsarea Philippi that it was clear that Jesus had deliberately set Himself to fulfil prophecy in certain particulars that can be distinguished. This fact ought to facilitate the interpretation of other parts of the narrative also; it ought to provide a principle of exposition. There is perhaps no indication on the surface to show which these parts of the narrative are: on the whole, they are those which do not contain uncialized words in Westcott and Hort's text. For instance, we have seen how large a portion of Rom. 8 is overwritten, as the Germans would say, upon Ps. 89, no less than eleven consecutive expressions having been transferred from the old to the new, several of these being characteristic, including the long compound συναντιλαμβάνεται; yet these have been overlooked. And the present writer is prepared to find that he has overlooked very many more that were before his very eyes (see p. 379). Then Ps. 89 has been also the key to the understanding of Cæsarea Philippi; yet no uncializing of the text! The very great importance of this Psalm has not been fully appreciated for the New Testament. And one reason is that we have failed to appreciate first and foremost its paramount importance in having guided many of the movements of the Master-prophet during His life on earth; for these movements must needs vibrate to the text of the New Testament as we shall see that they do.

Now in the Betrayal-narrative we are to see further effects of this Ps. 89, when we shall apply the principle of the Lord's intentional fulfilment of prophecy. At some point of His life—it is doubtful if there will ever be any large measure of agreement as to what point— He resolved to be Messiah. If we deny this we side with John and accept (whether consciously or not) a mountain of difficulties, indeed a whole Himalaya, the first of which is that we must throw over the Synoptists in regard to such cardinal points of the Life as the Temptation, the Agony, and all the human sympathy of Christ. Instead of the last we may accept a superhuman sympathy, as Bacon has observed on John $11^{4, 15}$. Instead of the Agony we may accept John $12^{22\,ff}$, an agony in the presence of the Greeks and of the crowd in Jerusalem, but the fourth Gospel positively vetoes the Agony in the Garden. Instead of the Temptation, which John not only omits but cannot on his principles possibly admit, we have nothing. The question cannot be argued here, and must be left to the reader's quiet consideration.

The Triumphal Entry.

However, the Lord, having set Himself to be the Christ, deliberately determined to do His duty in fulfilling prophecy. He was aware of the bearing of Zech. 9⁹, for instance, upon Himself—

> Zech. 9⁹ Rejoice greatly, daughter of Sion; proclaim it, daughter of Jerusalem : behold thy king cometh, unto thee righteous and saving, himself meek and riding upon an ass, even upon a young colt.

This, as He knew, was only a more detailed reproduction of another prophecy—

> Isa. 62¹¹ For, behold, the Lord maketh a thing heard to the end of the earth : Say ye to the daughter of Sion, Behold, thy Saviour hath come to thy side, *with his own reward*, and his *work before him*.

But *his reward* here mentioned is one form of that *compensation of thy Christ* which we saw was recently the theme of His discourse at Cæsarea. His *work before him* was His duty to fulfil prophecy to the best of His power, *to fulfil all righteousness*, to leave nothing undone that He could do, leaving the rest to God.

But here is another case where John throws over the Synoptists with no unsparing pen. They have narrated the Master's minute instructions to the disciples to secure Him the ass whereon He is to ride, and their narrative is altogether credible. John will have none of it. Jesus, he says (John 12¹⁴), "found an ass and sat upon it" (apparently after the crowd had "come to meet him" with Hosanna), " as it is written, Fear not (this is a loose quotation), daughter of Sion, behold thy king cometh unto thee sitting upon an ass's colt." And he proceeds, " These things his disciples knew not (οὐκ ἔγνωσαν) at the first, but when Jesus was glorified they remembered then that these things had been written of him *and these things they did to him.*" *They did to him* does not mean that *the disciples* had done anything to Him, though Westcott here harmonizes by such an opinion ; the disciples had done nothing whatever according to John ; the crowd

THE BETRAYAL

had done everything except that Jesus had *found an ass*. John is determined to exclude all those preparations for the entry which Mark, Luke, Matthew so carefully ascribe to the Master. The disciples, he says, did not recognize *these things;* later they remembered that *these things* were prophesied; and that the crowd fulfilled the prophecy in doing *these things*.* Westcott's view is that the disciples had performed the preparations in ignorance of the application of Zech. 9^9. If so, this does not prevent the Master's thought of it. It is conceivable, but unlikely, that He locked within His breast His own intention to fulfil this prophecy. The disciples were not His domestic servants. How does John 15^{14} *my friends* suit with Westcott's explanation? It would be hard to suppose that the " *no longer* do I call you servants " applies to the preparation just because it was four days earlier than the saying? The Master-prophet must needs be training His disciples in the interpretation of prophecy: but it would indeed be a strange way of training them to maintain such silence and secrecy at a great crisis. Though Mark and Luke do not record the fulfilment of Zech. 9^9 as such, their narrative is quite in keeping with the view that He had acquainted His disciples with the thoughts of His heart at the time. The fact that John ascribes the meeting and jubilation of the crowd to their knowledge of the raising of Lazarus, shows John's desire to enhance the effect of " the sign." It also makes us ask with amazement why the Synoptists knew nothing of the raising of Lazarus.

The eating of the Passover.

The next preparation at this time deliberately made by the Lord is that for the Passover (Luke 22^8), where

* This is just like Acts 17^{11}, where the Bereans "examined the scriptures daily, to see if *these things* (ταῦτα) were so." One thing is the event, one thing is the scripture compared with it; the result is *these things*. See *St. Luke the Prophet*, Ch. II.

Matthew and Mark, however, attribute the first proposal to the disciples. Is it not plain that in Zech. 9[11], the next verse but one to that of the Triumphal Entry, there is a suggestion of the Last Supper?

> Zech. 9[11] And thou *by the blood of the testament* sendest forth thy captives from the pool that has no water.

This has been interpreted (quite correctly, as far as the words go) to convey the release of " the spirits in prison " ; in fact, it is one of the chief foundations of the doctrine of 1 Pet. 3[19]. That their release was held to be effected by the preaching *after* the crucifixion does not prevent the blood of the cross being identified with the cup of the Last Supper for this purpose. The Master prepared the cup; He could not prepare the cross, which He seems, however, to have anticipated. What He says in Luke 22[20] is—

> This cup is the new testament in my blood—the cup which is poured out for you.

The form of the words proves that *the new testament in my blood* was in no ordinary shape, it was to be seen in the shape of a cup of wine poured out before them and for them to drink and to be strengthened by it. The blood which was to give efficacy to His fresh will, made fresh by an obedience unknown hitherto to God's will, was *the blood of the will* in Zech. 9, as He understood it at this moment. Assured that His blood would soon be shed, He resolved that it should be the means of a new will. This death, then, should be a " release to the captives " (Isa. 61[1], $αἰχμαλώτοις$, here $δεσμίους$)—mankind, a release such as that which He had come to preach and declared as His divine purpose and mission on the first day of ministry at Nazareth. *The pool that has no water* became within a century a

* See Hart, *Expositor*, Jan. 1907.

THE BETRAYAL

phrase for the unbaptized: but at present it meant for Him the misery of this evil world. And had it not been prophesied that "he should be as a river rushing gloriously *in a thirsty land*" (p. 315)?

The Two Swords.

The next preparation that He (shall we say?) deliberately makes is—

Luke 22[36] But now he that hath a purse, let him take it, and likewise a scrip, and he that hath no sword, let him sell his garment and buy one. For I say unto you that this which is written must be fulfilled (τελεσθῆναι) in me, And he was numbered with the lawless (μετὰ ἀνόμων), for that which concerneth me hath an end (τέλος). And they said, Lord, Behold, here are two swords. And he said unto them, It is enough.

This much-controverted passage is guaranteed by its very obscurity as genuine in some sort. If, however, instead of wondering at the absurdity of physical resistance on the part of twelve, or of two, sworded men in the time of crisis we try to estimate the data correctly, we may yet perhaps be enabled to see some light upon the action. There was a prophecy to be fulfilled in Him, written in Isa. 53[12], and He was consciously contributing to the fulfilment of it, as is proved by *For I say unto you.* A point that may or may not be important in this prophecy is that the chief term in it is *the lawless*, which is here found in LXX though with a different preposition (ἐν τοῖς ἀνόμοις): so that while it is not an exact quotation from LXX it is probably to be classed as a quotation, especially as the Hebrew *transgressors* is not nearly so often translated by ἄνομοι as by some other term. What meaning, then, we ask, did He attribute on this occasion to the prophecy? It behoves us to dismiss from the mind, if possible, the general conviction that the great prophecy of Isa. 53 was about to be fulfilled by Him and that He knew it, if only because this general fulfilment, which few would now be found to deny, has never to this day enabled any one to feel sure of the particular meaning of the two swords—I refer to modern times, later than the Holy Roman Empire with the sword of Christ and that of Cæsar. Perhaps the possession of two swords among twelve men does not by itself entitle them or their Chief to be *numbered with the lawless*. And yet it is just possible that in conjunction with a fulfilment of prophecy in a highly-charged atmosphere it might do so. Let us first observe what the position of *the lawless* is in—

Isa. 53 (LXX) ⁵ But he is wounded because (διά) of our lawless actions (A).
⁸ From (ἀπό) the lawless acts of my people he is led to death.
⁹ For he did not do lawlessness.
¹² And because (διά) of their [lawless actions, *or*] sins *he is delivered up*.

Do these passages lead us to a train of thought suitable to the conditions? *Lawless*, we have seen above (Chap. I), is an epithet and almost a synonym of Herod: but we can hardly see that connection here. The fear of Antipas, if ever it existed, is long past. But some breach of the Mosaic law would naturally be meant, of the Sabbath law, for instance. Or a rebel against the state or government would fall under the term. In fact, Absalom's rebellion is so termed (2 Sam. 19¹⁹). So that the treachery of Judas prefigured by Ahithophel is not improbably included in *lawlessness*. Thus the train of thought would be, He was the son of David, the lawful King of the Jews, the enemy of all rebellion. Yet rebellion caused His delivery; He was wounded; He was led to death, because of the rebellion of one of our

THE BETRAYAL

number, said the disciples. But this they could not say till after the Passion. At present He could say that He had a rebel among those with whom he was classed, and He had said, a few minutes before, But behold, the hand of him that *delivereth me up* is *with me* (μετ ἐμοῦ) on the table. Here is the very preposition (μετά) in a very uncommon sense, joined with the very word *delivered up*, which occurs next to the quotation in the same verse of Isaiah. And He proceeds to say—

> Luke 22[22] For the Son of man indeed *goeth his way* (πορεύεται) as it hath been determined (κατὰ τὸ ὡρισμένον), but woe unto that man through whom *he is delivered up*.

The latter words show that Isa. 53[12] was in His mind.

But what is more to our present purpose, *goeth his way* as *it hath been determined*, is an expression of particular meaning, and leads us back to the journey of David in 2 Sam. 15[20]. Our monosyllabic language is incapable of doing justice to πορεύομαι and ὑπάγω: if *journey* is ponderous, *go* is quite inadequate. There are those who will maintain that *goeth his way* must needs have a far more important meaning than going to Olivet—it must have a cosmic meaning: that *determined* must have a cosmic meaning. But there is no need to deny this if we assert also the more immediate and intelligible sense of the words. Certainly *delivered up* bore that immediate meaning, however momentous the result of the action: it is a relatively common term. As to *determined*, it is used of human action in the New Testament, but much oftener of divine. Nor would the divine aspect be excluded if here we took it of His determination to fulfil the history of David as if it were a prophecy, so far as this was a consequence of going His way to Olivet according to His custom. That which was determined was determined by Him, and was simply the performance of His duty, "spending the days in the Temple teaching, and going out to pass the nights on the Mount *of Olives*, as it was called " (Luke 21^{37}). This *as it was called* is a reminder of Geth-*semane* (press of *olives*) which Luke does not name expressly. The whole story of David's journey was in His mind, and quite naturally *the kingdom* is the theme of nearly all His sayings.

> Luke 22^{25} The kings of the Gentiles . . . but ye shall not be so. ^{29} And I bequeath to you, as my father bequeathed to me, a kingdom, that ye should eat and drink at my table in my kingdom.

Hence in addressing Simon concerning the request by Satan, the words, *Turn thou about and strengthen thy brethren* sprang to His lips from 2 Sam. 15^{20}. And it is conceivable that Peter made the ready reply in almost the words of Ittai, *Lord, I am ready to go my way with thee both* to prison *and to* death, but only on the assumption that the Lord had discussed the journey of David with His disciples already. If this assumption is denied, we are hopelessly reduced to the conclusion that the entire Gethsemane incident was constructed long after the event upon the basis of the history of David in 2 Sam. If it is admitted, it is only upon the earlier basis that the Prophet of Nazareth did discuss one Old Testament passage after another with His disciples. If He was not a prophet, then the evangelists in describing Him as such were bankrupt of a history to narrate, and yet would seem to have hit upon a marvellous device for helping out their labouring imagination with borrowed tags of antiquity.

No such basis for the two swords is provided in 2 Sam., but possibly it may be found in some other scriptures. The sword of Peter which cut off Malchus's ear was probably one of these two swords; the other might have belonged to Judas, who, it seems from Luke, had not yet

THE BETRAYAL

left the company. We therefore turn once more to the passage in Deut. 32[39-41], which has been quoted. But why have we not quoted it further? It has been before our eyes and yet the significance of it has till now escaped us!

> I will make my arrows drunk with blood, and *my sword shall devour flesh from the blood of the wounded and of the captives, from the head of the rulers my foes* (or, *the rulers the Gentiles*, ἀπὸ κεφαλῆς ἀρχόντων ἐχθρῶν, or ἐθνῶν).

It is impossible not to see that the ear of the high priest's servant, which the disciple took off (ἀφεῖλεν, Luke, Matthew, Mark), or cut off (ἀπέκοψεν, John), answers to this prediction—*flesh from the head of the rulers my foes*. The servant was one *of the rulers*. So much is clear. *Rulers* is a common term in the New Testament. He was one of the *rulers my foes :* but was he one *of the Gentiles* (A) ? John alone gives his name as Malchus, which points to a Jew. But John alone recognizes the crowd as partly Gentile in composition, for he makes the Roman *cohort* come with the crowd *from the high priests and Pharisees*, for which Matthew gives *high priests and elders of the people*, Mark *high priests and scribes and elders*, Luke *a crowd* merely. It is very remarkable that precisely where the LXX has a doubtful reading of Deut. 32[42], the four Gospels give an uncertain answer accordingly.*

How far is the Malchus Story manufactured ?

Some would be disposed after making this discovery to throw up the story of the two swords along with the

---

* On turning to the Hebrew we find that *Gentiles* has no business here, but belongs to the following verse. Therefore the Alexandrine MS. is here wrong in its translation of the Hebrew. But as neither *my foes* nor *the Gentiles* is necessary to the story, the question is unimportant for our purpose. The A reading could be translated *of the rulers who ruled* (in this case) *the Gentiles* by bending them to their will,

story of Malchus, which as soon as it steps beyond the fact of a scuffle must be pronounced unhistorical. A reader who has read to this page will perhaps agree that the evangelists here refined too much in making the incident out of the Ode of Moses. One expression of the Ode, *and no one shall take [pluck] them out of my hand[s]* had been taken by the Lord into his own lips in the discourse in Solomon's porch (John 10^{28}, though the language is not LXX), and repeated generally in John 17^{12}, and then John 18^9 finds a fulfilment of His own words (which are essentially these) in the narrative of the capture. But, as Bacon observes, John 18^9 spoils the effect of John 17^{12}. However, the main question for us now is, Does this suffice to show that the Ode was being carefully studied by the disciples under the Lord's tuition at the time? Hardly. Therefore they could not have been prepared by this means, by the study of this passage, for the purchase of the swords. The Ode, it rather seems, was brought into play long afterwards when the Gospels were being composed. There is a reason for this in the fact that *Moses and Jesus son of Nauê* spake it in the ears of the people (Deut. 32^{44}). Mark knows nothing of the healing of the ear. Luke introduces it, but Matthew has not followed him though he records the rebuke of the smiter. And even John has not followed Luke. But all, with the possible exception of Mark, have used the Ode as a source (see p. 364). The conclusion is difficult to avoid that this is a case of *ex post facto* construction of history. On the other hand, this conclusion may be false, and, if so, here is one of the most amazing fulfilments of prophecy—because of its obscurity of origin—in all the Bible.

Or can we, again, draw a line between the story of wounding Malchus and the story of Malchus healed? There is nothing very improbable in the Marcan account that an (anonymous) disciple cut off the ear of the

THE BETRAYAL 381

(anonymous) servant of the high priest. This implies that he had a sword to cut with. Does not the difficulty come in with Luke, who introduces the healing? But then Luke it is who introduces the purchase of swords and the two swords. And then Luke, Matthew, John, have all applied Deut. 32, which possibly Mark has not. This leads to the conclusion that Deut. 32 and the healing in Luke, and the mention of the fulfilment in Matthew, and the *I am* in John, were all later importations into the simple narrative of Mark. The words, *and no one shall take*, etc., may (or may not) have been due to the influence of Deut. 32^{39}.

Are the Swords for Fighting?

But after all, to what does all this digression bring us? We have seen that *the lawless* may have been the rebel Judas who was in the Lord's mind a few verses before He makes the quotation, and that one of the swords may have been that of Judas. And in favour of this view we may take Luke 22^{52}: "Are ye come out as against a thief *with swords* and staves?" These words, however, were addressed to "them that had come against him, chief priests and captains of the temple and elders," and Judas was not himself one of these, though he was with them. If Judas had been *the lawless* a few verses before, Jesus was now *numbered with the lawless*, for Judas was His friend of an hour ago, and the two swords were now crossed in fight, one on behalf of the *numbered with the lawless*, the other joined in treachery with the swords of the lawful authorities, representing the Mosaic Law. Before this symmetrical and dramatic situation is dismissed from the mind, it is worth while to observe that there is prophetic warrant for it, and it is found in two passages—

Zech. $10^{3\,ff}$ Mine anger is kindled against the shepherds (the *lawful rulers*), and I will visit upon the lambs;

and the Lord God Almighty *will visit His flock* the house of Judah (the Lord and disciples), and will order them as his goodly horse in battle . . . And they shall be as warriors treading mire in the streets in battle, *and they shall fight* (παρατάξονται), for *the Lord is with them* ("God with us," Immanuel), and the riders on horses shall be confounded. And I will strengthen the house of Judah and will save *the house of Joseph*, and I will resettle them, for I love them, and they shall be as if I had not turned away from them.

Zech. 14³ And the Lord shall come forth and fight with those nations, as in the day of his fighting, *and his feet shall stand* in that day on the mount of Olives before Jerusalem on the east. And in that day there shall be a great amazement from the Lord upon them [who assail Jerusalem], and each one shall take hold of his neighbour's hand, and his hand shall cleave unto his neighbour's hand. *And Judas* (ὁ 'Ιούδας) *shall fight* (παρατάξεται) at Jerusalem, and shall gather the strength of all the peoples round about, gold and silver and raiment unto a great multitude.

The two passages * taken together in the subsequent light of Judas's treason would appear to have predicted a serious encounter : the Lord had marshalled His force on one side, Judas had marshalled his on the other : for Judah and Judas being identical names in Greek can be placed on the same side or on opposite sides according to requirement of sense. The Lord's *feet standing on the Mount of Olives* gives a pointed touch in connection with the fact that he went by custom thither. The name *Immanuel* and the *house of Joseph* are two features, however, that are wholly outside the contemporary record, if we may so call it, of the history : they do not

* Between the two occurs that text (Zech. 13⁷) *Smite the shepherd* . . . which has rather lost its point in its applications.

come into any relation with the acts and words of Jesus, and only appear when Luke and Matthew first appear.* There is nothing to show that the Master Himself regarded these particular prophecies as a direction of His movements. There is every reason to see that they would be applied to them in a later generation. And from the connection of *a sword* [36], and the *two swords* [38], with the sword [49], and swords [52], it is likely that the two earlier mentions were intended by Luke to lead up to the two later. Between the two passages Luke has inserted the contrast of the stillness and solitude of *the place* on Olivet, where very briefly and simply he describes the Agony. But we have seen that the use of the sword against the high priest's servant is the cause of an undue application of prophecy by Luke, and it is therefore probable that Zech. 10^3 and 14^{13} are to be traced only to Luke's mind and not to the Lord's. Judas the lawless by joining the "lawful" rulers gave the crowning proof of their lawlessness; their forces were joined against Immanuel and the little flock. But the nature of the fighting was misunderstood by the disciples, and the misunderstanding has been perpetuated by Luke in the matter of the two swords.

What, then, was the true understanding which escaped them? I believe Prof. Burkitt has hit the mark when he says: † "They are among the saddest words in the Gospels, and the mournful irony with which they are pervaded seems to me wholly alien from the kind of utterance which a Christian evangelist would invent for his Master . . . It is all a piece of ironical foreboding." But is there not in the same context another instance of

* There are some rather doubtful signs that John had these two prophecies of Zechariah in view when he wrote $18^{1\text{-}11}$: there is συνήχθη, 18^2—very strange, perhaps from Zech. 14^{14}; then the organized force ("cohort," etc.) of 18^3 may be based upon Zech. 14^{14}; the ἔπεσαν (18^6) may look back to πτῶσις, Zech. 14^{12}, but much more to Ps. 40^{14}.

† Burkitt, *The Gospel History*, etc., 140.

the same irony? It has long seemed to the present writer that no explanation but that of irony can be found for the words: "that ye may eat and drink at my table in my kingdom, and sit upon thrones judging the twelve tribes of Israel." First of all, there seems to be no basis for this saying in the history of the tribes. The period to which any such prediction might be expected to belong is that of Joshua, otherwise called Jesus of Nauê, who was, in fact, succeeded by the Judges, but in quite a different way from this saying. And no word of Jesus of Nauê seems to be applicable to such a word of Jesus of Nazareth. Secondly, the reality of the saying is hardly credible. For at one of the most impressive moments the disciples had repeated, or else commenced, the unseemly strife, which of them should be the greatest. John so far agrees with Luke that this was the occasion of that strife as to record the feet-washing, which we may almost call the sacrament of humility, as we may call the other two sacraments of purity and of love.

The Sword of Justice.

At the same time, if we allow ourselves to imagine the Christian life to be subject to analysis at all and divisible into qualities at all, we cannot stop short at the trio of humility, purity, love—we must admit that justice shall make it a quartet. Justice, the first attribute of God, cannot be absent from the Life that He prescribes to man. Now the sword is the emblem of justice.

Deut. 32⁴¹ For I will sharpen as lightning my sword, and my hand shall lay hold of judgment (κρίματος).

This text is the true origin of the Sword of Justice. Therefore when the Lord prescribed that a sword should be purchased He was carrying further the idea of the rulers of the twelve tribes who were expressly described as *judging* them (κρίνοντες [30]). The irony was all the sharper, "more cutting than any two-edged sword" (τομώτερος

THE BETRAYAL 385

ὑπὲρ πᾶσαν μάχαιραν δίστομον, as Heb. 4¹² might have said) because it came so very near to the truth of actual life. "Yea, yea, prepare ye a sword, ye rulers! ye judges! Have ye then twain? Two swords for twelve judges! It sufficeth. For is it not written—

> Isa. 32¹ A righteous king shall reign and rulers *with judgment* shall rule?"

The Irony of Anguish.

Now it is barely credible that in the same breath in which He rebuked their personal self-seeking He should promise them each a several place and throne as Judge of one of the twelve tribes of Israel. (Is this the reason why Matt. 19²⁸ has placed the saying earlier, before the final approach to Jerusalem?) On the other hand, how probable that He should have said something like it in an irony of sadness, seeing that all His teaching had been thrown away! Words are quite inadequate to convey the anguish of His soul, but there is a passage in Isaiah that may have come to His mind—

> Isa. 21¹ Oh that a whirlwind might come through the desert, from the desert coming on the land. A terrible vision and a hard is declared unto me. He that disregardeth disregardeth, he that *is lawless is lawless* . . . Now will I groan and comfort me. Wherefore my loins are filled with infirmity, and pangs take hold of me as of her that travaileth. I did wrong in that [they] did not hear: I was eager in that [they] did not see. My heart wandereth and *lawlessness* baptizeth me, my soul hath turned unto fear. Prepare *the table, eat ye, drink ye:* rise up, *ye rulers* (οἱ ἄρχοντες), and prepare ye shields . . .

There is a scornful irony, a melancholy, in this passage, and its kinship with the context of Luke 22 is obvious. (The above translation is given as the one that seems

c c

most appropriate to the occasion.) The idea of rulers may well have suggested a reference to the rulers of the twelve tribes—indeed the number of the twelve may have a relation to that of the tribes of much earlier standing than is supposed—where (Num. 1^5) Moses and Aaron make a ruler of every tribe (ἄρχοντες τῶν φυλῶν) for census purposes.

And on this question the curious may observe that some of the twelve rulers can be identified with some of the twelve apostles in name. The first of the rulers is Elizur = *my God is a rock*, which bears a remarkable resemblance to the first of the apostles, *Peter*. The last of the rulers is Ahira = *brother of evil*, a term that fits the traitor: but what is more remarkable, the Greek for this is ’Αχειρέ. Let this be the name of the father of Judas; then, prefixing to it *Ish* = *man*, we have for *Judas* himself the name ’Ισαχειριώτης, " the man belonging to Ahira," shortened to ’Ισχαριώτης. This account of the origin of the term may be added to the many already current—it is as probable as many of them. One of the rest is *Nathanael*. A fourth is Elishama = *my God will hear*. But *Simon*, for Simeon, = *hearing:* this, then, is a fourth identity. A fifth is Eliasaph = *whom God added*, which is another term for *Matthew* = Mattithiah = *gift of the Lord*. We may perhaps add the name which is second on the list—Shemiel = *friend of God*—as a fair equivalent of John = *grace*. And perhaps also Thaddeus, if (as Dalman * supposes) it = Theodas for Theodatos, *gift of God* in answer *to prayer*, representing Pagiel, *prayer of God*, i. e. *answer to prayer*. That as many as seven coincidences can be found is remarkable, for to arrive at the true names of the twelve is no easy matter apart from any prophetic parallels.

But, lastly, it is clear in any case that the sense in Luke is broken and incoherent. The strife for pre-eminence

* *The Words of Jesus*, p. 50.

THE BETRAYAL

has brought its reproach and an appeal for service. But then comes a promise of lordship, and this lordship is a reward for services done, by fidelity in His temptations. How does this cohere with the previous warning? Then follows the address to Simon, most abruptly: and how does this attach to the previous promise? For if the disciples were all to be judges of the tribes, seated on thrones, they would be already qualified, and would not need the strengthening of one who had himself turned again. And, next, immediately there follows Peter's promise, and the prediction of his denial. The present arrangement is a collection of disjointed fragments.

To resume after this long digression. We cannot say that the episode of the two swords is a case of the Lord's preparing deliberately for the fulfilment of prophecy, and we conclude that it is not in line with the preparation of the ass and of the passover. Luke thought it was, and by inserting *that which concerneth me hath an end* he marks the end, the last act, of those preparations which, as he thought, were deliberate on His part with the exception of His wonted retirement by night to Olivet which he had already mentioned.

The name Gethsemane. The Cup.

An effort of mind is required to dismiss the idea that Gethsemane was a current name at the time of the Agony. It is certain that the Hebrew of 2 Sam. knows nothing of such a place as a station of David's retreat. Why, then, should we suppose that tradition was busy with the name or even with the place? It is certain also that the Greek only presents the name in a roundabout fashion. For here it is duplicated and diverges widely from the Hebrew. 2 Sam. 15^{18} (LXX): " And they tarried at the Far House. And all his servants ($\pi\alpha\tilde{\iota}\delta\varepsilon\varsigma$) passed up beside him; and all the Hittites and all the Pelethites, and they stood *at the olive* in the wilderness: and all the people went on their way beside him, and all who attended on him and all the stalwart men and all the warriors, six hundred men, and they were beside him: and all the Cherethites and all the Pelethites and all the Gittites (Γεθθαῖοι), the six hundred men who came on their feet *to Geth* and were going their way before the king." The only way in which the name Gethsemane is constructed at all is by joining *Geth*, which stands for the Philistine city in the Hebrew, where we should translate *from Gath* instead of *to Geth*, to the Hebrew for *olive-oil* (*shemen*) five lines above. (The question how *at the olive* " came into the LXX " at all is one that cannot be discussed here.) Of the three names which obviously in the LXX refer to one and the same spot, the Far House, the Olive, the Press, the first would be the only possible term for any one to use in David's time: the other two are not likely to have been made into a name by Jesus; and they are not likely to have been so compounded till Mark. Then Matthew adopts it, but Luke and John do not. It is worth notice that Mark and Matthew interpose between His leaving the city and reaching Gethsemane the incident of *All ye shall be offended* and the prediction of the denial, which corresponds to the *Simon, Simon* . . . of Luke. But, in fact, Gethsemane must, by 2 Sam. 15, have been almost contiguous to the city wall. Luke has antedated the incident in the upper room, although it corresponds with the conversation of David with Ittai, where the words *turn thou round* . . . and *there shall thy servant be* occur. Did Luke, then, fail to apprehend the parallel between David and David's son? This view cannot be entertained. Relatively to the prototype the order preserved by Luke is generally correct, but he has taken the liberty of putting back the incident, without precisely dating it, because he wished to sharpen the contrast to *and that ye may sit upon thrones*. . . .

THE BETRAYAL

Luke is thus free from topographical difficulties, and can say merely *When he came to the place.* . . . John, as we have seen, makes the party to cross over the brook Kedron. *The place* (τόπου, τόπον) (Luke, John) bears a slight touch from Ittai's words, 2 Sam. 15²¹. The expression of David's resignation, *Let him do to me* . . ., is relatively slightly earlier in 2 Sam. 15²⁶ than in Matthew, Mark, and Luke. For the *worship* of God by David is distinctly on the ascent or at the head of Olivet. The words of the prayer, *Abba, Father*, are those of Ps. 89, as we have seen before. No more fruitful or uplifting spring of prayer can be imagined. *All things are possible unto thee* (πάντα δυνατά σοι) recalls—

Ps. 89⁹ Lord God of the powers (δυνάμεων), who is like unto thee: powerful (δυνατὸς) art thou, O Lord, and thy truth round about thee.

Let this cup pass from me refers to—

Ps. 75⁸ For there is a cup in the hand of the Lord; of strong wine full of mixture, and he poureth from this into that: but [still] the dregs thereof are not emptied out, and all the sinners of the earth shall drink.

Of this passage it seems only possible to say, whether or not we introduce the comparison of—

Isa. 51¹⁷ Awake, awake, arise, Jerusalem, thou that *shalt drink* of the hand of the Lord *the cup of his wrath:* for *the cup* of trembling (falling), the beaker of his wrath thou hast drunk up, and emptied out. . . .

that all lines of interpretation seem at length to run out into a cosmic meaning. If the king of Judah is lamenting over Jerusalem, this is not all. *He poureth from this into that.* The LXX has hit upon a marvellous and mysterious and graphic thought, of eternal suspense, eternal passion, eternal pain. Prostrate before God He represents Jerusalem which killed the prophets (Matt. 23^{37}), but Jerusalem is not the world. He had read—

Ps. 89^{11} Thou hast founded the earth and the fulness thereof.

Was the sinless to drain really the cup of wrath which was appointed for all the sinners of the earth to drink? To resign the story of the Agony, to abolish it, as John has done, would be indeed to resign one of the most powerful impressions that the world has ever felt. It has come to us not only with the true stamp but with the intentional stamp of the Master's choice, when He chose to go to Olivet, to the place which Mark and Matthew have called Gethsemane.

The Opportunity of Judas.

And the act of Judas was also an intentional fulfilment of the story of Ahithophel. "Judas also knew the place" (John 18^{2}), and therefore the time. It has commonly been supposed, rather in extenuation of his action, that he wished to force the Lord's hand, to make Him declare Himself the Christ openly, and this is a very intelligible opinion, especially in view of his gross misunderstanding, in which he was not alone, that he should sit upon a throne judging one of the twelve tribes of Israel in the approaching kingdom. But the evidence seems to show that he was also possessed of the Lord's previous application to Himself of the retirement of King David to Olivet. He was in the secret place of the interpretation of prophecy. He knew how the prophecies of Zechariah had absorbed the thought of Jesus and the disciples, and therefore how Zech. 14^{14} had pointed to himself by name: it seemed to tell him to gather together the armed strength of the Romans as for a fight (p. 382), and to promise that he should reap some great harvest of " gold and silver and raiment." He had heard " Hosanna to the son of David,

THE BETRAYAL 391

the king of Israel, that cometh in the name of the Lord." He may be called intoxicated with prophecy and with avarice, a mingled drink; he is called one "into whom Satan entered." He resolved impetuously to be the Ahithophel to the king of Israel, and to do what Ahithophel counselled. His father's name, let us suppose (p. 386), was *Aḥir'a*, originally *Aḥire'a, brother of a friend*, or *brother of a shepherd*. This very name pointed to Aḥithophel, *brother of folly*. The fact would encourage him, not discourage him, for Ahithophel's counsel had been itself good for its purpose, had it only been followed. Coarse in phrase and confident in tone, this counsel would have been successful. If tried now, it would be successful. The *elders of Israel* were marked out as the negotiating party. The arrest should be made *by night*, when He was weary; the disciples *would flee* and He would be captured *quite alone*, by the prearranged *signal of a kiss;* the disciples would be left *in peace*. The exact terms of his action were prescribed for him in 2 Sam. 17, save that twelve thousand men were neither available nor necessary. The design was performed within a day or two of its conception.

The question may here be asked, What relation Ps. 41^{10} bears to 2 Sam. 17 : for if Ahithophel is the false friend of that psalm and is fulfilled in Judas, and if 2 Sam. 17 is also fulfilled in him, does it not appear as if these two Old Testament passages combined to produce the Judas of the Gospels, who had otherwise no existence ? In other words, is it credible that one historical person can fulfil at the same time and in the same particulars two ancient independent prophecies ? The answer to this question is that the two prophecies are not independent. The psalm is definitely called " For the end : Psalm of David " (εἰς τὸ τέλος · ψαλμὸς τῷ Δαυείδ). Without treating this psalm, the superscription of which resembles many others, as claiming David's composition, we know that the title was read by the Lord as part of the psalm. It is therefore certain that as He expected *the end* (Luke 22[37]) He would especially study and pray this group of psalms. And Judas would also study them in his fashion. He would read Ps. 41[8] thus, regardless of the punctuation of the line before it—

Ps. 41[8] Shall he that sleepeth not be made to awake?

In other words, Might not the sleeping title of Messiah be awakened by Judas's own action? Out of this he would make an excuse to force a declaration of the Christ. That Judas was—

> The *man of my peace* [my familiar friend] in whom I trusted, who *eateth my loaves* [at the Last Supper], hath made great scorn of me—

he realized, but cared not, in the pursuit of his vast and far-reaching design. But this expression, *the man of my peace*, is a proof, in connection with the whole tenour of the psalm, that it was composed in poetical illustration of 2 Sam. 15–18 and its touching and beautiful story of David's sorrow. Another instance of a psalm, also entitled *For the end—a psalm of David*, reproducing the thought of 2 Sam. 15[26], is—

> Ps. 40[8 f] Then said I, Lo, I have come—in the volume of the book it is written of me—*to do thy will*, my God, I have chosen ($\dot{\epsilon}\beta o\nu\lambda\eta\theta\eta\nu$).

I suggest that while *the volume of the book* is a sufficiently comprehensive expression to include other passages, such as Deuteronomy and Isaiah, one meaning, and indeed the first and original meaning, of it is 2 Sam. 15. Where else in the Old Testament can be found this willing *delight* in doing God's will? The answer usually made to this question is, Nowhere, but the psalm is idealizing Deuteronomy. This may be so, but the concrete, if we can find it, is the true basis of ideals, and may

THE BETRAYAL

it not be that 2 Samuel is *the book*, for it contains the concrete example of David ? The remarkable fact is the presence of *delight* in 2 Sam. 15^{26}: "If the Lord say I have no delight in thee," and as the key-word in Ps. 40^6: "Sacrifice and offering thou *hast no delight* in," and ^{8}, "*I delight* to do Thy will." Thus Ps. 40^8 has been the means by which 2 Sam. 15^{21} has come into the Gospels. Again, one chief reason for assigning Deuteronomy as *the book* is that in the captivity sacrifices were disused. But here again the time of David's exile equally meets the case, and even better; he was by exile cut off from the sacrifices. The date of the composition of the psalm is altogether less important than the theme of it. That many of the psalms are poetic meditations on lessons of the Pentateuch has been demonstrated.* The same might be shown in regard to the Davidic narratives.

Judas deliberately fulfils Scripture.

There is therefore but one scripture that Judas intentionally set himself to fulfil, that of 2 Sam. That he used the LXX for this purpose and not the Hebrew is quite clear from the fact that the LXX alone has the portion which he fulfilled, *even as a bride turneth to her husband*, and he took it in a different way from the LXX, where it is not a sign but merely a simile *as easily as*. The title (Matt. 26^{50}, ἑταῖρε ἐφ' ὃ πάρει) *Friend* . . . is not unsuited to Judas in the capacity of Ahithophel, though not applied to him in LXX; the title *Friend* is applied by Absalom to Hushai. But the very idea of the traitor kissing the Lord is so repugnant to John that he will not have it, and makes it impossible. Luke before him had felt some hesitation in permitting the actual kiss. He seems to have had before him—

Ps. 38^{10f} My heart is troubled, my strength faileth me :

* By Dr. Büchler and by Dr. King, *The Psalms*, etc., see Part III. Introduction.

and the light of my eyes is no longer with me. *My friends* and my neighbours *draw near* against me (ἐξ ἐναντίας μου ἤγγισαν) and stand, and they that were nearest me stand *afar off*" (μακρόθεν).

Therefore Luke has made "Judas *draw near* to Jesus to kiss him. . . . But the disciples, seeing what would follow, said, Lord, shall we smite with the sword?" Luke does not say that the kiss took place. He also presently says that Peter, as though he represented Ittai, *nearest to the Lord* (see p. 352 n.), followed *afar off* (μακρόθεν), as if from this psalm. So Mark and Matthew. But John disapproved of this, and based his narrative on other psalms.

Ps. 27[2] When evil-doers drew near against me to eat up my flesh, they stumbled *and fell*. Even if an *encampment* should fight against me, yet will not my heart be afraid.

Encampment (παρεμβολή) is so often used for the *castle*, *Turris Antonia* (Acts 21 ff), that it could not fail to suggest the garrison of it.

Ps. 91[5] Thou shalt not be afraid for a terror *by night*, for an arrow that flieth by day, for a *deed that walketh in darkness*, for destruction and devilry at midday. *A thousand* shall fall beside thee, and ten thousand at thy right hand, but *he shall not come nigh* thee.

Hence John, after emphasizing the deed of darkness in the simple and telling words *And it was night, by night* (13[30]), has brought the Roman cohort of six hundred men, besides others, to make the arrest; and "Judas *stood with them*"; but before any kiss could be given "they went back *and fell* to the ground." John particularly mentions the "chief captain," or *chiliarch*, commanding *a thousand men*, as present. Having declined the phrase of Psalm 38, John declines to say that Peter followed *afar off :* but he *followed.* Where was the King's friend now (see p. 241), the steward on whose shoulder the key of David had been laid, the minister whose place was by the King's side ? He was to learn, as he had not yet learned, what following meant.

CHAPTER XIII

WHAT, THEN, DID PAPIAS WRITE?

IN * the course of the great controversy thirty-five years ago between Dr. Lightfoot and the author of *Supernatural Religion*, the work of Papias of Hierapolis in five books, entitled, *Expositions of Oracles of the Lord* (λογίων κυριακῶν ἐξηγήσεις) was a subject of discussion, partly as to the nature of its contents, of which only a few meagre fragments survive, but chiefly as to the value of its evidence for the existence of our evangelical narratives. We have now to examine into the exact meaning of the title of this work in the light of the history of the terms involved, and in the light of the contemporary apostolic fathers, as well as of the fragments themselves.

Title of the Work of Papias.

It was taken for granted by the two controversial champions that Papias's title was fairly translated by *Expositions of Oracles of the Lord, Explanations* † *of Dominical Oracles, Explanation of Sayings of Jesus that were oracular*, whether to include acts along with sayings, as Lightfoot contended, or not. Obviously the principal question in connection with the title is the meaning of λόγια, and the next to it is the meaning of κυριακά. The

---

* This was written before I had seen a most convincing work on this subject, *The Oracles ascribed to Matthew by Papias of Hierapolis*, 1894 (anonymous), pp. 274. I leave this chapter, however, just as it was written, while recommending the above "Contribution to the criticism of the New Testament." It is strange that it has escaped the notice of nearly all readers.

† Dr. Abbott is probably right in saying *Exposition*, not *Explanation* (*Enc. Bib.*, " Gospels," col. 1810).

WHAT, THEN, DID PAPIAS WRITE? 397

object of this chapter is to show that another meaning is alone able to satisfy the conditions.

To deal first with κυριακά. The meaning is not clear if we translate it *of the Lord, dominica,* for it might then mean *of God,* and there are several passages which this translation would never suit. Rev. 1¹⁰, " I was in spirit on God's day " would not serve, whether the meaning were the seventh or the first day of the week : it is neither. The meaning is, " I was (*i. e.* had become) in spirit (*i. e.* prophetically by means of the ecstatic state) on the Messianic Day," the Judgment Day. The only possible meaning of the adjective is that of κύριος χριστός as about to judge the world in righteousness : it is eschatological or nothing. Again, 1 Cor. 11²⁰, " This is not to eat the Lord's supper." Certainly here we could not substitute " God's supper." But neither could we adequately translate " Christ's supper " : it is the Messianic supper in the same sense of the word as Rev. 1¹⁰; as St. Paul proceeds to say, " As often as ye eat this bread and drink this cup, ye proclaim the death of the Lord *until he come.*" This adjective κυριακός is not used except in the sense of the first or second coming of Christ, until we pass beyond the New Testament scriptures, and even then, when it begins to be applied to the first day of the week, it is at first applied in connection with the same view κατὰ κυριακὴν ζῶντες ἐν ᾗ καὶ ἡ ζωὴ ἡμῶν ἀνέτειλεν, " The Lord's day on which dawned the Dayspring of our life " (Ign. *Mag.* 9). Afterwards this view naturally wore off. But as late as Clem. Al. (*Strom.* viii. 1, 1) the scriptures of the Lord (αἱ κυρ. γραφαί) = *testimonies of the Lord* (τὰ μαρτύρια κυρίου).

This Messianic meaning of κυριακά, therefore, is so far clear that when the word is applied to Logia we expect to be guided towards something of a Messianic meaning for it, towards the Messianic side of its meaning. After a prolonged observation of the use of the Old Testament in the New, one comes to the persuasion that the Old

Testament texts quoted are used without any regard to the context from which they are taken, and with a sole regard to the purpose which they are intended to serve, that of proving that Jesus is the Christ, and the necessary inferences from that conclusion. It would not be too much to say that the final cause of the Old Testament was to be Messianic, to provide Christian proofs, to be an armoury of Christian weapons. But now all these weapons, these proof-texts, are words of a certain kind and purpose, sought out for it and discovered, and stored up for future use. That is to say they are just Logia, *precious words*, oracles, utterances, extracted from the treasury of God.

In the Greek Bible the word λόγιον is a favourite with the translator of the 119th Psalm. He uses it eighteen times for the *precious word* of God (five of the eighteen times it is in the plural). In the remaining places it bears just the same meaning, even when the " precious word of the Lord is full of wrath " (Isa. 30^{27}). (See above, p. 244.) But for a translation we must have one word for one word, and " oracle " is the best that we can use; understanding it to be the spoken oracle, not the oracular authority which speaks it.

" The Oracles " in the New Testament.

When we come to the New Testament we find the same consistent usage in the four places—only four—where it occurs. St. Stephen (Acts 7^{38}) says, " Moses received living *oracles* to give unto you," and surely the Decalogue, to be the foundation of the sermon on the Mount, was a thing of precious words. And these were the oracles above all others that St. Paul meant when he said (Rom. 3^2) that the first advantage of the Jews over the Gentiles was " that they were entrusted with *the oracles* of God "—first in time, and first in importance. He also is distinctly thinking of Sinai; for he immediately proceeds, "What if some did disbelieve?" We then come to Heb. 5^{12}, where the Hebrews "have need for one to teach them what are the elements of the beginning of *the oracles* of God." Here we begin to have the real New Testament sense of the word, for in the two last passages St. Stephen and St. Paul are both speaking of early Old Testament times when the oracles were only in the hands of the children of Israel. But here they are to be in Christian hands, and what for? In order to be used in the manner stated above, for the more confirmation of the faith, by investigation of select passages bearing on the Christ that was to come and had now come. The Hebrews were mere infants, in need of milk instead of solid food. He urges them to pass on to full growth, yet without anticipating the course of nature. The passage is one of great importance, and brings out the exact meaning of *Logia* very clearly.

For immediately afterwards we have a repetition in other words of the same idea. He says, (6^1) "Leaving the argument of the origin of the Messiah, let us move on unto full growth." "The beginning of the Messiah" can be no other than "the elements (or rudiments) of the beginning of *the oracles* of God," or, the alphabet of the oracles of God. Now, although even the alphabet has a beginning, the usual meaning of *alphabet* is *beginning*, and therefore we are to equate the origin (of the Messiah) with the alphabet (of the oracles of God). It follows that the oracles of God are oracles of the Messiah—that is to say, they are oracles delivered by God concerning the Messiah, discovered by man rightly in the scriptures of the Old Testament. What he says, then, amounts to this: "I have now sketched for you the outline of Messianic teaching in the Old Testament on the person of the Son in relation to angels, of Jesus in relation to Moses, and have begun to deal with His priesthood in relation to Melchizedek. But on this I have much to say and what is hard *to interpret*. I have been dealing with *Logia* throughout, but I am conscious of taxing your dulness; you have in truth never been drilled in the alphabet of *Logia*, in the simplest rules for taking and finding passages of the Old Testament which bear upon Jesus as the Christ. However, I must take you on with me. I must leave the rudimentary *Logia*, assuming your knowledge of them, as I assume your knowledge of the four duties of repentance from dead works and faith in God and baptisms (compared with baptism) and confirmation, and of the two great doctrines of resurrection and judgment. (Διδαχῆς has got shifted from its proper line, where it should be after νεκρῶν.) And I must take you to some more advanced *Logia*." He has given them some thirteen *Logia* and is going to give as many more. The present passage forms a break in the argument which serves at once as a space for rest and for solemn exhortation. The apology for *his* abstruseness takes the quaint form of an apology for *their* childish dulness.

The last New Testament passage is 1 Peter 4^{11}: "If any man speak, let him speak as speaking oracles of God." For "man" we are justified here in saying "prophet," for he has just before said, "Each as he received a gift"; but the gift may be of substance, in which case they are to minister it to one another as good stewards of the manifold grace of God—and equally so if it be of spirit, and then if the gift is of spirit, a prophet is to speak as conscious that he speaks *oracles* of God. Why does the Revised Version make this verse cloudy and difficult? Why does it drag in "speaking *as it were* oracles of God? This is very unnecessary and harmful. The prophet did speak oracles of God. That was his duty and privilege. To say *as it were* implies that he did not speak oracles of God, but something else requiring no less solemnity and earnestness.

The prophet spoke according to the rules clearly set

WHAT, THEN, DID PAPIAS WRITE? 401

forth by St. Paul in 1 Cor. 14$^{23\text{-}33}$. He spoke *Logia* in combination with other *Logia* or with recent events, His " revelations " were similar in kind, in *genus* but not in *species*, to the Revelation of St. John the Divine.*
Here it need only be said that in a passage of any length in the New Testament dealing with the work of the Christian prophets we are likely to find something said concerning *interpretation* or *discrimination*, and accordingly in 1 Cor. 14$^{27\text{ f}}$ we have the order " let one (only) be interpreter (διερμηνευέτω means as *between the two* speakers with tongues, or at the most three who speak in turn), and if there be no interpreter, the person is to be silent in church, speaking only to himself and to God. And as to prophets, let two or three (only) be speaking (in turn), and let the other (prophets) *discriminate*." The *Logia* required this discrimination, a disentanglement of various trains of thought being very necessary when all contexts were apt to be disregarded and prophecies from different authors combined together.†

That we have no definite declaration by authority of what a *Logion* was is not surprising, considering that it was taken for granted in apostolic times that every reader knew: and it so happens that only four times is the word mentioned in the New Testament. But the case of Heb. 5^{12} makes it abundantly clear. Any Messianic passage of the Old Testament was a *Logion*, and, further, any passage might become a Messianic passage if duly sub-

---

* See *The Christian Prophets*, Ch. III.
† It may be worth while to mention here that the absurd term κυβερνήσεις (1 Cor. 12^{28}) translated " governments "—which has no sort of support in the context or anywhere else—is probably nothing more than a miswriting of ἑρμηνεύσεις. But some copyist thought he would explain it, and so put in ἀντιλήμψεις which now stands before it. Strike out ἀντιλήμψεις, κυβερνήσεις, and read ἑρμηνεύσεις, and then verse 28 is simply read over again interrogatively in 29 and 30. The case is then one that proves itself. Then the χαρίσματα are altogether set in sharpest contrast with the ὁδὸς of 13^1; *the Gifts* are all inferior to *the Method* of love.

D D

mitted by a prophet speaking in ecstasy according to rule and submitting his revelation to the verdict of the umpires who were also prophets, and receiving their sanction. Gradually this rule was relaxed. It is not hazardous to say that the texts of the Old Testament in St. Peter's speeches, Acts 1-4, were among the earliest *Logia;* likewise Mark 1^2, 11^9 and 12^{10}. These would be the rudiments, the alphabet of *Logia*. But they were the alphabet of a copious language. For it has been demonstrated above, for instance, that not merely several expressions, but substantially every word except "Mary" and except the dreams in the story of the Magi, is from the Old Testament in Greek. But this story would certainly be an example of most advanced study of oracles and it could not have been composed till after the disparagement of dreams had ceased, and after the time when every oracle had to be submitted by a prophet in esctasy to the discrimination of the other prophets.

"*The Oracles*" *in the Apostolic Fathers and in Philo.*

We now pass to the passages where the term is used in the Apostolic fathers, and for this purpose Lightfoot's *Essays on Supernatural Religion,* Ch. V. should be consulted. Let us take Clem. R. 53. He says, "Ye know and know well the holy scriptures, beloved, and ye have dived into (ἐγκεκύφατε, stooped to look in) the oracles of God; we write these things, therefore, to put you in remembrance." Lightfoot is urging that *Logia* is a synonym for the scriptures, and says that Clement proceeds to quote Deut. $9^{12\,f}$ and Exod. 32^7, "of which the point is not any divine precept or prediction, but *the example of Moses.*" Lightfoot is traversing the statement in *Supernatural Religion,* that "*the oracles* was not then at all applied to doings as well as sayings," and he proves on the contrary that "the oracles" can be found in historical as well as prophetical passages of the Old Testament. But that is not the precise meaning of "the oracles." The scriptures are not oracles until they are consulted and quoted as need arises. The scriptures are holy, but are not all equally "precious" until the need arises: then, and just so far, they are "oracles." "Oracles" is a relative term in regard to the person consulting the oracle and receiving what he finds them to give. Oracles need interpretation, as we saw in Heb. 5^{11}. We may be permitted to say that "oracles" is subjective, and "scriptures" objective—with the due apology for those much-abused expressions.

Further consideration of all the passages where "oracles" are mentioned will show how entirely this distinction is borne out. In the above passage Clement means, "Let me underline for your guidance the example of Moses." The writer of Hebrews has said the same: he has underlined thirteen texts. Even the maker of a genealogy of Christ had underlined names of obscure persons in Ruth and Chronicles. The scriptures become *oracles* when they are found to exhibit traces of the great purpose of God to those who seek it. In quoting Philo* perhaps Lightfoot has not done full justice to this subjectivity. Philo is talking of the supreme grandeur of Moses, and he says that from his ancestor Levi's birth he was "joined to the Lord" alone: in return for which consistent worship God gives Himself as his inheritance. "My argument," says Philo, "is confirmed by an *oracle* in which it is said—

Deut. 10^9 The Lord himself is his inheritance according as the Lord thy God promised him."

This is an instance of the first of Philo's three classes of oracles, those which proceed "from the very face of

* *De conf. quær.*, 24 (p. 538).

God* through the divine prophet as interpreter; the second class being of answers after inquiry; the third class proceeding from the face of Moses possessed by inspiration. The unsought promise of God making for the good of men, as Philo says, is surely a very precious passage of scripture, especially for those who benefit directly by it. The other text concerning the mark on Cain is thus introduced : "The death of the fratricide is nowhere found in the law; indeed, there is an *oracle* uttered upon him thus—

> The Lord set a mark upon Cain, lest any one finding him should kill him.

Why? I suppose because the impiety is a thing without an end." He then quotes the *Odyssey* and the *Theætetus* in further illustration of the purpose of God. Here the *oracle* on Cain is the correlative to the mark on Cain.

A few more occurrences of the term *oracles* require to be noticed in the Apostolic fathers and Irenæus.

Clement (Cor. 19), after quoting Ps. 51 to show how David obtained a good report, says that his and others' humility " has through obedience made better not only us but also the generations before us, even them that *received His oracles in fear and truth.*" This emphasizes the attitude of mind, the conscious effort on the part of the recipients who resolved to accept wholly (καταδεξαμένους) the fulfilments of prophecy on which the structure of the Church was raised. No such conscious effort could be required to accept scriptures of the law and the prophets on which their minds had been nurtured.

Polycarp, writing to the Philippians (7), says, "And whosoever confesseth not the testimony of the cross is of the devil: and whosoever perverteth *the oracles of the Lord* to his own lusts, and says that there is neither

---

* Philo, *Vit. Mos.*, 3[23], p. 163. *De profugis*, 11, p. 555.

resurrection nor judgment, he is the firstborn of Satan."
On this Lightfoot strangely observes (p. 174), " How much he included under this expression we cannot say, but it must be observed that he does not write τὰ κυριακὰ λόγια, *the dominical oracles,* or τὰ λόγια, *the oracles* simply—the two expressions which occur in Papias—but τὰ λόγια τοῦ Κυρίου, *the oracles of the Lord,* which form of words would more directly suggest the Lord as the speaker." This is going too far, for it maintains that *the oracles of the Lord* is more likely to be a subjective genitive, meaning " oracles spoken by the Lord," than an objective genitive, " the oracles spoken concerning the Lord." This cannot be maintained. It seems as if Lightfoot had not considered this point of view—that possibly Logia did not mean *words of Christ* (with or without *dealings*) or anything like it, but scripture passages referring to the Christ and discovered in the Old Testament. He does indeed once say *oracles of* (or, *relating to*) *the Lord :* but there he leaves the latter alternative meaning, which alone is right. And yet all along Lightfoot has been showing (p. 173) that the oracles were *the scriptures of the Old Testament* and nothing less or more. Why, then, just when he comes to Polycarp, A.D. 150, does he forget this and think only of the *scriptures of the New Testament?* What if Polycarp was still, as a disciple of John, sufficiently in full touch with the oracles of the Old Testament to be thinking only of them? What if he meant Jesus by the Lord, and when he said *the oracles of the Lord* meant the Old Testament passages concerning the Lord Messiah ? If he did so, then all would be perfectly clear. There were always some, like the mockers of 2 Pet. 3^3, whether Gnostics or not, who perverted the oracles. For instance, here is a passage taken at random to exemplify *the perversion of the oracles of the Lord.* Isa. 41^8, 43^{1f} are acknowledged to be Messianic passages; they must belong to the oracles of the Lord. But this is the kind of stuff that the Naassene

heresy (of Jewish origin, otherwise called Ophite, worshipping the serpent) makes out of them, according to Hippolytus (Hær. 5³), "*When thou passest through rivers* means the moist substance of generation, and *fire* means the impulsive principle; *thou art mine, fear not.*" Again, in Ps. 24, "*Who is this king of glory?* A worm, and not a man, an outcast of the people: himself is the king of glory and powerful in war. And by war he means the war that is in the body, because its frame has been made out of hostile elements, Remembering (Job 40²⁷) *the war that is in thy body.*"

"Such, then, is their system" — says Irenæus of another school, the Valentinians — "one that neither prophets announced, nor the Lord taught, nor apostles delivered, but of which they boast they have a complete knowledge beyond all others." Exactly the same is his meaning in regard to perversion (I. 8¹): "They (the Gnostics) transpose and transform, and by making one thing out of another they lead many astray by their ill-constructed fancy of *the oracles of the Lord* as they are made to suit the case." ... "They want to make *the oracles of God* suit their own fables." On the other hand, if the oracles were the sayings (and doings) of Jesus it is not easy to see how the perversion of them, so repeatedly mentioned, would ever have taken place. The complaint of Polycarp is that the oracles were *perverted to their own lusts*, as few sayings (or doings) of Jesus could possibly be *perverted*. The denial, which Polycarp proceeds forthwith to mention, is a different matter from perversion, and while denial of the resurrection and the judgment could be denial of some of those sayings (and doings), it could equally well, and indeed far more consistently, mean the oracles concerning the Lord which were found in the Old Testament.

The Apostolic Fathers in their regard for the Old Testament.

Before, however, we go to Papias himself let us briefly notice the use of scripture by Clement and Barnabas. Clement's Epistle to the Corinthians consists of about 1,160 lines, of which no less than 346 are quotations with or without notes of quotation (λέγει γὰρ or the like) introducing them: not far short of one-third of the whole is quotation. This enumeration does not take account of many isolated expressions which would reduce the proportion very nearly to half-and-half. But, what is even more remarkable, of the passages quoted the proportion of the New Testament verses to those of the Old Testament and Apocrypha is as seventeen to two hundred and forty-five. Now the number of pages of the Old Testament to the New Testament is three and a half to one, while these quotations show a proportion of the Old Testament to the New Testament of nearly fourteen to one. In the case of the Epistle of Barnabas the disproportion is no less remarkable: one-fourth of the whole contents is quoted matter. But of the quoted matter no less than one hundred and fifty-seven verses are from the Old Testament against eleven from the New Testament, apart from unverified quotations: as fourteen to one.

There is only one explanation of this disproportion as we think it, true proportion as they thought it: the Old Testament was more important to them than the New, which appeared to them in the light of a commentary on the Old, a fulfilment of it, but in such a way that what was fulfilled was *at that time* more important than what fulfilled it, in point of literature or scriptural value at least. Justin Martyr would not have been content to speak of the Gospels as "memoirs" if he had attributed to them the relative importance which they commanded two centuries later, and fourteen centuries later.

The importance of this fact is enormous when we come to consider the meaning of Papias's title, which we may assume to correspond fairly with the contents of his work. The two works of which we have analyzed the quotations belong to the same date as Papias, and both are epistles, where we expect or are entitled to expect more instruction and exhortation than quotation. But if epistles are crowded with quotation from the Old Testament, what is *an explanation of scriptures* (not so say *oracles*) to be expected to contain? Lightfoot says, " if Papias entitled his work " thus, " there is nothing to show that he did not include narrative portions of the Gospels, as well as discourses; though from the nature of the case the latter would occupy the chief place." This statement involves two great assumptions, first, that *oracles* in *Papias's* title of contents is used in the more comprehensive sense, which tended to become, as we know, in the course of years A.D. more and more comprehensive till it meant nothing more or less than scriptures; secondly, that it must mean words spoken *by* the Lord Jesus (and probably deeds done by Him) instead of meaning words written by the prophets of the Old Testament *concerning* the Lord Christ which were duly fulfilled by the Lord Jesus, so that the whole work in five books amounted to a proof from the prophetic side that Jesus was the Christ, intended to serve as a *vade-mecum* for devotional or meditative or controversial purposes. It would seem that Lightfoot had never thought of this point of view at all. And yet, considering how much of the Gospels and Acts is directed to the Argument from Prophecy, it is antecedently probable that some such work would at the time be in existence.

The Extant Contents of Papias.

Let us therefore interrogate Papias if we can, and let us assume Lightfoot's dates for him: born A.D. 60–70. We are not at all concerned to show that the work did not

WHAT, THEN, DID PAPIAS WRITE? 409

contain acts of Jesus. Upon the theory now propounded it did. In fact, in proportion to the originality of Jesus, if the term may be allowed, "the authority with which He taught," the sayings of Jesus were drawn less from the Old Testament than any man's sayings. They were His own. The other prophets, whether of the Old Testament or the New Testament, were borrowers of Isaiah, verbally speaking, far more than He was. The theory now propounded is that Papias dealt with fulfilments, and from the nature of the case these were to be found far more in His acts and sufferings than in His sayings. But in fact, since Lightfoot has said so much concerning His sayings, as if that were the meaning of *oracles*, our path henceforward is rather divergent from his, and it essays a positive result which, should it be established, would throw new light upon the earliest form of the Christian faith. We may take the fragments of Papias in the order in which they are given in Lightfoot's volume, *The Apostolic Fathers*, and make observations on each in succession.

(I, II) Papias was said by Eusebius to be known to be a hearer of John the Divine and Apostle. Eusebius "charges Irenæus with confusion" on this point (Eus., H. E. iii. 39; Iren. v. 33, 4) [Lightfoot, *Ign.* i. 426]. This is the author of the Apocalypse. Like master, like pupil. There is no writer of the New Testament who is half so full of the spirit and letter of the Old Testament as he is. The Apocalypse contains five hundred and eighteen quotations from the Old Testament in twenty-two chapters, on a moderate estimate by Westcott and Hort's list! The "hearing," if it means discipleship, of such an author was no sort of preparation for a collection of the sayings and doings of Jesus, which are hardly referred to or recognized in Revelation. The whole bent of his mind was towards the imagery and phraseology of the Old Testament.

(III, 1, 2) The term ἀρχαῖος ἀνήρ, applied to Papias,

means " an old-fashioned man," just as Mnason was "an old-fashioned disciple " in the opinion of Luke (Acts 21[16]). Here we have the opinion of Irenæus. As Luke looked back from after A.D. 70 upon the ultra-Jewish Christianity of fifteen years before, when a Christian was at the same time a sincere Jew, and maintained the position described in Acts 2[41-47], etc., so Irenæus looked back upon Papias who found his great interest in the Old Testament scriptures fulfilled in Christ and only a lesser interest in details of His life apart from such fulfilments. And this accounts too for the *expositions* or *explanations* in the title (unless we suppose, what is far the simplest meaning, that *expositions* are the texts as set forth). There are numerous quotations of the Old Testament that, as applied to Jesus, require explanations, and many such explanations occur in Acts (2[29, 34], 4[25], 7[37, 49], 8[31 f]). But what is most remarkable about our Gospels is generally the absence of explanations, so that we are surprised to find, *e.g.*, the parable of the Sower followed by an explanation. Irenæus (A.D. 177) wrote a long generation after Papias, very likely two generations, and by that time the canon of the New Testament had become far more settled, and the disproportionate value of the Old Testament (as we think it) was reduced. Irenæus saw the New Testament large while Papias had seen it small, in proportion to the Old Testament.

The next point to notice is that the work, according to Papias's own statement, consisted of at least two parts: " the interpretations " ($\dot{\epsilon}\rho\mu\eta\nu\epsilon\acute{\iota}\alpha\iota\varsigma$), and " all that he had learnt carefully and remembered carefully in time past from the elders," which he arranged alongside of the former ($\sigma\nu\gamma\kappa\alpha\tau\alpha\tau\acute{\alpha}\xi\alpha\iota$). It must be allowed that when Lightfoot translates the last word " to give a place " for you, he hardly does justice to the word. There is *arrangement* in $\tau\acute{\alpha}\xi\alpha\iota$, there is *orderly* arrangement in $\kappa\alpha\tau\alpha\tau\acute{\alpha}\xi\alpha\iota$, and there is this *alongside* of something else in $\sigma\nu\gamma\kappa\alpha\tau\alpha\tau\acute{\alpha}\xi\alpha\iota$.

How can justice be done to the expression with less ? It seems to imply nothing less than an arrangement in columns, probably three columns : the texts, the interpretations, the comments of the elders (if any). But suppose Lightfoot's view to be right, the columns would still be three : the sayings and acts of Jesus, the interpretations, the comments of the elders (if any). If the first column consisted of our Gospels, as Lightfoot supposes, this would make a somewhat formidable volume, not so much because of the third column as because of the second. For the idea of the sayings and acts of Jesus being accompanied by *interpretations* is even more serious than that of *explanations*. However, the two terms, unless we have already disposed of *explanations*, must surely be synonymous, or else—worse still—we should have a Tetrapla, a work in four columns ! And five books of it ! And all written by a very narrow-minded man (says Eusebius), though bishop of the important city of Hierapolis in Phrygia. If, however, the text was that of the prophecies fulfilled, it would be most natural that it should be attended by *interpretation* (see pp. 83, 102, 293, etc. above) in the second column, and by the comments of the elders in a third.

When Papias said concerning Matthew that " he composed the oracles in the Hebrew language, and each (reader) *interpreted* them as he was able," his meaning was the same that is here given. Besides the translation of the oracles into Greek which many Greek readers would require, the interpretation would be necessary to all readers, that is to say, the application of the Old Testament passage to its environment or event in the life of Christ. It is plain that Papias's work was an improved edition of " Matthew's," adapted in an *exposition* (the texts) for Greek scholars by a very scholarly Greek writer, as Jerome has remarked, and accompanied by *interpretations* which were more or less authoritative in conse=

quence of Papias's diligent inquiries of all who came to him from the headquarters of " the Truth," and also by "*illustrative traditions.*" *

(III, 3, 4) Papias says that he did not care for " those who related *the foreign commandments.*" This is a strange expression, but it derives some light from its correlative expression, " but those which have been given from the Lord to *the faith.*" Now it so happens that we have this very combination, of "*the commandments of God* and *the faith* of Jesus," in Rev. 14^{12}, to "guard which is the endurance of the saints." Does not this point to the idea that St. John the Divine held the two to be on the same level, and to be inseparable? And so they were then. The (τὰς) "foreign commandments" may be Jewish ordinances of circumcision and lustration; and the contrary includes those authoritative interpretations of the Old Testament passages which set all these aside as the Lord did in Mark 7^{19}, "making all meats clean." When Papias was born the Jewish law was not a foreign commandment, but when he wrote it had become so, and this was very largely due to the interpretation of prophecy in accordance with the teaching of Jesus and the belief in Him.

The expression is translated by the author of *The Oracles of Papias* as " the commandments of another man," but it does not appear to be explained further, and who is supposed to be meant is not stated. If Moses is meant, the sense will be as in the text above. If " any other man than Jesus " is meant, we should expect not ἀλλοτρίας but τῶν ἄλλων. Lightfoot translates " foreign commandments," omitting " the," and gives no explanation, so far as I can find. Valois's (in Routh) " nova quædam et inusitata præcepta " seems quite wrong. The expression seems rather to have escaped notice.

It was quite fatal to the Church to allow the Jewish scriptures to occupy the preponderating place which they

* *Enc. Bib.*, "Gospels," Abbott, col. 1814.

WHAT, THEN, DID PAPIAS WRITE? 413

occupied for the readers of Clement and Barnabas, unless at the same time the Christian readers were supplied with weapons to controvert the Jews, who defended their law in and by those very scriptures. To suppose that the Christian life and experience in the year A.D. 100 with the Greek Bible in its hand was strong enough to convert the synagogue into the Church without careful and considered interpretation would be to take a sanguine view of the difficulties. To suppose that it could do so with the Hebrew Bible instead of the Greek is to assume an utter impossibility. But given, first of all, the Greek Bible, and given, next, those lines of interpretation with which the modern mind is partly familiar, the task, so far as theory went, was capable of achievement and, as we know, was abundantly achieved. I say partly, because a careful search will disclose beneath every page of Acts the Old Testament passages—the oracles—which were actuating the minds of the characters and of the writer to act and to say and to write as we see them doing. For instance, we find that St. Peter, meditating on the supersession of circumcision by baptism, had his trance at Joppa; we find that Philip, meditating on the conversion of Egypt, received in ecstasy the angel's message to go to "the desert." In either case the trance was accompanied by a train of reasoning which some patience will be required to discover underlying the materials of the narrative. It will be found that the reasoning follows a line of oracles in every case, for there was nothing else to follow (see pp. 202, 232 n.)

Translation of some of Papias's Expressions.

One rubs his eyes at reading in Lightfoot's Translation of Papias (*The Apostolic Fathers*, p. 528, and *Essays*, p. 143) the following: " I did not take pleasure in those who have so very much to say, but in those who teach the truth, nor in those who relate foreign commandments, but in those [who record] such as were given from the Lord to the

Faith, and are derived from the Truth itself." (Οὐ γὰρ τοῖς τὰς τὰ πολλὰ λέγουσιν ἔχαιρον ὥσπερ οἱ πολλοί, ἀλλὰ τοῖς τἀληθῆ διδάσκουσιν, οὐδὲ τοῖς τὰς ἀλλοτρίας ἐντολὰς μνημονεύουσιν, ἀλλὰ τοῖς τὰς παρὰ τοῦ Κυρίου τῇ πίστει δεδομένας καὶ ἀπ' αὐτῆς παραγιγνομένας [-νοις] τῆς ἀληθείας.) The last six words are ambiguous. Any English reader who did not refer to the Greek would suppose that Lightfoot meant that the commandments given from the Lord were derived from the Truth. But what Papias says is quite different. He says *those who relate them are derived*—to use Lightfoot's expressions—from the truth itself. But then, again, to say that *persons are derived* from any but their own ancestors is an awkward expression. But again—most important—that is not the meaning of παραγίνεσθαι, which invariably means *arrive*, come *to the side of*, and never once in the New Testament, where it occurs thirty-seven times, does it mean *come from the side of*, or *be derived from*. It is to be feared that the English reader is not the only person who has gone astray here. Translate, "and who came to me straight from the Truth itself,"—reading with Gebhardt, Harnack and Zahn παραγινομένοις. If, however, we retain παραγινομένας, we translate "and come to me from the Truth itself." Either the reporters or the reports "come to me," says Papias, or "used to come."

And this following of the parallels of the oracles (παρακολουθεῖν, Luke 1[3]: see p. 82 above) is exactly in accordance with what Papias says: "For I did not think that I could profit so much from *the* (*texts*) *out of the books* (τὰ ἐκ τῶν βιβλίων) as from the (comments upon them) by a living and abiding voice." Once more, a respectful protest must be raised against the omission of *the* by Lightfoot before *books*. To make Papias disparage books generally is hardly fair. Such a generalization is only a translator's confession of ignorance, in a case where a slight effort of imagination would have pointed him the way to knowledge. It is only fair to allow Papias, who is throughout maintaining his carefulness in sifting and comparing the statements of eyewitnesses and earwitnesses, to have some consciousness of responsibility; but then in the same breath to make him disparage " the contents of books " is nothing less than a contradiction. In one place, however, Lightfoot does partly explain himself by a paraphrase, " the capricious interpretations which Papias found in current books " (p. 160). This comes to nothing definite. What Papias means is that *the texts from the books of the Old Testament* by themselves are valuable, but that the descriptions by the Lord's then surviving disciples of the occasions on which they were fulfilled are still more valuable, including, as they must by hypothesis include, the aforesaid texts. Further, these comments embodying those of Jesus upon selected texts have come to constitute *a body of tradition* (παράδοσις, represented by Papias's expression δεδομένας παρὰ τοῦ Κυρίου τῇ πίστει) now *attached to the faith* and requiring to be guarded as " the very commandments of God," in contrast to the old law, which is now become *foreign*. There now appears to be no difficulty whatever in understanding Papias's position.

(5–7) Eusebius professes to be not quite clear as to the problem of two Johns at Ephesus which he commends to the attention of readers, but he could hardly give more clearly his own opinion that the teacher of Papias was the author of Revelation, and that Papias claims to have heard him with his own ears and to have included his traditions in the five books.

(8–10) The other passages of Papias, in which he records some other wonderful events likewise, as having come down to him by tradition, do not now concern us. Philip's daughters living at Hierapolis were the medium of two of these, the raising of a corpse and the drinking of poison by Justus Barsabbas unharmed.

(11-12). Then it seems that Papias put in his second or third column (παρατέθειται) " some strange parables of the Saviour and teachings of his and some other statements of a rather mythical character," including a period of some thousand years after the resurrection and a material form of Christ's kingdom on the earth. After the clear statement by his master in Rev. 20^{4f} Papias is not to be blamed for this. Whether the term of a thousand years is predicable of any but a "material" reign is purely a metaphysical question.

(13-14) Then Eusebius judges him a man of very mean capacity, or narrow-minded; but adds that he influenced Irenæus and others because of his old-fashioned character. It was easier for Eusebius in A.D. 300 than for Irenæus and his contemporaries in 180 to discern and characterize the historical phases through which the Christian faith passed in the two first bewildering centuries of its life.

"Peter's Instructions."

(15) " Peter adapted his instructions to the needs (of his hearers) but had no intention of giving a connected arrangement of the Lord's oracles "—says Papias. Once more let us translate τῶν κυριακῶν λογίων,* *the oracles about the Lord.* Now this clearly implies that Peter's *instructions* (διδασκαλίας) had something to do with the *oracles* that he used. We know that he used them freely in Acts. He has employed no less than a dozen prophecies of the Christ, most of which are cardinal supports of our Christian theology to-day. But has it ever been supposed

---

* λογίων is the reading of Routh and of Gebhardt, Harnack and Zahn. Papias goes on to mention τα λόγια (Ματθαῖος μὲν οὖν 'Εβραΐδι διαλέκτῳ τὰ λόγια συνεγράψατο). Is there any reason why λογίων should be altered into λόγων? Is there any sense in λόγων from any point of view? It will hardly be contended that λόγων included the actions of the Lord. Dr. Abbott (*Enc. Bib.,* "Gospels," col. 1812) gives λόγων (*v. r.* λογίων).

WHAT, THEN, DID PAPIAS WRITE? 417

that Peter had designed to write a biography of Christ that would be called a Gospel? There is, indeed, in 2 Pet. 1^{15} ("but I will give diligence that ye may be able at every time also after my decease to call these things to your remembrance"), an intimation that Peter planned the production of some written work. This is the only possible meaning, as Zahn has shown (*Einl.*, ii. p. 47). Now 2 Pet. goes on to give an idea of the sort of work it would be, for he refers to the Transfiguration as an example of the fulfilment of a *prophecy* (2 Pet. 1^{20}) namely, Ps. 2^6, "his holy mountain," where "the Lord said unto me, Thou art my Son," etc. This is exactly an instance of *the oracles of the Lord* of which Papias's work was an *exposition*. Peter did not design to leave behind him even an ordered collection (σύνταξιν) of the oracles, but he may have intended to see that some collection of them was made. The fact is that Mark has preserved three of the twelve oracles quoted in Acts by Peter, many others of the twelve being such as to fall naturally outside the scope of his Gospel. But it is quite possible that the idea ascribed to Peter by the anonymous elder whom Papias reports in this negative way, and claimed by 2 Pet. 1^{15} more positively, developed into Mark or Luke and Acts. Also it is possible that the elder was mistaken. In any case it was much more his object to assert the carefulness and the accuracy of Mark than to affirm anything else about him. He assumes that Peter required an interpreter in any case, because (if for no other reason) he was an imperfect scholar in Greek composition. The present writer hopes to have shown in *St. Luke the Prophet* that Luke was the Silvanus who is said in 1 Pet. 5^{12} to be the medium who wrote that Epistle.

E E

The Oracles of Papias still founded on the Old Testament.

(16) The next fragment is, " Matthew then composed the oracles in the Hebrew language, and each [reader] interpreted them as he was able." The usual translation of this statement may perhaps be right, making *interpreted* mean only translated from Aramaic into Greek. But it is a question whether it does not mean a previous or subsequent *interpretation* of sense rather than language. For when " the elder " used the same term, *interpreter of Peter*, as applied to Mark (though we are not told that Matthew's composition is reported by Papias from the *same* elder), it is quite possible that it meant expositor as much as translator. It is a pure assumption on the part of some persons that the meaning of the statement is generally that our Matthew is a translation from the Aramaic. Our Matthew cannot be called a translation, and again and again it is found to be built up, apart from its quotations from the Old Testament, on the Greek Bible. Of the quotations, those which are peculiar to Matthew (see list in Westcott, *Intr.*[5], p. 225) are taken into our Matthew from this collection of *the oracles in the Hebrew language*. Here, then, we have the exact limit of the Hebrew (Aramaic) original of our Matthew. And it must be remembered that this statement of Papias is no sort of proof of the authorship of our Matthew.

(IV) The *pericope adulteræ* (John 7[53 ff]) is supposed by Lightfoot to be one of those illustrative anecdotes which Papias derived from the report of the elders, and which he did not scruple to arrange alongside of the interpretations of the oracles, and this is most probable. We need not discuss it further than to say that it belongs to the class of passages where the Law of Moses was " fulfilled," this time in immediate practice, by Him who " came not to destroy but to fulfil." This, again, exactly exemplifies

WHAT, THEN, DID PAPIAS WRITE? 419

the *Exposition of the Oracles Concerning the Lord.* What could be better than this incident to show that " a greater than Moses is here "? Its character, therefore, does throw light upon the nature of *the oracles* as drawn from the Old Testament.

(V-X) We can pass over these references to Papias with two remarks : that Georgius Hamartolus says that Papias mentions John's death at the hands of Jews after *fulfilling Christ's prophecy.* It is one that on every account deserved to be included with the *oracles* concerning the prophet of Nazareth, especially because it fulfils the words applied by Tertullian (*c. Marc.* 4[39]) to apostles killed by the Jews—

> Ps. 116[13] I will *drink the cup* of salvation and call upon the name of the Lord. Precious in the sight of the Lord is *the death of his saints*—

And, secondly, that Jerome has bluntly translated Papias as saying " *Books to read* do not profit me so much," etc., where he has utterly failed to see the point of τὰ ἐκ τῶν βιβλίων, thereby drawing after him much people. The interpolation of " to read " is gratuitous. Then he says, " he has not leisure or power to translate into Latin such important matters as neatly as they are written." If the *Exposition of the Oracles* had been an explanation of the Gospel accounts, as Lightfoot maintains—" the main object of the work "—would it not have been a worthy task to have done this, even at a comparative loss of neatness ? If, on the other hand, the book was a *pugio fidei* or *vado mecum* of prophecies fulfilled in Christ, it might well have been worth less than Jerome's while, about A.D. 400, to translate it. Jerome's statement, therefore, is quite intelligible. No regret need be felt about the loss of the translation by itself, for Jerome has mistranslated Irenæus's remark about Papias when he said that Irenæus makes Papias a hearer of *the evangelist*

John. This is a good instance of the persistent tendency to put the clothes of the apocalyptist on the back of the evangelist.

(XI) The short fragment on " the angels to whom He gave the rule of the administration concerning the earth " would have much more place among *oracles concerning Christ* than among " sayings and doings of Christ." For it would be an explanation of the original high estate of the angels when they were all *ministering spirits* and all worshipped God (Heb. $1^{6,7}$), as Deut. 32^{43} and Ps. 104^4 taught, with the proviso given in Heb. 2^5; while their fall, which he proceeds to mention, is described in the phraseology of Rev. 12^9, by Papias's master. It is quite clear that the fragment might well be an explanation of the saying of Jesus in Luke 10^{18}: " I beheld Satan as lightning *fallen from heaven*." But this would not be enough : for this expression itself is a fulfilment of—

Isa. $14^{12, 17}$ How doth he fall out of heaven, the morningstar that dawneth betimes ! He is *dashed down to the earth*, he who sendeth forth [*his angels*] into all the nations . . . he who maketh *the whole world* desert.

Thus the fragment is equally suitable to either theory of the contents of the book, as Lightfoot would probably have admitted (p. 200).

(XII, XIII) Anastasius of Sinai calls Papias " the Great (ὁ πολύς)" and an expositor, and says that he took all the work of " the six days " as referring to Christ and his Church. This remark does not belong very well to the sayings and doings of Jesus. But it suits well with the idea of Clement of Alexandria (Strom. 5^{10}, 6^{16}), whose application of Ps. $19^{2\,\text{ff}}$ suggests its use by Papias as an oracle of the Lord. Anastasius considers that Papias is spiritual in regard to his views of paradise, thus differing from Eusebius's remark above, where he called him materialist.

WHAT, THEN, DID PAPIAS WRITE? 421

"*The vine with ten thousand shoots*," etc.

(XIV) We now come to the well-known passage concerning the vine with ten thousand shoots, which again Lightfoot supposes to be an illustrative story derived from oral tradition, relating what the elders said that John said that the Lord said, and he would place it in the third column of Papias's work. There we might leave it, as it would not conflict with our theory. But it is perhaps worth while to point out what may probably be the origin of the idea. In Isa. 7[23] (Greek) shortly after the Immanuel prophecy, the impending punishment by the king of Assyria is predicted. Now we know from Justin Martyr (*Dial.* 77 and 103), that the king of Assyria was identified with Herod; and this idea has been traced back at least as far as Acts 12[23] in the New Testament. Then follows the prophecy that "Herod" shall be shaven bare, and every one that is left on the land shall eat (nothing more than) butter and honey.

> Isa. 7[23]. And it shall be in that day that wherever there are a thousand *vines* of a thousand shekels they shall become earth and thorns.

Now we saw that after the devastation of the land in consequence of Herod, who is a form of Antichrist—and this became clear from a study of the prophecies in the light of Justin Martyr's idea—there must follow a Restitution of all things, an ἀποκατάστασις πάντων (Acts 3[21]), in the time of Christ, and so these vines must become far more fruitful than before. Isaiah proceeds in the next two verses to deal with the crops of arable land, just as the Papias fragment does with *wheat;* the harmony of the *animal creation* in the time of Christ follows in Isa. 11, and this last passage is actually transcribed by Irenæus in this connection. May we not infer from Irenæus's words that he is here concerned to justify Papias, whom he has summoned to his support? This is what Irenæus says: "The Lord said, they shall see who shall come to those (times)." [Thus far is quoted by Lightfoot. But Irenæus proceeds:] "These times then (*ergo*) are prophesied by Isaiah, who says (*Haec ergo tempora prophetans Esaias ait*): The wolf shall feed with the lamb, etc. (as Isa. 11$^{6-9}$, Greek). And again: The wolves, etc. (as Isa. 65^{25}). I am not unaware, however, that some persons try to take these verses as meaning wild men, both of divers nations and different works, who believe, and after their belief agree with the righteous. But although this may now be the case with some human beings who come from various nations into the agreement of the faith, still in the resurrection of the righteous it will so happen with the animals, as it has been said, For God is rich in all things. And it is right that when creation is restored" (here again is a reference to the ἀποκατάστασις πάντων just mentioned) "all the animals shall obey and be in subjection to man" (as Papias said in the passage quoted from him) "and revert to the food originally given by God—for they had been originally subjected in obedience to Adam—namely, the fruits of the earth. But this is not just the occasion to show that the lion feeds on straw. Still, this shows the size and richness of the fruits: if the lion feeds on straw, what must the wheat be like that produces such straw?"

That Irenæus is led away from his subject, the bodily resurrection, to a digression upon the animals is caused by the last three lines of Papias's fragment, which deal with the animals. Does it not seem far more probable that Papias himself had been quoting Isa. 11? and is not the *ergo* of Irenæus almost a proof of it? Lightfoot takes the same view (p. 198), but draws no inference from it as to "the main object of Papias's work." The point that Lightfoot does not show, and probably it is beyond a man's power to show it, is how " the interpretation of the sayings and doings of Christ recorded in the written

WHAT, THEN, DID PAPIAS WRITE? 423

Gospels" is apt to prove " characteristically millennial " (*Essays, S.R.* p. 159). The subject and the predicate here are utterly out of harmony. In other words, Papias's second column, so to speak, of *interpretations characteristically millennial* would, upon Lightfoot's theory, be hopelessly incompatible with the text of his first column, the sayings (and doings) of Christ. Had it been possible for the evangelical narratives to be travestied in this characteristically millenarian fashion throughout the space of five books, and had they been so travestied at the hands of the orthodox bishop of Hierapolis, the result would have been to strangle the Christian faith. We must bear in mind that Papias himself, to do him justice, said of this report of the elders, " But these things are credible [only] to them that believe." It would be hard to deny that Irenæus, who has probably embodied much of the substance of Papias's work in his own, is himself just as millennial as Papias, as Lightfoot admits (p. 151). He also wrote in five books; but then he is not a professed expositor of the evangelical narratives. On the other hand, there was room for much fantastical interpretation by Papias if he took for his text the prophecies concerning Christ as he found them in the Greek Bible. For instance, Papias reports the elders as saying, " When any of the saints shall have taken hold of one of their clusters, another shall cry, I am a better cluster; take me, *bless* the Lord *through me.*" Can there be any doubt that the origin of this is found in the passage just mentioned—

> Isa. 65⁸ Thus *saith the Lord,* As *the grape* shall be found in *the cluster,* and they shall say, Injure it not, for *a blessing is in it,* so will I do on account of him that is my servant, for his sake I will not destroy all ?

Then follows immediately a very important Messianic passage (Chap. III above). We have seen how almost any *oracle of the Lord Jehovah* was liable to be treated as an *oracle of the Lord Christ* in the first century. The medium of the Greek Bible is just the element in the problem which Lightfoot has overlooked.

Meanwhile, we are still waiting to see whether Lightfoot has yet supplied us with any fragment of Papias to put into his second column, "the interpretations which explained the text, and which were the main object of the work" (p. 157). The *pericope* is gone (nineteen lines) into the third column. The *vines* (twenty lines) are gone, as being likewise elders' illustrations. The *Judas* fragment (seventeen lines) has yet to be considered, and where will it go?

(XV-XVII) The Messianic feast which Papias mentions is a reminiscence of Rev. 3^{20}, etc. But these again are based on older prophecies, such as—

> Isa. 9^3 They shall rejoice before thee as they that rejoice in harvest, and like unto them that divide spoils.
> Isa. 56^7 I will bring them into *my holy mountain* and gladden them in my house of prayer: *their whole burnt-offerings* and their sacrifices shall be acceptable upon my altar.

(XVIII) The horrible symptoms preceding the death of Judas are partly to be found in Ps. 69^{25}, from which passage the quotation in Acts 1^{20} is taken, and are partly exaggerations on similar lines (see Ch. VIII). The miserable traitor was to be loaded with such a list of bodily torments as not even the Old Testament vocabulary could provide. Once granted that there was to be a traitor, this heightening of his misery was inevitable. But the position of the fragment, however repulsive—and it seems to be genuine Papias, not the report of elders' sayings—would be more appropriate or at least intelligible among oracles concerning the Christ than among the sayings and doings of Jesus. It could not be claimed for any one of Lightfoot's three classes, or columns, and he

WHAT, THEN, DID PAPIAS WRITE? 425

has said nothing about it in the *Essays*. The present theory would find a place for it in Papias's second column, as an explanation of an oracle in Ps. 69.

(XIX, XX) are of no value to us here.

Ignatius and St. John on " filtration " of the Church from Judaism.

To conclude briefly. Lightfoot's theory is that " Papias, like Irenæus after him, undertook, we may suppose, to stem the current of Gnosticism " (p. 166); perhaps " he fell into the opposite error, so that his Chiliastic doctrine was tainted by a somewhat gross materialism." But there is not a single trace of gnosticism as the adversary assailed in Papias's work. Why go to Irenæus a long generation or two generations later? Why bring in Hippolytus, later still? Why bring in the Ophites? Why suppose or suggest that Papias wrote his work late in life? If he was born A.D. 60–70, then A.D. 120 is a fair average for the date of his writing, and this would be two good generations earlier than Irenæus. There was not much time for Basilides (fl. 117–138, Alexandria) to have become formidable in Hierapolis before that. Lightfoot suggests that because the epithet *foreign* (ἀλλότριος) is applied to the Gnostic teaching by Ignatius (? 117 A.D.), it is equally applied to the same in Papias. But if we look at the Ignatian passages we shall doubt this way of putting the case.

Thus (Ign. *Rom.* pref.) " Ignatius . . . unto them that are filled with the grace of God without wavering and are filtered clear from every *foreign* stain." Had the Roman Christians, then, come through Gnosticism to Christ, leaving their sediment behind? Not at all, but they had come through Judaism, and a better figure could hardly be employed than *filtration*. Again, " I exhort you—yet not I, but the love of Jesus Christ—take ye only Christian food, and abstain from *foreign* herbage which is heresy " (Ign. *Tral.* 6). Here, undoubtedly, there is a reference, as elsewhere in this Epistle, to the Docetic heresy which denied the real passion of Christ, a form of Gnosticism indeed, but very different from the wild fancies of Basilideans and Valentinians. But this heresy was quite as much a form of Judaism as of Gnosticism, and it existed long before Gnosticism, having been implicitly rebuked as an error by St. Paul when he said to Festus and to the Jew Agrippa II who believed the prophets (Acts 26[23]), "*how that the Christ must suffer*"— a new word "sufferable," being coined, we may almost say, to convey this most vital idea. A large class of Jews had always refused to apply the sufferings of Isa. 53 to the Christ. Once more (Ign. *Phil.* 3) the same idea occurs: "If any man walketh in a *foreign* doctrine, he hath no fellowship *with the suffering* [of Christ]." In each of these passages, then, it would be truer and clearer to say that the lingering errors of Judaism within the Christian Church were being combated, the process of filtration being still incomplete, and the predominant use of the Old Testament in the epistles of Clement and Barnabas illustrates this incompleteness.

But the use of ἀλλότριος, meaning *Jewish*, had begun within the canon of the New Testament (John 10[5])—

> But *a stranger* will they not follow, but will flee from him, for they know not the voice of *the strangers*.

If Ignatius alone concerned the reader, the words should be translated *foreigner(s)*. They are no older than Ignatius. They can only be understood in the light of the second century. The writer of the Gospel is so conscious of this anticipation of history that he says—

> This *parable* said Jesus unto them, but *they knew not* what things they were which he spake unto them.

WHAT, THEN, DID PAPIAS WRITE? 427

The relation of these *strangers* or *foreigners* (ἀλλότριοι) to the Church appears on further study of the *parable*. The *door* through which the shepherd entereth into the sheepyard of the ancient church is the *door of faith* (Acts 14^{27}) which God had opened to the Gentiles in the ministry of St. Paul, by contrast with the door of circumcision. Hence, the faith-door is presently identical with the shepherd himself, since faith in Christ is actually Christ Himself: " the wealth of the glory of *this mystery* among the Gentiles *which* is *Christ in you*, the hope of the glory " (Col. 1^{27}). This personal union with Christ is expressed by " the sheep hear his voice, and he calleth his own sheep by name and *leadeth them forth*" (ἐξάγει, compare the idea of filtration) out of the sheepyard of the Jewish Church. After putting out (ἐκβάλῃ) all his own sheep, he goeth on the way (πορεύεται) before them, never to return to the sheepyard, but to find pasture elsewhere. Others who go up from elsewhere (ἀναβαίνων ἀλλαχόθεν) are thieves and robbers. The covenant of circumcision is done with; only its deadening effect is hinted at : " the thief cometh only to steal and *kill* (θύσῃ) and destroy." The Fourth Gospel, as Bacon * has clearly demonstrated, is the Pauline Gospel developed. Our bodies are to be presented a living sacrifice (θυσία), says St. Paul (Rom. 12^1, etc.) : the Jewish system would make them a dead sacrifice, would *kill* them (θύσῃ, John 10^{10}).

And still we ask which of the fragments of Papias can, upon Lightfoot's theory, be placed in the second column of his work—" the interpretations " which " were its main object." The asking of this question is far from interfering with Lightfoot's main contention that there were in Papias's work quotations from our Gospels, while it is here suggested that they were cited by Papias in proof of the fulfilment of the ancient oracles which he explained of the Christ.

* Bacon, *The Fourth Gospel in Research and Defence*, passim.

CHAPTER XIV

DR. SCHWEITZER'S QUESTIONS

DR. SCHWEITZER, in his valuable and instructive and appreciative work, *The Quest of the Historical Jesus*, presents a *résumé* of criticism of the Gospels for the last century and a half, and comes at length to the comparison between his own work, *The Secret of the Messiahship and the Passion*, and that of Wrede, *The Messianic Secret in the Gospels*. In the course of this comparison he propounds some forty questions bearing upon the Marcan narrative,* and embodying the main issues of the Gospel problem as they emerge in the twentieth century. "They are the enigmas which the consentient critical induction offers to modern historical theology" (p. 335). While, then, these questions require the attention of all thoughtful persons, they especially challenge the consideration of any theory which essays a new point of view, and proposes a fresh treatment of the problem accordingly. If the theory of the preceding pages is worth anything, it will welcome the application of the test which they provide for it, and it does so.

First of all, it is to be noted that the crucial difficulty which the two eminent modern critics have singled out for the titles of their works is the Messianic secret, the secret of the Christ. Differing from each other as "thoroughgoing scepticism (Wrede) and thoroughgoing eschatology (Schweitzer)," in the description of the latter, they agree in this as in other points of their argument.

---
* *The Quest*, etc., p. 332.

They agree in focussing the attack upon the secret of the Christ as the principal key to the main position. Thus several of Schweitzer's questions are directed to this objective.

The Messianic Secret.

"Why is His Messiahship a secret and yet no secret, since it is known, not only to the disciples, but to the demoniacs, the blind man at Jericho, the multitude at Jerusalem, and to the High Priest?" "Why does Jesus, in Mark $4^{10 ff}$, speak of the parabolic form of discourse as designed to conceal the mystery of the Kingdom of God, whereas the explanation which He proceeds to give to the disciples has nothing mysterious about it?" "What is the mystery of the Kingdom of God?" "Why does Jesus forbid His miracles to be made known even in cases where there is no apparent purpose for the prohibition?"

But the question "What is the nature of the Messiah-secret?" is one for which we search in vain among Schweitzer's forty. Its nature is one of deliberate prophetic interpretation in act. The answer to the questions of this class has been provided in the preceding pages (50, 61, 315 ff, etc.). So far from being "the literary invention of Mark himself,"* the Secret is an oracle of Isaiah, which the Lord resolved to fulfil. Let us quote once more—

> Isa. 31^9, 32^1 Thus saith the Lord, Blessed is he that hath in Sion a seed, and men of his house in Jerusalem. For behold, a king, a *righteous* [king] shall reign, and rulers with judgment shall rule. And THE MAN shall be *hiding his words* (καὶ ἔσται ὁ "Ανθρωπος κρύπτων τοὺς λόγους αὐτοῦ), and he shall *be hidden* as from rushing water: and he shall appear in Sion as a river rushing gloriously in a thirsty land. And they shall no more be confident upon men (ἔσονται

---
* *The Quest*, p. 342.

πεποιθότες ἐπ' ἀνθρώποις), but they shall give their ears to hear.

Hiding his words: therefore He used parables. *Be hidden:* therefore the Messianic secret. This whole prophecy the Lord had resolved to fulfil as the Son of David, for whom Ps. 89 was rich in promises—

Ps. 89[36 ff] Once for all I sware by [in] my holy one that I will not be false to David. *His seed* shall endure for ever, and his throne as the sun before me, and as the moon prepared for ever: and the witness (ὁ μάρτυς) in heaven is faithful (πιστός). But thou hast thrust away and set at nought, thou hast put off thy Christ (τὸν χριστόν σου).

The testimony of the Baptist was widely current, that the Prophet of Nazareth was the Son of God, the beloved in whom He was well pleased. The trust in pedigree or in Holy Writ made Him the Son of David. The conviction of the demoniacs was one of divine Holiness. The information of the High Priest was derived through Judas. The mystery of the kingdom of God is a truth of the spiritual order, formerly secret and now made known. Exactly how much was known to each individual at each separate moment is more than we can expect to know. But the inner circle of disciples, to whom "it was given to know it," was, by hypothesis, more capable of this truth than the world was.

THE MAN in the Book of Wisdom.

But this is an opportunity to mention a very important passage of the Wisdom of Solomon which has only received a passing mention above. The Lord, as He pondered Ps. 89[48], concerning the MAN of *all the sons of men*, compared with it not only Isa. 32[2], but a fuller description of Himself in Wisd. 2, where *the righteous* of Isa. 32[2] is persecuted by the ungodly—

Wisd. 2¹⁰ Let us oppress the poor *Righteous Man* (πένητα δίκαιον). . . . Let our strength be the law of righteousness, for that which is feeble is proved unprofitable. And let us *lie in wait* for the Righteous Man, for he is ill-profitable to us, and he opposeth *our works*, and he upbraideth us with sins of the law, and he allegeth against us sins of our discipline. He professeth to have *the knowledge of God*, and calleth himself *the Lord's son* (παῖδα). He was made to reprove our thoughts (εἰς ἔλεγχον ἐννοιῶν ἡμῶν). He is grievous unto us even to behold, for his life is not like other men's, and his ways are diverse. We are esteemed of him as base metal, and he abstaineth from our ways as from *uncleannesses*. He pronounceth the end of the righteous to be blessed, and boasteth that *God is his father*.

¹⁷ Let us see if his words be true : and let us *tempt* (πειράσωμεν) what [shall happen] in *his outgoing* (ἐκβάσει). For if he is *the Righteous Son of God*, He will help him, and *deliver him* from the hand of his adversaries. Let us examine him with shameful treatment (ὕβρει) and torture, that we may learn his gentleness (ἐπιεικίαν) and judge his forbearance (ἀνεξικακίαν). Let us condemn him with a shameful death (ἀσχήμονι), for he shall be visited out of his own words.

²¹ These things they imagined, and they were deceived, for their own wickedness blinded them. And they knew not *the mysteries of God*, neither hoped they for the wages of holiness, nor discerned a reward for blameless souls. For God created THE MAN for incorruption (ἔκτισεν τὸν ῎Ανθρωπον ἐπ᾽ ἀφθαρσίᾳ), and made him *the image** of His own being (εἰκόνα τῆς ἰδίας ἰδιότητος).

How easily is the general bearing of the whole remark-

* We compare Acts 2³¹, 13³⁴ ᶠᶠ and Heb. 1³, etc.

able passage, especially the latter portion, converted into the particular, and applied to the Christ! The Prophet of Nazareth having resolved to be the Righteous One, knew that His very poverty exposed Him to persecution; and how could His disciples escape it? He could not but arraign the *law of righteousness* of the Scribes and Pharisees, and equally He could not fail to read in this chapter withal the whole course of His ministry to its outgoing, its *exodus*, in Jerusalem (see above, p. 279. The closeness of ἐκβάσει and ἔξοδον, Luke 9^{31}, is very suggestive). He read here that He would enrage them by *testing their thoughts* — nevertheless He tested them in Mark 11, 12 by differing from their *notions of uncleanness;* nevertheless He set forth His law of uncleanness (Mark 7^{19}) by *differing from their ways*; nevertheless He was the friend of publicans and sinners by *opposing their works* (Matt. 23^3); He opposed them by naming Himself *God's child*, and claiming God's *knowledge*; He did not deny the inferential claim to be *God's son*, and to offer them a *knowledge* of God like unto His own (John $10^{36\,\text{ff}}$). All this He had read in Wisd. 2,* and when, in Luke 11^{54}, the Scribes and Pharisees *lay in wait* for Him to catch something *out of His mouth*, we can see that the idea is based on Wisd. $2^{12,\,20}$. Then the reproach of the high priests with the scribes and elders, in Matt. 27^{43}, is not wholly drawn from Ps. 22^8, for the words, "For he said, I am God's son," which are not in the psalm, are present in Wisd. 2^{18}: "If he is the Righteous *Son of God*." . . . Again, Luke 22^{28}: "Ye are they that have continued with me *in my temptations*," as also Luke $22^{40,\,46}$: "Pray ye that ye may be spared entering *temptation*," is based upon Wisd. 2^{17}: "Let us *tempt*."

* After Him St. Paul had read in it of *the strength* which they claimed for *the law*, and he wrote that *circumcision had no strength* (Gal. 5^6), and *the law was feeble* (Rom. 8^3), and *he opposed its works*. The clear reference in Rom. 5 to *death entering into the world* in this same passage (Wisd. 2^{24}) has been mentioned.

Thus, with all this amount of other reference to the ministry and death of the Righteous, we cannot hesitate to say that 2[22], *and they did not know the mysteries of God*, has been applied by the evangelists to *them that are without, the rest, the others*, by which vague terms they denoted those for whom Wisd. 1, 2, has hardly any term at all, except the vague term, "impious men" (ἀσεβεῖς) in 1[16]. Once more the uncertain character of the ancient scripture is reproduced in the New Testament. The parable was the only form of discourse that conceivably could serve as a test for *those who were without,* therefore He employed it (Mark 4[11], Luke 8[10], Matt. 13[11]).

The Resolution of the Christ.

We pass to another group of Schweitzer's questions. " Why does Jesus first reveal His Messiahship to the disciples at Cæsarea, not at the moment when He sends them forth to preach?" "How does Peter know without having been told by Jesus that the Messiahship belongs to his Master?" "Why must it remain a secret until the ' Resurrection ' ?" "Why does Jesus indicate His Messiahship only by the title, Son of Man?" "And why is it that this title is so far from prominent in primitive Christian theology?"

The first question is one that probably involves an error. We have said above (p. 392) that the resolution to be the Christ rested in the Lord's own will. "He learned the obedience from the things which he suffered " (Heb. 5[8]), and these things are the whole of His earthly experience, not only His death. Neither Greek scholarship nor just thought would permit *the things* to be limited to His death. The divine obedience was a continual strain of endeavour : " If thou walk in my ways and keep thyself in my commandments " is the sublime and solemn condition of Zech. 3[7] (p. 313). Therefore

F F

we have to suppose that the Prophet of Nazareth had trained His disciples in many scriptures before He sent them forth to preach. It is not conceivable that they had not been instructed in Ps. 89 before Cæsarea. They knew both the testimony of the Baptist and his Davidic sonship. The question, therefore, "how Peter knew," seems to have been answered on p. 317. The next question should be put differently, not "until the Resurrection," but "until He appeared at Sion," and has been answered by Isa. 31^9. The next, on the use of the Son of Man as the only title, is answered by Ps. $89^{48\ f}$. The Firstborn, the Elect, the Man, the representative Man, the seed of David, the Christ, though they do not all mean the same thing, all mean in that psalm the same person; all or most imply the same effort, the same holy resolution in Him. The title Christ, used twice in the same psalm, and a third time by implication of the corresponding verb, was more concrete and terse and intelligible and picturesque; perhaps this may account for its prevalence over the other.

Partial Discoveries of the Christ.

We pass to another group. "How do the demoniacs know that Jesus is the Son of God?" They had become aware of His holy character and mission by hearsay, like the multitude (Mark 3^8). Is it too much to suppose that with the belief of those days that epileptics were the thralls of Satan, they were the loudest in proclaiming the divinity of their deliverer? "Why does the blind man at Jericho address Him as the Son of David, when no one else knows His Messianic dignity?" Hearsay again. He had heard, says Mark, that Jesus of Nazareth passeth by. One of the disciples had told him that Jesus was the Son of David, foretold in Ps. 89. This is not surprising, since the Son of Man had been the subject of talk in the previous verse, and *the compensation of the Christ* is there mentioned only in slightly altered terms

DR. SCHWEITZER'S QUESTIONS

from those of Ps. 89 (λύτρον ἀντὶ for ἀντάλλαγμα; in 1 Tim. 2⁶ ἀντίλυτρον occurs). The disciple might have thought there was little harm in acquainting a blind man with more than the Master permitted. " How was it that these occurrences did not give a new direction to the thoughts of the people in regard to Jesus ? " But how do we know that they did not ? Within a day or two the triumphal entry took place. He was at Sion, if not " in Sion," where He was to " appear as a *river rushing gloriously* in a thirsty land." He was to " come on behalf of Sion as the Deliverer and turn away impieties from Jacob," when " the wrath from the Lord " should " have come as a *violent river*." (Isa. 59$^{20, 19}$). Perhaps this answers the next question, " How did the Messianic entry come about ? " There were crowds of Galileans at the city for the feast. " How was it possible without provoking the interference of the Roman garrison ? " But this was what would seem a very mild procession, and challenged no notice at all. " Why is it ignored in the subsequent controversies ? " This question provides the answer to the one before it. " Why was it not brought up at the trial of Jesus ? " Because, in fact, the sole importance of it lies in the sphere of prophecy, which the Romans could not have comprehended.

The Lord and the Forerunner once more.

We pass to the fourth group. " What is the meaning of the statement that Jesus discovered a difficulty in the fact that the Messiah was described as at once David's son and David's Lord ? " But there was no difficulty whatever for the true interpreter of Ps. 89. If David's son meant one who was only descended from David, one of the many, one who was an ordinary citizen, this person was not meant in the text. The scribes were too easily content with a pedigree man, and ought to raise their thoughts higher to a Son of the Highest.

David himself looked for the Highest, as the object of his worship. "How are we to explain the fact that Jesus had to open the eyes of the people to the greatness of the Baptist's office subsequently to the mission of the twelve, and to enlighten the disciples themselves in regard to it during the descent from the mount?" The latter part of the question has been answered above (Ch. X, p. 290 etc.) : the former is not a great difficulty, for we have no means of determining whether one multitude is wholly or partly different from another, we only know that two multitudes are never quite composed of the same people. There were people who, though they had heard of John before, would benefit by hearing of him again. "Why should this be described as a mystery difficult to grasp (Matt. 11$^{14\,f}$. ' If ye choose to receive it . . . He that hath ears to hear, let him hear) ' " ? Schweitzer here is in grievous error : *choose* (θέλετε is not *can*, though Schweitzer says so thrice. " Wenn ihr es fassen *mögt* " might pass muster, though less good than Luther; but " fassen *könnt* " (*bis*) could not pass. Luther gives " so ihr es *wollt* annehmen ") is a concession by the Lord to the multitude who were unduly convinced, over-convinced of the actual identity. They refused to see any mere figurative or prophetical identification or fulfilment : they were sure John was actual Elias. He says : " If you choose to accept the figurative truth in such a positive way, accept it : there is truth in it." Hence the warning which follows, He that hath ears, let him hear. On the last expression see pp. 102^f above, and p. 317. When Isa. 32^3 says, "But they shall give their ears to hear," the contrast is with his previous words, " They shall cease to trust upon men." It was possible to trust too much even upon John as Elias, and indeed it was now time for them to be " no more so confident upon men." Jesus foresaw that John would not ascend to heaven in a fiery chariot.

"What means He that is least in the kingdom of heaven is greater then the Baptist?" (Luke 7^{28} = Matt. 11^{11}). This very difficult text has hitherto received a translation which is disparaging to the Baptist, and it is doubtful whether it increases our knowledge of the conditions of the kingdom of heaven. Can one really suppose that such a comparison could have been drawn by the Lord between the Baptist with all his earnestness, sincerity, courage, and *him that is least in the kingdom of heaven* to the advantage of the latter? Even if we allow that personal character is nothing and position or date is everything (and who would allow it?) the sentence is too severe upon the author of the first witness to the Lord. The Lord has not finished His course before He excludes His own Forerunner—by this translation—from His kingdom! One is compelled to inquire earnestly whether the translation is correct. One is strongly inclined to think it is not. Another, therefore, is here proposed in the belief that all we like sheep have gone astray in a false translation from which a single breath or change of breathing would have saved us. The great lesson of the Baptist's life, as of the Saviour's, is self-effacement, than which there is no greater for all time. *And he that is lesser*, as John was lesser, *in the kingdom of heaven is greater than himself* (ὁ δὲ μικρότερος ἐν τῇ β. τ. θ. μείζων αὐτοῦ ἐστίν). I venture to suggest that αὐτοῦ should be read for αὐτοῦ.* That there is no parallel to the usage in the New Testament is not surprising, for the instances of the idiom in classical Greek are not frequent, though well known. An αὐτός before αὐτοῦ is not necessary:

* There were no breathings for some 300 years after the first copy of a gospel. Scrivener, *Introd.*, p. 43.
Since writing the above I have seen Dr. Abbott's explanation (*The Son of Man*, 3523)—that *the lesser is* Christ. I still think, however, that the assertion would have undone the self-effacement, and prefer to read αὐτοῦ and avoid all comparison.

(compare αὐτῆς εὐγενεστάτη, Soph. frag. 786). The context shows that John is the subject of praise by Jesus: the praise culminates in *there is no greater prophet than John*. Then to introduce a *but* and therewith to dash John to the ground in comparison with *the lesser* Christian is a very wanton course of translation, however acceptable it might be to the churchman of the second century. The lesson is the same that the Lord teaches in Luke 9[48], *He that is lesser among you all, he is great* (ὁ γὰρ μικρότερος ἐν πᾶσιν ὑμῖν ὑπάρχων οὗτος ἐστιν μέγας), and in Luke 14[11], 18[14], "He that humbleth himself shall be exalted." Is it likely that the Lord would have taught this beautiful and divine lesson in Luke 9[48] if He had taught almost the opposite lesson, a lesson of competition, in 7[28]? Is it likely that after depreciating John and his baptism, Luke 7[29] would have gone on to describe the thronging of the people (of Israel) to the baptism of John? Quite the reverse. He describes the thronging because he had just described the appreciation of John by Jesus. And this appreciation was in strict accordance with scripture, with the high charter of John in Mal. 2[6] (see above, Ch. VII, p. 188), though only Mal. 3[1] is here cited by Luke, but this citation is enough to prove the train of thought.

The questions put by Schweitzer continue: "Does the Baptist then not enter into the kingdom of Heaven?" Most certainly he does. How else can we read those profoundly touching words of the Forerunner in Mal. 2[5], "My covenant was with him of life and of peace, and I gave them to him that he may fear me with a [right] fear and stand in awe before my name?" "How is the kingdom of Heaven subjected to violence since the days of the Baptist?" "Who are the violent?" "What is the Baptist intended to understand from the answer of Jesus?" The last question has been answered in the pages above (p. 277). The *violent* are first of

DR. SCHWEITZER'S QUESTIONS

all Herod Antipas (Matt. 11¹²); for was not Herod "the river strong and great " (Chap. I), and is not *violent* (βίαιος) the epithet of the river to which " the wrath from the Lord " is compared (Is. 59¹⁹) ? and after him *until now*, until the time when Matthew was written—the words are parenthetic as " until this day " in Matt. 28¹⁵—the persecutors. But there is scriptural warrant for saying that the violent men *plunder* it (ἁρπάζουσιν), for, says

Ps. 89⁴¹ " *All* that journey by the way do *plunder* him " *
(David, διήρπασαν : see Ch. X, p. 307).

Luke 16¹⁶ is probably not essentially different in meaning—*every man forceth his way into it*—*every* traveller plunders it.

Jesus, the Twelve, and the Multitude.

The questions continue: " What importance was attached to the miracles by Jesus Himself ? " " What office must they have caused the people to attribute to Him ? " Here we must not be too precise. The " sons of Israel " also " cast out devils," as we know, and yet the fact did not cause the people to deem them Christs. It is safe to say that the delivered held Him to be " the Holy One of God." To Jesus Himself they were an assurance that He was still fulfilling the condition of Zech. 3⁷, " If thou walk in my ways and keep thyself in my commands," even when the Baptist's witness

* The context was about to be applied, soon after Jesus spoke this, to John's death, as we have seen above; may we go so far as to suppose that in the interval of his imprisonment, when the expectation of the people that he would ascend to heaven as Elias did was still at its height, this verse was also in the Lord's mind in that very connection ? At least here are the two passages where ἁρπάζειν is to *plunder*, whereas the verb is always in the New Testament used for to *snatch away*. It seems as if Matthew at any rate took the idea of Ps. 89 in the Lord's mind to be that of *plunder* in the person of John; whether John 6¹⁵ took it to be that of *snatching away* to make *Jesus* king, although the latter view does not accord with the context of Ps. 89, is another question.

was under a cloud. They were signs of the Messiah, indications ($\sigma\eta\mu\varepsilon\tilde{\iota}\alpha$, not amounting to proofs $\tau\varepsilon\varkappa\mu\acute{\eta}\varrho\iota\alpha$, which occurs only in Acts 1³). The question is too large for discussion here. But the position that "miracles" were then the order of the day, as now they are not, is as defensible on the grounds of evidence in a then court of law as the other position that no " miracles " ever happened. A then court of law would have to accept them, though it would also be responsible for not seeing a miracle where there was none, as, *e. g.*, at the Baptism : for trances were not miracles. A modern court would require proof of relevancy and sanity before accepting miracles.

" Why is the discourse at the sending out of the Twelve filled with predictions of persecutions which experience had given no reason to anticipate, and which did not, as a matter of fact, occur ? " The question seems to refer to Matt. 10¹⁷ ff, *They shall deliver you up* . . . which in Mark and Luke is a part of the Olivet discourse (see above, Ch. XI). It is appropriate there, but not in its place in Matt. 10. The "reason to anticipate" has been given above in Wisd. 2¹². The persecutions occurred later, and how do we know that some did not occur earlier, though unmentioned ? A similar answer may be given to the next question, " What is the meaning of Matt. 10²³ about the imminent coming of the Son of Man, seeing that the disciples after all returned to Jesus without its being fulfilled ? " They returned after a brief and partial mission, but the fact is undeniable that they had not "finished ($\tau\varepsilon\lambda\acute{\varepsilon}\sigma\eta\tau\varepsilon$) the cities of Israel before the Son of Man came " in the Death and Glory, " His life rescued by God from the hand of hell " (Ps. 89⁴⁹). It must be remembered still that He was the Coming One from the first, from the Baptism and before. At the close of the four Gospels He had come. It is arbitrary to say that no other passage but Dan. 7¹³, " Behold, [one] *like* the Son of Man was coming with the clouds of heaven," is here intended by Him. To represent Elias as being *He that cometh*, as Schweitzer does, is to run counter to all evidence, whatever misconception may have existed among the multitude (see Ch. VI, p. 167). John $1^{26\,f}$ correctly uses *He that cometh* of the Christ; so, I have contended (pp. 146 ff), does the true reading of Luke 3^{23}. The assertion of Schweitzer that Jesus was the first and only person who made John to be Elias rests on the palpable mistranslation mentioned above.

" Why does Jesus leave the people just when His work among them is most successful and journey northwards ? " The answer is in Ch. X above (pp. 303 ff). " Why had He, immediately after the mission of the Twelve, manifested a desire to withdraw from the multitude who were longing for salvation ? " This is in Matt. 11^1 only, and the answer is there given—He left them in order " to teach and preach in their cities "—unless I have misapprehended the question. For any other withdrawal Isa. 32^2 would account, as we saw. " How does the multitude of Mark 8^{34} suddenly appear at Cæsarea Philippi ? " The neighbourhood was crowded. " Why is its presence no longer implied in Mark 9^{30} ? " " How could Jesus possibly have travelled unrecognized through Galilee, and how could He have avoided being thronged in Capernaum although he stayed at ' the house ' ? " These questions, if I apprehend them aright, assume that if the prophet of Nazareth were once known to be the son of David, the Holy One of God, His footsteps must be dogged incessantly by a multitude. But this assumption implies too much. No spell of His life and presence, no power and authority of His teaching, would rivet a multitude to Him in those days, still less the same multitude always. The life was incomplete. " How came He so suddenly to speak to His disciples of His suffering and dying and rising again, without, more-

over, explaining to them either the natural or the moral
'wherefore'?" "All attempt," observes Wrede, "to
aid the understanding of the disciples is lacking." Perhaps this is the sort of question on which the pages above, especially Ch. X, may throw light.

"Did Jesus journey to Jerusalem with the purpose of working there, or of dying there?" Ps. 89[48] said *He shall not see death.* This was all. He did not know the time or the season, for the prophecies did not tell Him, though they told Him to go there and He had resolved to fulfil them. "How comes it that in Mark 10[39] He holds out to the sons of Zebedee the prospect of drinking His cup and being baptized with His baptism?" "And how can He, after speaking so decidedly of the necessity of His death, think it possible in Gethsemane that the cup might yet pass from Him?" (See above, Ch. XII, pp. 374, 389). "Who are the undefined *many*, for whom, according to Mark 10[45], 14[24], His death shall serve as a ransom?" This admits of a very clear answer from the oracles. The *many* are those of whom it was written—

Isa. 53[12] And himself bare (ἀνήνεγκεν, the sins as an oblation) the sins *of many*, and
Isa. 53[11] the Lord willeth to . . . justify the Righteous one in his good service (εὖ δουλεύοντα) *to many*.
Ps. 34[22] The Lord shall ransom (λυτρώσεται) the lives of his servants.

But the *ransom* is essentially *the compensation of the Christ*, Ps. 89[51] (see above, Ch. X, XII).

"How came it that Jesus alone was arrested?" See Ch. XII, pp. 355, 390. "Why were no witnesses called at His trial to testify that He had given Himself out to be the Messiah?" This was no charge for a Roman judge and Roman law: the charge of claiming to be a king in that fashion fell utterly flat, save as a whip for

DR. SCHWEITZER'S QUESTIONS 443

Pilate in the hands of the Sanhedrin, and a source of the mockery. The trial before the high priest was very hurried, and no time had been left for collecting evidence, the passover being near. " How is it that on the morning after the arrest the temper of the multitude seems to be completely changed, so that no one stirs a finger to help Him?" The multitude itself was different, and no reliance can ever be placed upon " the multitude " remaining the same for two days together, either for practical or for historical purposes.

" In what form does Jesus conceive the resurrection which He promises to His disciples, to be combined with the coming on the clouds of heaven, to which He points His judge?" This has not been told us. See Ps. 89[49].

> He told it not, or something sealed
> The lips of that evangelist.

" In what relation do these predictions stand to the prospect held out at the time of the mission of the Twelve, but not realized, of the immediate appearance of the Son of Man?" This question implies by *immediate* that it was within a very few weeks, and the interpretation will be considered below, as also the two remaining questions on Mark 14[28], 16[7], " I will go before you into Galilee."

" *The Cities of Israel.*"

I have answered these questions more for my own satisfaction than with a sense that the answers are correct, and these I put down before reading the subsequent pages of Schweitzer. To some of his answers I respectfully take exception. That the violent men who plunder (or snatch up) the kingdom of heaven are " repentant sinners, converted by the Baptist, who force on and wrest from God the kingdom," is an interpretation which puts a strain upon the words *until now*, *violent*, and especially *wrest*. Again, in spite of the fact that Isa. 6^{9f}, quoted so often in the New Testament, bears so strong a predestinarian ring, it is a great extension of this doctrine which Schweitzer presents when he identifies belief with election (p. 356), or even when he resorts to the will of God (p.353) to modify the hard law of predestination. Nor does he allow enough for the disability of the original LXX to convey niceties of thought and doctrine. Again, is it conceivable that the disciples had "finished the cities of Israel" when they returned to Jesus ? or that Matthew intends us to think that they had ? To say that the words mean " completed a hasty journey through the cities of Israel to announce the kingdom " is strange, for to "finish " is not to "complete a hasty journey through." And then to say the verse means " this and nothing else," is to tie one's colours to the mast of Matthew rather tightly and to throw over Mark and Luke, who have made the discourse to which the words belong part of the Olivet discourse. At best it must be very doubtful whether this verse is worth anything at all. But the work supposed to be set to the disciples simply could not be done in the time that Schweitzer allows for it before the impending harvest-season—even if each of the Twelve took one-twelfth of the cities (and villages) of Israel and did no more than stand in the fountain-space of each city and deliver a peremptory announcement and flee—for the context is of fleeing to another city rather than of preaching. This interpretation of Matt. 10^{23}, instead of discrediting the expectation of Jesus, discredits either Matthew or the author.

But, unfortunately, it is just this verse, thus interpreted by Schweitzer, which is made a cardinal verse : it gives "the first postponement of the Parousia," "the first significant date in the history of Christianity : it gives to the work of Jesus a new direction, otherwise inexplicable." " Without Matthew 10, 11, everything remains enigmatic." To examine the verse more closely. The reading *of Israel* is doubtful. Hort has bracketed the definite article [τοῦ] ᾿Ισραήλ. If τοῦ is omitted with B D, then πολειςιςραηλ presents the double ις, which therefore becomes suspicious, as if πολεις had suffered a false reduplication of its last two letters before ἕως—πολειςιςεως—and some scribe seeing ις supposed it right to supply ραηλ after it. Certain it is, though surprising, that *the cities of Israel* is found hardly anywhere else (just three times) in the Bible. And even this fact alters the aspect of the verse. I do not feel quite confident of what is about to be said as an explanation, but at present would suggest that the passage on which Matthew is working is—

> Isa. 40⁹ Lift up in strength thy voice, thou that *bringest the gospel* to Jerusalem. Lift ye up, *be ye not afraid:* say thou *to the cities* of Judah, Behold your God. *Behold, the Lord cometh* with strength, and his arm with authority; *behold,* his reward is with him and his work before him. As a shepherd he will shepherd his flock, and with his arm will he *gather* [the] lambs, and will comfort them that are with young.

If we are to suppose Matt. 10²³ to refer to the Twelve sent forth to preach, they are *bringing the gospel,* and not only to Jerusalem but *to the cities.* Then in Matt. 10²⁶, ²⁸ He does tell them *be ye not afraid.* Then it is plain from Matthew that the burden of their preaching is, as Isaiah says, *The Lord cometh.* Then in Matt. 10¹⁶ he says, *Behold,* I send you forth as sheep in the midst of wolves, implying that they are no sheep of an ordinary flock, but one which has a heavenly ever-present Shepherd—which is Isaiah's thought.

Again, since this same chapter, Isa. 40³, contains the Baptist's motto, *The voice of one crying,* etc., it is most easy to suppose that the context was also found to contain matter relevant to the gospel. It is easy to suppose that the Lord Himself dealt with that context in discourses with the Twelve and used the actual words of Matt. 10^{28}. But then, did He use them in the sense of Schweitzer? The answer should be in the negative, for—

Zec. 14^7 There shall be one day, and that day [is] known unto the Lord—

is a text which He must have considered long before the mission of the Twelve. Granted that His expectation was that the end would fall within the generation, there is not evidence to show that He expected it within a few weeks of the mission.

For the natural translation is just this: Ye *certainly will never finish* (οὐ μὴ τελέσητε) the cities before the Son of Man comes, not because He comes so quickly, but because the task is too great for twelve men to accomplish even in forty years. Again, there is one fact that shows that Matthew did not interpret as Schweitzer: Matthew says, "But when they persecute you in one city, flee unto another," implying the need of some considerable time for persecution to arise; for heralds who shouted an announcement only would not be persecuted for so harmless a proceeding.

"*I will go before you.*"

There are two other passages in Mark 11^{16} and Mark 14^{28} which may here be explained out of the same portion of Isa. 52$^{11, 12}$ and with a much greater degree of probability. The former is "He suffered not that any one should *carry a vessel* through the Temple," and it is given as part of the purgation of the temple. But the source seems to be—

Isa. 52^{11} Stand off, stand off, come ye out thence [from Sion], and touch not an unclean thing; come out

DR. SCHWEITZER'S QUESTIONS

of the midst of her, be separate, ye that *bear* the *vessels* of the Lord.

The other is a passage of which Schweitzer makes much : " I *will go before you* (προάξω, lead you forward) into Galilee." This is from the next verse—

Isa. 52¹² For ye shall not come out with tumult nor go your way in flight; for the Lord *will go* his way *before you* (πορεύσεται πρότερος ὑ.), and he that *gathereth* you is the God of Israel.

We note that *gathereth* (ἐπισυνάγων) takes up the *gather* (συνάξει) of Isa. 40¹¹ above (see p. 445) where it is applied *to the flock*. This is immediately after the quotation from Zech. 13⁷, " I will smite the shepherd," etc.; consequently we know that in Mark 14²⁸ *I will go before you* means *as a shepherd* before his flock. Few readers would see this in Mark, though an Eastern reader, conversant with the practice of Eastern shepherds, would see it. But the remarkable thing is that in Isa. 52 there is not a word or suggestion about shepherds and sheep, for (συνάξει) *gather* is not in itself suggestive of sheep. Therefore it seems clear that the connection by Mark of Isa. 52¹² with the oracle of Zech. 13⁷ is due to the fact that *gathereth* was held to be filled with the pastoral meaning drawn from *gather* in Isa. 40¹¹.

What inference is to be drawn from this fact is not quite so clear as the fact itself. That Galilee was " home " to most of the disciples, and was the natural sphere of their activity, is a fact that points to their going there first if ever they left Jerusalem. But whether the Lord Himself had said this or it was put into His mouth is a question not easily determined. For there is always the hypothesis that several oracles, especially some in Isaiah and Zechariah, had some fulfilment, and if so the particular fulfilment had to be discovered for them. That the Lord resolved to fulfil many prophecies and did fulfil them is a fact, but that He did not fulfil everything that was written is also a fact, and between the fulfilled and unfulfilled there is a considerable margin of those for which fulfilments were imagined by the evangelists and the disciples upon evidence now more now less trustworthy. This margin presents the sphere of real difficulty for criticism in the future.

The point of Schweitzer's argument here is precarious in the extreme. He claims that " it is quite evident that Jesus is not speaking of sufferings after His death, but of sufferings that will befall the disciples as soon as they have gone forth from Him." He then makes a dangerous assumption : " If the theology of the primitive Church had remoulded the tradition, it would have made Jesus give His followers directions for their conduct after His death. That we do not find anything of this kind is the best proof that there can be no question of a remoulding of the life of Jesus by primitive theology. How easy it would have been for the early Church to scatter here and there through the discourses of Jesus directions which were only to be applied after His death. But the simple fact is that it did not do so." Did it not ? What, then, we must ask, has this argument to say to the Olivet discourse ? Did Jesus suppose that the whole of the phantasmagoria of Matt. 24 = Mark 13 = Luke 21 would have time to be enacted in the few weeks before His death —they were then a few days ? Armies gathering and encircling the city, the abomination of desolation being set up, disciples flying after praying that their flight be not in the winter, and suffering all sorts of betrayal, treason, despite and persecution. Upon any showing here are " directions for their conduct after His death," in a " discourse of Jesus," " remoulded by primitive theology," upon a " tradition." Schweitzer, in fact, ignores the Olivet discourse, which is, however, far more likely to have over-

DR. SCHWEITZER'S QUESTIONS

flowed into Matt. 10, 11 than they to have overflowed into it.

His next paragraph, which shews that the sufferings foreshadowed at the mission of the Twelve are "four times unhistorical," is one that will seem mistaken to a reader of Wisd. 2 (see above, p. 431), which Jesus had certainly read and knew as certainly that the disciple was not above his Lord (Matt. 10²⁴—a verse which accounts for the insertion of these predictions there). However, if all this part of the discourse is "unhistorical," how can it possibly be held that Matt. 10²³ is historical, cardinal, and vital for the life of Jesus at this particular point in it?

The form of the saying, and its substance too, is very much like that of Olivet—

MATT. 10²³	MATT. 24³⁴, MARK 13³⁰, LUKE 21³²
For *verily I say unto you,* Ye *shall not have* finished (οὐ μὴ τελέσητε) the cities *till* (ἕως) the Son of Man be come (ἔλθῃ).	*Verily I say unto you,* This generation *shall not have* passed away (οὐ μὴ παρέλθῃ) *till* (ἕως) all these things be accomplished.

There is a certain want of restraint in this portion of the book, which becomes more pronounced when we are told that to all the other phenomena that He expected full speedily to occur we must find room to add the outpouring of the Spirit in Joel 2. Why is this? Simply because Joel 3¹³ describes the judgment as the harvest-day of God, and this is a ", remarkable parallel" to Matt. 9³⁸, Pray ye therefore *the Lord of the harvest* . . . But we have seen in the Olivet discourse that it was held by the Lord to be possible for the Day to fall in *the winter*, which is not harvest. If this argument is held to be based on anything like evidence, the pages of this volume, now closing, may hope to receive an equal indulgence.

LIST OF ORACLES, ETC., QUOTED

GEN. 3^{15}, 366
19^{17}, 328
49^9, 226
49^{22}, 173
Exod. 4^{22}, 5
19^4, 48
24^{1f}, 266
34^{34}, 293
40^{34f}, 131, 281
Num. 5^{21f}, 225
17^{21f}, 169
$24^{17, 21}$, 22, 310
24^{23}, 257
Deut. 4^{48}, 271
18^{16f}, 280
32^{11}, 48
32^{30}, 261
32^{35}, 260
32^{39}, 343, 363, 379
32^{41}, 384
2 Sam. 5^{3f}, 150
15, 16, 17, 347 ff
17^{23}, 218
22^2, 231
1 Kings 17^{10}, 288
22^{19}, 77
2 Chr. 21^8, 220
Ezra 1^{1f}, 155
$5^{2,8}$, 155
Job 2^8, 227
Ps. $2^{6f, 6}$, 200, 270, 306
12^6, 244
14^3, 227
16^{10}, 7, 330
17^{10}, 226

Ps. 18^{30}, 244
22^{14}, 361
27^2, 394
34^{22}, 442
38^{10}, 393
40^8, 392
41^8, 392
41^{10}, 218
42^6, 362
$69^{22, 25}$, 218f
72^{10}, 16
74^{2-13}, 305
75^8, 389
78^{67}, 173
81^6, 173
82^6, 241
89^4, 151, 155
89^{8ff}, 310ff, 389
89^{14}, 301
89^{19-23}, 123, 177
89^{26-29}, 121ff, 313
89^{35-41}, 74, 151, 177, 306, 430, 439
89^{48}, 136
91^5, 394
92^{10}, 364
$96^{10, 13}$, 134, 367
$97^{1, 4, 7}$, 133
99^8, 286
105^{41}, 231
$109^{8, 18f}$, 218ff
116^{13}, 419
118^{22}, 154
118^{26}, 149
119^{40}, 244
132^3, 66

Ps. 132^{10}, 177
132^{11}, 127
133^3, 271
148^1, 76
Isa. 1^3, 74, 138
4^{2-5}, 40, 43, 119, 128
5^{25}, 264
6^{8-10}, 103, 264
7^{10ff}, 4, 52, 130
7^{23}, 421
8^1, 79
8^4, 17
8^{6-8}, 8, 45, 59, 310
8^{9f}, 11
8^{19}, 258
9^{1-4}, 28, 70, 166, 168, 197
9^3, 424
9^7, 77, 130, 171
9^{18f}, 71, 328
10^1, 79
10^5, 72
10^{13}, 90
10^{14}, 22, 30
$10^{16, 18}$, 90, 98
10^{17f}, 72, 89
10^{19ff}, 165
10^{22}, 175, 328
10^{24ff}, 12
10^{29}, 51
11^1, 72, 167, 172
11^6, 422
11^{8f}, 73
12^3, 45
13^{6ff}, 116, 328
13^{10ff}, 175, 328

450

LIST OF ORACLES, ETC., QUOTED 451

Isa. 14^{11}, 98f, 103, 238
$14^{12,17}$, 420
$14^{23\text{ff}}$, 105, 238
$17^{7\text{ff}}$, 17
$17^{12\text{ff}}$, 17
$19^{1,21\text{f}}$, 48
$21^{1\text{f}}$, 385
$21^{13\text{ff}}$, 28
$22^{4\text{ff}}$, 237ff, 242f
24^{16}, 328
26^{16}, 326
27^{12}, 14
27^{13}, 328
28^{16}, 154
$29^{9,14}$, 46
30^{27}, 398
30^{31}, 18, 89
31^{5}, 35
$31^{6,8}$, 21, 89, 101
31^{9}, 315, 429
32^{1}, 15, 61, 315, 385
32^{2}, 49, 317, 429
32^{3}, 103, 436
$32^{6\text{f}}$, 21, 29
$33^{3\text{f}}$, 18, 28
33^{7}, 76, 120
$33^{13\text{ff}}$, 18, 74, 117
34^{4}, 328ff, 333
35^{7}, 45
37^{30}, 77
37^{31}, 176
37^{36}, 90
$40^{9\text{ff}}$, 445
41^{18}, 232
$42^{4,7}$, 183
43^{5}, 49
$43^{12\text{ff}}$, 248
43^{19}, 232
43^{20}, 45
44^{3}, 45, 232
$45^{1\text{ff}}$, 156f
$47^{3\text{ff}}$, 262
48^{12}, 263
48^{14}, 252
$48^{20\text{f}}$, 232, 243, 252
$49^{1\text{ff}}$, 250f
$49^{6,9}$, 184, 251
49^{7}, 329
49^{12}, 252

Isa. 51^{1}, 234
51^{17}, 389
$52^{11\text{f}}$, 446
$53^{5\text{ff}}$, 376
$53^{11\text{f}}$, 442
$54^{8\text{f}}$, 45, 203
55^{1}, 45, 232, 329
55^{3}, 7
55^{5}, 328
55^{9}, 330
56^{1-7}, 206f, 424
$59^{7\text{ff}}$, 256,
59^{19}, 12
59^{21}, 328
$60^{1\text{ff}}$, 22, 24, 183
60^{3}, 11, 255
60^{6}, 16, 25
60^{10-16}, 253
60^{17}, 24
60^{22}, 261
62^{2}, 255
$62^{10\text{f}}$, 264, 372
65^{8}, 328, 423
65^{9}, 65
65^{25}, 422

Jer. $4^{23\text{ff}}$, 118
7^{11}, 206
18^{3}, 215
$19^{1\text{ff}}$, 216f
19^{8}, 227
19^{10}, 225
20^{4}, 41
21^{10}, 41
23^{4}, 42
27^{9}, 28^{1}, 32^{39}, 42
29^{10}, 263
31^{15}, 5, 50
50^{16}, 255
50^{17}, 42
51^{46}, 243

Ezek. $13^{0\text{ff}}$, 256
17^{10}, 179
34^{13}, 328
$37^{19\text{ff}}$, 169

Dan. 2^{28} 325
11, 12, 324ff

Hos. 1^{10}, 235
6^{2}, 309
9^{7}, 328
10^{6}, 10

Hos. 11^{1}, 4, 24
$11^{3,5}$, 21, 24, 49
11^{11}, 36
12^{1}, 258
12^{2}, 357ff
12^{9}, 49

Amos $1^{6\text{ff}}$, 6, 34
5^{15}, 176
9^{11}, 176

Jonah 1^{17}, 5
Mic. $3^{5\text{ff}}$, 78, 256
4^{9}, 32, 116
$5^{7\text{ff}}$, 23, 68, 76
6^{9}, 33
7^{6}, 33

Hab. 2^{3}, 147
Hag. 2^{4}, 342
Zech. $2^{6\text{ff}}$, 267f, 297f
$2^{13\text{ff}}$, 284
3^{2}, 306
$3^{3\text{f}}$, 341
3^{7}, 313
3^{8}, 126
3^{9}, 342
5^{11}, 248
$6^{12\text{f}}$, 23, 126
9^{9}, 372f
9^{11}, 309, 374
$10^{3\text{ff}}$, 118, 174, 381
$11^{4,7,11}$, 62, 209
$12^{3,6,12}$, 327
$13^{2\text{f,6}}$, 327
13^{7}, 247
$14^{1\text{f,7}}$, 327, 339, 446
14^{3}, 382

Mal. $1^{6,10}$, 196f
$1^{8,13}$, 62
1^{9}, 187, 198
1^{11}, 193, 197
1^{14}, 194
2^{5}, 188
$2^{6\text{f}}$, 180, 188, 192
$2^{10\text{f}}$, 193f, 229
2^{13}, 187, 193
2^{16}, 192
3^{1}, 147, 182, 184, 197, 204
3^{2}, 185, 206
3^{3}, 187, 189, 207

Mal. $3^5_?$, 185, 194
3^{7f}, 185, 193
3^{11}, 192
3^{16f}, 194
3^{18}, 198
4^1, 147, 185
4^2, 195

Mal. 4^4, 190, 289
Wisd. 2^{10-21}, 431
2^{21ff}, 292, 366
4^{15}, 221
5^1, 222
$7^{4,7,8}$, 77
$8^{10,16}$, 78f

Wisd. 9^8, 285
Ecclus. 16^{10}, 328
34^{1ff}, 42^{24}, 46
43^9, 76
48^{1ff}, 186
2 Macc. 6^{19}, etc., 108

www.ingramcontent.com/pod-product-compliance
Lightning Source LLC
Chambersburg PA
CBHW071222290426
44108CB00013B/1261